Machine Learning and Data Science Techniques for Effective Government Service Delivery

Olalekan Samuel Ogunleye
School of Computing and Mathematical Science, University of Mpumalanga, South Africa

A volume in the Advances in Electronic Government, Digital Divide, and Regional Development (AEGDDRD) Book Series

IGI Global
PUBLISHER of TIMELY KNOWLEDGE

Published in the United States of America by
IGI Global
Engineering Science Reference (an imprint of IGI Global)
701 E. Chocolate Avenue
Hershey PA, USA 17033
Tel: 717-533-8845
Fax: 717-533-8661
E-mail: cust@igi-global.com
Web site: http://www.igi-global.com

Library of Congress Cataloging-in-Publication Data

Names: Ogunleye, Olalekan Samuel, 1979- editor.
Title: Machine learning and data science techniques for effective government service delivery / edited by Olalekan Samuel Ogunleye.
Description: Hershey, PA : Engineering Science Reference, 2024. | Includes bibliographical references and index. | Summary: "This book investigates the development, management, and monitoring approaches to effective government services delivery through data science and machine learning"-- Provided by publisher.
Identifiers: LCCN 2024002231 (print) | LCCN 2024002232 (ebook) | ISBN 9781668497166 (hardcover) | ISBN 9781668497173 (paperback) | ISBN 9781668497180 (ebook)
Subjects: LCSH: Internet in public administration. | Machine learning. | Data mining.
Classification: LCC JF1525.A8 M336 2024 (print) | LCC JF1525.A8 (ebook) | DDC 352.70285/531--dc23/eng/20240214
LC record available at https://lccn.loc.gov/2024002231
LC ebook record available at https://lccn.loc.gov/2024002232

This book is published in the IGI Global book series Advances in Electronic Government, Digital Divide, and Regional Development (AEGDDRD) (ISSN: 2326-9103; eISSN: 2326-9111)

British Cataloguing in Publication Data
A Cataloguing in Publication record for this book is available from the British Library.

All work contributed to this book is new, previously-unpublished material.
The views expressed in this book are those of the authors, but not necessarily of the publisher.

For electronic access to this publication, please contact: eresources@igi-global.com.

Advances in Electronic Government, Digital Divide, and Regional Development (AEGDDRD) Book Series

ISSN:2326-9103
EISSN:2326-9111

Editor-in-Chief: Zaigham Mahmood, University of Derby, UK & North West University, South Africa

MISSION

The successful use of digital technologies (including social media and mobile technologies) to provide public services and foster economic development has become an objective for governments around the world. The development towards electronic government (or e-government) not only affects the efficiency and effectiveness of public services, but also has the potential to transform the nature of government interactions with its citizens. Current research and practice on the adoption of electronic/digital government and the implementation in organizations around the world aims to emphasize the extensiveness of this growing field.

The Advances in Electronic Government, Digital Divide & Regional Development (AEGDDRD) book series aims to publish authored, edited and case books encompassing the current and innovative research and practice discussing all aspects of electronic government development, implementation and adoption as well the effective use of the emerging technologies (including social media and mobile technologies) for a more effective electronic governance (or e-governance).

COVERAGE

- Emerging Technologies within the Public Sector
- E-Citizenship, Inclusive Government, Connected Government
- Case Studies and Practical Approaches to E-Government and E-Governance
- Knowledge Divide, Digital Divide
- Frameworks and Methodologies for E-Government Development

IGI Global is currently accepting manuscripts for publication within this series. To submit a proposal for a volume in this series, please contact our Acquisition Editors at Acquisitions@igi-global.com or visit: http://www.igi-global.com/publish/.

The Advances in Electronic Government, Digital Divide, and Regional Development (AEGDDRD) Book Series (ISSN 2326-9103) is published by IGI Global, 701 E. Chocolate Avenue, Hershey, PA 17033-1240, USA, www.igi-global.com. This series is composed of titles available for purchase individually; each title is edited to be contextually exclusive from any other title within the series. For pricing and ordering information please visit http://www.igi-global.com/book-series/advances-electronic-government-digital-divide/37153. Postmaster: Send all address changes to above address.

Titles in this Series

For a list of additional titles in this series, please visit:
www.igi-global.com/book-series/advances-electronic-government-digital-divide/37153

Futuristic e-Governance Security With Deep Learning Applications
Rajeev Kumar (Moradabad Institute of Technology, India) Abu Bakar Abdul Hamid (Infrastructure University Kuala Lumpur, Malaysia) Noor Inayah Binti Ya'akub (Infrastructure University Kuala Lumpur, Malaysia) Madhu Sharma Gaur (G.L. Bajaj Institute of Management and Technology, India) and Sanjeev Kumar (G.L. Bajaj Institute of Management and Technology, India)
Information Science Reference • copyright 2024 • 276pp • H/C (ISBN: 9781668495964) • US $275.00 (our price)

Handbook of Research on Network-Enabled IoT Applications for Smart City Services
K. Hemant Kumar Reddy (VIT AP University, India) Diptendu Sinha Roy (National Institute of Technology, Meghalaya, India) Tapas Kumar Mishra (SRM University, India) and Mir Wajahat Hussain (Alliance University, India)
Information Science Reference • copyright 2023 • 409pp • H/C (ISBN: 9798369307441) • US $315.00 (our price)

Smart Village Infrastructure and Sustainable Rural Communities
Mohammad Ayoub Khan (University of Bisha, Saudi Arabia) Bhumika Gupta (Govind Ballabh Pant Institute of Engineering and Technology, India) Agya Ram Verma (Govind Ballabh Pant Institute of Engineering and Technology, India) Pushkar Praveen (Govind Ballabh Pant Institute of Engineering and Technology, India) and Cathryn J. Peoples (Ulster University, UK)
Engineering Science Reference • copyright 2023 • 343pp • H/C (ISBN: 9781668464182) • US $250.00 (our price)

AI, IoT, and Blockchain Breakthroughs in E-Governance
Kavita Saini (AMET University) A. Mummoorthy (Malla Reddy College of Engineering and Technology, India) Roopa Chandrika (Department of Information Technology, Malla Reddy College of Engineering and Technology, India) and N.S. Gowri Ganesh (Saveetha Engineering College, India)

For an entire list of titles in this series, please visit:
www.igi-global.com/book-series/advances-electronic-government-digital-divide/37153

IGI Global
PUBLISHER of TIMELY KNOWLEDGE

701 East Chocolate Avenue, Hershey, PA 17033, USA
Tel: 717-533-8845 x100 • Fax: 717-533-8661
E-Mail: cust@igi-global.com • www.igi-global.com

Table of Contents

Detailed Table of Contents

A new age in public administration has been brought about by the rapid advancement of technology in the twenty-first century, which is marked by the incorporation of machine learning (ML), data science, and artificial intelligence (AI) into government services. This chapter thoroughly analyzes how these technologies are revolutionizing e-government, providing creative answers to age-old problems and altering the dynamics of public service delivery. The first section of the chapter explores the foundations of AI, data science, and ML, explaining their main ideas and applications to e-government. It highlights how new technologies can revolutionize processes, improve decision-making, and offer data-driven insights for creating policies. The conversation also touches on practical uses for these technologies, including fraud detection, effective resource allocation, public health predictive analytics, and traffic management optimization.

This chapter proposes how to implement in-house polymathic enterprise architecture-based generic learning processes (PEAbGLP) that can be the fundament of a generic and transcendent enterprise's artificial intelligence (AI) concept (EAIC). Generic and transcendent means that it supports and interfaces with all AI and technology domains, like machine learning (ML), deep learning (DL), data sciences (DS), and others (simply intelligence). The EAIC uses the author's polymathic transformation framework that is specialized in enterprise transformation projects (ETP). ETPs have an extremely high level of failure rates, and added to this fact, AI products force siloed integration approaches, which are risky undertakings. The EAIC ensures business sustainability and operational excellence for the enterprise (simply entity), and the main problem is the adoption of a holistic and polymathic learning process (LP). The PEAbGLP presents how an entity can integrate intelligence, which can be supported by the author's (already mature) applied holistic mathematical model (AHMM) for LP-based AI.

It is important to recognize that a well-run judicial system contributes to the formation of a favorable atmosphere that fosters national growth. The efficient administration of justice is just as important to the court's efficacy as its capacity to be impartial, firm, and fair at all times. Notwithstanding these vital functions of the court, Nigeria's legal system is sometimes unsatisfactory and sluggish moving. People no longer trust the courts because of this, as most people think that justice postponed is justice denied. In recent times, machine learning methods have been used for predictive purposes in several domains. In this work, the authors used 5585 records of precedent rulings from the Supreme Court of Nigeria (SCN) between 1962 and 2022 to construct a prediction model for the categorization of judgments. Primsol Law Pavilion, an independently owned data repository, provided the data. Following data annotation and feature extraction, three classification methods (decision tree, multi-layer perceptron, and kNN) were used to construct the model.

This chapter first discusses what good governance means and why it is so important for society. It is the public governance that lacks a centralized AI framework. Several key characteristics of good governance have been identified, including active participation of citizens in the governance process, transparency, accountability, and empowerment of women. These attributes are essential to achieving good governance. However, many other traits can help create good governance in organizations. Next, the authors explain the good governance characteristics that AI can manage, and some sample use cases for the same have been provided. They also explain how the government could organize itself to use AI best. These examples can help establish

are playing a crucial role in many applications. The chapter focuses on development, monitoring, and management approaches to machine learning implementation for effective government service deliveries. Government forms different policies and aims to successfully pass them to the citizens. The government service deliveries include many sectors like healthcare system, education policies, foreign policies, infrastructure and construction policies, public transportation policies, etc. Machine learning (ML), deep learning (DL), and artificial intelligence (AI) provide many methods like time series analysis, regression, classification, reinforcement learning, clustering, dimensionality reduction, long short-term memory, etc. These methods help retrieving meaningful data from the large volume and predict the desired results. These technologies already revolutionized many sectors like automating the application processes, fetching the relevant and required data instantly, etc.

This chapter explored the transformative impact of data science and VGI on public service provision. VGI, as user-generated content, has played a significant role in democratizing geographic information, empowering users to actively participate in data generation and curation. The integration of VGI into government operations has presented new opportunities for improving service delivery across various domains like education, health, transportation, and waste management. Additionally, data science has complemented VGI by utilizing advanced techniques such as AI, IoT, big data, and blockchain, thereby revolutionizing the entire landscape of government service delivery. However, the successful utilization of VGI in public sector delivery requires addressing critical challenges, including data quality, security, inclusivity, technological infrastructure, and specialized skill sets. Collaborative efforts involving governments, volunteers, and academia can enhance the quality of VGI data.

Preface

In an era where machine learning algorithms are reshaping sectors and data is worth as much gold, these technologies will unavoidably and significantly improve how government services are delivered. The book *Machine Learning and Data Science Techniques for Effective Government Service Delivery* explores how modern technology may transform public sector operations, policy-making, and citizen involvement in a relevant and innovative way.

The idea for this book came from the realization that. In contrast, the private sector has quickly embraced data science and machine learning and profited greatly from them. Still, despite their enormous promise, the public sector has taken these technologies more slowly. Globally, governments are the guardians of vast and diverse data sets. When properly examined and used, this data can result in better-informed decisions, more effective service delivery, and ultimately higher citizen satisfaction.

This book aims to close the knowledge gap between data science technology and its useful implementation in government services. It is designed for academics, data scientists, policymakers, and government officials leading the way in incorporating technology into governance.

This book's chapters are carefully crafted to address various subjects. We start by outlining the fundamental ideas of data science and machine learning so that readers with no prior technical knowledge can still understand the main points. After that, the book explores more advanced topics, including natural language processing, AI-driven policy analysis, and predictive analytics, presenting real-world case studies of these technologies' effective integration into government services.

The difficulties and moral issues involved in using data science in the public sector are covered in great detail throughout the book. A full discussion of data privacy, security, and algorithmic bias risk is provided, giving readers a clear picture of the duties involved in managing public data.

Furthermore, government organizations wishing to start their digital transformation path might use this book as a guide. It provides helpful guidance on developing data science skills, establishing cooperative ecosystems, and encouraging an innovative culture in government agencies.

As we wrap up the book, we consider the future of government service delivery in light of evolving technologies. We talk about how developments like blockchain and quantum computing might affect public services in the future and how governments can prepare for them.

Machine Learning and Data Science Techniques for Effective Government Service Delivery is not merely a list of approaches and case examples. It's a picture of a time when governance and technology work together for the common benefit. It is a call to action to innovate, work together, and change how governments run and provide services to the general public.

As editor, let me express my sincere gratitude to the subject-matter experts who have contributed their knowledge and experiences to this book. The breadth and caliber of the information offered demonstrate their commitment to the subject.

We hope this book will help our readers on their road to using data science and machine learning to improve public governance and service delivery by acting as a resource and source of inspiration.

Kind regards,

Olalekan Samuel Ogunleye
School of Computing and Mathematical Science, University of Mpumalanga, South Africa

Chapter 1
Using Artificial Intelligence to Enhance E-Government Services Delivery Through Data Science and Machine Learning

Olalekan Samuel Ogunleye
School of Computing and Mathematical Science, University of Mpumalanga, South Africa

ABSTRACT

A new age in public administration has been brought about by the rapid advancement of technology in the twenty-first century, which is marked by the incorporation of machine learning (ML), data science, and artificial intelligence (AI) into government services. This chapter thoroughly analyzes how these technologies are revolutionizing e-government, providing creative answers to age-old problems and altering the dynamics of public service delivery. The first section of the chapter explores the foundations of AI, data science, and ML, explaining their main ideas and applications to e-government. It highlights how new technologies can revolutionize processes, improve decision-making, and offer data-driven insights for creating policies. The conversation also touches on practical uses for these technologies, including fraud detection, effective resource allocation, public health predictive analytics, and traffic management optimization.

DOI: 10.4018/978-1-6684-9716-6.ch001

The first section of the chapter explores the foundations of AI, Data Science, and ML, explaining their main ideas and applications to e-government. It highlights how new technologies can revolutionize processes, improve decision-making, and offer data-driven insights for creating policies. The conversation also touches on practical uses for these technologies, including fraud detection, effective resource allocation, public health predictive analytics, and traffic management optimization.

The thorough case studies and success stories from different nations are essential to this discussion. These illustrate these technologies' widespread influence and variety of uses in the public sector. Examples include Singapore's Smart Nation program, Estonia's well-known digital governance model, and the UK's use of AI in public health.

However, obstacles are involved in integrating AI and data-driven technology into government functions. The essay critically analyzes the problems with data privacy, security, morality, and the possibility of prejudice in AI. It talks about how important it is to overcome the digital gap, maintain ethical standards in modern technologies, and guarantee transparency, accountability, and equal access to technology-driven services.

The article looks ahead, projecting future e-government trends and directions. It forecasts a sustained trend toward increasingly complex AI applications, the emergence of blockchain technology for increased transparency, and the increasing significance of individualized, citizen-focused services. To fully fulfill the potential of e-government, the essay highlights the necessity for a balanced strategy that harmonizes technological innovation with ethical governance. It also highlights the collaborative effort that is required among diverse stakeholders.

1. INTRODUCTION

E-government has transformed public administration using digital platforms to improve efficiency, accessibility, and transparency. E-government, propelled by the Internet and digital technologies, aims to be more citizen-centric and responsive than just digitizing services (Dunleavy et al., 2006).

E-government has entered a new age with AI. The power of Artificial Intelligence (AI) to learn, adapt, and make judgments offers unmatched prospects for improving service delivery. Governments can examine big data, automate regular processes, and personalize services via AI (Meijer and Thaens, 2018).

AI subsets data science and machine learning are important to e-government. They help analyze large databases, identify trends, and optimize service delivery (Janssen et al., 2017). Machine learning algorithms can find patterns and insights in government data to improve decision-making, resource allocation, and policymaking (Mergel et al., 2018).

Government agencies use digital technologies and systems to improve access to and delivery of government services to citizens, corporations, and other entities. It uses ICT, primarily the Internet, to increase government transparency, efficiency, and public participation (UN E- Government Survey, 2020). With the broad usage of the Internet in the late 1990s and early 2000s, e-government began. The initial focus was government websites and portals providing public service and contact information (West, 2004). As technology advanced, e-government expanded from informational webpages to interactive platforms. This lets citizens file taxes, apply for licenses, and pay fees online. Governments integrated back-office systems to streamline operations and improve service delivery (Ho, 2002).

Adding AI to e-government services is a strategic and technological enhancement. Citizens expect more responsive and tailored services from governments; therefore, they must innovate. This chapter explains how the public sector can use AI and its benefits and drawbacks (Bertot et al., 2010).

Artificial Intelligence, Data Science, and Machine Learning can transform e-government service delivery. The chapter will explore e-government, the basics of AI and related topics, and actual applications and case studies. The chapter will also discuss government AI deployment difficulties and ethics.

Following this introduction, the chapter will be divided into several sections, each focusing on different aspects of AI in e-government. It will discuss future trends and a call for continued research and development in this vital area.

2. THE LANDSCAPE OF E-GOVERNMENT SERVICES

E-government has emerged and evolved as the digital revolution has transformed government services. E-government, or electronic government, uses information and communication technology (ICT), notably the Internet, to improve government service delivery to consumers, corporations, and other entities (United Nations E-Government Survey, 2020).

E-government initially meant creating websites and portals for government agencies to provide public service information (West, 2004). Early e-government platforms were static and limited in contact and transaction. Increasing government information access was the main goal throughout this period, which improved openness and public participation.

As internet technology advanced, e-government became increasingly interactive and transactional. This move from digital presence to performance allowed citizens to locate information and complete tasks like submitting taxes, applying for licenses, and participating in public consultations online (Ho, 2002). This era prioritized service efficiency and citizen access to government.

The e-government landscape further evolved as services from different government departments and agencies were integrated. This integration aimed to give users a seamless experience by providing access to various services through a single interface, often termed a "one-stop government" (Dawes, 2008). The shift to integrated services reflected a more citizen-centric approach to governance and technology advancement.

The advent of Social media and the proliferation of smartphones and mobile technology ushered in what is often referred to as E-Government 2.0. This phase emphasizes government- citizen dialogue using social media for information sharing, feedback gathering, and public participation (Linders, 2012).

Advanced technologies like AI, blockchain, and the Internet of Things are transforming e- government (IoT). These technologies enable smart governance to ensure that government services are online and more personalized, predictive, intelligent and efficient by using AI and data analytics to improve policymaking, enhance public services and automate routine administrative tasks (Gil-Garcia et al., 2019).

This implies that a larger digital revolution in society is reflected in the development of e- government. E-government has constantly evolved to take advantage of technology breakthroughs, from early digitization initiatives to the present investigation of AI and IoT. This continuous evolution aims to satisfy the public's growing demands for responsive, effective, and easily available government services.

a. Core Components of E-Government Services

E-government services are multifaceted, consisting of multiple fundamental elements that improve the effectiveness, accessibility, and openness of government functions. These elements are necessary for the effective execution and operation of e-government programs.

Online Service Delivery

Online service delivery is one of the main elements of e-government. Government services are being digitalized to facilitate online transactions between residents and businesses. These services cover many duties, from straightforward ones like paying fines or renewing licenses to trickier ones like filing taxes or requesting government assistance. Convenience is the main advantage of online service delivery, as it allows customers to obtain services whenever they want without physically visiting government offices (Jaeger, 2007).

Information Dissemination

Public information dissemination is one of the main purposes of e-government. This includes details regarding government programmes, policies, services, and opportunities. Transparency is ensured, and public faith in the government is bolstered by effective information dissemination through e-government websites. Additionally, it is essential to inform the public about their rights, obligations, and the resources at their disposal (Bertot, Jaeger, & Grimes, 2010).

E-Participation

The use of ICT by governments to interact with the public, solicit their opinions, and facilitate their participation in decision-making is known as "e-participation." By encouraging two-way communication between the government and its constituents, this e-government feature increases inclusivity and democracy in governance. E-participation can take many forms, such as social media interaction, online polls, petitions, and public consultations (Macintosh, 2004).

E-Administration

The internal workings of government agencies are included in e-administration, which emphasizes using ICT to boost productivity, reduce paperwork, and strengthen cooperation between agencies. This includes using enterprise resource planning (ERP) systems, digital record-keeping, and automating administrative procedures. E-administration results in more efficient government procedures and better public sector management (Cordella & Bonina, 2012).

Integration and Interoperability

The integration and interoperability of many government systems and services is a crucial facet of e-government. This guarantees effective data and resource sharing between government departments and agencies, giving users a consistent and smooth service experience. Integration is essential for cutting administrative expenses and preventing duplication of work (Pardo, Gil-Garcia, & Burke, 2008).

Security and Privacy

Because a large portion of the data handled in e-government services is sensitive, security and privacy are critical. Strong cybersecurity measures must be put in place by governments to guard against data breaches and guarantee citizen data privacy. This entails following privacy rules and regulations, encrypting, and maintaining safe databases (Bélanger & Carter, 2008).

b. E-Government Frameworks and Strategies

The foundation of digital transformation comprises e-government frameworks and strategies, which direct the deployment and administration of online government services. These frameworks cover a wider range of topics than just technology; they also cover policy creation, service delivery models, public involvement, and interagency cooperation. E- government frameworks offer organized models and directives that support the systematic creation and implementation of digital government services. Typically, these frameworks cover many e-government topics, from service optimization and user engagement to technological infrastructure and user engagement. They are necessary to ensure that e- government projects complement public administration's overarching objectives, including improved efficiency, accessibility, and openness. The different e-government frameworks and tactics used to address various e-government features are provided in this section.

Theoretical Frameworks in E-Government

Theoretically, digital government projects can be developed and understood with the help of e-government frameworks. These frameworks often incorporate models for service delivery, citizen interaction, and internal government operations.

1. **Service Delivery Models**: Service delivery frameworks concentrate on the digital presentation and accessibility of government services for users. Models like the "Stage Model," which outlines the progression of e-government services from simple information distribution to fully integrated service portals, are examples of this (Layne & Lee, 2001).
2. **Citizen-Centric Frameworks**: They highlight citizens' role in actively participating in e-government. The elements impacting citizen participation and utilization of e- government services are analyzed by frameworks such as the 'Citizen Adoption Model' (Carter & Bélanger, 2005).
3. **Interoperability Frameworks**: Focus on the organizational and technical components that enable various government systems to function smoothly.

This covers policies for collaborative platforms, system integration, and data standards (Pardo, Nam, & Burke, 2012).

Strategic Planning and Implementation

Strategically planning is essential to the effective execution of e-government projects. It entails establishing precise goals, determining the required resources, and creating a development and deployment roadmap.

1. **Developing E-Government Strategies**: involves evaluating needs, establishing realistic goals, and matching those goals with general government objectives. A multi- stakeholder strategy comprising various government agencies, business partners, and citizen groups is frequently necessary (Heeks & Bailur, 2007).
2. **Implementation Models**: Provide detailed procedures for implementing e- government services. This could entail service monitoring and evaluation on an ongoing basis, phased adoption, and pilot testing (Gil-Garcia & Pardo, 2005).

Policy and Regulatory Frameworks

Policy and regulatory frameworks provide the moral and legal foundation for e-government activities. They cover cybersecurity, data privacy, accessibility, and digital inclusion.

1. **Data Protection and Privacy Laws**: An essential component of e-government frameworks are regulations that guarantee privacy and preserve citizen data. This comprises regulations and recommendations on data collecting, storage, and dissemination (Bélanger & Carter, 2008).
2. **Cybersecurity Policies**: Frameworks are essential for safeguarding e-government infrastructure and portals against cyberattacks. These cover data encryption, incident response, and network security standards and protocols (Dawes, 2009).

Global and National E-Government Frameworks

Various national and international e-government frameworks can be compared and contrasted to gain insights into diverse strategies and best practices.

1. **Global E-Government Standards**: National policies can benefit from the recommendations and benchmarks for e-government development provided by

organizations such as the OECD and the United Nations (UN E-Government Survey, 2020).

2. **National Frameworks and Case Studies**: Analyzing particular national frameworks provides useful insights into tactics and execution that work, such as the digital governance model in Estonia or the e-Government Action Plan in Singapore (Kumar & Best, 2006).

c. User Engagement and Participation

E-government has transformed the connection between governments and citizens. The idea of user engagement and participation—a paradigm shift toward more inclusive, interactive, and responsive governance—lays the groundwork for this change. This feature of e-government improves the credibility and efficacy of public administration in addition to democratizing the decision-making process (Macintosh, 2004). Thus, user participation and engagement are essential to the success and long-term viability of e-government programs. This suggests that governments can enhance the democratic process and raise the standard of their services by promoting a culture of involvement.

The Essence of User Engagement and Participation

The involvement of citizens in the digital public sphere, which includes everything from information access to active participation in governance processes, is referred to as "user engagement" in e-government.

1. **Information Accessibility**: A fundamental aspect of citizen participation is guaranteeing that pertinent government information is accessible to the public. This is essential for transparent involvement and knowledge (Bertot, Jaeger, & Grimes, 2010).
2. **Interactive Platforms**: E-government systems provide citizens with access to information and enable citizens and government personnel to engage. These exchanges may occur through talks, consultations, and feedback systems (Linders, 2012).

Mechanisms and Tools for Participation

The digital era has facilitated several tools and methods to improve citizen participation in government.

1. **Online Consultations and Surveys**: Governments can conduct online surveys and consultations using digital platforms to get feedback from the public on policies and services (Thomas & Streib, 2003).
2. **E-Petitions and Digital Forums**: Citizens can voice their concerns, propose policies, and participate in public discourse through e-petitions and forums (Panopoulou et al., 2014).
3. **Social Media as a Tool for Engagement**: Social networking sites now provide a forum for in-the-moment communication and feedback, making them effective tools for increasing user engagement (Mergel, 2013).

Challenges in User Engagement

Although digital platforms present novel avenues for interaction, several obstacles continue to exist.

1. **Digital Divide**: Not every citizen has equal access to online resources, so the digital gap continues to be a major obstacle (Ragnedda & Muschert, 2013).
2. **Engagement Quality**: It can be difficult to guarantee the effectiveness and caliber of involvement. Mechanisms are required to ensure the significance and influence of citizen input (Bonsón et al., 2012).

Case Studies and Best Practices

Examining successful case studies yields important information about user interaction tactics that work.

1. **Local Government Initiatives**: Examples from local governments that have successfully implemented participatory platforms can serve as practical models (Criado et al., 2013).
2. **Global Examples**: Global examples, like the European Union's e-participation programs, provide a more comprehensive understanding of engagement tactics (Alford & Hughes, 2008).

d. Impact Assessment of E-government Services

Understanding the effects of e-government services is essential to determining their efficacy and efficiency. Analyzing how digital efforts have changed public service delivery, citizen involvement, and overall governance is known as impact assessment in e-government. This evaluation aids in determining the elements that contribute to success, areas in need of development, and the wider social effects of digital government services (Heeks & Bailur, 2007). Impact assessment is, therefore, essential for determining the effectiveness and future trajectory of e-government initiatives. Governments may guarantee that their digital services adequately address citizen requirements and enhance governance by conducting thorough and multifaceted evaluations.

Frameworks for Impact Assessment

Several frameworks are available for e-government impact evaluation, each focusing on a distinct aspect of the influence.

1. **Service Delivery and Efficiency**: Assessing how e-government efforts have improved the effectiveness and caliber of public service delivery. This involves tracking decreases in expenses, processing times, and user satisfaction (West, 2004).
2. **Transparency and accountability**: evaluating the impact of e-government services on increasing accountability and transparency in governmental operations (Bertot, Jaeger, & Grimes, 2010).

Methodologies for Measuring Impact

The impact of e-government services is evaluated using a variety of approaches, from quantitative measurements to qualitative studies.

1. **Quantitative Metrics**: Provide information about user volume, service adoption, and efficiency measures such as time and money-saving. Survey and feedback forms frequently measure user happiness and service quality (Jaeger & Mattson, 2009).
2. **Qualitative Assessments**: Involving case studies, focus groups, and interviews to comprehensively understand the socio-political implications and user experience of e- government services (Dawes, 2008).

Challenges in Impact Assessment

Assessing the impact of e-government initiatives is not without challenges.

1. **Data Availability and Reliability**: Getting hold of accurate and thorough evaluation data might be difficult (Thomas & Streib, 2003).

2. **Attributing Outcomes**: Because of the impact of other factors, it might not be easy to explicitly link e-government activities to advances in governance and service delivery (Gil-Garcia & Pardo, 2005).

Case Studies and Comparative Analysis

Examining case studies of e-government projects that have been both successful and unsuccessful yields useful information about effect assessment.

1. **Best Practice Examples**: E-government initiatives showing notable benefits can be examined to identify best practices and critical success criteria (Criado et al., 2013).
2. **Comparative Studies**: E-government project comparisons between various nations or areas can demonstrate how contextual factors affect results (Kumar & Best, 2006).

e. Future Trends in E-Government

The increasing demands of citizens and the rapid growth of technology drive constant changes in the e-government scene. To forecast changes in digital governance and become ready for the opportunities and problems they provide, it is imperative to understand future trends. Anticipating how emerging technology, societal changes, and policy innovations will shape and be shaped by digital governance also requires examining future trends in e-government. Governments must adopt a forward-looking viewpoint to provide the necessary tools to capitalize on emerging prospects and improve public service delivery and citizen participation (Gil-Garcia, Helbig, & Ojo, 2019).

Owing to those above, this section's analysis looks at new technology, changes in strategy, and how they affect public administration. This is because fascinating technological developments and strategic advancements will characterize the future of e-government. To truly reap the rewards of digital transformation, governments must carefully handle these advancements, addressing issues like technological accessibility, privacy concerns, and ethical governance.

Emerging Technologies in E-Government

The integration of emerging modern technology has the potential to transform e-government services completely:

1. **Artificial Intelligence (AI) and Machine Learning**: AI's automation and predictive analytics are revolutionizing e-government. One example is the City of Los Angeles' usage of artificial intelligence (AI) in its "Chip" chatbot, which responds to thousands of citizen inquiries daily and increases productivity and user pleasure. However, depending too much on AI raises questions about decision transparency and algorithmic bias (Meijer & Thaens, 2018).
2. **Blockchain Technology**: Blockchain technology is used by Estonia's e-governance system, which is a trailblazing example of safe data management and digital identity verification. By integrating many government databases, the Estonian X-Road system improves data integrity and public trust. However, there are still issues like scalability and technical complexity (Ojo, Janowski, & Estevez, 2018).
3. **Internet of Things (IoT)**: IoT is used in smart city programs, such as those in Singapore, to monitor the environment and manage traffic. These use cases show how IoT can improve the efficiency of urban governance and urban livability. However, many obstacles exist, such as the digital divide and data privacy (Anthopoulos, 2017).

Strategic Shifts in E-Government Methodological Advancements Are Equally Influential in Shaping E-Government's Future

1. **User-Centric Design**: The use of e-government must increase to justify the change towards user-centric design. This method is demonstrated, for example, by the Government Digital Service (GDS) of the United Kingdom, which redesigns digital services in response to user demands and feedback, increasing user engagement and improving service efficiency.
2. **Cross-Agency Collaboration**: The "Joined-up Government" program from the Netherlands exemplifies how crucial interagency cooperation is to e-government. The strategy has enhanced service delivery and streamlined procedures by merging services across departments.

Social and Policy Implications Additionally, as E-Government Develops, Social and Policy Issues Become More Prominent

1. **Digital Inclusion**: It is essential to guarantee fair access to e-government services. South Korea's "Digital Inclusion Policy" bridges the digital divide

and improves social inclusion in digital governance by giving access and training to marginalized communities.

2. **Privacy and Ethics**: Privacy and ethical issues are becoming more pressing as e- government services rely more heavily on data. The General Data Protection Regulation (GDPR) of the European Union provides a framework for resolving these concerns, which strongly emphasizes user privacy and data protection in digital services.

Global Perspectives and Comparative Analysis Global Developments in E-Government Reveal Various Applications and Problems

1. **Global Best Practices**: As demonstrated by the United Nations E-Government Survey, benchmarking against international norms aids in assessing and enhancing national e-government initiatives. For instance, Denmark's strong digital infrastructure and citizen-focused services are credited for its high rating.
2. **Local Context Adaptation**: It's crucial to modify e-government for regional settings. The necessity for context-sensitive techniques is highlighted by India's Aadhaar program's difficulties in addressing privacy and data security issues despite its scope and effectiveness in providing digital IDs.
3. **Fundamentals of AI, Data Science, and Machine Learning:** At the vanguard of the digital transformation of government services are three technologies: machine learning, data science, and artificial intelligence (AI). Government operations, decision-making, and citizen interactions are changing due to their integration into public administration. The delivery of e-government services has enormous potential to be revolutionized by AI, Data Science, and Machine Learning. By utilizing these technologies, governments can increase productivity, make wiser decisions, and give citizens better services. However, issues pertaining to ethics, privacy, and workforce development must be addressed to achieve their potential in public administration.

Core Concepts and Definitions

1. **Artificial Intelligence (AI)**: In e-government, artificial intelligence (AI) refers to the process of simulating human intelligence in machines so that those

machines may carry out tasks that would normally need human intelligence. This includes the ability to solve problems, make decisions, and process natural language (Russell & Norvig, 2016).

2. **Data Science**: Data Science in e-government entails extracting insights and knowledge from huge amounts of data. Studying and comprehending complex data sets integrates several disciplines, including machine learning, statistics, and data analysis (Provost & Fawcett, 2013).
3. **Machine Learning (ML)**: ML is a branch of AI that creates algorithms that let computers learn from their experiences and get better at them. Machine learning algorithms have the potential to enhance service delivery, automate procedures, and forecast trends in e-government (Bishop, 2006).

Real-World Applications and Case Studies

1. **Predictive Analytics in Public Health**: the US Centers for Disease Control and Prevention (CDC) applies data science and machine learning to predictive analytics in public health. For instance, during the COVID-19 pandemic, ML models were used to anticipate outbreak trends and inform policy decisions.
2. **AI in Taxation and Revenue Collection**: AI is used by HM Revenue and Customs (HMRC) in the UK to improve fraud detection and tax compliance. Artificial intelligence (AI) systems examine tax returns to spot trends that point to possible fraud, greatly enhancing the effectiveness and precision of audits.
3. **Machine Learning in Traffic Management**: One outstanding example is Singapore's use of ML for traffic control as part of its Smart Nation strategy. Machine learning algorithms examine traffic patterns to optimize traffic light timings, minimise traffic jams, and enhance road safety.

Statistical Analyses and Expert Opinions

- According to a McKinsey Global Institute report, artificial intelligence (AI) may generate an extra $13 trillion in global economic activity by 2030, boosting the world GDP by roughly 1.2 percent yearly (McKinsey, 2018).
- Experts such as Google Brain co-founder Andrew Ng highlight the transformational potential of AI and ML in government. These domains include resource allocation, environmental monitoring, and predictive maintenance of public infrastructures.

Potential Challenges and Ethical Considerations

1. **Data Privacy and Security**: Data security and privacy are issues brought up by using AI and data science in governance. It is critical to preserve sensitive citizen data (Bélanger & Carter, 2008).
2. **Bias and Fairness**: Bias in AI systems is becoming a major worry. Governments must make sure AI systems are impartial and do not reinforce preexisting prejudices (Barocas & Selbst, 2016).
3. **Skill Gap and Capacity Building**: Knowledgeable personnel (i.e., employees) in these technologies are necessary to implement AI and ML in government services. It is imperative to tackle the skill gap to successfully implement AI and ML in e- government (West, 2018).

4. APPLICATIONS OF AI, DATA SCIENCE AND MACHINE LEARNING IN E-GOVERNMENT

Integrating Artificial Intelligence (AI), Data Science, and Machine Learning (ML) into e- government signifies a paradigm shift in public service delivery. These technologies offer innovative solutions for complex problems, ranging from resource optimization to enhanced citizen engagement. This section explores their diverse applications, supported by case studies, statistical data, and expert opinions. Therefore, AI, Data Science, and ML applications in e-government transform public administration, leading to more efficient, transparent, and responsive services. However, addressing challenges related to ethics, privacy, and technology implementation is essential for harnessing the full potential of these technologies in the public sector.

a. AI-Enhanced Public Service Delivery

1. **Automated Customer Service**: Government agencies increasingly use AI-powered chatbots for customer service. For example, the U.S. Citizenship and Immigration Services (USCIS) employs a virtual assistant, Emma, who handles millions of inquiries annually, significantly improving response times and accuracy (USCIS, 2020).
2. **Document Analysis and Processing**: AI algorithms are employed for document classification, data extraction, and processing. The Canadian government uses AI to process immigration applications, reducing processing times and increasing efficiency (Canada Immigration, 2019).

b. Data Science in Policy Making and Governance

1. **Predictive Analytics in Public Health**: Data science methodologies have been pivotal in public health management. During the COVID-19 pandemic, the CDC used predictive modeling to forecast virus spread and resource requirements, informing policy decisions and health interventions (CDC, 2020).
2. **Resource Allocation**: Data-driven insights assist governments in optimizing resource allocation. For instance, the city of Chicago leverages data science for predictive analytics in law enforcement deployment and public health resource distribution (Chicago Data Portal, 2018).

c. Machine Learning for Efficiency and Transparency

1. **Fraud Detection**: ML algorithms are increasingly deployed for fraud detection in government transactions. The UK's Department for Work and Pensions employs ML to identify patterns indicative of benefit fraud, significantly reducing illegal claims (DWP, 2021).
2. **Traffic Management and Smart Cities**: ML is crucial in smart city initiatives. Singapore's Intelligent Transport System uses ML algorithms for real-time traffic prediction and management, enhancing urban mobility (LTA Singapore, 2019).

d. Statistical Analyses and Expert Opinions

- A study by Accenture revealed that AI could double annual economic growth rates by 2035 by changing the nature of work and creating new relationships between humans and machines (Accenture, 2016).
- According to an expert in AI policy, Jack Clark, deploying AI in government can lead to more informed decision-making processes and improved public services. Still, he stresses the importance of transparency and accountability in these systems.

e. Challenges and Ethical Considerations

1. **Data Privacy and Security**: Using AI and ML to handle personal data raises significant privacy concerns. Data protection and compliance with regulations like GDPR are crucial for maintaining public trust (EU GDPR, 2018).

2. **Bias and Fairness in AI**: There is an ongoing debate about bias in AI algorithms. Ensuring that these technologies are fair and do not perpetuate existing societal biases is a challenge that governments need to address proactively (Buolamwini & Gebru, 2018).

5. CASE STUDIES AND SUCCESS STORIES

The greatest way to demonstrate the revolutionary effects of AI, Data Science, and Machine Learning on e-government is through case studies and success stories from the real world. These examples show how these technologies can be used in real-world scenarios and improve policymaking, public service delivery, and citizen involvement. This section explores several noteworthy case studies from various global locations. These case studies show how AI, data science, and machine learning have great potential to transform e-government. They emphasize how technology can improve government, policymaking, and public services. But for these technologies to be successfully implemented, privacy, moral usage and public participation must also be resolved.

a. Case Study 1: Estonia's E-Residency Program

- **Implementation**: Estonia's E-Residency program is a pioneering initiative offering digital identity and e-services to non-residents.
- **Results**: The program has attracted over 70,000 e-residents, contributing significantly to Estonia's economy (Korjus, 2019).
- **Lessons Learned**: The importance of robust digital infrastructure and international collaboration in digital governance.

b. Case Study 2: AI in Traffic Management in Tokyo, Japan

- **Implementation**: Tokyo uses AI to analyze traffic data and optimize signal timings, reducing congestion.
- **Results**: Reports indicated a reduction in traffic congestion by up to 20% in targeted areas (Tokyo Metropolitan Government, 2020).
- **Lessons Learned**: Tailoring AI solutions to specific urban challenges can yield significant improvements in city management.

c. Case Study 3: South Korea's Disaster Response with Data Science

- **Implementation**: South Korea's use of data science for disaster response, particularly during the COVID-19 pandemic, involved extensive data integration and analysis for contact tracing and resource allocation.
- **Results**: Rapid and efficient response measures significantly contained the spread of the virus (Park, 2020).
- **Lessons Learned**: The critical role of real-time data analysis and transparent communication in crisis management.

d. Case Study 4: AI-Powered Health Diagnosis in the UK

- **Implementation**: AI-based techniques for early cancer diagnosis and individualized treatment plans have been deployed by the National Health Service (NHS) in the United Kingdom.
- **Results**: Improvement in early cancer detection rates and patient outcomes (NHS, 2021).
- **Lessons Learned**: Healthcare service delivery can be greatly improved by AI. However, data privacy and ethical issues must be carefully considered.

e. Case Study 5: Predictive Policing in Los Angeles, USA

- **Implementation**: The LAPD uses predictive policing algorithms to anticipate crime hotspots and optimize patrolling.
- **Results**: A reported reduction in burglaries and violent crimes in areas where the program was implemented (LAPD, 2019).
- **Lessons Learned**: There is a need to balance technological innovation in law enforcement with privacy and civil liberties concerns.

f. Case Study 6: Brazil's E-Voting System

- **Implementation**: Brazil implemented an electronic voting system to streamline the electoral process.
- **Results**: Significant reduction in vote counting time and instances of electoral fraud (TSE Brazil, 2018).

- **Lessons Learned**: The potential of digital solutions to enhance the efficiency and integrity of electoral processes.

g. Case Study 7: Digital Land Registry in India

- **Implementation**: Blockchain technology is being used in multiple Indian states to create a digital land register system to decrease fraud and increase transparency.
- **Results**: Enhanced availability of land data, decreased incidence of property conflicts and fraudulent activities (NITI Aayog, 2020).
- **Lessons Learned**: Blockchain technology can be a powerful tool for ensuring transparency and security in public records.

6. CHALLENGES AND ETHICAL CONSIDERATIONS

Artificial Intelligence (AI), Data Science, and Machine Learning (ML) combined with e- government projects have created previously unheard-of chances for better public involvement, more effective policymaking, and better service delivery. Nevertheless, there are difficulties in using these cutting-edge technologies in the public sector. These difficulties include a wide range of topics, including the digital divide, transparency, justice, privacy issues, and moral conundrums. Ensuring that the advantages of technological breakthroughs in e-government are fairly distributed while preserving citizen rights and trust is not only a technical but also a moral and social necessity. The application of AI, data science, and machine learning (ML) in public administration presents various complicated issues and ethical dilemmas, which are examined in this section.

A cautious and thoughtful approach is required due to the challenges surrounding using AI, Data Science, and ML in e-government. It is crucial to balance the potential advantages of emerging technologies and the necessity to address their societal, ethical, and legal ramifications. Sustaining the democratic ideals at the core of public administration, preserving public trust, and guaranteeing fair service delivery all depend on striking this balance.

a. Data Privacy and Security

- **Issue**: The collection and processing of large volumes of personal data raise significant concerns about privacy and data security.

- **Impact**: Potential risks include data breaches, unauthorized access, and misuse of sensitive information.
- **Mitigation Strategies**: Strict adherence to data protection laws like the GDPR and robust cybersecurity measures are essential (EU GDPR, 2018).

b. Bias and Fairness in AI

- **Issue**: AI algorithms can reflect and perpetuate existing biases, leading to unfair and discriminatory outcomes in public service delivery.
- **Impact**: This may result in systemic inequalities affecting marginalized communities.
- **Mitigation Strategies**: Ensuring diversity in training data and regular audits for bias are necessary steps (Buolamwini & Gebru, 2018).

c. Transparency and Accountability

- **Issue**: The opacity of certain AI systems, known as the 'black box' problem, poses challenges for transparency and accountability.
- **Impact**: Lack of clarity in AI-driven decisions can undermine public trust in government services.
- **Mitigation Strategies**: Implementing explainable AI and maintaining human oversight are key (Ribeiro et al., 2016).

d. Digital Divide and Accessibility

- **Issue**: Disparities in access to digital technologies can exacerbate social inequalities.
- **Impact**: Citizens lacking digital access or skills may be disadvantaged in using e- government services.
- **Mitigation Strategies**: Policies promoting digital inclusion and accessibility are critical (Ragnedda & Muschert, 2013).

e. Workforce Implications

- **Issue**: AI and automation may disrupt job markets, leading to displacement and new skill demands.

- **Impact**: Government employees may face job insecurity and require reskilling.
- **Mitigation Strategies**: Focus on workforce training and developing new roles complementing AI technologies (West, 2018).

f. Ethical Use of AI

- **Issue**: Ethical complexities arise in deploying AI in sensitive areas of public administration.
- **Impact**: Misuse or unethical application of AI can have serious societal ramifications.
- **Mitigation Strategies**: Establishing ethical guidelines for AI use in government is crucial (Floridi et al., 2018).

g. Legal and Regulatory Challenges

- **Issue**: Rapid technological advancements often outpace the existing legal and regulatory frameworks.
- **Impact**: This can create ambiguities and challenges in governance, compliance, and liability.
- **Mitigation Strategies**: Legal adaptation and international collaboration are required (Weber, 2017).

7. FUTURE TRENDS AND DIRECTIONS

As the twenty-first century progresses, quick technological advances and changing social demands will likely shift the e-government scene significantly. The way governments and individuals engage is already changing due to the integration of artificial intelligence (AI), data science, and machine learning (ML) in public sector activities. It is anticipated that in the future, these technologies will bring about even more significant changes, opening up new avenues for digital administration. This section examines the future of public administration and service delivery and how developing technologies, societal changes, and policy innovations are anticipated to affect these developments. In addition to highlighting technology developments, the investigation considers the wider ramifications for public participation, ethical governance, and policy.

a. Advanced Technologies Reshaping E-Government

- **AI and Advanced Analytics**: AI will be used in e-government in increasingly advanced ways, such as real-time decision-making analytics and predictive public policy modeling (Russell & Norvig, 2016).
- **Blockchain for Transparency and Security**: Blockchain technology is predicted to completely transform voting and public record systems, as well as data quality and transparency in e-government applications (Ojo, Janowski, & Estevez, 2018).

b. Personalization and Citizen-Centric Services

- **Customized Service Delivery**: AI and ML will make it possible for e-government services to be more individualized and citizen-centric, adjusting their offers to suit each person's requirements and preferences (Linders, 2012).
- **Enhanced Citizen Engagement**: More sophisticated data analysis technologies will enable a more in-depth understanding of public opinion, resulting in a more adaptable and interactive government (Gil-Garcia, Helbig, & Ojo, 2019).

c. Smart Cities and IoT Integration

- **Smart Urban Governance**: The proliferation of IoT devices will boost smart city projects by combining AI and ML for effective urban administration, including environmental monitoring, public safety, and traffic control (Anthopoulos, 2017).
- **Real-Time Data Utilization**: The real-time data of IoT devices will be increasingly utilized in public resource management and urban planning to support dynamic decision-making.

d. Ethical AI and Governance

- **Development of Ethical Frameworks**: AI will be used increasingly in e-government. Hence, it will be essential to create ethical frameworks and regulations to control its use (Floridi et al., 2018).

- **Addressing AI Bias and Transparency**: Governments will prioritize addressing the issues of AI bias and guaranteeing openness in AI decision-making procedures (Buolamwini & Gebru, 2018).

e. Overcoming Challenges and Building Trust

- **Bridging the Digital Divide**: Priorities include closing the digital gap and guaranteeing fair access to e-government services (Ragnedda & Muschert, 2013).
- **Cybersecurity and Data Protection**: Strengthening cybersecurity measures and protecting citizen data will maintain public trust in digital government services (EU GDPR, 2018).

8. CONCLUSION

a. Digital Transformation in Government: A Reflection

It is clear from our examination of artificial intelligence (AI), data science, and machine learning (ML) in e-government that these technologies are changing how public administration is conducted and how individuals and governments engage with one another. The integration of these technologies signifies a substantial change towards more efficient, transparent, and responsive governance, ranging from blockchain-enhanced transparency and citizen-centric service delivery to AI-driven traffic systems and predictive analytics in public health management.

b. The Promise and Challenges of AI and Data Science in Public Sector

AI, ML, and data science have enormous potential to revolutionize e-government. These technologies provide creative answers to persistent problems in public administration, such as service delivery, policy creation, and resource allocation. The global case studies and success stories—like Singapore's Smart Nation program and Estonia's digital government model— illustrate the significant effects that these technologies can have.

However, there are difficulties with this transition. Several obstacles to overcome include concerns about data security and privacy, prejudice and fairness in AI, accountability and transparency, the digital gap, and the requirement for moral AI governance. The public, technologists, and policymakers need coordinated efforts to address these issues. It will be imperative to create strong legal frameworks, ethical standards, and open policies to guarantee that the advantages of new technology are achieved while protecting the rights and confidence of the public.

c. The Future of E-Government

The future of e-government appears to be full of opportunities. Government services may become more individualized, responsive, and effective in the future, according to the continuous developments in AI, Data Science, and ML. The way these technologies are incorporated into responsive public services, personalized healthcare, and smart cities will develop further, providing unmatched chances for innovation in government.

However, even as we welcome these technical developments, we must remain aware of their risks. It is crucial to close the digital divide, guarantee fair access to technology, safeguard citizen data, and uphold public confidence. The requirement for inclusive, open, and moral governance must coexist with the desire for innovation in government.

d. The Role of Stakeholders

For e-government to successfully integrate AI and data-driven technologies, multiple stakeholders must work together. Governments must collaborate closely with technology professionals, private sector partners, academic institutions, and citizens to create and execute effective digital solutions. By working together, we can make sure that these technologies are in line with the values and needs of the general public.

e. Embracing a Human-Centric Approach

A human-centric approach to applying these technologies in e-government is crucial as we move forward. While AI and data science offer powerful tools for automation and efficiency, the human element remains irreplaceable in terms of empathy, ethical considerations, and public engagement. Governments must strive to use these technologies to enhance, rather than replace, human decision-making and interaction.

f. Final Thoughts

In conclusion, the journey of integrating AI, Data Science, and Machine Learning into e- government is ongoing, filled with exciting possibilities and significant responsibilities. By navigating the challenges thoughtfully and prioritizing citizen welfare and rights, governments can leverage these technologies to revolutionize public services and foster a more engaged, informed, and empowered citizenry. The future of e-government, underpinned by these advanced technologies, holds the promise of a more efficient, transparent, and responsive governance landscape that effectively meets the needs and expectations of the digital era.

REFERENCES

Accenture. (2016). *Why Artificial Intelligence is the Future of Growth*. Author.

Alford, J., & Hughes, O. (2008). Public Value Pragmatism as the Next Phase of Public Management. *American Review of Public Administration, 38*(2), 130–148. doi:10.1177/0275074008314203

Anthopoulos, L. (2017). Understanding Smart Cities: A Tool for Smart Government or an Industrial Trick? *Public Administration Review*.

Barocas, S., & Selbst, A. D. (2016). Big Data's Disparate Impact. *California Law Review*.

Bélanger, F., & Carter, L. (2008). Trust and Risk in E-Government Adoption. *The Journal of Strategic Information Systems*.

Bertot, J. C., Jaeger, P. T., & Grimes, J. M. (2010). Using ICTs to Create a Culture of Transparency: E-government and social media as openness and anti-corruption tools for societies. *Government Information Quarterly, 27*(3), 264–271. doi:10.1016/j.giq.2010.03.001

Bishop, C. M. (2006). *Pattern Recognition and Machine Learning*. Springer.

Bonsón, E., Torres, L., Royo, S., & Flores, F. (2012). Local E-Government 2.0: Social Media and Corporate Transparency in Municipalities. *Government Information Quarterly, 29*(2), 123–132. doi:10.1016/j.giq.2011.10.001

Buolamwini, J., & Gebru, T. (2018). *Gender Shades: Intersectional Accuracy Disparities in Commercial Gender Classification*. Academic Press.

Canada Immigration. (2019). *AI in Canadian Immigration Processing*. Author.

Carter, L., & Bélanger, F. (2005). The utilization of e-government services: Citizen trust, innovation and acceptance factors. *Information Systems Journal, 15*(1), 5–25. doi:10.1111/j.1365-2575.2005.00183.x

Chicago Data Portal. (2018). Predictive Analytics in Public Services.

Cordella, A., & Bonina, C. M. (2012). A Public Values Perspective for ICT Enabled Public Sector Reforms: A Theoretical Reflection. *Government Information Quarterly*, *29*(4), 512–520. doi:10.1016/j.giq.2012.03.004

Criado, J. I., Sandoval-Almazan, R., & Gil-Garcia, J. R. (2013). Government Innovation through Social Media. *Government Information Quarterly*, *30*(4), 319–326. doi:10.1016/j.giq.2013.10.003

Dawes, S. S. (2008). The Evolution and Continuing Challenges of E-Governance. *Public Administration Review*, *68*(s1). Advance online publication. doi:10.1111/j.1540-6210.2008.00981.x

Dawes, S. S. (2009). Governance in the digital age: A research and action framework for an uncertain future. *Government Information Quarterly*, *26*(2), 257–264. doi:10.1016/j.giq.2008.12.003

Dunleavy, P., Margetts, H., Bastow, S., & Tinkler, J. (2006). *Digital Era Governance: IT Corporations, the State, and e-Government*. Oxford University Press. doi:10.1093/acprof:oso/9780199296194.001.0001

DWP. (2021). *Using Machine Learning to Detect Welfare Fraud. EU GDPR (2018).* General Data Protection Regulation.

European Union. (2018). *General Data Protection Regulation (GDPR).* Author.

Floridi, L., Cowls, J., Beltrametti, M., Chatila, R., Chazerand, P., Dignum, V., & Schafer, B. (2018). *AI4People—An Ethical Framework for a Good AI Society: Opportunities, Risks, Principles, and Recommendations. Minds and Machines.* Academic Press.

Gil-Garcia, J. R., Helbig, N., & Ojo, A. (2019). Smart Governance in the Context of Smart Cities: A Literature Review. *Information Polity*.

Gil-Garcia, J. R., & Pardo, T. A. (2005). E-government success factors: Mapping practical tools to theoretical foundations. *Government Information Quarterly*, *22*(2), 187–216. doi:10.1016/j.giq.2005.02.001

Heeks, R., & Bailur, S. (2007). Analyzing e-government research: Perspectives, philosophies, theories, methods, and practice. *Government Information Quarterly*, *24*(2), 243–265. doi:10.1016/j.giq.2006.06.005

Ho, A. T. (2002). Reinventing Local Governments and the E-Government Initiative. *Public Administration Review*, *62*(4), 434–444. doi:10.1111/0033-3352.00197

Jaeger, P. T. (2007). Deliberative Democracy and the Concept of E-Government. *Administration & Society*.

Jaeger, P. T., & Mattson, T. (2009). E-Government, the Information Society, and the Future of Public Administration. *Public Administration Review*.

Janssen, M., Van der Voort, H., & Wahyudi, A. (2017). Factors influencing big data decision- making quality. *Journal of Business Research*, *70*, 338–345. doi:10.1016/j.jbusres.2016.08.007

Korjus, K. (2019). *Estonia's E-Residency Program Success Metrics*. E-Residency Blog.

Kumar, V., & Best, M. L. (2006). *Impact and Sustainability of E-Government Services in Developing Countries: Lessons Learned from Tamil Nadu*. The Information Society.

LAPD. (2019). *Predictive Policing Program Analysis*. Author.

Layne, K., & Lee, J. (2001). Developing fully functional E-government: A four stage model. *Government Information Quarterly*, *18*(2), 122–136. doi:10.1016/S0740-624X(01)00066-1

Linders, D. (2012). From E-Government to We-Government: Defining a Typology for Citizen Coproduction in the Age of Social Media. *Government Information Quarterly*, *29*(4), 446–454. doi:10.1016/j.giq.2012.06.003

Macintosh, A. (2004). Characterizing E-Participation in Policymaking. *Proceedings of the 37th Annual Hawaii International Conference on System Sciences.*

McKinsey Global Institute. (2018). *Notes from the AI Frontier: Modeling the Impact of AI on the World Economy*. Author.

Meijer, A., & Thaens, M. (2018). Digital Government Transformation: A Structural Analysis of Digital Government's Impacts. *Public Administration Review*.

Mergel, I. (2013). Social Media Adoption and Resulting Tactics in the U.S. Federal Government. *Government Information Quarterly*, *30*(2), 123–130. doi:10.1016/j.giq.2012.12.004

Mergel, I., Edelmann, N., & Haug, N. (2018). Defining digital transformation: Results from expert interviews. *Government Information Quarterly*.

NHS. (2021). *AI in Healthcare Delivery*. NHS.

Ojo, A., Janowski, T., & Estevez, E. (2018). Blockchain for Government and Public Services: A Systematic Literature Review. *Government Information Quarterly*.

Panopoulou, E., Tambouris, E., Tarabanis, K. (2014). E-participation Initiatives: How is Europe Progressing? *European Journal of ePractice*.

Pardo, T. A., Gil-Garcia, J. R., & Burke, G. B. (2008). Governance Structures in E-Government: Are They Changing? *International Journal of Electronic Government Research*.

Pardo, T. A., Nam, T., & Burke, G. B. (2012). E-government interoperability: Interaction of policy, management, and technology dimensions. *Social Science Computer Review*, *30*(1), 7–23. doi:10.1177/0894439310392184

Park, S. (2020). Data Science in South Korea's COVID-19 Response. *Journal of Public Health Policy*.

Provost, F., & Fawcett, T. (2013). *Data Science for Business*. O'Reilly Media.

Ragnedda, M., & Muschert, G. W. (2013). *The Digital Divide: The Internet and Social Inequality in International Perspective*. Routledge. doi:10.4324/9780203069769

Ribeiro, M. T., Singh, S., & Guestrin, C. (2016). Why Should I Trust You? Explaining the Predictions of Any Classifier. *Proceedings of the 22nd ACM SIGKDD International Conference on Knowledge Discovery and Data Mining*. 10.1145/2939672.2939778

Russell, S., & Norvig, P. (2016). *Artificial Intelligence: A Modern Approach* (3rd ed.). Pearson.

Thomas, J. C., & Streib, G. (2003). The New Face of Government: Citizen-Initiated Contacts in the Era of E-Government. *Journal of Public Administration: Research and Theory*, *13*(1), 83–102. doi:10.1093/jpart/mug010

Tokyo Metropolitan Government. (2020). *AI Traffic Management Initiative*. Author.

United Nations. (2020). *E-Government Survey 2020*. Author.

USCIS. (2020). *Emma: Virtual Assistant*. U.S. Citizenship and Immigration Services.

Weber, R. H. (2017). Regulating the Internet: The New Battle against Chaos. *International Journal of Communications Law and Policy*.

West, D. M. (2004). E-Government and the Transformation of Service Delivery and Citizen Attitudes. *Public Administration Review*, *64*(1), 15–27. doi:10.1111/j.1540-6210.2004.00343.x

West, D. M. (2018). *The Future of Work: Robots, AI, and Automation*. Brookings Institution Press.

Chapter 2
Enterprise Transformation Projects:
The Polymathic Enterprise Architecture-Based Generic Learning Processes (PEAbGLP)

Antoine Toni Trad
https://orcid.org/0000-0002-4199-6970
IBISTM, France

ABSTRACT

This chapter proposes how to implement in-house polymathic enterprise architecture-based generic learning processes (PEAbGLP) that can be the fundament of a generic and transcendent enterprise's artificial intelligence (AI) concept (EAIC). Generic and transcendent means that it supports and interfaces with all AI and technology domains, like machine learning (ML), deep learning (DL), data sciences (DS), and others (simply intelligence). The EAIC uses the author's polymathic transformation framework that is specialized in enterprise transformation projects (ETP). ETPs have an extremely high level of failure rates, and added to this fact, AI products force siloed integration approaches, which are risky undertakings. The EAIC ensures business sustainability and operational excellence for the enterprise (simply entity), and the main problem is the adoption of a holistic and polymathic learning process (LP). The PEAbGLP presents how an entity can integrate intelligence, which can be supported by the author's (already mature) applied holistic mathematical model (AHMM) for LP-based AI.

DOI: 10.4018/978-1-6684-9716-6.ch002

INTRODUCTION

The PEAbGLP is based on empiric busines (and non-business) cases and experiences, which can be described by using a Natural Language Programming (NLP) that can be integrated by using Enterprise Architecture (EA) concepts and design languages. An AR based LP supports an Entity wide Polymathic learning strategy. The PEAbGLP offers a set of recommendations and an adapted IHITF that includes AI/LP, EA, business engineering, managerial, and technical propositions. The PEAbGLP can be used by executive managers, ETP managers, business architects/analysts, and Intelligence implementation engineers to enable solutions to transform business, and LP based AI environments. The RDP uses a Polymathic approach and applies an interdisciplinary AR based LP. The AHMM4AI based PEABGLP, combines various EA, AI, Mathematical Modelling (MM), academic/educational, and ETP (simply *Project*) domains. These domains can be: Business engineering, IHITF, (Re)Organization concepts, Major/frequent changes, Financial engineering, AI, Project Management (PM), MM/algorithms, Information and Communication Systems (ICS), EA, geoeconomics/geopolitical analysis, and other. This article is linked to all the author's works and their RDP findings (Trad, 2023a, 2023b). This RDP is not a simplistic quantitative, but a complex qualitative one that is based on Polymathics, which can appear as complex for the reader. Polymathic research is needed because the rate of failures in such Projects is about 95%.

LP related topics/domains that includes: 1) An adapted evolutive RDP; 2) Enriches the IHITF, to avoid locked-in; 3) Uses a methodological approach that is based EA and AR/LP/AI; and 4) A Polymathic and Interdisciplinary Engineering Project Work (PIEPW) (Trad, 2023a, 2023b) to support Entity's Knowledge Management System (KMS). The PIEPW is used to integrate LPs as shown in Figure 1. The PEABGLP use integrated: Critical Success Areas (CSA), Critical Success Factors (CSF), Key Performance Indicators (KPI), Concrete ICS variables (CSAs, CSFs, KPIs, and concrete ICS variables, or simply Factors), The LP uses the HDT to support the

Figure 1. The integration of the LP in the project

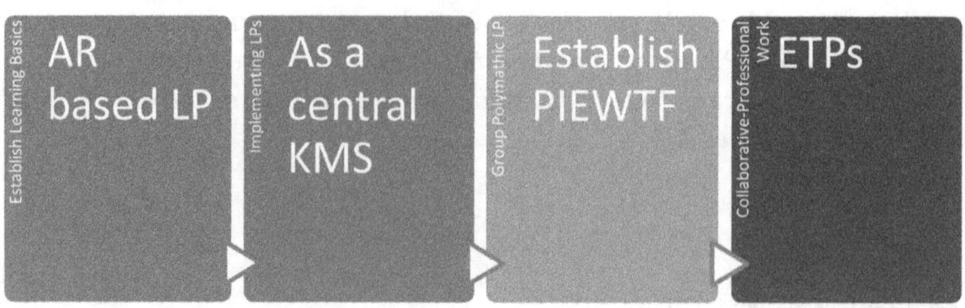

DMS. Projects need Polymathic profiles which are extremely rare and they intensive LP based coaching. The PEAbGLP manages acquired experiences from encountered problems. The PEABGLP links Project topics like in Architecture in civil engineering and help teams in modelling activities; and the Entity's engineers have the needed LP implementation skills. The PEABGLP can be based on existing Project frameworks like: 1) EA environments to support LPs (Pushpakumara, Jayaweera, & Manjulan, 2021); 2) An IHITF and an MM like the AHMM4AI (Trad, & Kalpić, 2019a); 3) Unbundled Entity's services pool (Trad, 2015a, 2023e); 4) EA and AI domains (Trad, & Kalpić, 2022a, 2022b); 5) A scalable ICS and an agile PIEPW (Trad, 2023d); 6) A PIEPW based PM method (Spencer, 2016); 7) A transformable PEABGLP (Trad, & Kalpić, 2021b); and 8) The PEABGLP problem solving is supported by the KMS (Blackburn, & Rosen, 1993). .

PEABGLP's Characteristics

Polymathic skills and characteristics for Projects are developed and improved along the Project. The PEABGLP needs an LP based DMS/KMS in order to solve all Project's types of problems and to optimize PMs' schedules. This chapter uses an IHITF, which is the author's Transformation Research Architecture Development framework (*TRADf*) that includes: 1) ICS, PIEPW, EAIC, and corresponding LP patterns; 2) The DMS/KMS; 3) PEABGLP generators; and 5) An RDP, which is the 1st CSA and its heading are in fact the initial set of CSFs.

Figure 2. The interaction between the project and the RDP

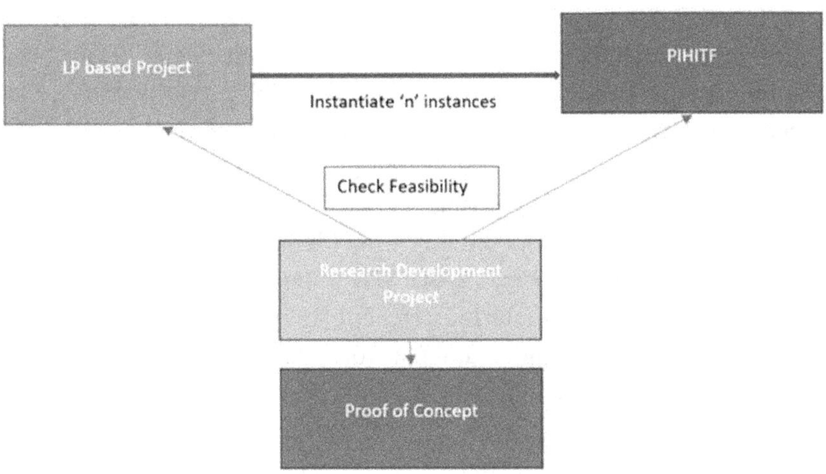

THE RESEARCH DEVELOPMENT PROJECT

A Different Innovative Concept and Managing Complexity

This version of the RDP is based on the following facts and objects: 1) Projects, and AI/LP are environments; 2) A Project needs an MM based metamodel; 3) Needs an established IHITF that links various ICS/AI components, concepts and methodologies; 3) Uses essentially a qualitative approach and vulgarizes simplistic quantitative methods, which are the origin of Projects' failures; 4) This RDP is complex and needs experiences and knowledge in various domains; 5) Uses a Polymathic approach; 6) If the valuable reader finds this chapter complex, then he can refer to the conclusion section; and 7) How to implement the EAIC and a generic LP concept; 8) ICS/AI, and EA domains, use a large number of definitions and abbreviations… This is a qualitative framework oriented research, and therefore the inclusion of the IHITF's is inevitable. The next step is to identify the Researched Literature Review (RLR) and RDP's Gap.

The RLR, Related Works, and RDP's Gap

Projects' very high rates of failures are the result of the lack of Polymathic skills and that Projects have exclusively financial goals; which creates siloed ICSs. Projects need the AHMM4AI to supports LP based HDT, which in turn supports the DMS (Trad, & Kalpić, 2014a). This chapter's Research Question (RQ) is: "How can the PEABGLP support AI based Projects?" This chapter (like all the author's works) is based on *TRADf* and his previous works like: 1) Academic and Educational Transformation Projects-The Role Team-Based Learning in Polymathics (RTBLP) (Trad, 2023a); 2) The Business Transformation Project's Holistic Agile Management (Trad, & Kalpić, 2022c); 3) The Selection, and Training Framework selection and training framework (STF) for Manager's in Business Innovation Transformation Projects–Educational Recommendations (Trad, & Kalpić, 2014b); 4) The business transformation enterprise architecture framework for innovation: The role of artificial intelligence in the global business education (RAIGBE) (Trad, 2021b); 5) Using Applied Mathematical Models for Business Transformation (Trad, & Kalpić, 2019a); 6) A Transformation Framework Proposal for Managers in Business Innovation and Business Transformation *Projects*-An ICS's atomic architecture vision (Trad, 2015b). 7) Using a Generic Artificial Intelligence Pattern for Business Transformation (Trad, 2022a); 8) An Intelligent Neural Networks Micro Artefact Patterns' Based Enterprise Architecture Model (Trad, & Kalpić, 2017a); 9) Applied Mathematical Model for Business Transformation Projects: The Intelligent Strategic Decision-Making System (iSDMS) (Trad, 2020a); 10) An Applied Mathematical Model for

Business Transformation and Enterprise Architecture: The Holistic Organizational Intelligence and Knowledge Management Pattern's Integration (Trad, 2021); 11) Proactive monitoring and maintenance of intelligent control systems: a design pattern for autonomous systems (Trad, & Kalpic, 2004); 12) Proactive monitoring and maintenance of intelligent control systems: a design pattern for autonomous systems (Trad, & Kalpic, 2004); 13) The Selection and Training Framework (STF) for Managers in intelligent city Innovation Transformation Projects-Managerial Recommendations (Trad, & Kalpic, 2014); 14) Using a Generic Artificial Intelligence Pattern for Business Transformation (Trad, 2021); 15) Business Transformation Projects-An Intelligence Driven Development for Enterprise Architecture and Asset Management-The Proof of Concept (Trad, & Kalpic, 2018a); 16) The business transformation framework on Knowledge and Intelligence-Driven Development (KIDD) (Trad, & Kalpic, 2021a); 17) The Transformation Framework: The Role of Artificial Intelligence for Military Strategies (RAI4MS) (Trad, 2021d); 18) The Business, Societal, and Enterprise Architecture Framework: An Artificial Intelligence, Data Sciences-, and Big Data-Based Approach (Trad, 2021e); 19) The Business Transformation Enterprise Architecture Framework: Intelligent Strategic Development and Operations (iSDevOps) (Trad, 2021f); 20) Private Cloud based Transformation Projects (PCTP) for Business Intelligence (Trad, 2023c); 21) Business Transformation and Enterprise Architecture Projects: Natural Language Programming (NLP) (Trad, 2022b); 21) Strength, Weakness, Opportunity and Threat (SWOT) based Transformation's Organizational Risks' Management (STORM) (Trad, & Kalpić, 2023a); 22) Academic and Educational Transformation Projects-The Role Team-Based Learning in Polymathics For University Cycle (RTBL4UC) (Trad, 2023b); and others.

This RDP assesses and confirms the gap for the presented RQ, that is due to the following facts: 1) There isn't a no similar RDP approaches and IHITF; 2) Complexity and high failure rates; 3) There is nothing similar to the PEABGLP; 4) The author's absolute lead in Projects' research works; and 5) There are no LP based approaches for AI. The PEABGLP's Rating & Weighting Concept (RWC) is based on *TRADf's* Factors.

Factors' Integration and Management

TRADf is agnostic to any type of Project or AI domain and the PEABGLP selects its sets of Factors (where CSAs corresponds to a set of CSFs). A selected and tuned CSF is in turn a set of KPIs, and where each KPI (and its corresponding ICS concrete variable) maps to a single Project item/requirement. Each KPI can map to a real-world/concrete ICS programming language's variable, so Project's evaluation returns realistic statuses' values. Where each Project requirement relates to a column of the HDT based Tables (Putri, & Yusof, 2009). In the RDP's and hence Proof of Concept's (PoC) 1st phase (or feasibility phase), which checks the selected sets of Factors, which are persisted in Decision Tables (DT); where delivers recommendations and Project actions.

Based on RDP's RLR and Factors' evaluation by TRADf's rules: 1) PEABGLP's/ Project's related references must to be credible and are estimated by the researcher(s) by using the LP based DMS; 2) These references must be conform to TRADf's classification structures; 3) Project's phases are evaluated by using Factors; 3) The used EA and AI modelling capacities and their mappings to Factors' (KPIs and ICS' variables); 4) Apply the Architecture Development Method (ADM) to manage PEABGLP's implementations; 5) The ADM manages TRADf's iterations and Factors' RWC based evaluations; and 6) If the aggregations and evaluations of all the Project's DTs are positive (then the results are persisted in LP based Tables) and if these results exceed the initially defined *project's* minimum, then the Project continues to PoC's execution (or the 2nd phase), which uses the selected ACSs.

Project's Selected ACSs

This RDP is one of the Project's CSA, and the PoC is based on PEABGLP's set of ACSs, which are combined with a common EA/ADM and Project based ACS that originates from the Open Group. The EA based ACS covers Project ICS, EA/ AI, modelling, linking KPIs, and basic Project scenarios with ICS variables. The selected ACSs present PEABGLP's capabilities and PIEPW integration concepts. PEABGLP's Factors are integrated, automated, tuned, and measured by HDT's RWC. The RWC is superficially used the 1st Project's iteration and then (re)evaluated by using subsequent ADM coordinated iterations. In each of ADM's iterations, the PEABGLP's status and progress (or regression) is evaluated by the DMS. ADM's iterations enrich LPs by the gained experiences and used actions, which is optimal and typical for AR based education. The selected Factors (and especially CSFs) are essential for the Project and the. selected ACSs are:

- The insurance domain (Jonkers, Band, & Quartel, 2012a), which is used for ICS, MMs, and EA topics;
- Polymathic characteristics (Clark, Johnson, Turner, 2004).
- A ICS case study presents how to integrate PIEPW, cross-functional collaboration in *Entities*. This ACS present cross-functional teams and the main aim was to build Polymathic LP. Another major aim was to manage DMS in PIEPW based interactions; and checks the *Engineer's* cross-functional professional capacities. A crucial Factor, is the impact of collaboration when

using LPs in Polymathic fields like ICS, which can be represented by a model of cross-functional collaboration that is shown in Figure 4 (Morse, 2020).

- This ACS is related to digital equity and educational inclusion during an emergent COVID-19. Presents perceptions and practices related to the rapid rise in remote-environments during coronavirus (COVID-19) crisis.
- Investigating the role of EA in AI/BigData analytics; an ACS in a large public sector organization. This ACS shows how EA supports various phases of AI/ BigData integration (Adhytia, Kurnia, Dilnutt, R., Hidayanto, 2023).

ADM's Application

The LP based DMS, and ICS' subsystems, need an ADM to synchronize Project's activities. A Project should use an IHITF, like the author's TRADf, and its HDT to solve PEABGLP's problems (Markides, 2011). The DMS delivers solutions, actions… TRADf synchronizes Project's and ADM activities, as shown in Figure 3. PEABGLP and ADM integration can be modelled by the AHMM4AI.

Figure 3. ADM's phases
(The Open Group, 2011a, 2011b)

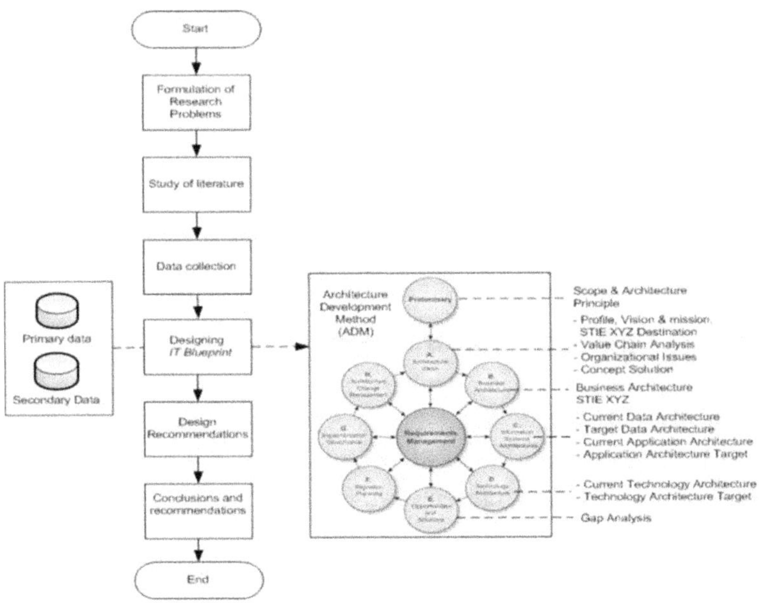

The AHMM4AI

Polymathic modelling concepts and AI models, are supported by the AHMM4AI, which uses an unbundling process. The AHMM4AI based DMS uses sets of Factors and defined sets of actions, to manage LP based HDT. The RLR used the following facts and resources: 1) Works/articles and resources related to Transformations, Projects, AI/LP, ICS reengineering, and other…; 2) Other author's works, and *TRADf*; 3) Project's and PoC's feasibilities; 4) Selected Factors and the RWC; and 5) Thus RDP uses the Empirical Engineering Research Model (EERM). A Polymathic-Mathematical Model (PMM) is a subset of concrete and existing concepts, behaviours; and that a PMM is a description of a precise realities (Polderman, & Willems, 1998). The PMM has the following characteristics:

- Abstracts a physical system (Hinkelmann, 2016).
- EA is a descriptive process that validates the PMM principles (Sankaralingam, Ferris, Nowatzki, Estan, Wood, & Vaish, 2013).
- Can model AI, and LP based HDT modules.
- There is a gap in Polymathic Project's management (Syynimaa, 2015).
- Optimizes *Projects* by applying Factors (Dogan, Çalgici, Arditi, & Gunaydin, 2015).
- Enables AHMM4AI's implementation (Giachetti, 2012).
- Describes an *Entity,* Project, and PEABGLP (Sankaralingam, Ferris, Nowatzki, Estan, Wood, & Vaish, 2013).
- Multi-criteria or a multi-Factors model(s) needs a mixed method (qualitative and quantitative) like the LP based HDT (Zandia, & Tavana, 2011; Kim & Kim, 1999).
- Is optimal for the usage of the EERM (Easterbrook, Singer, Storey, & Damian, 2008).

PMM's Basic Elements and Artefacts

Factors define initial HDT's nodes that are important to solve problem types. AHMM4AI's basic elements are used in DMS' requests processing and the PEABGLP. AHMM4AI's nomenclature is presented in Figure 4:

- The symbol $\sum$ indicates summation of RWC's elements and actions, denoting the weighting/importance of the elements. RWC uses integers ranging in ascending importance from 1 to 10.
- The symbol $\underline{\text{U}}$ indicates sets union.

Figure 4. AHMM's nomenclature
(Trad, & Kalpić, 2019a)

Basic Mathematical Model's (BMM) Nomenclature

Iteration	= An integer variable "*i*" that denotes a *Project/ADM iteration*	
microRequirement	= (maps to) KPI	(B1)
CSF	= Σ KPI	(B2)
Requirement	= (maps to) CSF = $\bigcup$ microRequirement	(B3)
CSA	= Σ CSF	(B4)
microMapping microArtefact/Req	= microArtefact + (maps to) microRequirement	(B5)
microKnowledgeArtefact	= $\bigcup$ knowledgeItem(s)	(B6)
neuron	= action->data + microKnowledgeArtefact	(B7)
microArtefact / neural network	= $\bigcup$ neurons	(B8)
microArtefactScenario	= $\bigcup$ microartefact	(B9)
AI/Decision Making	= $\bigcup$ microArtefactScenario	(B10)
microEntity	= $\bigcup$ microArtefact	(B11)
Entity or Enterprise	= $\bigcup$ microEntity	(B12)
EnityIntelligence	= $\bigcup$ AI/Decision Making	(B13)
BMM(*Iteration*) as an instance	= EnityIntelligence(*Iteration*)	(B14)

The Generic AHMM's Formulation

AHMM	= $\bigcup$ ADMs + BMMs	(B15)

AHMM's Application and Instantiation for AI (and PEABGLP)

Domain	= RAD	(B16)
AHMM4(*Domain*)	= $\bigcup$ ADMs + BMMs(*Domain*)	(B17)

- The AHMM4AI enables that a Project and PEABGLP can be presented models, by using Factors and RWC.

The RWC

TRADf (or an IHITF) needs an internal and open/generic RWC or it can use an external one. *TRADf's* RWC proposes the following rules and definitions:

- The weighting for each CSA is CSA_WGT ϵ { 0.00% … 100.00% } are floating point percentage values, which are derived from DTs (One CSA has one DT and a set of CSFs).
- A weighting is defined for each PEABGLP's CSF, and a rating for each KPI.

- The selected corresponding weightings for CSFs is CSF_WGT ϵ { 1 … 10 } are integer values.
- The selected corresponding ratings to KPI KPI_RAT ϵ { 0.00% … 100.00% } and is derived from: 1) An ICS application/module variable(s) (simply VAR); or 2) Estimated by the IHITF or a domain specialist.
- The AHMM4AI applies the HDT, which uses the RWC.
- RWC (Project-iteration *i*) = ∑CSA*CSA_WGT.
- CSA_WGT = ∑CSF*CSF_WGT.
- CSF_WGT = ∑KPI*KPI_RAT.
- KPI_RAT = ∑VAR*VAR_RAT.

Otherwise the RWC can use standard external solutions like:

- Like the one proposed by the Object Management Group's (OMG) (OMG, 2022): 1) The Decision Model and Notation (DMN); 2) The DMN can be used for implementing business decisions and business rules; and is optimal for Project's status checking; and 3) The DMN can be used for Tables' evaluation and HDT's operations.
- The weighted criteria matrix is a DMS that can evaluate Projects; and is based on the evaluation criteria (that has weighted by ratings). By evaluating alternatives based on KPIs with respect to defined criteria.

The PEABGLP uses the HDT which is mainly qualitative method and has specific calls to quantitative methods. And such complex artefacts need an EERM.

The EERM and the HDT

The EERM is optimal for complex artefacts (Johnson & Onwuegbuzie, 2004; Easterbrook, Singer, Storey & Damian, 2008), which can be enforced with calls to Quantitative Analysis for AI and LP (QNA4LP) and with a central Qualitative Analysis for AI and LP (QLA4AI). These methods differences are in the scope and depth of the research process. The EERM checks if PoC (or experiment) is valid, where a PoC links to dependent-variables (in the form of Factors) and checks relationships exist between these Factors. To Solve a PEABGLP problem type (or RQ, or to evaluate a Factor); and HDT's results/findings enhance LPs. The defined PEABGLP problems (and related Factors) are initialized in the Project's preliminary phase (or the 1st iteration). Then, the HDT (uses data sets, constraints/rules, and goal functions) is launched. Primitive QNA4LP is limited but the QLA4LP uses LPs to improve the DMS; which enables cross-functional linking of LPs which support the Project's Applied Learning Transformation MM (ALTMM) (Hine, 2013).

The ALTMM

The AHMM4AI has: 1) A static view; 2) A dynamic (or behavioural) view; and 3) Access to LPs' storage. The Project is modelled by using the ALTMM that contains:

AHMM4AI=Weigthing_1* QLA4AI +Weigthing_2* QLA4AI (B18).

AHMM4AI = $\sum$ AHMM4AI for a Project iteration (B19).

ALTMM = $\sum$ AHMM4AI instances (B20).

Weigthing_1 and Weigthing_2 are delivered by the RWC and they are ϵ { 0.00% ... 100.00% } and is derived from: 1) Weigthing_1 + Weigthing_2 = 100%; or 2) Weigthing_1 and Weigthing_2 are tuned by the IHITF.

ALTMM's Objective Function (OF) optimization is processed by applying constraints and help variables that need to be interface and calibrated. These variable (for maximization or minimization) can be, for example: ICS' capacities, Project's status, or another condition. For the PoC the success is the constraint can be quantified as a binary 0 or 1, where the OF minimizes *ALTMM's* risks and identifies PEABGLP's efficiency. The *ALTMM* combines various methodologies and the AHMM4AI. Where the AHMM is the skeleton of *TRADf* that used scenarios to support PEABGLP requests (Kim, & Lennon, 2017). In the *Project's* initial phase PEABGLP problem types are selected and processes and needs an LP Polymathic domains, which is the second CSA (Agievich, 2014).

AI AND LP POLYMATHIC BASICS AND DOMAINS

Needed Polymathic Capacities and Approach

Projects needs capacities to implement, structure, design, develop, and transform LPs; where LPs need continuous evolution (Crittenden, 2005). The PEABGLP uses: 1) Evolutive quality concept; 2) Enhancements' concepts; 3) Polymathic implementation; 4) Use of LP patterns; and 5) AI/LP and ICS bridging; 5) ICS' evolution; 6) Building an AI/LP metamodel; 7) Factors management by the ADM (Thune, 2011); 8) To support concurrent LPs; and 9) The ADM, Unified Modelling Language (UML), can be adapted to offer the Transformation Development Method (TDM). The PEABGLP aligns: 1) LPs implementation visions; 2) Supporting LP modelling principles; 3) LPs management; 4) Interfacing external LPs; and 5) Defining optimal granularity and Unit of Work (UoW).

Figure 5. Polymath basic activities
(Cotellessa, 2018)

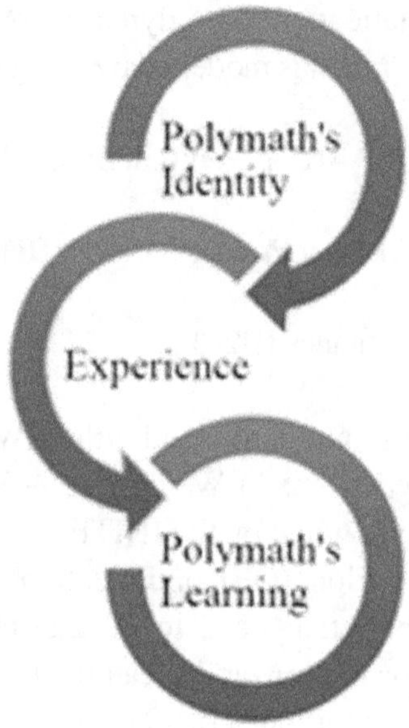

Optimal Granularity and the UoW

The PEABGLP supports design of LPs by using avant-garde activities like brainstorming sessions; Mind mapping, SWOT, UML, ... (Ahmad, 2020). The PEABGLP needs to inter-connect various domains and as shown in Figure 5, to support basic Polymath activities (Cotellessa, 2018). For such activities there is the need to define the Projects granularity and the UoW which align/synchronize *Project's* resources using a holistic "1:1" mapping concept. Projects face various types of problems which can be abstracted by the EAIC.

Applying the EAIC and Managing Complexity

PEABGLPs persist Project's experiences and the PIEPW supports LPs development. The EAIC abstracts concrete problems by using the HDT to solve complex problems. The EAIC supports Project's planning, EA/modelling, and implementation activities which are complex. This complexity to siloed approach which should be cross-functional. The EAIC manages Entity's products/services, employees' multi-tasking capabilities, regulations/governance, roles/responsibilities, frequency of change, application of new strategy... To manage complexities' effects, the EAIC offer an IHI Complexities Management Strategies (CMS) (Heywood, Hillar, & Turnbull,

Figure 6. The PEABGLP is an autonomous sub-system
(Woudenberg, & Unis, 2023)

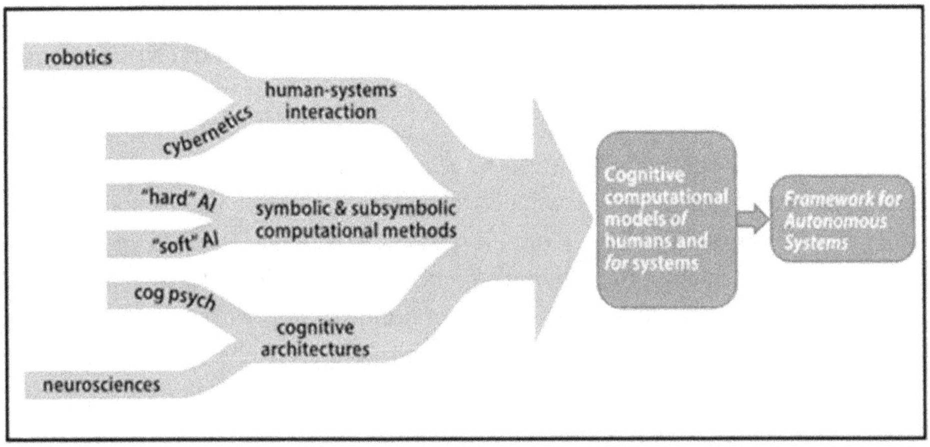

2010). The CMS inter-connects different domains (which are siloed) and manages also external Factors; which can be abstracted by the use of the *Global Simplicity Index (GSI),* which shows the level of complexities' reduction. The CMS uses the HDT for problem-solving and the improvement of LPs (Wikipedia, 2021, 2023). LPs are based on Polymathic thinking which interlinks many fields (Woudenberg, & Unis, 2023; Freeman, 1999) that makes the PEABGLP: 1) A holistic and systemized module; 2) It includes technical and business problem-solving capacities, as shown in Figure 6; and 3) Includes physical, logical, and human Factors.

Projects' complexities and ever evolving ICS/technologies (and AI), have generated a new transformational challenge that can handled by the IHITF. This shift has imposed a Polymath thinking concept and collaboration (Orayer, 2023); and that needs a well-integrated PEABGLP.

THE PEABGLP

LP Basics

The LP tries to simulate the functions of the human-brain which is an empirical concept, and such an LP is based on beam-search and AR that are the fundament of the HDT (Trad, 2019a). The evolution of Entity's Intelligence, depends on LPs, which are capable of handling complex Project problems. LPs depend on the situation/context with respect to finance, history/experiences, real-time events and time. LPs correspond to business functional architectural model.

AR-Based LR

Intelligence includes a cognitive process and attempts to replicate human-intelligence and behaviour; and also tries to apply heuristics/HDT by using an IHI NLP, as shown in Figure 7. Heuristics based Intelligence is a sequential set of actions that starts from an initial state to a solution-state(s). At each state the Intelligence offers a set of actions to find solution(s) that can be less valuable solution, or good solution (or a goal state). Intelligence uses the HDT that has root-node and each new state-node it delivers possible solutions or new problems. These nodes that can learn, use RWC, and produce solutions. When the number of available nodes becomes large, the HDT (and its constraints and Factors) can decide to stop. When a solution-node was selected, then it changes the *Project* (Mobus, & Fisher, 1999).

The HDT NLP's Integration

HDT's NLP (a set of actions-based scenarios) searches for the best-solution(s) that can achieve Project's objectives. Best solutions depend on Factors and OF(s). Intelligence tries solve problems by NLP actions, where the structure of a solution (or a goal states). Each solution is related to set of actions which outputs change HDT's states and modify the Project and related LPs. Selecting the best solution depends on the access to data and actions. The EAIC and PEAbGLP use NLP scripts to interface the HDT in-order to solve problems and enhance LPs. The PIEPW supports integration of an NLPs uses standard tools and development environments,

Figure 7. NLP's integration

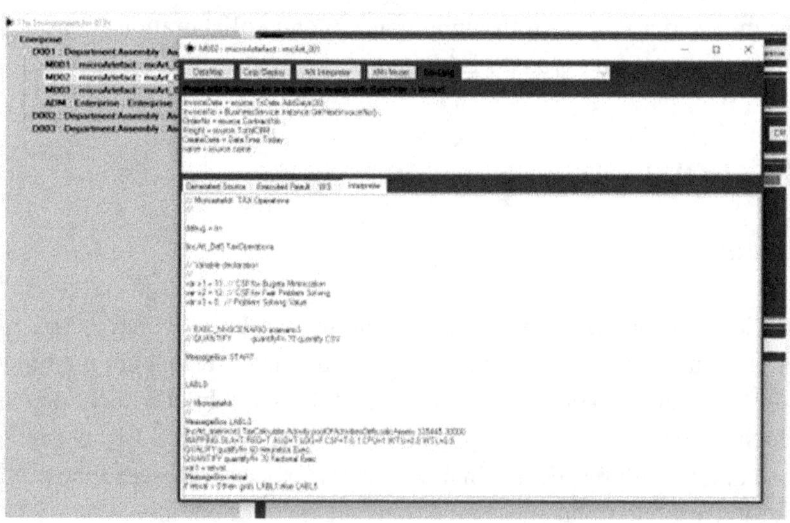

as shown in Figure 7. Heuristics-based reasoning emerged as an Intelligence domain in the middle of the 20th century; and in 1950, Alan Turing developed a fundamental test for machine logic, which is known as the *Turing Test*. The term AI was coined in the proposal for a seminal AI domain's conference that took place at Dartmouth in 1956 (Schmelzer, 2021).

LP and AI Domains

The PEABGLP offers a PIEPW based-interface to AI domains like Operation Research (OR), ML, DL, and other. These domains can be generalized by using the generic EIAC and HDT, this can achieved by: 1) PEAbGLP modelling; 2) Implementing LP interfaces for ML, OR …; 3) Intelligence' integration; 4) The EAIC abstracts OR, ML…; and 5) Using complex algorithmics? Domains like OR, has important advantages as shown in Figure 8 (Kapoor, 2021).

The HDT makes calls to AI domains like ML, OR and other (Trad, & Kalpić, 2021b, 2021c) by:

- Use Artificial Neural Networks (ANN) that promotes iterative LPs, which can be 1) Supervised; 2) Semi-supervised; or 3) Unsupervised.
- OR methods are applied to deliver information for developing optimal decisions, for production or scheduling.
- Many fields like logistics uses OR for optimizing their processes, like for example the optimization of the vehicles routing. OR is used to coordinate operations, processes and activities in *Entities* and is based on mixed methods

Figure 8. LP interfaces OR for Hyperautomation
(Kapoor, 2021)

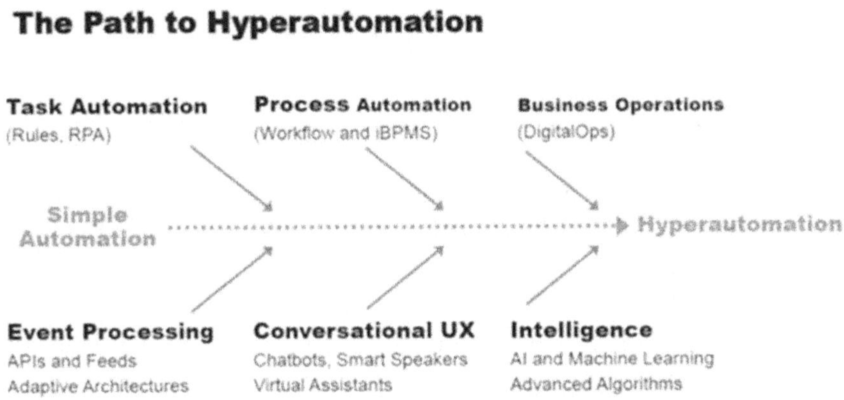

Figure 9. Subfields of AI and OR
(Dornemann, Rückert, Fischer, & Taraz, 2020)

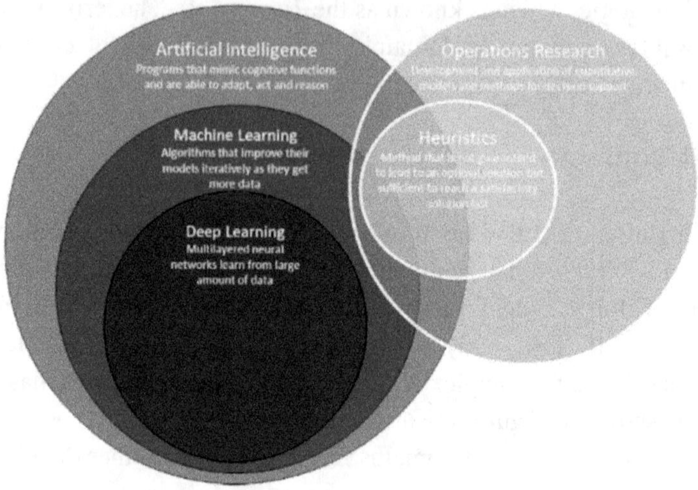

combining quantitative models, with the aim to deliver the optimal solution for a planning problem.

The EAIC interfaces OR fields: Linear Programming Domain (LPD), Mixed (MIP), and Non-Linear Programming (NP). It includes also: simulations, Markov chains and game theory. These fields need important computing resources. Domains like ML and OR enhance LPs by recursively partitioning problem sources' into subtypes. DLD's uses Deep Neural Networks (DNN), that uses different layers to abstract complexities as shown in Figure 7, and illustrates the EAIC's abstraction of AI domains. The PEAbGLP uses OFs to optimize which measures discrepancy between outputs, and causes that the LPs' predictions are enhance (trained), by persisting solution's path and the target, which can be done by the HD, which can also interface Data Science (DS) (Trad, & Kalpić, 2021b), as shown in Figure 9.

Interfacing DS

DS is the process of finding patterns-meaning in data-stores by using AI-technics, like ML, DL, OR, or other, which enhance LPs. LPs can interface DS and OR for optimizing planning, inventory, transportation… And offers two models: 1) Deterministic models that includes NP, which is an optimization problem using an OF, and 2) LPD is applied to find optimal solution(s); and 2) Stochastic models that include: a- Markov process, which tries to proactively estimates changes; b-

Discrete-Time Markov Chains (DTMC) that uses sets of just in time independent variables (Factors); c- A Continuous-Time Markov chain (CTMC) is always an available stochastic process that for all states, it can modify its HDT state's contents; d- Queueing Theory (QT) is an MM that describes waitind ng objects, known as queues. EAIC offer an AI Polymathic model.

The EAIC a Polymathic Model

Polymathic model's basics are (Schmelzer, 2021): 1) Use classifications and unbundling; 2) LP and interfaces with OR (or other) is optimal for HDT; 3) The IHITF supports EAIC. Polymathic models uses the HDT and the RWC (Della Croce, & T'kindt, 2002). The HDT uses: 1) ANNs that has a set of connected tree-nodes named Artificial Neurons (AN); 2) LPs uses OR algorithms. This part (or CSA) shows clearly that the Entity has to establish a LP based Polymathic Entity Metamodel (PEM).

THE PEM

There are many approaches for building a PEM, where a PEM is essential for Projects that take many years to finalize; and in-order to avoid Entity's locked-in commercial ICS and AI products, a possible and fairly straight-forward approach can the application of a Relational DataBase (RDB) based PEM.

An RDB-Based PEM

The RDB-based PEM can be gradually implemented by using Entity's ICS/data-storage without the need for continuous colossal investments in siloed-external products. Such a PEM supports a Project, because the RDB is used in all ICS' subsystems. The main advantage is that RDBs contain all the essential information, structures, integrity-checking controls, and applied MM constraints/constructs (Trad, 2023f).

An Asset Management-Based PEM

A Project can use the Holistic Project Asset Management Concept (HPAMC) to support a PEM. The HPAMC manages Entity's assets that includes on all its resources/assets: 1) Business cases, requirements, and processes; 2) Financial and real-estates assets; 3) Software, DBs, ICS components; and other types of assets (Trad, & Kalpić, 2020a). The PEM delivers a transcendent and generic approach.

A Transcendent and Generic Approach

The EAIC is an AI driven-concept that offers LP templates and patterns to support Entity's Intelligence; and is also coupled with a mapping concept for the requirements and other Project's parts. A generic approach needs a successful unbundling of the legacy ICS and AI-modules. The Polymathic Unbundling/conversion Process (PUP) of the legacy ICS needs an IHI Methodology, Domain, and Technology Common Artefacts Standard (MDTCAS) that can map existing Microartefacts, Building Blocks (BB)... to a Project and EIAC (Trad, 2023e). The MDTCAS, as shown in Figure 10, maps also to existing methodologies, like the Object Oriented (OO) Methodology (OOM), UML, The Open Group's (TOG) Architecture Framework's (TOGAF)/ ADM... BBs contain Intelligence and Application services and can be modelled by using EA and NLP. There is the need to apply the "1:1" mapping concept for unbundled BBs. The EAIC and PEAbGLP use complex communication interfaces to interact with various NLP scripts which main aim is: 1) HDT solutions; 2) Locate fallouts; 3) Interface different ICS-languages; 4) Interfaces EA and MDTCAS; and 5) Accesses dictionaries and registries.

Dictionaries and Registries

The NLP uses the Universal Description, Discovery and Integration (UDDI) to access services' catalogues and Business Processes (BP). Such an environment links Intelligence services and combine them with BP. The PEM can use the registry

Figure 10. MDTCAS' implementation

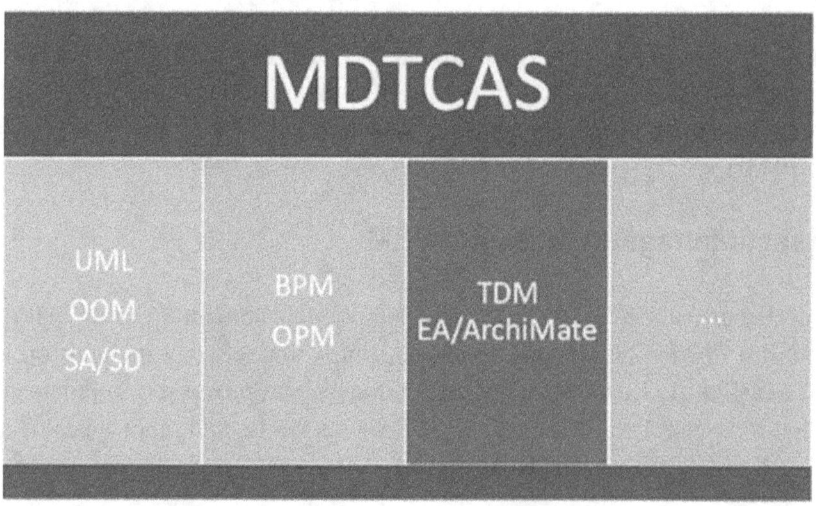

Figure 11. EAIC2FAC's structures

```
SWOT2CSA
{
        S_Value                  = HDT.eval( CSA.S_Value);
        W_Value          = HDT.eval( CSA.W_Value);
        O_Value          = HDT.eval( CSA.O_Value);
        T_Value          = HDT.eval( CSA.T_Value);
};
CSA2CSF
{
        S_Value                  = HDT.eval( CSF.S_Value);
        W_Value          = HDT.eval( CSF.W_Value);
        O_Value          = HDT.eval( CSF.O_Value);
        T_Value          = HDT.eval( CSF.T_Value);
};
CSF2KPI
{
        S_Value                  = HDT.eval( KPI.S_Value);
        W_Value          = HDT.eval( KPI.W_Value);
        O_Value          = HDT.eval( KPI.O_Value);
        T_Value          = HDT.eval( KPI.T_Value);
};
Interfacing to Concrete Artefacts
KPI elements map/link to VAR by using the KPI2VAR structure:
KPI2VAR
{
        S_Value                  = HDT.eval( BB.VAR.S_Value);
        W_Value          = HDT.eval( BB.VAR.W_Value);
        O_Value          = HDT.eval( BB.VAR.O_Value);
        T_Value          = HDT.eval( BB.VAR.T_Value);
};
```

to interface high level Entity components, like SWOT, where elements map/link to Factors by using the EAIC to Factors (EAIC2FAC) class-structure. Each CSA contains related CSFs and in turn KPIs where each KPI links to an ICS variable (VAR, which is a BB's attribute and is represented as BB.VAR) (Javatpoint, 2021; Trad, & Kalpić, 2023a), and the various structures are shown in Figure 11.

Interfacing Project Implementation Environments

PEM's (and EAIC) EAIC2FAC can be used to interface all existing environments:

- Behaviour Driven Development (BDD) that is influenced by NLP's systems thinking.
- Modelling Language-ArchiMate that includes behavioural and structural elements; with a wide range of elements and relationships. ArchiMate-elements are grouped into the layers of ArchiMate Framework (Hosiaisluoma, 2021).
- Application cartography tools and diagrams like
- TOGAF's the Application Communication Diagram (ACD), which depicts all used models and mappings related to communication between applications.
- Application Programming Interface's (API) management tools (Patni, 2017).
- Test Driven Development (TDD) is a manual approach and a concept where software developers design the test first (Janzen & Saiedian, 2005).
- Acceptance Test-Driven Development (ATDD) is used to make collaborate business clients, *Project* engineers, *Project* testers and software engineers and to assist their communication (Koudelia, 2011). Based on standard TDDs, the standard ATDD methodology is based on developing tests where tests represent the results of the requirement's behaviour of a set of NLPs and BDDs.
- Requirements' implementation uses NLP scripts and methodologies like UML.
- PEM's and EIAC's capabilities enable a successful integration of Intelligence.

INTELLIGENCE

Adapting AR to LP and Intelligence

AR's main characteristics to adapt to LP and hence Intelligence, are (Burns, 2015; O'Leary, 2007):

- AR is optimal for LPs, because its empirical approach that enriches reflective practice and local practical inquiry.
- AR tackles concrete problems in participatory, collaborative, and cyclical ways in order to produce IKIs and LPs.
- Can be: Positivist, Interpretive, and Critical; and supports basic operations that are shown in Figure 12 (BRM, 2022).

Figure 12. AR's basic operations
(BRM, 2022)

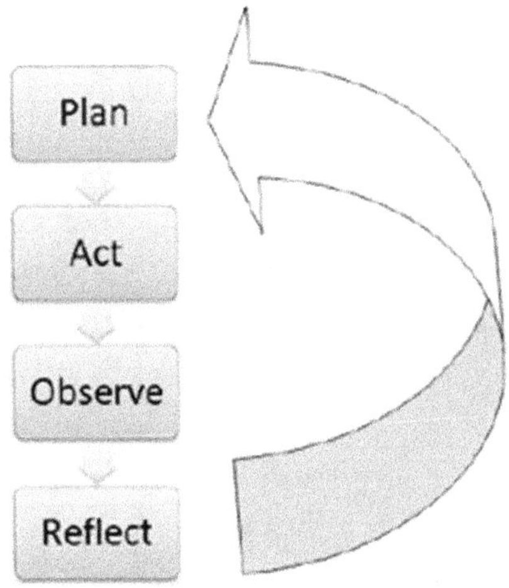

AR based Intelligence Basics

An Entity and its Projects are supported the PEABGLP and its related HDT which forms the Entity's Intelligence. Intelligence manages Return On Experiences (ROE). ROEs are enriched by solutions for encountered problems. Solutions are compound objects that contain actions, recommendations, and business cases, which 7improve transformational changes' success rates. Therefore, the PEABGLP minimizes Project risks' (Hussain, Dillon, Chang & Hussain, 2010). The PEABGLP manages ROEs which are sets of Intelligence Knowledge Items (IKI), where and ROE is a set of interlinked IKIs and enhanced *Intelligence*… PEABGLP supports Intelligence to establish problem-solving strategies, patterns-actions… Besides empirical concepts, the PEABGLP includes a Data Modelling Concepts (DMC).

The DMC

The DMC offers access management for data through a dynamic data architecture which is a layered group of data-models that is based on Data BBs (DBB) which that can be represented with class-diagrams. The DMC includes: 1) The Class-diagram and mapping concepts, supports the establishment of data architecture and modelling artefacts; and concentrates business aspects; 2) Data Solution Blocks (DSB) that includes NLP scripts that manages data accesses; and 3) Engineering patterns, use mapping mechanisms to support interoperability various fata-sources and strategic Intelligence subsystems.

Figure 13. Complex system's approach
(Daellenbach & McNickle, 2005)

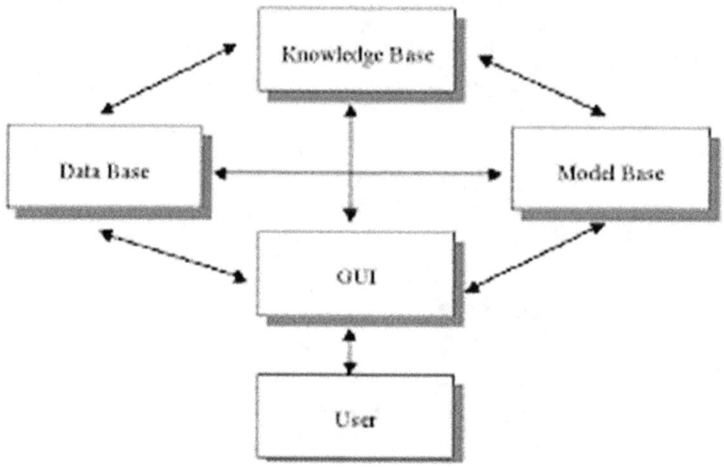

Strategic Intelligence Subsystems

Integrating Intelligence is complex undertaking which includes the integration of subsystems like OR, DS/systems' analysis, various AI domains and systems' modelling, as shown in Figure 13. Intelligence is supported by the EAIC to automate IKIs and to unify AI-domains integration (Daellenbach & McNickle, 2005). Such an automation needs LP Patterns (LPP).

LPPs can conform to existing standard formats like (Trad, & Kalpić, 2021a): Project Management XML (PMXML) used by the project management body of knowledge (PMBOK); Architecture XML (ArchiXML); System Modelling XML (SysML); Representational State Transfer (ReST) Web Application Description Language (WADL); RESTful API Modelling Language (RAML); The Information Technology Infrastructure Library (ITIL) that uses the Data Centre XML (DCML); Control Objectives for Information and Related Technology (COBIT) using the Governance, Risk, and Compliance XML (GRC-XML); Business Reporting XML (BRL); Business Process Modelling Notation (BPMN); Business Process Execution Language (BPEL); Client side frameworks (NodeJS); Entity Relational Modelling (ERM) using the XML Scheme Diagrams (SD); TDD; BDD; Business Rules Management (BRM); and others.

EA for AI and PEABGLP

The TOAF/ADM based IHITF can be adapted to support EAIC, because provides a methodological approach to Project's activities like planning, designing, and other. Therefore PEABGLP is enforced with workflow automation, customer service enhancement, predictive analytics… These facts enforce Business Architecture (BA) LPs, where Figure 14 shows the inter-action between the various parties, core processes, LPs, and the Entity (Crosley, Indrajit, & Dazki, 2023).

Intelligence as an Expert System

LP based Expert Systems (LPES) like the ones used for medical, geopolitical, conflicts/wars, financial, and military analysis, which makes them more than strategic. LPES can be for example, applied for: 1) Military analysis and related geopolitical risks' estimations. LPES balances risks related to military technologies. The evolutive capabilities is seeing important changes in the fields of: Cyber, electronic warfare, sensors, data, networks, cloud computing, AI, autonomy/robotics, genomics, biotech and synthetic biology; 2) The integration of Internet of Things (IoT) devices, AI-domains like Business Intelligence (BI), which have increased 300,000-fold from 2012 to 2018, which is doubling every few months, As shown in Figure 5 (Trad, 2021d).

Figure 14. BA that is supported by LPs
(Crosley, Indrajit, & Dazki, 2023)

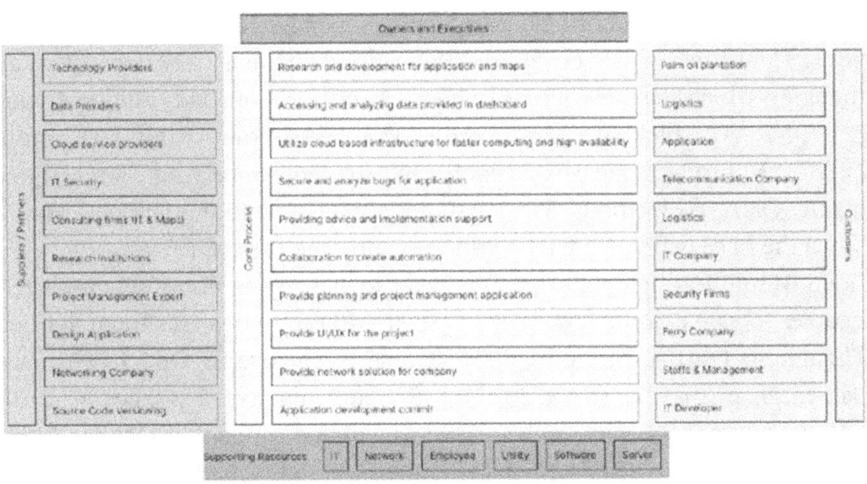

Figure 15. AI projects' trends
(Trad, 2021d)

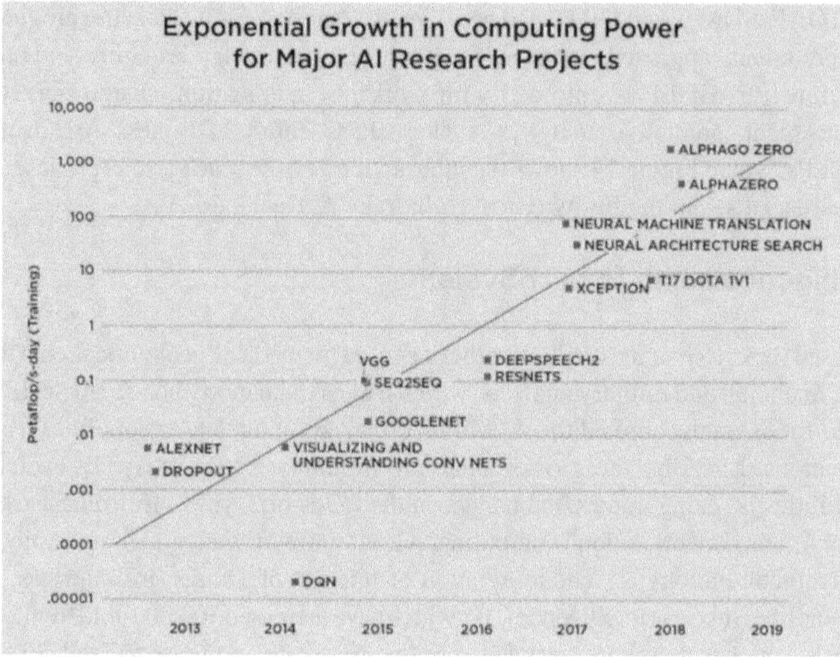

Cloud LP-Based BI

The advantages of Cloud LP based BI services are accessible on various ICS nodes. The Cloud serves as BI's infrastructure and LPs' processing. LPs are sets of choreographed services that are used to solve problems. LPs based BIs provide Entities with access to data-based dashboards, business KPIs and other business analytics. The LP based BIs cover all APplication Domain's (APD) analytics and BI strategies, which includes access to business-critical data and solutions; which is just a QNA4AI which needs to be mixed view like in the AR/HDT (Klipfolio, 2022). Most BI products have exclusively QNA4AI approach. And Cloud BI tools use mainly QNA4AI methods. The EAIC supports Cloud to migrate data-sources and when the PUP is finalized, then which enables the PEAbGLP.

Cloud BI solutions integrate data platforms to interrogate Entity's data-sources, that enables to gain a *360-degree* view of their APD activities, as shown in Figure 16 (ThoughtSpot, 2023; Klipfolio, 2022). Cloud BI can use BigData mechanisms. BigData mechanisms offer (SAS, 2021): 1) Supports massive, fast accesses; 2) The three V's:: Volume, Velocity, and Variety; 3) Volume supports collecting from a variety of sources; 4) Velocity supports speed and scalability; and 5) Variety supports various types of formats.

Figure 16. A BI dashboard presenting 360 numbers around customers (ThoughtSpot, 2023; Klipfolio, 2022)

EIAC and PEAbGLP Skills

The needed set of skills are (Trad, 2021b, 2021g): 1) Detailed LPs modeling; 2) AI components' design; 3) PEAbGLP application services; 4) Requirement engineering; 5) Standardized ICS/AI/LP services integration; 6) EA and related Business, Data, Application, and Technology Architectures; 7) Generic skills like leadership; 8) Business engineering; 9) PM technics; 10) ICS technologies; 11) Business use cases design BP process modeling; 12) Standard frameworks; and other.

Standards Frameworks

EAIC interfaces market frameworks like risk frameworks; where the most popular is Committee of Sponsoring Organizations of the Treadway Commission (COSO), which is shown in Figure 17. The EAIC consults executive directors, Project-members, and is designed to identify risks (Trad, 2021i).

The COSO framework include components, a common language and offers a roadmap for risk-management, which enhances LPs. And the EAIC includes security mechanisms like: Managing Passwords, Firewalls, Secure Development and Operations, Antivirus, Wireless Fidelity, Malware, Security Monitoring and Logs...

Figure 17. The COSO framework
(Curtis, & Carey, 2012)

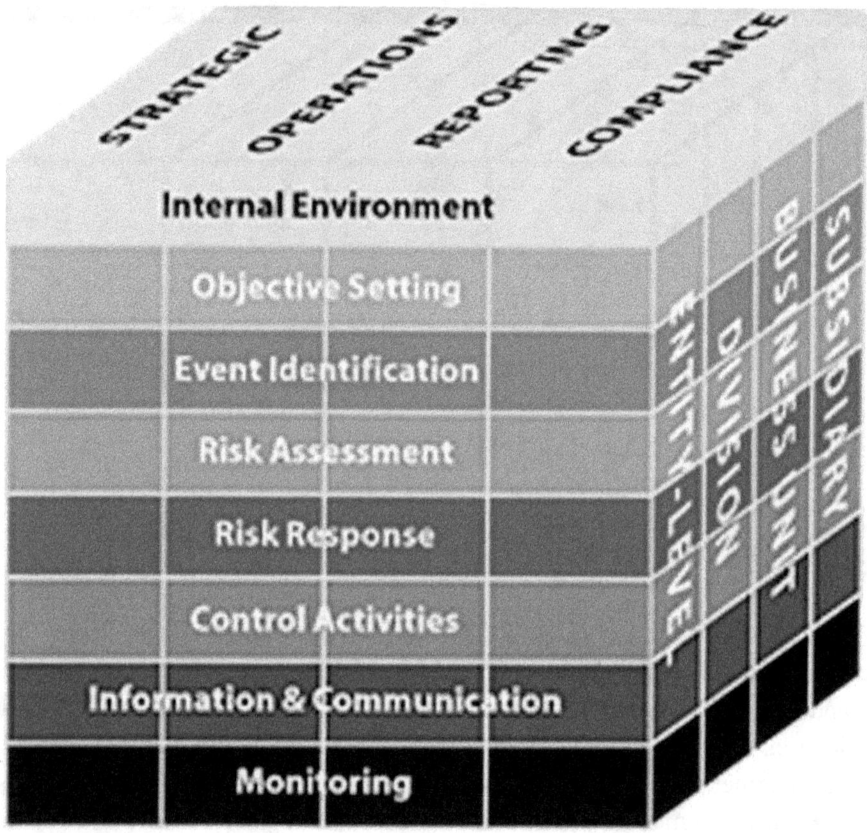

THE PROOF OF CONCEPT

The PoC uses the selected ACSs and its objective is to show that the EIAC support PEABGLPs and LPs.

PEABGLP-Based Scenarios

The Project uses and manages the selected Factors and a common ACS (EA based transformation concept as shown in Figure 18). PEABGLP's actions in ADM phases, are: 1) Phase A: To setup PIEPW services' roadmap; 2) Phase B: To setup PEABGLP's target architecture; 3) Phase C: To model EAIC's application landscape; 4) Phase D: Manages the gap analysis; and 5) Phases E/F: Verifies PEABGLP's implementation and evaluate Project's status.

Figure 18. Transformation goals
(Jonkers, Band, & Quartel, 2012)

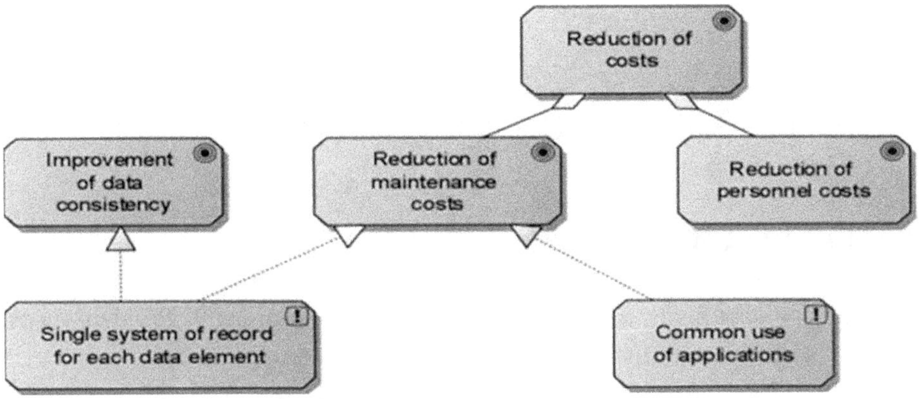

Factors and Constraints Setup

In this case OR's integration is considered and execution starts with the use the prepared sets of data, then the execution of the HDT follows, and delivers optimal solution(s).

RDP's Phases

This RDP's concept proposes a standardized and automated manner to evaluate the RLR. If RWC's evaluation is successful, then the PoC is completed. RDP's Phase 1 constraint is that CSAs that have an average result below 8.0 will be ignored. As shown in Table 1, the results justify (with an average of 8.15) the usage of the EAIC

Table 1. The PEABGLP RDP's outcome is (rounded) 8.15 Poc's Ececution

CSA Category of CSFs/KPIs	Transformation Capability	Average Result	Table
The RDP's Integration	Usable-Mature	From 1 to 10 9.20	1
AI/LP Polymathic Basics	Transformable-Possible-Complex	From 1 to 10 8.10	2
The PEABGLP	VeryComplex	From 1 to 10 7.00	5
The PEM	Transformable-Possible-Mature	From 1 to 10 9.00	4
Intelligence	Heterogenous-Complex	From 1 to 10 7.80	5

Evaluate First Phase

and HDT can be used and that Phase 2 can be done. The PEABGLP (and EIAC) interfaces Intelligence and its Factors which are presented and evaluated (by the RWC) in Table 1.

The NLP scripts manages Factors and link to AHMM4AI's instance and it's HDT. Table 1 presented results concludes PoC's first phase, which shows that the PEABGLP is very complex.

The HDT and Offered Solutions

The HDT contains nodes that use: 1) Actions; 2) Constraints; 3) Problem types; and 4) A set of possible solutions/recommendations. An HDT node contains a CSF proposal/state. A state contains an aggregate of a resource linked with a 1:1 mapping link.

Then the HDT delivers a set of solutions which are in fact transformational actions. As shown in Figure 19, the EAIC's layers are: 1) EA/EAIC link to OR; 2) The client side includes AI-modules which interface: RDBs, and various types of interfaces; 3) Application services; 4) Resources management system; and 6) ICS' platform. The HDT interfaces uses Google's OR library (Google Developers, 2021) and the used OF tries to deliver the best solution(s) for the PoC's problem. HDT's (and using OR) results are delivered as a set of solutions. The defined OF helps to find the best solution, and the EAIC delivers the needed packages. The PoC's problem is execute a transaction that supports the transport vehicles to end-users. Where it assigns modules to vehicles, and then chooses the optimal route. OR finds the route with optimal costs, calculated distance travelled by the vehicle, and other constraints and Factors. The best solution is OF's best value (maximum or minimum). OF and selected constraints are linear expressions, which defines the problem and are fed in NLP scripts. The next step was is to tune the OF and constraints, by using LP which is called from an HDT node, like all QNA4AI methods. OR/LP inputs an array of arguments: 1) OF pointer; 2) Constraints; and 3) Decision variables/Factors.

Figure 19. The activation of OF

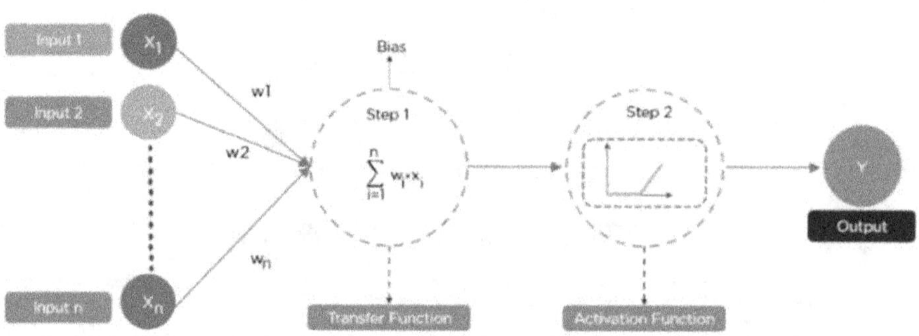

Figure 20. Interacting SWOT

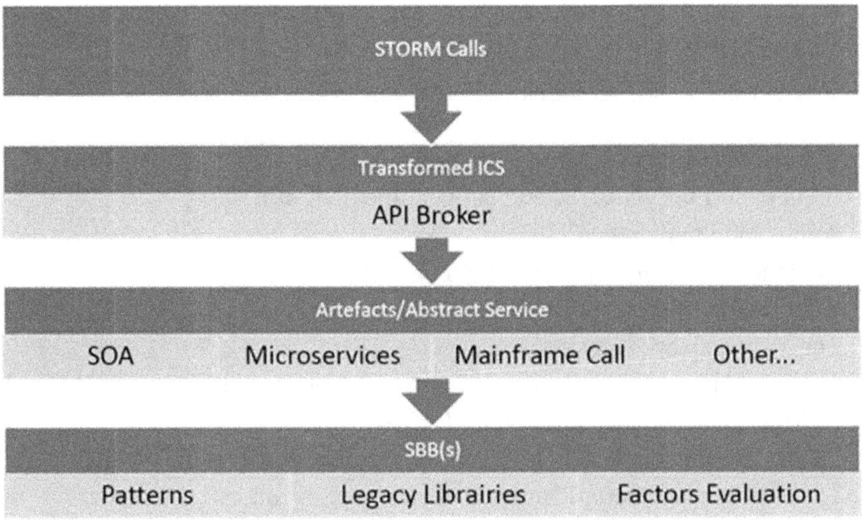

Interfacing High-Level Methods

Using Factors to interface SWOT as shown in Figure 20 and EAIC executs the following steps:

- Linking EAIC to SWOT.
- Factors tags are linked to various SWOT scenarios. Links Factors to structures, like CSA2CSF…
- Intelligence and its HDT to deliver SWOT's output/solutions.

The used SWOT are: EAIC2FAC, CSA2CSF, CSF2KPI, and KPI2VAR; and then IHITF's frontend mapping actions are activated by: 1) Selecting HDT nodes that contains the Factors, and 2) .Selecting the problem to be solved. SWOT uses Intelligence to generate actions to solve a request.

SOLUTION AND RECOMMENDATIONS

This chapter proposes a set of architecture, refinement, technical and managerial recommendations:

- Implement an IHITF and MDTCAS.

- The author uses his *TRADf* to show how and Entity can build an IHITF.
- Using an IHI EA (for defining the *target architecture*), which can support the PEAbGLP.
- EA serves as a methodology and tool to provide the link between the EAIC, PEAbGLP, and LPs.
- The ADM manages design, PUP, and EAIC activities.
- Implement Entity's TDM and delivers the pool of BBs.
- Apply and finalize the PUP.
- Implement a flexible and scalable ICS.
- Establish an optimal PEM.
- The NLP concept is mature.
- The EAIC is complex and is feasibility; and interface PEM with EAIC.
- A Project uses scripts to integrate Intelligence.
- Efforts must be applied to integrate PEAbGLP in whole the Entity.
- The PEABGLP's complexity lies in ICS heterogeneous components.
- Apply AR based LPs.
- Collect ROEs to enhance LPs.
- The Project uses PIEPW to integrate PEAbGLP.
- Intelligence interfaces existing AI-domains like ML, DL, OR, LP,…
- To use RWC based DT to filter and weight CSAs.
- Use the HDT to solve problem.
- The ADM4AI support the PEAbGLP.
- The Project defines a strategy to persist the Entity's LPs.
- EIAC interfaces high-level methods like SWOT.
- Accumulated IKI/knowledge/experiences are fed in the Entity's storage.
- This RDP uses a multi-dimensional concept, because it has: 1) An adapted mixed research concept; 2) Shows how to build an internal methodology framework; and 3) A methodological approach based on EA and AI.
- The RLR proved the existence of an important knowledge gap.
- To use a mathematical model (like the AHMM4AI) and LP based HDT, to support Intelligence's operations.
- Cross-functional/Polymathic skills are needed for such Projects.
- The PEABGLP coordinates LPs integration to deliver knowledge blueprints, patterns, …
- To implement a PIEPW based teamwork.
- PEABGLP is optimal because it promotes Polymathism, critical-thinking, and opinion-based concepts.

FUTURE RESEARCH DIRECTIONS

The *TRADf* future research efforts will focus on building a meta-model for Projects.

CONCLUSION

This version of RDP is part of a series of publications related to IHITF, Projects, and AI. This research is based on mixed-method the HDT that combines QLA4AI and QNA4AI research models. Factors are selected and tuned by the RWC to diminish risks and improve success rates when building an EAIC and PEAbGLP in Projects. In this chapter, the focus is on PEAbGLP, where it proposes a structured concept to implement LPs. The most important managerial recommendation that was generated by the previous research phases was that the Project's manager must be an architect of adaptive business systems or BTPAP. The PoC was based on the selected Factors that were linked to RDP resources and Intelligence's model. Intelligence represents the relationships between AI, HDT, LPs, Project requirements, BBs/microartefacts and Factors. The final result shows that EAIC and PEAbGLP are complex but the transformation process is possible. Therefore, the author recommends an iterative Project. The complexity is due to siloed AI and Project's concepts and implementation teams lack of PEABGLP, EAIC, EA, AI, and ICS skills. The Project teams must use PIEPW for AI related implementation; and the PEABGLP uses PIEPW services. The PEABGLP is needed to manage LPs to improve the Entity's Intelligence. Because of the low score, 8.15, Table 1 shows that PEABGLP's integration is very complex but possible. And the most important recommendations are:

- The EAIC and PEABGLP are strategic and need specific skills.
- The EAIC and PEABGLP have tangible and intangible values.
- AHMM4AI combines QNA4AI and QLA4AI, where the QLA4AI is for intangible values.
- Requirement engineering includes AI modules like AR based LPs; which enrich Entity's Intelligence.
- The EAIC interfaces various AI-domains like BigData, DS, ML, DL, which are commercial products.
- The PEABGLP uses a specific mixed approach.
- Projects and AI transformations haves very low success rates.
- Cloud based AI solutions are extremely expensive and are risky.
- The EAIC and PEABGLP support business secrecy and avoid Business as a Service (BaaS).
- The EAIC and PEABGLP support business sustainability.

- LPs need polymathic architecture and Project teams.
- Avoid siloed commercial AI products, which locked in Entities and blocks their evolution.

REFERENCES

Adhytia, B., Kurnia, Sh., Dilnutt, R., & Hidayanto, A. (2023). *Investigating the Role of Enterprise Architecture in Big Data Analytics Implementation: A Case Study in a Large Public Sector Organization. ACIS 2023 Proceedings Australasian*. ACIS.

Agievich, V. (2014). *Mathematical model and multi-criteria analysis of designing large-scale enterprise roadmap*. PhD thesis.

Ahmad, G. (2010). *Domain-Oriented Modeling of Indian Education System Through UML*. IUP.

Blackburn, R., & Rosen, B. (1993). Total quality and human resources management: lessons learned from Baldrige Award-winning companies. *Academy of Management Perspectives, 7*(3).

BRM. (2022). *Action Research*. Business Research Methodology. BRM.

Burns, A. (2015). *Action Research*. UNSW Sydney.

Clark, W., Johnson, K., & Turner, C. (2004). *Cross-Functional Student Teams as a Teaching Tool for Enhanced Learning*. East Tennessee State University, Johnson City.

Cotellessa, A. (2018). In Pursuit of Polymaths: Understanding Renaissance Persons of the 21st Century. Department Human and Organizational Learning and International Affairs. The Faculty of The Graduate School of Education and Human Development of The George Washington University.

Crittenden, V., & Wilson, E. (2006). An Exploratory Study of Cross-Functional Education in the Undergraduate Marketing Curriculum. *Journal of Marketing Education, 28*(1), 81–86. doi:10.1177/0273475305284643

Crosley, N., Indrajit, R., & Dazki, E. (2023). TOGAF Framework For an AI-enabled Software House. *Sinkron: Jurnal dan Penelitian Teknik Informatika, 8*(2). doi:10.33395/sinkron.v8i2.12390

Curtis, P., & Carey, M. (2012). *Committee of Sponsoring Organizations of the Treadway Commission-Risk Assessment in Practice*. Deloitte & Touche LLP.

Daellenbach, H., McNickle, D., & Dye, Sh. (2012). *Management Science. Decision-making through systems thinking* (2nd ed.). Plagrave Macmillian.

Della Croce, F., & T'kindt, V. (2002). A recovering beam search algorithm for the one-machine dynamic total completion time scheduling problem. *The Journal of the Operational Research Society*, *53*(11), 1275–1280. doi:10.1057/palgrave.jors.2601389

Dogan, S., Çalgici, P., Arditi, D., & Gunaydin, H. (2015). *Critical success factors of partnering in the building design process. METU JFA 2015/2*. Department of Architecture, İzmir Institute of Technology.

Dornemann, J., Rückert, N., Fischer, K., & Taraz, A. (2020). *Artificial intelligence and operations research in maritime logistics. Econstor*. Leibniz Information Centre for Economics.

Easterbrook, S., Singer, J., Storey, M., & Damian, D. (2008). *Guide to Advanced Empirical Software Engineering-Selecting Empirical Methods for Software Engineering Research*. Springer.

Google Developers. (2021). *Get Started with OR-Tools for C#.* Google. https://developers.google.com/optimization/introduction/dotnet

Heywood, S., Hillar, R., & Turnbull, D. (2010). *Insights into organization-How do I manage the complexity in my organization? Organization Practice*. McKinsey & Company.

Hine, G. S. C. (2013). The importance of action research in teacher education programs. In *Design, develop. evaluate: The core of the learning. environment. Proceedings of the 22nd Annual Teaching Learning Forum, 7-8 February 2013*. Murdoch University. http://ctl.curtin.edu.au/professional_development/conferences/tlf/tlf2013/refereed/hine.html

Hinkelmann, K. (2016). *Modelling in Enterprise Architecture. University of applied sciences northwest Switzerland*. Business School.

Hosiaisluoma, E. (2021). *ArchiMate Cookbook-Patterns & Examples*. Hosiaisluoma.

Hussain, O., Dillon, Th., Chang, E., & Hussain, F. (2010). Transactional risk-based decision making system in e-business interactions. *International Journal of ComputSystSci & Eng, 1*, 15-28.

Janzen, D., & Saiedian, H. (2005). *Test-driven development concepts, taxonomy, and future direction. Computer, 38(9).*

Javatpoint. (2021). *Understanding SWOT Analysis*. Javatpoint. https://www.javatpoint.com/swot

Johnson, R., & Onwuegbuzie, A. (2004). *Mixed Methods Research: A Research Paradigm Whose Time Has Come*. Sage Journals.

Jonkers, H., Band, I., & Quartel, D. (2012a). *ArchiSurance Case Study*. The Open Group.

Kapoor, A. (2021). *Artificial intelligence and machine learning: 5 trends to watch out for in 2021*. AI Zone. https://dzone.com/articles/artificial-intelligence-amp-machine-learning-5-dev

Kim, J., & Lennon, Sh. (2017). *Descriptive Content Analysis on E-Service Research. International Journal of Service Science, Management, Engineering, and Technology*. doi:10.4018/IJSSMET.2017010102

Klipfolio. (2022). *What is Cloud Business Intelligence?* https://www.klipfolio.com/resources/articles/what-is-cloud-business-intelligence

Koudelia, N. (2011). *Acceptance test-driven development* [Master Thesis]. University of Jyväskylä.

Markides, C. (2011, March). Crossing the Chasm: How to Convert Relevant Research Into Managerially Useful Research. *The Journal of Applied Behavioral Science*, *47*(1), 121–134. doi:10.1177/0021886310388162

Mobus, G., & Fisher, P. (1999). *Foraging Search at the Edge of Chaos*. Lawrence Erlbaum & Associates.

Morse, M. (2020). *Making a Difference Through Collaboration: A Case Study Exploring Cross-Functional Collaboration Within an Urban High School in the Northeastern United States* [Doctoral thesis]. The College of Professional Studies of Northeastern University.

O'Leary. (2007). *Action Research-Research Methodologies Guide. A collection of resources describing research.* Academic Press.

OMG. (2022). *Decision model and notation (DMN).* OMG. https://www.omg.org/dmn/

Orayer, O. (2023). *Is Polymath Thinking the Answer to Thriving in the AI Era?* Medium. https://medium.com/@opher.brayer/is-polymath-thinking-the-answer-to-thriving-in-the-ai-era-d269000163a3

Patni, S. (2017). *Pro RESTful APIs Design*. Build and Integrate with REST, JSON, XML and JAX-RS. doi:10.1007/978-1-4842-2665-0

Pittman, J., Severino, L., DeCarlo-Tecce, M., & Kiosoglous, C. (2021). An action research case study: digital equity and educational inclusion during an emergent COVID-19 divide. *Journal for Multicultural Education*.

Polderman, J., & Willems, J. (1998). *Introduction to Mathematical Systems Theory: A Behavioral Approach* (2nd ed.). Springer Verlag. doi:10.1007/978-1-4757-2953-5

PushpakumaraH.JayaweeraP.ManjulanW. (2021). *Using the Open Group Architecture Framework (TOGAF) for Quality Assurance in Higher Education Teaching and Learning*. doi:10.2139/ssrn.3808691

Putri, N., & Yusof, S. M. (2009). Critical success factors for implementing quality engineering tools and techniques in malaysian's and indonesian's automotive industries: An Exploratory Study. *Journal Proceedings of the International MultiConference of Engineers and Computer Scientists.*, *2*, 18–20.

Sankaralingam, K., Ferris, M., Nowatzki, T., Estan, C., Wood, D., & Vaish, N. (2013). *Optimization and Mathematical Modeling in Computer Architecture*. Morgan & Claypool Publishers.

SAS. (2021). *History of Big Data*. SAS. https://www.sas.com/en_us/insights/big-data/what-is-big-data.html

Spencer, M. (2016). *Agile EA – the MVP – enterprise architect-Building the Business Value Chain…* https://enterprisearchitect.wordpress.com/2016/04/11/agile-ea-the-mvp/1/2

Syynimaa, N. (2015). *Enterprise Architecture Adoption Method for Higher Education Institutions* [Doctoral Thesis]. Informatics Research Centre Henley Business School University.

The Open Group. (2011a). *Architecture Development Method*. The Open Group. https://pubs.opengroup.org/architecture/togaf9-doc/arch/chap05.html

The Open Group. (2011b). *TOGAF 9.1*. The Open Group. https://www.opengroup.org/subjectareas/enterprise/togaf

ThoughtSpot. (2023). *Understanding cloud business intelligence: Definition, benefits, and use cases. Business Intelligence*. ThoughtSpot Inc. https://www.thoughtspot.com/data-trends/business-intelligence/cloud-business-intelligence

Thune, T. (2011). Success Factors in Higher Education–Industry Collaboration: A case study of collaboration in the engineering field. *Tertiary Education and Management, 17*(1), 31–50. doi:10.1080/13583883.2011.552627

Trad, A. (2015a). *A Transformation Framework Proposal for Managers in Business Innovation and Business Transformation Projects-Intelligent aBB architecture*. Centeris.

Trad, A. (2015b). *A Transformation Framework Proposal for Managers in Business Innovation and Business Transformation Projects-An ICS's atomic architecture vision*. Centeris.

Trad, A. (2021b). The business transformation enterprise architecture framework for innovation: The role of artificial intelligence in the global business education (RAIGBE). The Business & Management Review, 12(1), 82-97.

Trad, A. (2021c). *Using a Generic Artificial Intelligence Pattern for Business Transformation. Book*. IGI Global.

Trad, A. (2021d). *The Transformation Framework: The Role of Artificial Intelligence for Military Strategies (RAI4MS). Book: Technological Development and Impact on Economic and Environmental Sustainability*. IGI Global.

Trad, A. (2021e). *The Business, Societal, and Enterprise Architecture Framework: An Artificial Intelligence, Data Sciences-, and Big Data-Based Approach. Book: Handbook of Research on Applied Data Science and Artificial Intelligence in Business and Industry*. IGI Global.

Trad, A. (2021f). The Business Transformation Enterprise Architecture Framework: Intelligent Strategic Development and Operations (iSDevOps). *International Journal of Distributed Artificial Intelligence, 13*(1), 74–101. doi:10.4018/IJDAI.2021010104

Trad, A. (2021g). *The Business Transformation Enterprise Architecture Framework for Innovation-The Role of Artificial Intelligence in the Global Business Education (RAIGBE)*. ICBED. doi:10.24052/BMR/V12NU01/ART-08

Trad, A. (2021i). The transformation framework The role security in the global education system. International *Journal of Higher Education Management, 8*(1).

Trad, A., (2022a). *Using a Generic Artificial Intelligence Pattern for Business Transformation*. Academic Press.

Trad, A. (2022b). *Business Transformation and Enterprise Architecture Projects: Natural Language Programming (NLP). Book: Handbook of Research on Applying Emerging Technologies Across Multiple Disciplines*. IGI Global.

Trad, A. (2023a). *Academic and Educational Transformation Projects-The Role Team-Based Learning in Polymathics (RTBLP)*. IGI Global.

Trad, A. (2023b). *Academic and Educational Transformation Projects-The Role Team-Based Learning in Polymathics For University Cycle (RTBLP4UC)*. IGI Global.

Trad, A. (2023c). *Private Cloud based Transformation Projects (PCTP) for Business Intelligence*. E-Leaders. g-casa.com

Trad, A. (2023d). *Business Transformation Project's-The Impact of Rise of Over-the-Top (OTT)*. IGI-Global.

Trad, A. (2023e). *Organizational and Digital Transformation Projects-A Mathematical Model for Building Blocks based Organizational Unbundling Process*. IGI-Global.

Trad, A. (2023f). A Relational DataBase based Enterprise Transformation Projects. *International Journal of Mathematics and Computers in Simulation, 17*, 1-11.

Trad, A., & Kalpic, D. (2004). Proactive monitoring and maintenance of intelligent control systems: a design pattern for autonomous systems. *26th International Conference on Information Technology Interfaces*, 637-642.

Trad, A., & Kalpić, D. (2014a). The Selection and Training Framework for Managers in Business Innovation and Transformation Projects-An applied mathematics hyper-heuristics model. *Proceedings of the 2014 International Conference on Mathematical Methods, Mathematical Models and Simulation in Science and Engineering (MMSSE 2014)*.

Trad, A., & Kalpić, D. (2014b). *The Selection, and Training Framework selection and training framework (STF) for Manager's in Business Innovation Transformation Projects–Educational Recommendations*. Journal EDEN.

Trad, A., & Kalpić, D. (2014c). *The Selection and Training Framework (STF) for Managers in intelligent city Innovation Transformation Projects-Managerial Recommendations*. IEEE.

Trad, A., & Kalpić, D. (2017a). *An Intelligent Neural Networks Micro Artefact Patterns' Based Enterprise Architecture Model*. IGI-Global.

Trad, A., & Kalpic, D. (2018a). Business Transformation Projects-An Intelligence Driven Development for Enterprise Architecture and Asset Management-The Proof of Concept. *ICAMCS Journal*.

Trad, A., & Kalpić, D. (2019a). *Using Applied Mathematical Models for Business Transformation*. IGI Global.

Trad, A., & Kalpić, D. (2020a). *Business Transformation and Enterprise Architecture: The Holistic Project Asset Management Concept (HPAMC). Book: Handbook of Research on Strategic Fit and Design in Business Ecosystems*. IGI Global.

Trad, A., & Kalpić, D. (2021a). *The business transformation framework on Knowledge and Intelligence-Driven Development (KIDD). Book: Encyclopaedia of Organizational Knowledge, Administration, and Technology*. IGI Global.

Trad, A., & Kalpić, D. (2021b). Transformation and Enterprise Architecture Projects-The Integration of Operational Research. *The 3rd International Conference on Machine Learning and Intelligent Systems (MLIS 2021)*.

Trad, A., & Kalpić, D. (2021c). Business transformation project's architect's profile (BTPAP). *The Business & Management Review.*, *12*(2), 137–153. doi:10.24052/BMR/V12NU02/ART-11

Trad, A., & Kalpić, D. (2022a). Business Transformation Projects based on a Holistic Enterprise Architecture Pattern (HEAP)-The Basics. IGI.

Trad, A., & Kalpić, D. (2023a). *SWOT based Transformation's Organizational Risks' Management (STORM)*. E-leaders conference, Check Republic. www.g-casa.om

Wikipedia. (2021). Polymath. In *Wikipedia*. https://en.wikipedia.org/wiki/Polymath

Wikipedia. (2023). *Complexity management*. Wikipedia.

Woudenberg, M., & Unis, C. J. (2023). *Systems Thinking-Skills and Insights to Resolve Wicked Problems. Systems Thinking*. https://www.polymathicbeing.com/p/systems-thinking

Zandia, F., & Tavana, M. (2011). *A fuzzy group multi-criteria enterprise architecture framework selection model*. Elsevier.

Chapter 3
An Anticipatory Framework for Categorizing Nigerian Supreme Court Rulings

Sabyasachi Pramanik
https://orcid.org/0000-0002-9431-8751
Haldia Institute of Technology, India

ABSTRACT

It is important to recognize that a well-run judicial system contributes to the formation of a favorable atmosphere that fosters national growth. The efficient administration of justice is just as important to the court's efficacy as its capacity to be impartial, firm, and fair at all times. Notwithstanding these vital functions of the court, Nigeria's legal system is sometimes unsatisfactory and sluggish moving. People no longer trust the courts because of this, as most people think that justice postponed is justice denied. In recent times, machine learning methods have been used for predictive purposes in several domains. In this work, the authors used 5585 records of precedent rulings from the Supreme Court of Nigeria (SCN) between 1962 and 2022 to construct a prediction model for the categorization of judgments. Primsol Law Pavilion, an independently owned data repository, provided the data. Following data annotation and feature extraction, three classification methods (decision tree, multi-layer perceptron, and kNN) were used to construct the model.

DOI: 10.4018/978-1-6684-9716-6.ch003

INTRODUCTION

Maintaining the rule of law at all times and defending and upholding the constitution are among the judiciary's fundamental goals as the third branch of the government (Ahmad et al., 2021). Today's highly advanced and industrialized human society has produced tremendous advancements, particularly in the fields of technology and architecture (Bhilare et al., 2019). Among the most integral achievements of humanity are law and society. The development of the legal system started with the rise of human civilization. Communities bound to a certain legislature have experienced significant disruptions and anxiety as a result of the lack of openness and ignorance of the legal procedures. As data becomes more widely available, the necessity for established standards and methods becomes even more critical (Medvedeva, 2023). Many European national and international courts strive for openness by following the regulation to encourage the reuse and accessibility of public sector information and to post their records online (Marković, 2018). An exceptional chance to handle this material automatically on a broad scale is presented by digital access to a substantial body of published case law.

Computers are now machines that can learn without supervision and adapt to new inputs without needing to be reprogrammed. This is due to recent advancements in data collection, aggregation systems, algorithms, and processing power (Ashley & Brüninghaus, 2009). In the past, there have been many efforts to anticipate court judgments using statistical techniques, such as factor and linear regression analysis. In 1957, Kort made an effort to use quantitative techniques to forecast Supreme Court rulings. Probability theory and quantitative approaches were suggested by Nagel (1960) and Ulmer (1963) for the analysis of court documents. These systems, however, were noise-sensitive and did not transfer to other legal areas (Cui et al., 2022).

Machine learning algorithms' ability to forecast court decisions has gained popularity (Aletras et al., 2016). Artificial intelligence has been used to build legal decision systems that help attorneys by automatically anticipating verdicts (Kelbert et al., 2012). Big data analytics proponents contend that it will lessen human prejudice and provide the legal system a scientific, evidence-based approach (Simmons, 2018; Završnik, 2018). In order to help judges in certain instances, machine learning has been used to provide answers known as algorithmic decision predictors (Ashley, 2019). These algorithms foretell the outcome of a case, which would normally be decided by a court or judges (e.g., guilty/not guilty, plaintiff/defendant ruling) (Medvedeva et al., 2020). It is sometimes said that algorithmic decision predictors increase the consistency and predictability of judicial decision-making, which is required under the equality principle.

These arguments contend that decision predictors may help judges make decisions that are more consistent, knowledgeable, and free of prejudice (Chalkidis et al., 2019; O'Neil, 2016). Machine learning classifiers use a traditional encoding method that does not capture the overall connections between predictor variables in a machine learning-based data set, even though selecting efficient predictors and using machine learning techniques on large data sets can yield impressive results (Alghazzawi et al., 2022). The studies conducted by Bhilare et al. (2019) and Shaikh et al. (2020) emphasized the use of manually derived characteristics from the court case dataset before using a series of machine learning algorithms to construct a prediction model that was based on performance. There have been claims that this technique can unintentionally reinforce prejudice and bias that are already present in training data (Liu et al., 2018).

Numerous efforts have been made in related literatures to use machine learning-based algorithms to the creation of prediction models for the legal system, using both structured and unstructured information. Studies that took into account the usage of unstructured information, however, run the danger of making it more difficult to accurately determine the semantic link using NLP algorithms (Medvedeva et al., 2023). Because of this, using structured datasets based on characteristics taken from court cases might be a good substitute; nevertheless, questions have been raised about the accuracy of the human feature identification method (Aletras, 2016). Greater issues have arisen as a result of the steady growth in the quantity of data being saved and the use of mobile devices to access this data. This is because information is difficult for human specialists to access properly, particularly with the introduction of big data.

Because of this, we decided to use unsupervised machine learning techniques to evaluate the dependency between characteristics in order to identify features that are redundant or irrelevant, which would increase the accuracy of the prediction model. In an attempt to assist Nigerian judges in making knowledgeable decisions about related cases in the future, the effect of two feature selection algorithms on the accuracy of three classification algorithms was tested in this paper using data gathered from historical (precedent) court cases from the Supreme Court of Nigeria (SCN). In this study, we used feature selection to determine the most significant characteristics that affect how Nigerian Supreme Court rulings are categorized. Additionally, we created a classification model utilizing three distinct machine learning algorithms—decision tree, KNN, and multi-layer perceptron—to forecast court case outcomes based on data that were retrieved. Lastly, we assessed the constructed prediction models' performance.

Supplies and Procedures

Nigerian Judicial Process Components

One fundamental tenet of Nigerian justice administration is judicial precedent. According to judicial precedence, issues that are similar should be resolved similarly (Ali, 2020). In circumstances when the facts are sufficiently comparable, it basically requires courts to follow decisions that have already been resolved (Ogbu, 2007). The stare decisis, or "stand by the decided," concept is used in accordance with the theory of judicial precedent. This essentially implies that lower courts must follow the rules of law established by higher courts in previous decisions.

This gives the law predictability and consistency. This concept states that a magistrate court must adopt a High Court's ruling in any case when the circumstances are comparable to those of a case that the High Court has determined. When the circumstances of a case determined by the Court of Appeal are comparable to a matter that is ongoing before a High Court, the High Court is also required to follow the Court of Appeal's judgment. When evaluating identical circumstances pertaining to both the case at hand and a matter that the Supreme Court has resolved, the Court of Appeal is required to adhere to the ruling of the Supreme Court.

A case law collection is a list of earlier decisions. It has significant weight in the Nigerian legal system and significantly influences judges' judgments. It is expensive for self-willed judges to arbitrarily depart from it since any judgment or choices these judges make might be overturned on appeal, making their process of making the decisions pointless. The Supreme Court follows its own prior rulings and will only stray from them if doing so will satisfy the essential standards of justice and fairness (Okeke, 2016).

Research Framework

Figure 1 displays a representation of the research framework that served as a guide for the investigation based on the techniques used. The processes of data identification, data collecting, feature extraction, preprocessing, and feature selection were carried out for feature identification and extraction.

Identification of Data

The Mendeley repository has the dataset that was gathered and utilized for this work (https://data.mendeley.com/datasets/ky6zfyf669/1). The dataset is described in detail in Ngige et al. 2023. The Supreme Court of Nigeria's decisions from prior criminal and civil appeal cases decided between 1962 and 2022 make up the dataset utilized in this research. The Primsol Law Pavillion, which runs a separate online archive of court cases that is accessible by subscription, supplied the supplementary dataset.

Figure 1. Conceptual view of the research framework

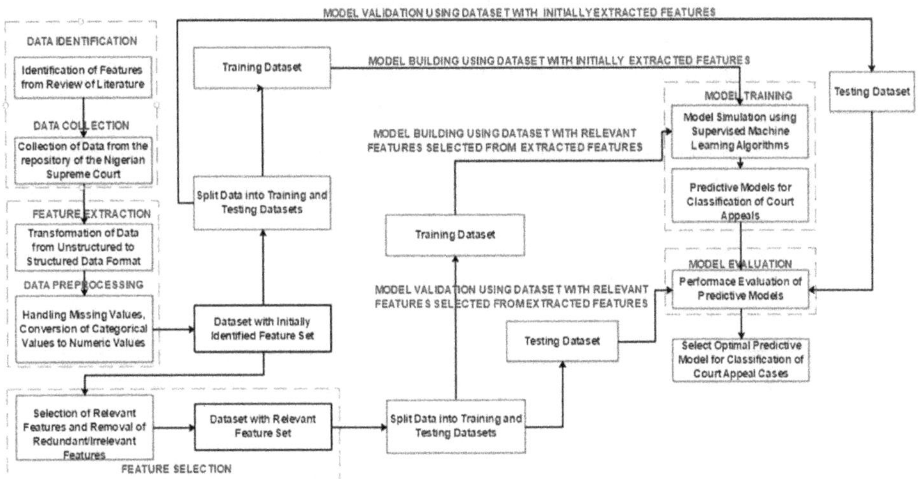

Choosing Features

We created a structured dataset for feature extraction, which can be shown as rows with details about each component for each case file and columns with the detected factors. This was accomplished by executing a Python script that parsed the document files as lists, after which the feature data was extracted, annotated, and saved with the corresponding data value.

The dataset's target variable was annotated with a categorical value, specifically: appeal denied or allowed. It was thus a binary classification issue since each row held information on case files that had been classed as either being granted or rejected. The finished dataset was kept in a format called comma separated values (.csv). After completing this activity, the dataset's worth decreased from 5585 appeal case records to 4696 case records because 889 records—or 15.9% of the total—were lost due to file damage. The bulk of the cases in the dataset were dismissed since it included information on 3109 dismissed cases and 1587 awarded ones.

It was necessary to do more research on the preprocessed dataset, which included details on the first discovered features that were taken from the case files, in order to choose the features. It was looked at how feature selection affected the process of identifying the most significant and pertinent characteristics that were connected to the categorization of the case outcomes. This led to the use of filter-based feature selection methods in this research. Their unsupervised machine learning techniques, which concentrate on finding characteristics that have a strong correlation with the target class but a weak correlation with each other, are the cause of this. This was done to see if using a small but significant number of features might maintain or enhance the performance of the classification model that was going to be created.

This is why the information-based and correlation-based feature selection methods were taken into account in this investigation. Furthermore, concentrating on the factors that are most important for influencing the result of appeal cases at the SCN was made possible by the identification of the pertinent features. The algorithm used in this study's feature selection procedure is shown in Figure 2.

Figure 2. Feature selection algorithm

Algorithm 3.1: Feature Selection Algorithm

INPUT:

$D = \{X, F\}$	*//A training data set with n appeal case records*
	//$X = \{X_1, X_2, .., X_n\}$ – Features from appeal cases
	// F labels – decision held for cases, n
X'	*//Predefined initial feature subset ($X' = \{\varphi\}$ or $X' \subset X$)*
θ	*//Stopping criterion*
OUTPUT: X'_{opt}	*//An optimal subset – relevant features*

Begin:

Initialize:

$X_{opt} = X'$; *//applying a search algorithm of choice*

$\theta_{opt} = E(X', I_m)$; *//evaluate X' by using an independent measure I_m*

do begin

$X_g = generate(X)$; *//select next subset of features for evaluation*

$\theta = E(X_g, I_m)$; *//X_g current subset evaluation by I_m*

If$(\theta > \theta_{opt})$

$\theta_{opt} = \theta$;

$X'_{opt} = X_g$;

repeat *(until θ is not reached)*;

end

return X'_{opt}; *//optimal set of relevant features for prediction*

end;

The input of the algorithm is a dataset *D,* which contains the extracted input features *X* and the target feature *F*. The algorithm starts by assuming an initial set of relevant features called *X'* for which a stopping criterion was proposed θ. The feature selection algorithm uses a metric I_m to assess the selected feature set *X'* which in turn is used to assess the stopping criteria θ. The value of the stopping criteria of each feature that is generated using X_g is assumed as the most optimal feature set X_{opt}. The process of generating feature and testing them with the metric I_m is repeated and compared until all the features have been fed and compared. The output of the feature selection algorithm is used to present the relevant features by ranking the features according the value of their metric. Therefore, the feature with the highest metric is the most relevant while the feature with the lowest metric is the least relevant.

In this study, two metrics were selected for the selection of relevant features, namely: information-based and the correlation-based metrics. The information-based metric considered was the mutual information ratio while the correlation metric considered was the Pearson correlation coefficient. The Python library that was used to implement the unsupervised machine learning algorithms was the *feature_selection* sub-library of sklearn. The independence measure I_m adopted by both feature selection has a value that explain higher relevance as a function of increasing value.

The mutual information gain (or Information Gain) is defined as a function of the entropy *H* of a feature as shown in Eq. 1. A feature *X is* deemed relevant for determining a target feature *Y* if the value of the mutual information *MI(X, Y)* is high. The entropy of a variable *X* called *H(X)* is the number of bits required in storing information about the feature *X*. Mutual information is also a function of the joint entropy of two features *X* and *Y*, namely: *H(Y|X)* and *H(X|Y).*

$$\begin{aligned} MI(X,Y) &= H(X) + H(Y) - H(X,Y) \\ &= H(Y) - H(Y|X) \\ &= H(X) - H(X \mid Y) \end{aligned} \tag{1}$$

where: *H(X) is the entropy of feature X and H(Y|X) is the joint entropy of Y wrt X.*

Every characteristic X is compared to the target feature Y to get the Pearson's correlation coefficient. The values fall between -1 and 1, but the absolute value—which falls between 0 and 1—is returned. The greater the link between traits X and Y, the closer the value of to 1. The formula for calculating each characteristic xi's Pearson's correlation coefficient (r) with regard to the target class (y) is given in Equation 2.

$$r = \frac{\sum\left(x_i - \overline{x}\right)\left(y_i - \overline{y}\right)}{\sqrt{\sum\left(x_i - \overline{x}\right)^2 \sum\left(y_i - \overline{y}\right)^2}} \tag{2}$$

where: r = correlation coefficient; x_i is the values of an input feature in dataset, $\overline{x}$ is the mean of the values of the input feature; y_i is the values of the target feature in dataset; and $\overline{y}$ is the mean of the values of the target feature.

Creation of the Classification Model to Forecast Legal Decisions

Several supervised machine learning methods were needed to build the prediction model for appeal case categorization. k-nearest neighbors (kNN), multi-layer perceptron (MLP) classifiers, and decision trees (DT) were the supervised machine learning methods that were used. While the target feature was used as the output features of the prediction models, the features that were found from the gathered dataset were used as input to the supervised machine learning algorithms. The prediction model for the categorization of appeal cases was developed using three datasets. The datasets comprised the one with data on the features that were first extracted and two more with data on the pertinent characteristics that were chosen via the use of Pearson's correlation and mutual information. Model formulation and model simulation were carried out with the goal of creating a classification model for forecasting court decisions.

With regard to model formulation, the original features found in the dataset of cases whose records were collected (the training dataset S) are represented by X_i, where i is the number of features found in the original dataset, and 〚X^'〛_j is made up of the features pertinent to the prediction of appeal case outcomes where j <i. The mapping Fs in Eq. 3 represents the feature selection process:

$$F_S : X_i \rightarrow X'_j \tag{3}$$

F_S: $X_i b$ relevant variables using the mapping in Eq. 4.

$$\begin{aligned} &\varphi : X_{jk} \rightarrow Y_k; \\ &\textit{defined as } \varphi\left(X_{jk}\right) = Y_k \textit{ for all cases, } k \end{aligned} \tag{4}$$

Where X_{jk} the set of attributes, j for cases, k and Y_k is the outcome of case, k. Hence, the selected machine learning algorithm model determine the best fit for $\varphi \in \mathbb{H}$ (the set of all possible mappings) based on the minimization of the loss function defined for each SML as the mapping in Eq. 5.

$$\mathbb{L}: \mathbb{Y} \times \mathbb{Y} \rightarrow \mathbb{R}+;$$

$$\text{defined as } \mathbb{L}(Y_a, Y_p) \tag{5}$$

Where $\mathbb{R}^+$ is a positive real number and Y_a, Y_p are the actual and predicted values of the target class respectively.

Three supervised machine learning algorithms were adopted in this study for the development of the predictive model required for the classification of the judgment of appeal cases brought before the SCN. Details of the three machine learning algorithms used for this study are presented below:

(i) The Algorithm Known as K-Nearest Neighbors (kNN)

This is a supervised machine learning technique that determined predictions by using brute force. The kNN classifier method used in this investigation is shown in Fig. The concept is to choose a random record's input values at random from the dataset that has to be identified. Next, using a distance measure, the values of this record are compared to the values of all the records that surround it that are adjacent. The k neighbors with the smallest distance are chosen after the distance between the search records Xab and those of the nearby records Xij is compared using the distance metric M. The class with the highest values Cm among the neighbors is identified after the value of the target class of the neighboring records N was recorded. The record Xab's prediction P is found using the value of the class with the maximum. Figure 3 displays the comprehensive method that was utilized to create the k-NN classifier. The Euclidean distance measure is the distance metric that was taken into consideration in this research in order to estimate the distance between records. The formula for calculating the Euclidean distance between two feature records is given in Equation 6.

$$\textit{Euclidean distace} = d\left(x_{i1}, x_{i2}\right) = \sqrt{\sum_{i=1}^{n}\left(x_{i1} - x_{i2}\right)^2} \tag{6}$$

Figure 3. The algorithm for the k-NN classifier

```
Algorithm 3.2:      k-Nearest Neighbours Algorithm

INPUT:
D = {Xij, Y}                  //dataset D containing the set of features, X and target class, Y
                              //Xij is a multi-dimensional array of feature space with i number of features and
                              j number of records
                              //Y is the target class – decision taken
k                             //number of neighbours
N                             //neighbouring records
Distance metric, M(X1, X2)    //estimator function for the distance between two feature examples.
d                             //distance between two feature space
OUTPUT:
predicted target class, P
-----------------------------------------------------------------------------------------------
Start:
Select a start search record Xab using a random generator = rand(a,b)
Compare the record with other records and calculate distance using metric
for (i=1, 1<=i, i++)
    for (j=1, 1<=j, j++)
    dn = Mn(Xab, Xij);                //estimate the distance between the search record and other records
Select k neighbours with the lowest values of d
    for(m=1, m<=k, m++)
        min(Nm)                       //select records with lowest distance value d
        Cm(Nm, Xab);                  //get the class values of the neighbours, Cm
return P = max(Cm)                    //return the class with maximum value
Stop.
```

ii. Decision Trees (DT) Algorithm

Using the features Xij as the nodes N and their values V as the edges of the tree in a top-down manner, this supervised machine learning algorithm creates a hierarchical tree structure that ends at the leaf (terminal node), which is where the target class name is located.

The decision tree classifier's implementation method is shown in Fig. 4. The approach employs a divide-and-conquer data partitioning mechanism, wherein an attribute selector method A is utilized to test for an attribute X that may be used to split the dataset across the target class values in the dataset. A leaf node with the name of the majority class C is created if every item in the dataset is part of that class. In contrast, dataset D is examined using dataset A to identify the characteristic that may be a contender for X if the dataset does not consist of a single class majority. Following the identification of the feature, two edges are extended from a node bearing the name of feature X. Using a split Criteria S, each edge V in the dataset determines how the records will be allocated across the node's values. A terminal node known as a leaf is formed if the edges include majority classes; if not, the process of further separating the dataset using newly produced candidate values for attribute X continues. Until no more splits can be performed, the characteristic X is eliminated before the formation of nodes required to divide the data for each new node created using it. The algorithm returned the final decision tree that it had constructed.

Figure 4. The algorithm for the DT classifier

```
Algorithm 3.3:        Decision Trees Algorithm
INPUT:
D = {Xij, C}                              //dataset D containing the set of features, X and target class, C
                                          //Xij is a multi-dimensional array of feature space with i number of features and
                                          j number of records
                                          //C is the target class – decision taken
Attribute List, L                         //L contains the set of features in the dataset
Attribute selection method, A(D, L)       //A function for assessing each feature's data partitioning strength
Splitting Attribute X                     //Attribute used to create a node
Feature Values, V                         //values of the feature used to split dataset
Split Criteria, S(criterion, X)           //A function for determining how targets values are split across feature values X
                                          //the function does this using a criterion to create binary splits
OUTPUT:
A Decision Tree
-----------------------------------------------------------------------------------------------
Start:
node = N
if records in D are all of the same class, C
        return leaf node(N) = C.          //tree is a single leaf node labelled with the name of the class of dataset
if (L = 0)
        return leaf(N) = max(C, D);       //return the node as a leaf node labelled with the name of the maximum class C
        X = A(D, L);                      //determine the best splitting criteria
        N = X                             //name the node with name of the splitting attribute X
        V = S(criterion, X);              //split the node into two edges based on majority class value
        L = {X};                          //Add X to attribute list and remove value from the dataset
        D = D – X;                        //remove attribute X from dataset
for (i=1, i<=V, i++)                      //check each value of the root node
        if(D = 0)                         //is the dataset empty?
        return leaf(V) = max(C, V)        //create a leaf node for each edge with the maximum class of each value V
        else
        for (i=1, i<=V, i++)              //for each value of the new node
                create node(X) = A(D,L) //generate new data partitions of new nodes for each value V
                        N = X;
                        V = S(criterion, X);
                        L = {X};          //add new node to each value edge
                        D = D – X;
        end for;
end for;
return N;                                 //return generated nodes/decision tree
```

iii. Multi-Layer Perceptron

The back-propagation technique, which uses the gradient-descent algorithm for back-propagation after feed-forward propagation, was used to construct the multi-layer perceptron. The input, hidden, and output layers comprise the three layers that make up the MLP. The input values from X to the I nodes on the input layers are accepted by the MLP model. At each of the M hidden levels, the MLP creates N nodes, which are ultimately coupled to two nodes at the output layer. Synaptic weights w(a, b) link each node on the MLP, extending from the input layer to the output layers. Using the corresponding activation functions AS and AL, the weights were utilized to create a sum of products of the values of the weights w(a, b) and the values of the nodes across all layers, depending on how layers b linked earlier layers a. From the input layers to the hidden layers and finally to the output layer, this was completed. Using an error function E, the value of the prediction p and the actual output Y were compared at the output layer. The value of E for each epoch's value e was calculated, and the gradient descent function G then utilized this value to calculate how much the value weights linking nodes needed to be modified in order to eliminate the error's influence on correctly predicting the class. The MLP model's predicted accuracy is increased by repeating this procedure of weight adjustment until the desired number of epochs is obtained while reducing the error value. The method utilized to create the MLP classifier is shown in Fig. 5.

Figure 5. The algorithm for the DT classifier

```
Algorithm 3.4:      Multi-Layer Perceptron: Back-Propagation Algorithm
INPUT:
D = {Xij, Y}                //dataset D containing the set of features, X and target class, C
                            //Xij is a multi-dimensional array of feature space with i number of
                            features and j number of records – all values are numeric and the target
                            class is binary
                            //C is the target class – decision taken
X                           //set of input variables
I                           //number of nodes at input layer
M                           //number of hidden layers
rand                        //random function
N                           //number of nodes at each hidden layer
w                           //weights used to attach a previous node to a subsequent node on next
layer
AS                          //Sigmoidal activation function for input and hidden layers
AL                          //Softmax activation function for binary output categorical nodes
b                           //bias of weighted sum of nodes
p                           //predicted value of judgement
E                           //error function prediction of judgement
G                           //gradient descent function
e                           //number of epochs
OUTPUT:  W                  //optimized weights
Start:
for(i=1, i<I, i++)                        //for all the nodes on the input layer
        for(n=1, n<=N, n++)               //for all the nodes at each hidden layer
                for(m=1, m<=M, m++)       //for all the nodes along each hidden layer
w(a, b) = rand();                         //create random values for weights connecting all nodes
                                          layer a with nodes in next layer b.
Q = Q(M,N,I)+Q(2);                        //create nodes from input layer (I inputs) across the hidden layers
                                          (N*M layers) to the output binary layer (value of 2)
for(i=1, i<I, i++)                        //for all the nodes on the input layer
        Generate S = SOP(w, X, b);        //generate sum of products of weights and nodes
        As = As(S)[-1, 1]                 //map output S into an output interval [-1, 1]
        for(n=1, n<=N, n++)               //for all the nodes at each hidden layer
                for(m=1, m<=M, m++)       //for all the nodes along each hidden layer
                As = As(S)[-1, 1]
                Generate S = SOP(w, A , b); //generate sum of products of weights and output from previous
        nodes
                p = AL(S)[-1, 1]          //map subsequent output into the interval [-1, 1]
                if(p=0)
                return "approved";        //return the outputs
                else
                return "rejected"
        end for
        if(E(Y, p)==0)                    //is error 0?
                return w(a, b);           //return the values of the weights
        for(j=1, j<=e, j++)
                G(w, E);                  //apply gradient descent to adjust the values of weights
                update w(a, b);           //update the weights with new values
        return w(a, b);                   //return the new values of weights connecting nodes
```

Method of Simulation

The holdout method was used in the simulation procedure to divide the data collected for this study into two (2) proportions, with the larger proportion being used to build (train) and the smaller proportion being used to validate (test) the predictive model. Five simulations were run in this research with training and testing percentage proportions of 50/50, 60/40, 70/30, 80/20, and 90/10. Using the datasets with the originally detected characteristics and the important features chosen using feature selection techniques, the simulation was run on the predictive model. A variety of performance assessment indicators were used to compare each simulation to the others.

Comparative Evaluation of Algorithms for Machine Learning

A conceptual representation of the comparative analysis technique is shown in Figure 6, which is used to suggest the best feature selection strategy and supervised machine learning algorithm combination for creating the predictive model that will be used to anticipate court appeal cases.

Figure 6. Conceptual view of the comparative analysis

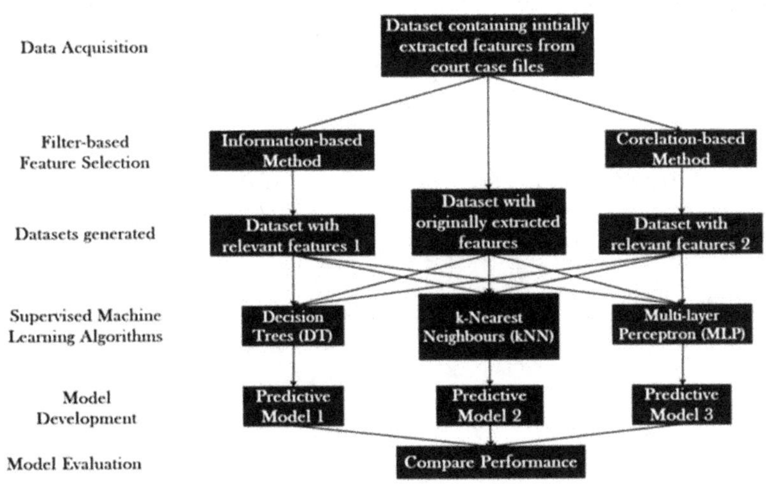

Three (3) feature selection techniques were used to extract the most relevant characteristics from the original dataset, as the graphic illustrates. New datasets with data on the characteristics that were shown to be most important for predicting court cases were created using the feature selection techniques. To create prediction models for the categorization of appeal case outcomes, three supervised machine learning algorithms were used to the three datasets. Using different ratios of the training and testing dataset, this procedure was carried out again for the five (5) selected simulations. There were a total of 45 simulations created in this research, with 15 simulations conducted for each dataset using several machine learning techniques. Several performance assessment measures were used to assess the supervised machine learning algorithms' performance.

An Assessment of the Forecasting Models' Effectiveness

A confusion matrix including the right and wrong predictions from the model validation using the test dataset was used to understand the outcomes of the simulation of the predictive model using the supervised machine learning techniques. A variety of performance assessment criteria, including as accuracy, recall, precision, and f1-measure, were employed to assess the predictive model's performance based on the number of accurate and wrong predictions made for the target class. The prediction model with the best performance was chosen after comparison using the simulations' performance evaluations as a foundation. A confusion matrix was used to evaluate each simulation, with positive instances being regarded as accepted appeals and negative ones as non-approved appeals. The right and wrong predictions provided by each predictive model used in this research are interpreted using a 2 by 2 confusion matrix. The confusion matrix for the categorization of testing data needed for model validation is shown in Fig. 7.

Figure 7. Confusion matrix for interpreting model validation

	PREDICTED CLASSES		
	Positive	**Negative**	
ACTUAL CLASSES	A	B	**Positive**
	C	D	**Negative**

It is evident from the confusion matrix in Figure 7 that the number of real records is given by the total of the horizontal cells, but the number of anticipated records is given by the sum of the vertical cells. As a result, A and D represent the quantity of properly categorized records, either positive (authorized) or negative (non-approved) (number of accurate classifications). The number of positive and negative records (number of inaccurate classifications) that were mistakenly categorized as positive and negative records, respectively, is B. Similarly, A+B and C+D represent the number of positive and negative records, respectively, while A+C and B+D represent the number of expected positive and negative records. The performance of the prediction models on the testing data for the five simulations was verified using the values found in the confusion matrix. The following is a statement of the metrics used for performance evaluation:

i. Accuracy: Using Equation 8, this was used to calculate the percentage of all properly categorized records for both groups. The model's ability to accurately identify authorized instances improves with accuracy getting closer to 100%.

$$Acccuracy = \frac{A+D}{A+B+C+D} \times 100\% \tag{8}$$

ii. Recall: This was used to determine the percentage of real records that fit the criteria for accurate classification in accordance with Eqs. 9a and 9b. After estimating the TP rate for the class, an estimate of the average will be made. The predictive model's ability to distinguish between appeals that are allowed and those that are denied based on the information presented increases with the value's proximity to 1.

$$TP\ rate_{Positive} = \frac{A}{A+B} \tag{9a}$$

$$TP\ rate_{Negative} = \frac{D}{C+D} \tag{9b}$$

iii. Precision: Using Eqs. 10a and 10b, this was utilized to determine the percentage of predicted records of a target class that were properly categorized. The average will be computed when the Precision for each target class has been assessed. The predictive model's classifications are better the closer the precision is near 1.

$$Precision_{Positive} = \frac{A}{A+C} \tag{10a}$$

$$Precision_{Negative} = \frac{D}{B+D} \tag{10b}$$

iv. The F1-score is a metric that combines recall and accuracy. Generally speaking, it is defined as the two's harmonic mean. An alternative method of calculating an average of values is the harmonic mean, which is often seen as being more suited for ratios (such accuracy and recall) than the conventional arithmetic mean. Equation 11 provides the formula for the F1-score in this instance. The predictive model's classifications are better the closer the precision is near 1.

$$F1 - measure = 2 \times \frac{Precision \times Recall}{Precision + Recall} \tag{11}$$

Outcomes and Discoveries

Ten of the thirteen characteristics that were first found demonstrated some degree of significance, according to the outcomes of the feature selection process based on mutual information. The trial court district, the proportion of male complainants, and the quantity of defense witnesses are the three characteristics that were eliminated. Based on the mutual information metric's value, the findings also demonstrated the significance of the pertinent attributes. The findings indicated that sentence, appeal court district, number of eye witnesses, offense committed, number of female appellants, number of female complainants, number of male appellants, number of complainants, and number of public witnesses were the most significant feature relevance. As a result, by using mutual information, the dataset was smaller than it was when the features were first extracted—by a percentage of 23.1%.

The characteristics that were less connected with one another were the most important features, while the features that were strongly associated with one another were redundant and needed to be removed, according to the findings of feature selection using the correlation-based technique. According to the Pearson's correlation measure, eight of the thirteen traits that were first extracted turned out to be the most important. The appeal court district, trial court district, offense, penalty, number of complainants, number of appellants, number of male appellants, and number of eyewitnesses are the characteristics that the Pearson's correlation measure determined to be significant. As a result, by using Pearson's correlation, the dataset was less than it was when the features were first extracted—by 38.5%. Table 1 illustrates this.

Table 1. Original extracted and relevant characteristics identified

S/N	Original Features	Feature Selection	
		Mutual Information	**Pearson's Correlation**
1	Appeal court district	■	■
2	Trial court district		■
3	Offence	■	■
4	Sentence	■	■
5	Number of complainants	■	■
6	Number of male complainants		■
7	Number of female complainants	■	
8	Number of appellants	■	■
9	Number of male appellants	■	
10	Number of female appellants	■	
11	Number of public witnesses	■	
12	Number of eye witnesses	■	■
13	Number of defense witnesses		
Proportion of features (%)		76.9%	61.5%

Table 2 shows the proportion of the records that were contained in the training dataset and the testing dataset that was performed over 5 simulations.

Table 3 shows the results of the simulation and the validation of the predictive models that were developed using the machine learning algorithms that were considered in this study based on the dataset containing the 13 initially extracted features. The results revealed that the best performance was achieved for each algorithm during simulation 5 when 90% of the dataset was used to build and 10% was used to validate the predictive model. The machine learning algorithm with the overall best performance in the development of the predictive model based on the dataset containing information about the 13 initially extracted features is the DT algorithm which is followed by the MLP and kNN algorithms.

Table 2. Results of the number of records stored in the training and testing records

Simulation#	Train/Test Proportion (%)	Train Records	Test Records
Simulation1	50/50	2348	2348
Simulation2	60/40	2817	1879
Simulation3	70/30	3287	1409
Simulation4	80/20	3756	940
Simulation5	90/10	4226	470

Table 3. Evaluation of simulation accuracy based on 13 initially identified features

Simulation#	Accuracy (%)		
	kNN	DT	MLP
Simulation 1	60.52	67.59	62.27
Simulation 2	62.16	68.39	64.98
Simulation 3	61.04	68.49	61.60
Simulation 4	63.30	69.47	67.04
Simulation 5	65.32	71.49	65.53

The depiction of the prediction models' accuracy throughout the course of the different simulations is shown in Figure 8. It is shown that throughout every simulation run for this investigation, the DT algorithm performed the best, followed by the MLP method.

Based on the dataset comprising the 10 pertinent characteristics that were chosen based on the mutual information metric, Table 4 displays the outcomes of the simulation and the validation of the predictive models that were created using the machine learning algorithms that were taken into consideration in this research. According to the findings, kNN performed best in simulation 4 when 80% of the dataset was used for training and 20% for testing, whereas DT and MLP performed best in simulation 1 when 50% of the dataset was utilized for both training and testing the model.

Figure 8. Graphical plot of accuracy of predictive models based on dataset containing 13 initially extracted features

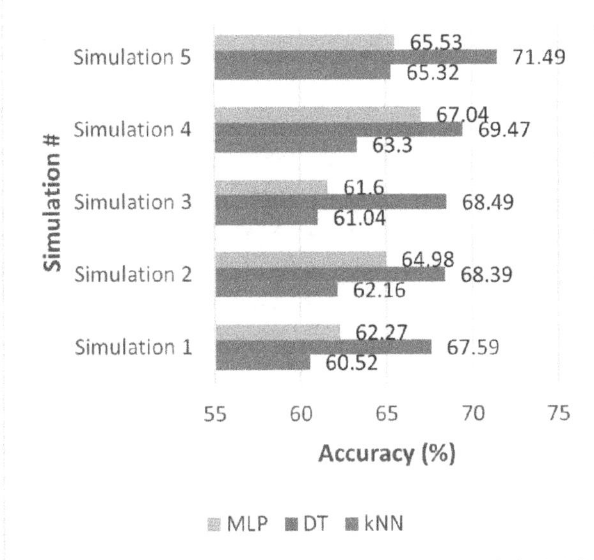

Table 4. Evaluation of simulation accuracy based on 10 features extracted by the mutual information metric

Simulation#	Accuracy (%)		
	kNN	DT	MLP
Simulation 1	62.95	69.12	64.52
Simulation 2	61.20	67.91	63.23
Simulation 3	63.73	67.78	63.59
Simulation 4	64.36	67.02	63.19
Simulation 5	59.36	65.53	61.06

The MLP and kNN algorithms come in second and third, respectively, to the DT algorithm, which has the overall best performance in building the predictive model based on the dataset containing details about the 10 relevant features that were chosen by the mutual information metric. The predicted models' accuracy throughout the course of the different simulations is illustrated in Figure 9. As can be seen, the DT method fared the best in each simulation; however, in simulations three and four, the kNN algorithm beat the MLP.

Figure 9. Graphical plot of accuracy of predictive models based on dataset containing ten relevant features selected using mutual information metric

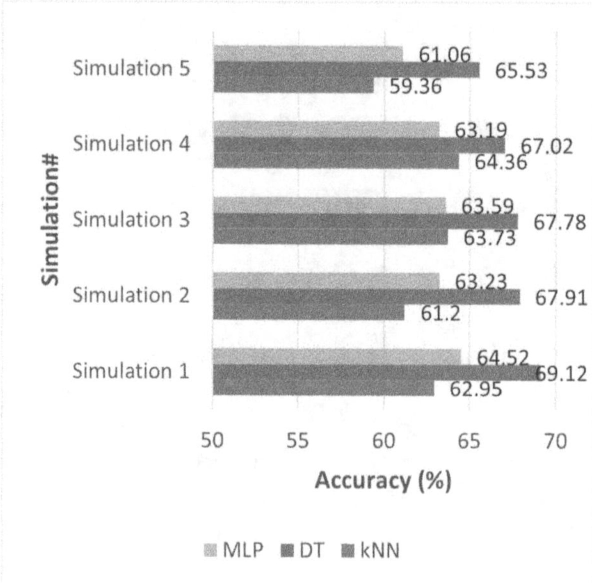

Based on the dataset comprising the eight pertinent characteristics that were chosen using the Pearson's correlation metric, Table 5 displays the outcomes of the simulation and the validation of the predictive models that were created using the machine learning algorithms that were taken into consideration in this research. According to the findings, kNN performed best in simulation 4 when 80% of the dataset was used for training and 20% for testing, whereas DT and MLP performed best in simulation 5 when 90% of the dataset was utilized for training and 10% for model testing.

The DT algorithm is the machine learning algorithm that performed the best overall in building the predictive model using the dataset that included details about the eight relevant features that were chosen using the Pearson's correlation metric. MLP and kNN, on the other hand, performed equally well. The accuracy of the predicted models throughout the several simulations is illustrated in Fig. 10. It is evident that the DT algorithm performed the best in all of the study's simulations. In simulations 1 and 4, it was found that the kNN method performed better than the MLP.

Findings from the analysis of how feature selection affects performance.

The accuracies of the kNN, DT, and MLP algorithms were 65.32%, 71.49%, and 65.53%, respectively, as a consequence of the simulation and validation of the predictive models that were created using the machine learning algorithms based on the dataset containing information about the 13 initially extracted features. Additionally, it was found that when the largest percentage of the training set was used to construct the model, the dataset produced the greatest results. A graphical depiction of the effect of feature selection methods on the prediction models' performance in relation to the dataset containing details about the 13 originally collected characteristics is shown in Figure 11.

Table 5. Evaluation of simulation accuracy based on 8 features extracted by the Pearson's correlation metric

Simulation#	Accuracy (%)		
	kNN	DT	MLP
Simulation 1	60.43	67.21	59.63
Simulation 2	62.00	69.08	63.81
Simulation 3	61.11	67.85	62.10
Simulation 4	66.81	68.94	64.79
Simulation 5	64.47	71.91	66.81

Figure 10. Graphical plot of accuracy of predictive models based on dataset containing 8 relevant features selected using Pearson's correlation metric

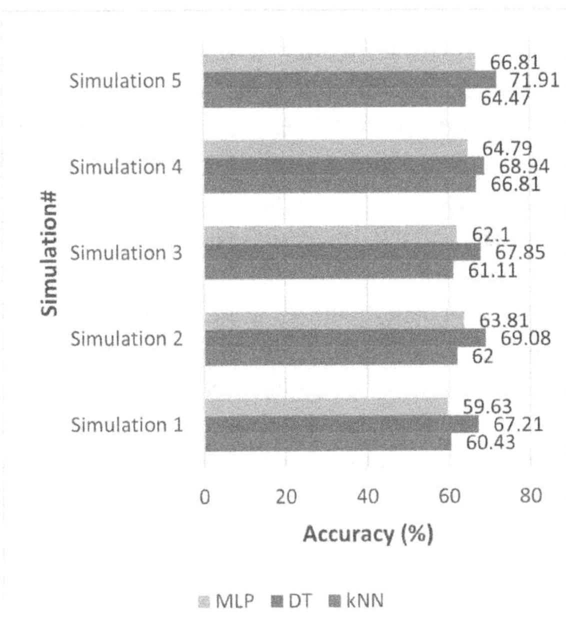

Figure 11. Graphical plot of the assessment of the impact of feature selection on the accuracy of predictive models

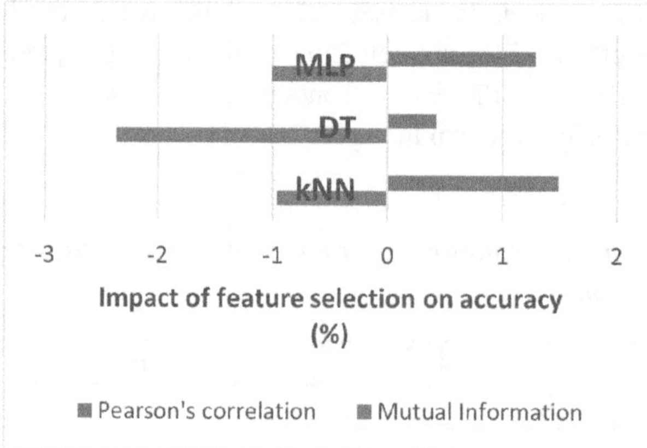

The results showed that the machine learning algorithms' performance was lowered when the dataset comprising details about the ten pertinent characteristics chosen based on the mutual information measure was used. It was found that there was a 1% reduction in MLP performance, a 2.5% reduction in DT performance, and a 1% reduction in kNN performance. The usage of the dataset including the characteristics chosen using the mutual information measure had a significant impact on the DT method. As a result, it was found that the attributes chosen for the categorization of the outcomes of appeal cases submitted before the SCN were not sufficiently relevant to be classified using information-based criteria.

In contrast to using the dataset containing information about the 13 initially extracted features, the predictive model performed better after adopting the dataset containing information about the 8 relevant features that were chosen using the Pearson's correlation metric. A 1.5% improvement in kNN performance, a 1.3% rise in MLP performance, and a 0.4% increase in DT algorithm performance were also noted. Additionally, it was observed that the kNN with the worst performance when using the dataset with data on the 13 originally extracted features performed the same when using the MLP algorithm when using the dataset with the 8 pertinent features chosen by the Pearson's correlation metric. Despite employing a training set with a smaller percentage than the MLP method, the kNN was nevertheless able to accomplish this increase. As a result, a small but significant number of traits that were more closely linked to the categorization of the results of appeal cases presented before the SCN were found via the use of correlation-based criteria.

Conversation

In order to create a prediction model based on data about these traits, this research concentrated on the discovery and adoption of certain factors that are connected to the results of appeal cases. After conducting a comprehensive analysis of related literature, the research determined certain characteristics linked to the resolution of court cases. Subsequently, pertinent data was obtained from a privately-owned online data archiving company. Files from many cases, including criminal, civil, and legal appeals heard by the SCN during a 60-year period, were housed in the archive.

After gathering the raw dataset and formatting it appropriately, it became clear that, in contrast to the recommendations of (de Oliveira et al., 2022) who examined the duration of the judgment, forecasting the outcome of appeal cases should be approached as a binary classification task. It goes without saying that a lawyer's most crucial responsibility is to consider all potential outcomes rather than how long a case may take to resolve in court. The destiny of the parties to such an appeal is determined by the result. The study demonstrated that a greater number of case files were gathered and used in the development of the predictive model, which is significantly more than the quantity taken into consideration in the study by (Lage-Freitas et al.,) which used over 3000 records for training in contrast to the use of 762 records for model building. The dataset that was gathered for this research contained instances of appeal that included violations of human rights, which was the subject of studies conducted by Medvedeva et al. (2023) and Park & Chai (2021).

Additionally, the study took into account the possibility that some features may have been more significant in influencing the outcome of appeal cases than others, as opposed to relying solely on the features that were initially identified from the literature from which data was extracted for this study. The majority of the reviewed literature failed to take into account the influence of pertinent features on the effectiveness of predictive models required to forecast case outcomes. For example, Shaikh et al. (2020) failed to take into account the identification of pertinent features or the effect that feature relevance had on the efficiency of machine learning algorithms. This research showed that feature identification may have a significant impact on how well machine learning algorithms work, but it also showed that choosing feature selection strategies carefully was necessary.

Additionally, it was noted that correlation-based feature selection techniques were more successful in locating pertinent features than information-based techniques in identifying the characteristics that enhanced the performance of machine learning algorithms. The district of the appeal court, the district of the trial court, the offense committed, the sentence of the trial court, the number of complainants—including the number of male complainants—the number of appellants, and the number of eyewitnesses were deemed to be the most pertinent factors that were significant in determining the outcome of appeal cases brought before the SCN. The capacity of the chosen characteristics to enhance the functionality of every machine learning algorithm used in this research served as justification for their relevance.

Furthermore, it was discovered that the kNN method performed on par with the MLP despite not meeting the MLP's expectations when utilizing the dataset that included details about the characteristics that were first detected. But according to the study's findings, the decision trees algorithm is the best machine learning algorithm for predicting how appeal cases that are submitted before the SCN would turn out. In contrast to the findings of studies by Bhilare et al., 2019 and Shaikh, 2020, the decision trees algorithm outperformed the kNN algorithm. It also outperformed the MLP algorithm, which was consistent with findings from a study by Park & Chai, 2021, which asserted that DT algorithms outperformed the MLP.

CONCLUSION

In this research, we have shown that by reducing the computational space and model complexity, identifying and eliminating elements that are unnecessary or redundant may speed up the computing process. Feature selection, when used in conjunction with feature extraction, may enhance the effectiveness of classifiers used to forecast court cases. The results of this study showed that, while correlation-based methods were more successful in identifying pertinent features and improving the performance of the algorithms, information-based feature selection methods were unable to identify the features that improved the performance of machine learning algorithms. But according to the study's findings, the decision trees algorithm is the best machine learning algorithm for predicting how appeal cases that are submitted before the SCN would turn out. In order to develop a better and more comprehensive consensus on the optimal algorithm for creating models to support Nigerian Supreme Court judges in rendering better, quicker, and more accurate verdicts based on prior court cases, we have also made available a new dataset that can be used in the future on other machine learning algorithms.

REFERENCES

Ahmad, H., Asghar, M. U., Khan, A., & Mosavi, A. H. (2021). A Hybrid Deep Learning Technique for Personality Trait Classification from Text. *IEEE Access : Practical Innovations, Open Solutions*, *9*, 146214–146232. doi:10.1109/ACCESS.2021.3121791

Aletras, N., Tsarapatsanis, D., Preotuic-Pietro, D., & Lampos, V. (2016). Predicting judicial decisions of the European Court of Human Rights: A Natural language Processing Perspective. *PeerJ. Computer Science*, *2*, 93–99. doi:10.7717/peerj-cs.93

Alghazzawi, D., Bamasag, O., Albeshri, A., Sana, I., Ullah, H., & Asghar, M. Z. (2022). Efficient prediction of court judgments using an LSTM+ CNN neural network model with an optimal feature set. *Mathematics*, *10*(5), 683. doi:10.3390/math10050683

Ali, R. (2020). *Predictive Modeling: Types, Benefits, and Algorithms*. Retrieved from Oracle Netsuite: https://www. netsuite. com/portal/resource/articles/financial-management/predictive-modeling. shtml

Ashley, K. (2019). A Brief History of the changing roles of case prediction in AI and Law: Law in context. *Socio-Legal Journal*, *36*(1), 93–112. doi:10.26826/law-in-context.v36i1.88

Ashley, K., & Brüninghaus, S. (2009). Automatically classifying case texts and predicting outcomes. *Artificial Intelligence and Law*, *17*(2), 125–165. doi:10.1007/s10506-009-9077-9

Bhilare, P., Parab, N., Soni, N., & Thakur, B. (2019). Predicting outcome of judicial cases and analysis using machine learning. *International Research Journal in Engineering Technology*, *6*, 326-330. Retrieved from https://www.irjet.net/archives/V6/i3/IRJET-V6I362.pdf

Chalkidis, I., Androutsopoulos, I., & Aletras, N. 2019. Neural Legal Judgement Prediction In English. *Proceedings of the 57th Annual Meeting of the Association for Computational Linguistics*, 4317-4323. 10.18653/v1/P19-1424

Cui, J., Shen, X., Nie, F., Wang, Z., Wang, J., & Chen, Y. (2022). *A Survey on Legal Judgment Prediction: Datasets, Metrics, Models and Challenges*. https://doi.org//arXiv.2204.04859 doi:10.48550

de Oliveira, R. S., Reis, J. A., & Sperandio Nascimento, E. G. (2022). Predicting the number of days in court cases using artificial intelligence. *PLoS One*, *17*(5), e0269008. doi:10.1371/journal.pone.0269008 PMID:35617285

Kelbert, F., Shirazi, F., Simo, H., Wüchner, T., Buchmann, J., Pretschner, A., & Waidner, M. (2012). State of online privacy: A technical perspective. In *Internet Privacy* (pp. 189–279). Springer. doi:10.1007/978-3-642-31943-3_4

Kort, F. (1957). Predicting Supreme Court decisions mathematically: A quantitative analysis of the" right to counsel cases. *The American Political Science Review*, *51*(1), 1–12. doi:10.2307/1951767

Lage-Freitas, A., Allende-Cid, H., Santana, O., & Lıvia, O. (2022). Predicting Brazilian court decisions. *PeerJ. Computer Science*, *8*, e904. doi:10.7717/peerj-cs.904 PMID:35494851

LiuH. W.LinC. F.ChenY. J. (2018). Beyond State v. Loomis: Artificial Intelligence, Government Algorithmization, and Accountability. *International Journal of Law and Information Technology, 27*(2), 122-141. https://ssrn.com/abstract=3313916

Marković, M., & Gostojić, S. (2018). Open Judicial Data: A Comprehensive Analysis. *Social Science Computer Review*, *38*(3), 295–314. doi:10.1177/0894439318770744

Medvedeva, M., Vols, M., & Wieling, M. (2020). Using Machine Learning to predict decisions of the European Court of Human Rights. *Artificial Intelligence and Law*, *28*(2), 237–266. doi:10.1007/s10506-019-09255-y

Medvedeva, M., Wieling, M., & Vols, M. (2023). Rethinking the Field of Automatic Prediction of Court Decisions. *Artificial Intelligence and Law*, *31*(1), 195–212. doi:10.1007/s10506-021-09306-3

Nagel, S. (1960). Using simple calculations to predict judicial decisions. *The American Behavioral Scientist*, *4*(4), 24–28. doi:10.1177/000276426000400409

Ngige, O. C., Ayankoya, F. Y., Balogun, J. A., Onuiri, E., Agbonkhese, C., & Sanusi, F. A. (2023). A dataset for predicting Supreme Court judgments in Nigeria. *Data in Brief, 50*. doi:10.1016/j.dib.2023.109483

O'Neil, C. (2016). *Weapons of Math Destruction: How Big Data increases inequality and threatens democracy*. Crown Publishing Group.

Ogbu, O. (2006). *Modern Nigerian Legal System* (3rd ed.). AP Press.

Okeke, G. N. (2016). Judicial precedent in the Nigerian legal system and a case for its application under international law. *Nnamdi Azikiwe University Journal of International Law and Jurisprudence*, *1*, 107–115.

Park, M., & Chai, S. (2021). AI Model for Predicting Legal Judgments to Improve Accuracy and Explainability of Online Privacy Invasion Cases. *Applied Sciences (Basel, Switzerland)*, *11*(23), 11080. doi:10.3390/app112311080

Shaikh, R. A., Sahu, T. P., & Anand, V. (2020). Predicting outcomes of legal cases based on legal factors using classifiers. *Procedia Computer Science*, *167*, 2393–2402. doi:10.1016/j.procs.2020.03.292

Simmons, R. (2018). Big Data, Machine Judges, and the Legitimacy of the Criminal Justice System. *SSRN*, *52*(2), 1067–1118. doi:10.2139/ssrn.3156510

Ulmer, S. S. (1963). Quantitative analysis of judicial processes: Some practical and theoretical applications. *Law and Contemporary Problems*, *28*(1), 164–184. doi:10.2307/1190728

Završnik, A. (2018). Algorithmic justice: Algorithms and big data in criminal justice settings. *European Journal of Criminology*, *18*(5), 623–642. doi:10.1177/1477370819876762

Chapter 4
Artificial Intelligence Is the New Secret Sauce for Good Governance

Dwijendranath Dwivedi
https://orcid.org/0000-0001-7662-415X
Krakow University of Economics, Poland

Ghanashyama Mahanty
https://orcid.org/0000-0002-6560-2825
Utkal University, India

Aditya Dhar Dwivedi
https://orcid.org/0009-0001-6189-0751
Dr. Ram Manohar Lohia Awadh University, Ayodhya, India

ABSTRACT

This chapter first discusses what good governance means and why it is so important for society. It is the public governance that lacks a centralized AI framework. Several key characteristics of good governance have been identified, including active participation of citizens in the governance process, transparency, accountability, and empowerment of women. These attributes are essential to achieving good governance. However, many other traits can help create good governance in organizations. Next, the authors explain the good governance characteristics that AI can manage, and some sample use cases for the same have been provided. They also explain how the government could organize itself to use AI best. These examples can help establish digital and trustworthy governance with the help of AI.

DOI: 10.4018/978-1-6684-9716-6.ch004

1.0 INTRODUCTION

The word "Governance" originated from the Greek word "Kubernaein, which means "to steer". There are many definitions of governance, but in a broad sense, governance refers to a set of well-defined principles and norms through which stockholders interact to steer towards creating a cohesive society (Mark, 2012). Governance is as old as human civilization. UNESCAP defines good governance means that "processes and institutions produce results that meet the needs of the society while making the best use of the resources at their disposal". Kofi Annan, the ex-Secretary General of the United Nations, once said, "Good governance probably is the single most important factor for eradicating poverty and promoting development".

Three sectors of society can facilitate good governance in any country (Sales, 1991). They are public, private and civil societies. While the public and private societies are well defined, civil society consists of a community of citizens linked by common interests covering. NGOs, Labor Unions, religious organizations, charities, professional associations and many more. Civil society, sometimes called the "third sector" organizations, are purely independent and voluntary that provide support and advocacy for specific people or causes in the community that may originate either from the public or private sector. Each of these entities needs governance to be effective and positively contribute to societal governance.

Civil society, by nature, is well organized. They play more of a voluntary role and fill the space untouched by the private and public sectors. The private sector, which is mainly driven by profit, got the necessary resources and framework for creating and implementing good governance. It's the public sector which provides public goods and governmental services, which is maximally controlled by the state and has the maximum complexity to deal. With rapid digitization and sharper societal need, the public sector is ill-equipped to provide good governance without adequate social and economic infrastructure. The paper aims to identify and explore areas where AI can be leveraged to transform governance. Artificial Intelligence (AI) is becoming a transformative force in the intersection of technology and governance, reshaping the principles of efficient governance in our current era. This article explores the significant impact of AI on improving the effectiveness, clarity, and agility of government operations, establishing it as the next key factor for promoting good governance.

Good governance is fundamentally defined by concepts such as accountability, openness, responsiveness, and inclusion. These principles are becoming more challenging to uphold due to the increasing population and complicated socioeconomic issues. Artificial intelligence, with its exceptional ability to process data, make predictions, and automate tasks, presents a new and effective way to address these difficulties directly. By incorporating artificial intelligence (AI) into many aspects of governance, such as public service provision and policy development, governments can tap into untapped possibilities for improving administrative effectiveness and enhancing public well-being. This study examines the diverse applications of artificial intelligence (AI) in governance, encompassing its contributions to refining decision-making processes, optimizing resource allocation, increasing public service delivery, and promoting more civic involvement. Additionally, it rigorously analyzes the obstacles and moral deliberations that arise when integrating AI into public administration, including issues related to privacy, algorithmic prejudice, and the digital divide.

This research endeavors to offer a thorough examination of how AI, when used wisely, can serve as a catalyst for positive governance. It attempts to achieve this by combining theoretical analysis with case studies, ultimately revolutionizing the operations and interactions between governments and their populations. By doing this, it aims to contribute to the current discussion on the overlap between technology and governance, providing valuable insights and ideas for politicians, technologists, and academics. To summarize, the potential of AI in transforming the realm of effective governance is vast. This paper will illustrate that AI is not merely a supplementary technology for contemporary governance, but rather an increasingly essential instrument that may facilitate better-informed decisions, streamlined processes, and ultimately, more efficacious government.

2.0 LITERATURE STUDY

I. Ulnicane et.al.(2021) explored the insights that AI governance, policy, and ethics can gain from other developing technologies in order to tackle issues and guarantee the socially advantageous development of AI. The approach highlighted the importance of inclusive governance, recognizing the various functions of the state, giving priority to social advantages, fostering international cooperation, and using insights from computer ethics and Responsible Innovation. Eva Erman et. al.(2022) described that effective AI governance should encompass not just the end results but also the procedural elements and political legitimacy. This paper establishes a conceptual framework for evaluating the political validity of global AI governance and evaluates the legitimacy of current global AI governance systems. M. Moon (2023) explored the impact of AI on promoting societal benefits, with a focus on utilizing participatory governance as a means of ensuring inclusive AI. The document provides policy suggestions to enhance the inclusivity and societal benefits of AI. Hepeng Jia (2020) offered an interview with Yi Zeng, a prominent authority in the field of AI ethics and governance. The text explores his involvement in AI governance concepts and his participation in several international organizations dedicated to AI ethics. A. Winfield & M. Jirotka()This study examines the ethical governance of robotics and AI systems, presenting a pathway that encompasses ethics, standards, legislation, responsible research, and public involvement. The statement underscores the importance of ethical governance in establishing public confidence in robotics and AI. J. Buenfil et.al(2019) presented a technique for AI robots to acquire ethical conduct by means of human-curated training utilizing online behavioral data extracted from social media. The text explores the necessity of governance in safeguarding individual rights and advancing the collective welfare in the extensive utilization of AI technologies. Michael Strange & Jason Tucker (2023) explored the political discussion surrounding AI in major global governance organizations, emphasizing the significance of 'crisis' situations in justifying significant changes in approach. The statement highlighted a transition in perceiving human health and healthcare from a state of 'crisis' to one where AI technology is portrayed as the solution. Thomas M. Vogl (2021) examined the utilization of artificial intelligence (AI) in local governments in the United Kingdom, highlighting significant obstacles and facilitators in the implementation of AI initiatives. It indicated that establishing fundamental governance structures at both local and national levels is necessary in order for AI technologies to contribute to effective government.

3.0 KEY CHARACTERISTICS OF GOOD GOVERNANCE

3.1 Participation of Citizens in the Process of Governance

Participation of citizens in the process of good government is a crucial component of democracy. A fundamental concept in democratic theory is that society benefits when all its citizens are involved. Nevertheless, a lack of participation in public affairs can cause several problems. Uninvolved citizens have unmet needs, affecting their quality of life and productivity. They may also turn to extreme measures such as populism. The relationship between political participation and government performance is substantial. According to the EIU and the World Bank, countries with the highest citizen participation have more effective governments. Similarly, nations with the lowest citizen participation score poorly on government performance. The results show that good governance is closely related to the level of participation of citizens. Also, reduction of the gap between the rich and the poor. Artificial Intelligence can help collect massive amounts of data from public participation and analyze them to understand their concerns and feedback. Citizen participation in government processes can be measured and analyzed by AI engines.

Recent reforms and citizen innovation have increased the number of avenues through which citizens can participate in government. As a result, citizens are increasingly engaged in more demanding forms of participation. In addition to direct contact with political leaders, more citizens are becoming members of civic associations, public interest groups, and other collective forms of action.

In addition to increasing citizen engagement, many governments have introduced a plethora of AI-driven programs to promote good governance. For example, the My Gov initiative aims to make government more transparent and responsive to citizens. Many other initiatives for good governance include RTI, E-Government, and Legal Reforms.

3.2 Transparency

Transparency is one of the key characteristics of good governance, and it is crucial for any organization to be transparent. This means having key contacts who can answer questions and explain reports and making sure that the reports contain enough information. Transparency also means being willing to disclose information to key stakeholders. Transparency helps create unity and trust amongst stakeholders, and it is essential for the functioning of any organization. Transparency enables employees to understand the strategic objectives of an organization and their role within the organization. Transparency is also increasingly important externally, as stakeholders increasingly demand that organizations demonstrate greater social responsibility. Transparency is also essential for internal and external relationships since transparency strengthens trust between employees and organizations. Transparency also enables organizations to take better decisions faster. Transparency allows people to predict outcomes and participate in decision-making. It is also crucial for ensuring accountability. When information is openly shared, people can judge how well government officials are performing their duties. Good governance fosters this kind of participation and accountability. Good governance also involves a strong legal foundation in a country, which must allow government officials to conduct their functions in accordance with laws and regulations. Transparency ensures that citizens can make informed decisions about the state of their government. It also allows citizens to identify where their elected officials have gone awry. Moreover, open data can be a useful tool in anti-corruption efforts. Besides improving citizens' rights, increased transparency also fosters the development of the economy.

AI-based data-driven decision processes can help establish transparency in decision making. Siloed echo chambers prevent key decision-makers from hearing diverse perspectives. Good AI practice and collaboration among agencies are crucial for good governance.

3.3 Accountability

Accountability is one of the most important aspects of good governance. It enables citizens to monitor their government's performance and determine where it may go astray. It also allows citizens to give direct input on their needs and identify inefficiencies. But not all accountability programs are effective. Many fail to address the needs of marginalized groups. To improve governance, accountability efforts should include participation and inclusion as key components. Accountability is the best way to ensure the effectiveness of government. Government decision-makers must be accountable to the public and to institutions. Data-driven AI systems can help agencies to be more accountable and explainable. In addition to transparency, good governance also calls for openness.AI systems can help such that everyone can make an informed decision. Good governance measures the efficient and ethical use of public resources. Often, accountability is pursued unilaterally, limiting participation in post-conflict political systems. For example, an accountability program that aims to reduce state capture can impose a narrow range of participation and lead to the perpetuation of marginalization. A socially responsible AI can help the government to detect the marginalization of certain segments and plan actions for the same.

3.4 Infrastructure Creation

When it comes to the country's infrastructure, the federal government has a responsibility. to make sure it remains in good condition. Much of this infrastructure is provided as part of a network, which requires consistent investments to ensure the network remains effective. The federal government may be better suited to oversee this infrastructure investment than the states. Modern economies rely on good infrastructure to function correctly. Without efficient transportation, communication, energy, and waste disposal systems, trade cannot thrive. In the United States, this infrastructure is ageing. That is a result of governmental neglect and lack. of funding. Therefore, maintaining the current infrastructure is crucial to maintain a healthy economy. In most countries, the government provides the necessary infrastructure for economic growth. This infrastructure is made up of many interrelated sectors, ranging from a water treatment plant to a wind farm, a gas line, and a broadband network. Often, the focus on infrastructure has led to unrealistic silver-bullet policy solutions. In fact, each sector of infrastructure has fundamentally different design frameworks, market attributes, and ownership structures.

In addition to these challenges, the federal government must ensure that infrastructure investment is provided most efficiently. Otherwise, the beneficiaries will use the infrastructure more efficiently than they should, and the government will not be able to get the full benefit. AI Engines are supporting smart city programs and many infrastructures design and maintenance.

3.5 Open Data and Data Marketplace

Governments should create Open data platforms for active participation by all communities. Open datasets are the government datasets that are made available for the public to use. These datasets can include maps, genomes, connectomes, chemical compounds, and scientific and mathematical formulas. They can also include data related to bioscience and medical practice. In many cases, these data are available for free and can be used by anyone for any purpose. Governments should make their data available in a timely manner. The ideal is to make the data available as close to when it was originally collected. In addition, there should be specific requirements to ensure that the government's data is accurate. Public data are also important because it can be used to inform public policy and to measure the impact of public programs. It also helps to generate insights, ideas, and value, resulting in better public services. Furthermore, it can help develop a better world for everyone. Therefore, it's important for governments to make their data open by default.

The success of the French National Address Database is an example of the power of open data. This collaboration between the government and private sector has improved government efficiency. The database includes over 25 million geocoded addresses but does not contain any personal information.

4.0 DATA DRIVEN MODELS OF GOOD PUBLIC GOVERNANCE

There is a need for governments to adopt a whole-of-government approach to leveraging data for better services. We need to make sure that it follows transparency, openness, collective governance, and value-based approaches. There are multiple models based on data-driven framework for developing and delivering public services. This framework allows outside stakeholders to participate in co-creating public services. The model also calls for governments to adopt a culture of data analysis and use. The use of data enables public services to identify new trends and needs, and to understand how to improve processes and dynamics. These capabilities will ultimately lead to improved service quality. By developing a data-driven culture, governments can anticipate and address the needs and challenges of their citizens.

4.1 OECD Data-Driven Models of Good Public Governance

The OECD has published a model for good public governance based on data. This model is called a data-driven public administration. It uses data-driven mission management to design effective public services. The OECD has also published a model for mission management in Norway. These models are becoming more widely used in government agencies. The OECD's Working Party on Security and Privacy in the Digital Economy has examined the breadth of attributes relevant to government-wide data policies. These attributes include open data, big data, and personal data. A data-driven public sector involves six key actors: the data subject, data producer, data controller, data analyst, and public decision maker.

The data-driven approach to public governance has several benefits. For example, it can facilitate better decision-making, enhance public services, and help organizations self-actualize value. Governments can use data in three broad stages: planning, evaluation, and monitoring. In some countries, this process is formalized, with the creation of chief data officers or data stewards.

The OECD report will consider the comparative experiences of OECD countries and will examine the conditions required for DDPS to be effective. It will also evaluate the importance of good leadership and the role of technological capabilities, as well as ethical management and preventative measures.

Data-driven models of good public governance can help governments better anticipate future needs and develop more effective policies. The key elements include an understanding of the challenges in the design and implementation of data-driven anticipatory governance. For example, data-driven Anticipatory Governance can require a policy maker to pre-figure the interactions and conditions that should exist for a policy to be effective.

Data-driven models of good public governance are increasingly becoming a mainstream way to monitor government performance. A government can benefit from predictive analytics by using data to predict changes in the state of the economy. It can use data to improve policies, reduce costs, and improve citizens' welfare. The OECD has conducted extensive research on the topic of data-driven public governance. The OECD has also identified the most effective ways to balance competing interests. This report will serve as a common reference for existing OECD legal instruments. It will also guide future OECD work in this area. To be effective in adopting data-driven models of good public governance, progressive governments should open their data by default. They must ensure that the data is reliable and timely, so that citizens can make use of the data. By making data available, progressive governments can circumvent the inherent political economy challenges of data governance. By opening data to the public, civic activists and regulators can hold governments to account

Figure 1. Four-stage model
(OECD)

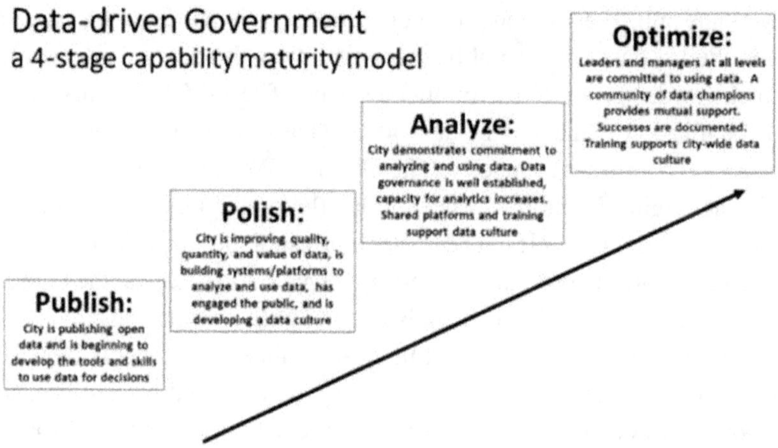

through the data they collect. And this data will also be useful in implementing artificial intelligence to improve government performance.

4.2 Norwegian Model

Data driven models of good public governance aim to make government more effective. The Norwegian public sector is highly sectoral and fragmented, with 70 executive agencies, 16 national ministries, and 358 municipalities. These organizations are largely autonomous, have strict boundaries, and enjoy a high level of trust from citizens. Modern governments often hold vast amounts of data about their subjects. The Nordic public sector is particularly data-rich, and the country is under pressure to use this data goldmine. Data driven public administration aims to harness this data as an asset and integrate it into policy- making, service delivery, organizational management, and innovation. The survey questions were designed to map the current state of data-driven public administration. The questionnaire also aimed to gauge challenges practitioners face. The participants were recruited from the Norwegian public sector AI forum, which brings practitioners together. The forum has 46 member organizations, ranging from planning to deploying data-driven practices. This sample includes organizations that are technologically advanced, such as government departments and local governments.

Data-driven public administration is a concept that is still in its infancy. It has many critics and advocates but is not an easy concept to implement. Yet it has enormous potential to improve governance. A number of studies have explored the potential of data-driven public administration in the United States. One such study, by Lipsky, focuses on data-driven practices in cities. The authors identify several challenges associated with data-driven public administration. Data-driven public administration will require countries to create effective data management approaches. This means developing the right data architecture, identifying the right talent, and building the right infrastructure. It also requires a national data-sharing strategy and infrastructure. To succeed, the challenge of building data-driven public administration is substantial.

Data-driven public administration is a promising trend for reforming government, but it remains an underdeveloped field of research. It will challenge traditional public administration and fundamentally change the way it engages and learns about its citizens. But it cannot be implemented overnight. Moreover, it must be rooted in a larger field of research. Data-driven public governance requires political leadership, commitment to technological progress, and an open approach to measuring success. While this is still an emerging area of innovation, pioneering government organizations have achieved impressive results through data-driven mission management. Although this process isn't yet commonplace, its adoption is expected to grow rapidly. Most agencies will publish key performance indicators (KPIs) in near-real-time, often using transparency portals. These metrics should be transparently visible and easily understood by citizens.

5.0 ROLE OF AI IN MEETING CHALLENGES THAT ARE SPECIFIC TO THE PUBLIC SECTOR GOVERNANCE

There are a lot of public sector-specific challenges that can be managed through artificial intelligence technology. It can also assist in the development of policy interventions. AI can provide an opportunity for the government to improve the delivery of public goods. Gagan, et. al. (2020) consolidated the extant literature

Figure 2. AI applications in government
(Gagan, 2020)

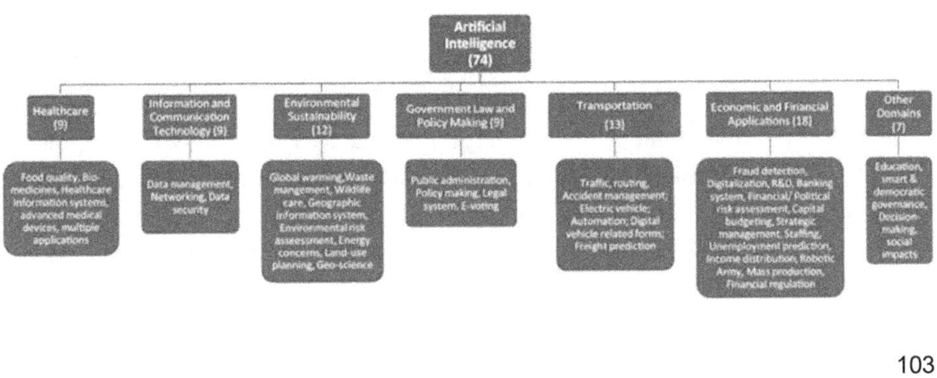

to find research gaps and suggests future research agendas for AI application in government sectors.

5.1 The Role of Artificial Intelligence in Government Policy Making

Governments around the world are exploring the role of artificial intelligence (AI) in policy- making. AI can be used for a number of purposes, including identifying voter sentiment, analyzing social media posts, and even drafting announcements. According to the Harvard Business Review, early AI experiments are underway in a variety of sectors. One example is postal services, which in the 1990s began using machine methods for recognizing handwriting and automatically routing letters.

However, while government policies are beginning to acknowledge the potential impact of AI, there is a need to define appropriate boundaries for the technology. While the AI Task Force Report recognizes the need for national security, it fails to discuss the implications of AI's use on human rights, especially privacy.

Governments are now looking at how AI can improve the performance of government agencies, from local to national levels. With the right data, AI can help identify policy priorities, evaluate hard-to-measure outcomes, and improve public services. And with AI, governments can make better use of their limited resources while still achieving the desired results.

In addition to the benefits of AI, government agencies are also looking at the ethical and social implications of AI. AI-related policies should focus on these ethical and social concerns. Even if a system can solve a complex problem, it does not necessarily mean that it is the right decision for the situation.

Aside from being efficient, AI-powered government systems should be fair. While a broad definition of fairness is necessary for regulating AI-based policies, these systems must be sensitive to the nuances of social justice. For example, the Indian Constitution envisions an equal society, with a welfare state embracing affirmative action policies. These policies may involve housing, education, and employment.

In addition to tackling these problems, AI can also help government agencies provide personalized education. It can analyze student progress and identify areas for improvement. It can also help governments automate emergency call lines and predict wildfires. Furthermore, AI can help predict the spread of diseases and other disasters.

In India, AI development is an emerging focus area for policy development. The country's burgeoning AI industry and ambitious governmental initiatives are contributing to the interest in AI in policymaking. The existing policy frameworks in India encourage the rapid development of AI for economic growth and social benefit, but they still highlight the limitations of data- driven decision-making.

Governments have embraced AI as the panacea for many problems. AI systems can analyze images from CCTV cameras and help governments identify individuals through video records. But this technology also raises ethical questions. IBM recently stopped offering facial recognition technology for mass surveillance due to concerns about human rights. Further, AI is not yet capable of distinguishing between factual and non-truthful speech.

The use of AI in government policymaking requires a combination of skills and technological advancements. Senior government officials should be agents of change and make AI a strategic priority. They should also provide the resources and the necessary support for AI implementation. In addition to creating a policy-making framework for AI, senior leaders should identify and empower influential leaders who are willing to take risks and innovate. Wim Naudé et.al. (2021) shared an all-pay contest model is developed to derive AI's implications for public policy. Euripidis Loukis et.al. (2019) proposed a policy analytics methodology for the exploitation of existing public and private sector data, using a big data oriented artificial intelligence technique, feature selection, in order to support policy making concerning one of the most serious problems that governments face, the economic crises.

5.2 Role of AI in Improving Government Infrastructure

Artificial intelligence has the potential to automate processes and increase efficiency in infrastructure development and maintenance. It can also optimize project scheduling and budgeting. Developing infrastructure is a time-consuming and costly process. Moreover, the demand for such services is often unpredictable, which makes it difficult to plan. Nevertheless, AI can make this process much easier by analyzing trends and forecasting future needs.

The use of AI in government can improve efficiency and effectiveness. It can also increase the performance of e-government services and systems. Moreover, it can alleviate mundane repetitive tasks. This can be beneficial for resource-constrained organizations that want to auto- mate more aspects of their processes. This way, they can focus on the more important aspects of governing their organization.

The increased penetration of AI is likely to boost global and national productivity. In 2015, a study of 17 countries showed that AI solutions improved growth by 0.37%. As a result, it could lead to better-paying jobs and more leisure time for workers. Moreover, AI could also help improve public service and enhance citizens' trust in government.

The conclusions of Saragih et.al .(2022) show that applying AI in the area of taxation can help tax authorities to enforce the law and offer taxpayers the convenience of fulfilling their tax obligations. Tan Yigitcanlar et. al. (2021) identified themes and ideas generated to inform municipal managers in their efforts to roll out AI in their local government activities and provide guidance for forward-looking research.

Besides its ability to automate tasks, AI can also help measure the resilience of infrastructure systems. For instance, AI can help detect oil spills and identify oil pollution. By analyzing historical events, AI can help assess the vulnerability of infrastructure systems. It can also help predict future events. AI can help governments better manage and prevent disasters. Christopher (2007) talks about the governments need detectors as a tool for gathering information digitally. Although AI is promising for improving infrastructure, it is not a panacea for all problems. Further research is needed to identify its limitations. It is a necessary step toward making AI technology more accountable. For example, it could improve the efficiency of government organizations by reducing the costs of maintaining infrastructure.

AI-based technologies could support the provision of health, food, water and energy services. They could also support the development of circular economies, smart cities, and low-carbon systems. If AI is used correctly, it can help governments achieve their goals. Despite its many benefits, AI cannot replace human labor or human decision-making.

A.Kankanhalli (2019) talked about the Artificial intelligence can play a catalytic role in developing many innovative services for citizens, governments, and companies. If the interaction is activated with various objects such as wearables, vehicles, industrial sensors, smart phones, surveillance cameras. V. Marda (2018) listed the huge AI potential in different government sectors such as, education, physical infrastructure, transportation, telecommunication, data security and management, finance, healthcare, research and development, policymaking, legal and justice system, etc. Also it is highlighted that the authorities need to recognize the need of quick implementation of the same in order to enhance the quality of life of citizens and the effectiveness of governance. U. Gasser et. al. (2018) focused on use of surveillance camera for public safety. networked cameras can be employed and used on roads; hotel stays, malls or any other public places to identify and theft and track criminals, also the location can easily be tracked by the police if the GPS is employed in these cameras for high-tech surveillance. Jun Lou et. al. (2018) explained and identified with the advent of AI, new opportunities are available for safety control. Matej Drev (2019) focused on government Embracing automation and artificial intelligence due to the momentous potential of associated productivity gain all the while simultaneously, and at the same time should ensure transitional support for displaced worker groups.

5.3 Role of Government as AI Regulator

The role of government in AI regulation is an important one, particularly in a market economy. This role is especially important for industries that may be impacted by AI. For example, the healthcare industry is heavily regulated and supplied by the government. The policy of the government regarding AI in healthcare should be closely scrutinized.

While AI is a growing and complicated field, governments around the world are increasingly looking at this technology as a national concern. With growing economic and academic com- petition in AI, some countries are worried that commercial enterprise alone will not be enough to keep their economies competitive. To deal with this growing problem, governments around the world are developing national strategies to promote AI development. However, they are struggling with the question of regulation.

The rapid development of AI raises serious ethical questions. The threat of AI to jobs and the potential interaction of AI and globalization is of particular concern. Further, some observers worry about the concentration of power and information because of the rapid development of intelligent machines. This can lead to greater information asymmetries, diminished individual consent, and more.

As AI continues to develop, government regulators will need additional expertise and regulatory powers. These powers should allow regulators to conduct audits, inspections, and assessments of AI systems. These processes should be carried out both before and after the deployment of an AI system. Furthermore, regulators will need the space and permission to experiment with new tools to monitor AI systems.

The Executive Order shows that the government is taking an active role in AI regulation. However, it must be noted that not all government agencies have the budget to undertake R&D. This makes it essential to develop systems that promote the exchange of knowledge and best practices. In the future, centralized platforms will play a critical role in facilitating knowledge sharing.

Currently, governments should develop legislation to regulate AI and ensure that it does not violate fundamental rights. Regulations should be cross-cutting, as AI has broad implications. Furthermore, governments should support regulators in building AI expertise. These agencies will also be responsible for setting general guidelines on AI regulation.

As AI continues to advance, governments face many new challenges. While there is considerable literature on various aspects of AI governance, the field of governance is still underdeveloped. Although new applications of AI offer opportunities for increased economic efficiency and quality of life, they also pose new risks and unintended consequences. The UK government is hoping to change this by taking an approach that is flexible enough to meet this challenge.

Governments can take steps to drive AI development by building coalitions with industry and academia. Such collaborations are necessary to realize AI's full potential. They can also direct applications in the right direction. In short, governments must take the lead in this important area.

John (2021) shared that US bank regulators issued a request for information on the financial institutions' use of Artificial Intelligence and Machine Learning (ML) . Hélène Benoist (2019). The regulators wanted to hear from the industry on how they would like to use AI/ML and what challenges they are currently experiencing with AI adoption. In the healthcare sector, AI is starting to shape the healthcare evolution with connected healthcare and AI transforming the lives of individuals and communities. AI offers great promises, it "holds the promise to improve safety, fairness, welfare, transparency, and other social goals".

5.4 Role of Government in Facilitating Building Marketplaces

To facilitate AI growth and faster adoption, government should build an AI marketplace. An online marketplace needs to be transparent about price and value. It should also be able to match customers and developers. It should also have the capability to share data and participate in federated learning. In addition, it should be possible to enforce data-centric regulations through an AI marketplace. An example of such regulation would be a high-risk area section. A public ledger could track the data provider and provide traceability of data. Similarly, smart contracts could be used to ensure that training data coverage is adequate.

A marketplace should also support federated learning, which allows consumers to train models without having to move the training data. The marketplace should also allow users to aggregate alternative datasets if they follow a similar distribution to the validation dataset. This is important because AI learning algorithms suffer from severe quality loss when trained on non-IID data.

Another challenge is regulating the marketplace. government should set up regulatory frameworks to ensure that the marketplace is compliant with these guidelines. For example, US regulations have created special licensing requirements for geospatial AI software.

As the world continues to digitize, countries would need more data centers and they will need more workers. Analysts predict that there will be 2.3 million full-time data center workers worldwide by 2025. Many businesses have built game-changing AI/ML systems in the cloud. However, this model is expensive, and companies are looking for more cost-efficient options. Government should facilitate policy so that larger data centers are set up to drive further AI growth.

6.0 CONNECTED GOVERNANCE

Connected governance is a way of running a business that can collaborate across boundaries. It enables the executive leadership to avoid needless bureaucracy and to establish a virtual governance layer that can span existing governing bodies. As strategic business challenges continue to cross the boundaries of geographical and enterprise boundaries, connected governance has become a critical tool for executives.

The key to successful collaborative governance is the ability of stakeholders to communicate and share knowledge. Although some stakeholders may be better equipped to participate continuously than others, collaborating can help build bridges between diverse perspectives and guide priorities. It is essential to set up decision rules that allow stakeholders to collaborate effectively. Otherwise, the rules could represent too much commitment from some groups.

Despite the benefits of collaboration, it may not be the best tool to manage uncertainty. In the short term, it may increase uncertainty. For example, stakeholders may try to change the context of an issue to avoid a straightforward resolution, while other stakeholders may have competing views of information. Finally, stakeholders may disagree on the information they are receiving, causing further uncertainty.

Collaborative governance must also address power imbalances and acknowledge them. This means setting clear ground rules for collaborative discussions and prioritizing the right metrics early. In addition, the collaborative process will be more effective if there is a specific leader who can steer the process and help weaker stakeholders participate more actively.

7.0 SUMMARY

AI can ensure efficiency in the entire public governance process. Starting from collecting inputs to taking the right decision to implement decision, AI can do it all at a faster and cheaper cost.

8.0 CONCLUSION

AI can ensure efficiency in the entire public governance process. Starting from collecting inputs to taking the right decision to implement decision, AI can do it all at a faster and cheaper cost.

Traditionally, efficiency has been defined in terms of increasing output. Later, this concept was reframed in terms of adding value. In connected governance, efficiency is concerned with achieving objectives. For example, when a government agency is running efficiently, the government should be able to meet the organization's goals. The concept of efficiency has been studied in connection with pandemic management. The study's findings suggest that using more resources does not always mean better management. For this reason, policymakers should pay special attention to resource allocation and budgetary constraints in the public sector. Another key to efficiency is learning from past mistakes. Experience in pandemic governance is an important factor in the creation of an efficient pandemic governance model. In fact, countries with pandemic governance experience have achieved the highest economic benefits.

Data availability statements: We do not analyze or generate any datasets, because our work proceeds within a theoretical and mathematical approach.

Conflict of Interest: The authors whose names are listed immediately below certify that they have NO affiliations with or involvement in any organization or entity with any financial interest (such as honoraria; educational grants; participation in speakers' bureaus; membership, employment, consultancies, stock ownership, or other equity interest; and expert testimony or patent-licensing arrangements), or non-financial interest (such as personal or professional relationships, affiliations, knowledge or beliefs) in the subject matter or materials discussed in this manuscript.

REFERENCES

Bevir, M. (2012). *Governance: A very short introduction*. Oxford University Press. doi:10.1093/actrade/9780199606412.001.0001

Buenfil, J., Arnold, R. D., Abruzzo, B., & Korpela, C. (2019). Artificial Intelligence Ethics: Governance through Social Media. *2019 IEEE International Symposium on Technologies for Homeland Security (HST)*. 10.1109/HST47167.2019.9032907

Dwivedi, D., Batra, S., & Pathak, Y. K. (2023). A machine learning based approach to identify key drivers for improving corporate's esg ratings. *Journal of Law and Sustainable Development*, *11*(1), e0242. doi:10.37497/sdgs.v11i1.242

Dwivedi, D. N., Mahanty, G., & Vemareddy, A. (2022). How Responsible Is AI?: Identification of Key Public Concerns Using Sentiment Analysis and Topic Modeling. *International Journal of Information Retrieval Research*, *12*(1), 1–14. doi:10.4018/IJIRR.298646

Dwivedi, D. N., Tadoori, G., & Batra, S. (2023). Impact of women leadership and ESG ratings and in organizations: A time series segmentation study. *Academy of Strategic Management Journal*, *22*(S3), 1–6.

Erman, E., & Furendal, M. (2022). Artificial Intelligence and the Political Legitimacy of Global Governance. *Political Studies*, *50*(4), 621–647. doi:10.1177/00323217221126665

Gasser, U., & Almeida, V. A. F. (2017). A layered model for AI governance. *IEEE Internet Computing*, *21*(6), 58–62. doi:10.1109/MIC.2017.4180835

Gupta, A., Dwivedi, D. N., & Shah, J. (2023a). Overview of Money Laundering. In Artificial Intelligence Applications in Banking and Financial Services. Future of Business and Finance. Springer. doi:10.1007/978-981-99-2571-1_1

Gupta, A., Dwivedi, D. N., & Shah, J. (2023b). Financial Crimes Management and Control in Financial Institutions. In Artificial Intelligence Applications in Banking and Financial Services. Future of Business and Finance. Springer. doi:10.1007/978-981-99-2571-1_2

Gupta, A., Dwivedi, D. N., & Shah, J. (2023c). Overview of Technology Solutions. In Artificial Intelligence Applications in Banking and Financial Services. Future of Business and Finance. Springer. doi:10.1007/978-981-99-2571-1_3

Gupta, A., Dwivedi, D. N., & Shah, J. (2023d). Data Organization for an FCC Unit. In Artificial Intelligence Applications in Banking and Financial Services. Future of Business and Finance. Springer. doi:10.1007/978-981-99-2571-1_4

Gupta, A., Dwivedi, D. N., & Shah, J. (2023e). Planning for AI in Financial Crimes. In Artificial Intelligence Applications in Banking and Financial Services. Future of Business and Finance. Springer. doi:10.1007/978-981-99-2571-1_5

Gupta, A., Dwivedi, D. N., & Shah, J. (2023f). Applying Machine Learning for Effective Customer Risk Assessment. In Artificial Intelligence Applications in Banking and Financial Services. Future of Business and Finance. Springer. doi:10.1007/978-981-99-2571-1_6

Gupta, A., Dwivedi, D. N., & Shah, J. (2023g). Artificial Intelligence-Driven Effective Financial Transaction Monitoring. In Artificial Intelligence Applications in Banking and Financial Services. Future of Business and Finance. Springer. doi:10.1007/978-981-99-2571-1_7

Gupta, A., Dwivedi, D. N., & Shah, J. (2023h). Machine Learning-Driven Alert Optimization. In Artificial Intelligence Applications in Banking and Financial Services. Future of Business and Finance. Springer. doi:10.1007/978-981-99-2571-1_8

Gupta, A., Dwivedi, D. N., & Shah, J. (2023i). Applying Artificial Intelligence on Investigation. In Artificial Intelligence Applications in Banking and Financial Services. Future of Business and Finance. Springer. doi:10.1007/978-981-99-2571-1_9

Gupta, A., Dwivedi, D. N., & Shah, J. (2023j). Ethical Challenges for AI-Based Applications. In Artificial Intelligence Applications in Banking and Financial Services. Future of Business and Finance. Springer. doi:10.1007/978-981-99-2571-1_10

Gupta, A., Dwivedi, D. N., & Shah, J. (2023k). Setting up a Best-In-Class AI-Driven Financial Crime Control Unit (FCCU). In Artificial Intelligence Applications in Banking and Financial Services. Future of Business and Finance. Springer. doi:10.1007/978-981-99-2571-1_11

Jia, H. (2020). Yi Zeng: Promoting good governance of artificial intelligence. *National Science Review*, *7*(12), 1861–1862. doi:10.1093/nsr/nwaa255 PMID:34676086

Jin, D. (2019). *Reconstructing our orders: Artificial intelligence and human society, no. 99*. Springer Singapore.

Kankanhalli, A., Charalabidis, Y., & Mellouli, S. (2019, April). IoT and AI for smart government: A research agenda. *Government Information Quarterly*, *36*(2), 304–309. doi:10.1016/j.giq.2019.02.003

Kovač, I. (2018). *At His Crossroad: Reflections on the Work of France Bucar*. His Crossroad Reflections Work Fr. Bucar. doi:10.1007/978-3-319-78331-4

Loukis, E., Maragoudakis, M., & Kyriakou, N. (2019). Economic Crisis Policy Analytics Based on Artificial Intelligence (vol. 11685). Springer International Publishing.

Marda, V. (2018, November). Artificial intelligence policy in India: A framework for engaging the limits of data-driven decision-making. *Philos. Trans. R. Soc. A Math. Phys. Eng. Sci.*, *376*(2133), 1–19.

Moon, M. (2023). Searching for Inclusive Artificial Intelligence for Social Good: Participatory Governance and Policy Recommendations for Making AI More Inclusive and Benign for Society. *Public Administration Review*, *83*(2), 366–378. doi:10.1111/puar.13648

Naudé, W., & Dimitri, N. (2020). The race for an artificial general intelligence: Implications for public policy. *AI & Society*, *35*(2), 367–379. doi:10.1007/s00146-019-00887-x

Pradani, D. A., Anwar, C., & Armeliza, D. (2021). Pengaruh Pemahaman Good Governance dan Penguasaan Teknik Audit Berbantuan Komputer terhadap. *Artificial Intelligence*, *2*(3), 496–516. Advance online publication. doi:10.21009/japa.0203.02

Rej, A. (2020, Nov. 27). Artificial Intelligence for the Indo-Pacific: A Blueprint for 2030. *The Diplomat*.

Sales, A. (1991). The Private, the Public and Civil Society: Social Realms and Power Structures. *International Political Science Review / Revue Internationale de Science Politique, 12*(4), 295–312. https://www.jstor.org/stable/1601467

Saragih, A. H., Reyhani, Q., Setyowati, M. S., & Hendrawan, A. (2022). The potential of an artificial intelligence (AI) application for the tax administration system's modernization: The case of Indonesia. *Artificial Intelligence and Law*, (0123456789). Advance online publication. doi:10.1007/s10506-022-09321-y

Sharma, G. D., Yadav, A., & Chopra, R. (2020). Artificial intelligence and effective governance: A review, critique and research agenda. *Sustainable Futures, 2*. doi:10.1016/j.sftr.2019.100004

Strange, M., & Tucker, J. (2023). Global governance and the normalization of artificial intelligence as 'good' for human health. *AI & Society*. Advance online publication. doi:10.1007/s00146-023-01774-2

Truby, J., Brown, R., & Dahdal, A. (2020). Banking on AI: Mandating a proactive approach to AI regulation in the financial sector. *Law and Financial Markets Review*, *14*(2), 110–120. doi:10.1080/17521440.2020.1760454

Ulnicane, I., Eke, D., Knight, W., Ogoh, G., & Stahl, B. (2021). Good governance as a response to discontents? Déjà vu, or lessons for AI from other emerging technologies. *Interdisciplinary Science Reviews*, *46*(1-2), 176–195. doi:10.1080/03080188.2020.1840220

Vogl, T. M. (2021). Artificial Intelligence in Local Government: Enabling Artificial Intelligence for Good Governance in UK Local Authorities. SSRN *Electronic Journal*. doi:10.2139/SSRN.3840222

Winfield, A., & Jirotka, M. (2018). Ethical governance is essential to building trust in robotics and artificial intelligence systems. *Philosophical Transactions. Series A, Mathematical, Physical, and Engineering Sciences*, *376*(2133), 20180085. doi:10.1098/rsta.2018.0085 PMID:30323000

Yigitcanlar, T., Agdas, D., & Degirmenci, K. (2022). Artificial intelligence in local governments: Perceptions of city managers on prospects, constraints and choices. *AI & Society*, (0123456789). Advance online publication. doi:10.1007/s00146-022-01450-x

Chapter 5
Unveiling the Power of Machine Learning Algorithms

Mehak Malhotra
Lovely Professional University, India

Amir Ahmad Dar
https://orcid.org/0000-0002-0379-2272
Lovely Professional University, India

Akshat Jain
Lovely Professional University, India

C. V. Adithya
Lovely Professional University, India

ABSTRACT

The study compares neural networks, k-nearest neighbors, decision trees, and support vector machines in various scenarios, exploring both supervised and unsupervised learning approaches. Benchmark datasets from the banking, healthcare, and image recognition sectors are used to validate the study. Performance metrics, including accuracy, precision, recall, and F1 score, are employed for a comprehensive analysis. The study addresses the transparency of machine learning algorithms, investigating ways to simplify complicated decision-making processes. It also explores how algorithmic performance is affected by parametric modifications to find the best configurations for specific applications. The report offers significant perspectives for professionals, researchers, and policymakers in sectors other than academia, boosting their basic understanding of machine learning technology in revolutionary domains. All in all, this study simplifies machine learning techniques and offers useful insights into their effectiveness and suitability in many fields.

DOI: 10.4018/978-1-6684-9716-6.ch005

1. INTRODUCTION

Machine learning, a subset of artificial intelligence, is a computer science dedicated to designing and developing algorithms that enable systems to automatically gain insights from data and then make predictions or judgments without additional programming. The basic concept focuses on the building of mathematical models, which undergo iterative modifications when exposed to large datasets to identify hidden patterns, infer correlations, and execute complex tasks. Supervised learning, a widely used framework, comprises training models using carefully labeled datasets, giving them the ability to predict outcomes for novel, previously unseen data instances. Unsupervised learning, on the other hand, explores unlabelled data in search of hidden patterns and deeper structures. Reinforcement learning adds an interactive component to learning by guiding algorithms through dynamic interactions with an environment via feedback mechanisms in the form of rewards or penalties. Machine learning's usefulness covers multiple fields, including healthcare, finance, and natural language processing, transforming decision-making processes and executing complex operations. The constant breakthroughs in algorithmic complexity, data-driven insights, and collaborative activities across interdisciplinary sectors highlight machine learning's continuous evolution, supporting its widespread impact on modern technology and social perspectives (Bishop, 2006; Domingos, 2012; Géron, 2022; Heaton, 2018; Krizhevsky et al., 2012; Sutton & Barto, 2018).

2. LITERATURE REVIEW

Machine learning is based on the idea that computers can learn from data without explicit programming. Basic learning algorithms were developed by pioneers such as Alan Turing and Arthur Samuel, whose early research in the 20th century laid the foundation for machine learning. Machine learning progressed from basic rule-based models to complex algorithms with the ability to process large amounts of data as processing power increased.

The story of machine learning unfolds throughout time, beginning in the mid-20th century with the early attempts of geniuses such as Arthur Samuel, who is credited with coining the phrase "machine learning." This era, which spanned the 1950s and 1960s, saw the birth of self-learning algorithms, as demonstrated by Samuel's construction of a checkers program designed to improve its performance via experience. Decision tree algorithms, an early expression of supervised learning, were introduced in the 1970s. As the 1980s progressed, the importance of symbolic learning and expert systems attempted to replicate human decision-making processes. The 1990s saw the rise of Support Vector Machines and neural networks, resulting in an evolution toward statistical methodologies. During this time, however, computational limits prevented wider adoption. Ensemble approaches caused an uprising in the late 1990s and early 2000s, boosting the effectiveness of machine learning models. By the mid-2000s, the convergence of large datasets and improved computer power had set the ground for the return of neural networks, resulting in significant advances in deep learning. Deep learning has risen in popularity in recent years, pushed by technological advances in technology and the widespread availability of large datasets. Milestones like AlphaGo's victory over a human champion in 2016 highlight the field's development, with the following advances in natural language processing enhancing its impact. Machine learning has entered the fabric of machine learning, easily integrating into numerous areas ranging from healthcare to finance. The historical timeline highlights a complicated interplay between algorithmic innovation, data accessibility, and computational capabilities, defining machine learning's history as a dynamic and pivotal domain within the larger landscape of artificial intelligence (Breiman, 2017; Dietterich, 2000; LeCun et al., 2015; Rumelhart et al., 1986; Samuel, 2000; Silver et al., 2016; Vapnik, 1999).

3. METHODOLOGY

The methodology utilized in this study to choose and evaluate machine learning algorithms was informed by both theoretical significance and real-world applicability. The selection of algorithms was predicated on the following factors: a wide range of representation of regression and classification techniques, relevance to the particular problem domain, and prevalence of the algorithms in the current literature. To ensure a comprehensive investigation, inclusion criteria focused on aspects like interpretability, robustness, and computational efficiency.

Data collection, which is the first step in the research process, involves gathering relevant datasets. To guarantee the quality of the data, preprocessing procedures like feature scaling and handling missing data are carried out. Next, in order to assess the performance of the model, the data is divided into training and testing sets. The study focused on supervised machine learning, emphasizing regression and classification algorithms using the R programming language.

Many algorithms are used for regression tasks, such as Polynomial Regression, Decision Tree Regression, Random Forest Regression, and Multiple Linear Regression. R-squared and Mean Squared Error are two examples of metrics used to evaluate the performance of each algorithm. Regression curves and scatter plots are two examples of visualizations that help with result interpretation.

Similar to this, algorithms such as Random Forest, K-nearest neighbors, Support Vector Machine, Decision Tree, Naïve Bayes, Gradient Regression, and Neural

Networks are used for classification tasks. Evaluation metrics such as F1-score, recall, accuracy, and precision are applied. Model performance is revealed by visualizations like ROC curves and confusion matrices.

4. TYPES OF MACHINE LEARNING

1. Supervised Machine Learning
    a. Regression Algorithm
        i. Simple Linear Regression
        ii. Multiple Linear Regression
        iii. Polynomial Regression
        iv. Decision Tree Regression
        v. Random Forest Regression
    b. Classification Algorithm
        i. Logistic Regression
        ii. Naïve Bayes
        iii. K-nearest neighbors
        iv. Support Vector Machine
        v. Decision Tree
        vi. Random Forest
        vii. Neural Network

5. SUPERVISED MACHINE LEARNING

An algorithm that uses labelled training data to learn how to make predictions or judgments without explicit programming is known as supervised machine learning. A dataset with matching labelled outputs for the input characteristics is used to train the algorithm. The algorithm modifies its parameters during training to reduce the discrepancy between the real labels and its anticipated outputs. Once trained, the algorithm may anticipate new, unknown data by generalizing what it has learned. To help the algorithm understand the underlying patterns and relationships in the data, the objective is to translate the input data to the proper output based on the labelled samples that have been supplied. Supervised learning is frequently utilized in tasks like regression and classification, in which the algorithm forecasts the category or value of the output variable.

5.1 Regression Algorithm

In machine learning, a technique known as regression is used to forecast a continuous output variable based on input data. To enable the algorithm to forecast fresh, unknown data, the objective is to describe the link between the input variables and the continuous target variable. Regression involves the algorithm learning from a series of labelled training instances that include the associated output values as well as the input attributes. To reduce the variation between the algorithm's anticipated outputs and the actual continuous values, the parameters are adjusted during the learning process. The regression model may be used to predict or anticipate the continuous result using fresh data once it has been trained.

Simple Linear Regression

The link between the independent (predictor) and dependent (responder) variables is examined using simple linear regression. Finding a linear equation with the formula

$$y = \beta_0 + \beta_1 x + \epsilon$$

In which x is the independent variable, y is the dependent variable, β_0 is the slope, and epsilon denotes error is the goal. To estimate β_0 and β_1, least squares minimize the squared gaps between expected and actual values. Regression is a widely used tool in domains such as finance and health to forecast future values and examine the relationships between variables. Linearity, homoscedasticity, independence, and error regularity are among the misconceptions. The coefficient of determination R^2, which shows how much of the variance in the dependent variable is explained, is one of the key metrics. The application relies on theoretical comprehension and visual inspection of scatter plots; it is appropriate when changes in the independent variable linearly impact the dependent variable. When measurement scales are suitable and, error variance is consistent, the model's dependability rises. The lm() function in R implementation syntax is employed for model fitting and summarization. This systematic procedure ensures consistent and intelligible outcomes, particularly when dealing with datasets exhibiting a reasonable linear connection. The syntax for this algorithm is

```
#Fit a simple linear regression model
model = lm(dependent_variable ~ independent_variable, data = your_data)
#Print the summary of the model
summary(model)
```

The predictor is the independent_variable, the dependent_variable is the predicted variable, and the your_data is the dataset that contains these variables. The summary function offers an extensive overview of the regression model, including coefficients and statistical measures of fit (Cohen et al., 2013; Fox, 2015; Kutner et al., 2005; Montgomery et al., 2021; Wasserman & Kutner, 1985).

Analysis for Simple Linear Regression

The data, which was obtained from Kaggle (https://www.kaggle.com/datasets/mohithsairamreddy/salary-data), includes characteristics like age, gender, years of experience, job title, education level, and salary. In this case, a good analytical approach is simple linear regression.

Read the data

```
dataset = read.csv("Salary_Data.csv")
```

Split the Data Into Test and Training Set

A fixed ratio of the dataset is split up into training and testing sets. To evaluate the algorithm's performance on a smaller subset of data, this first division is essential. If the algorithm produces appropriate results, it may then be used to forecast data on a larger scale. The data splitting procedure uses the "caTools" module, and a predefined seed set is used to guarantee consistent outcomes between runs. As part of this process, distinct training and test sets are created for further analysis.

```
install.packages("caTools")
library('caTools')
set.seed(123)
split = sample.split(dataset$Salary, SplitRatio = 2/3)
training_set = subset(dataset, split==TRUE)
test_set = subset(dataset, split==FALSE)
```

Making the Regressor

After the dataset is split into training and testing sets, the linear model is represented by the "lm()" function, which is used to build a regressor. Using this function, a model that builds a linear connection between the training set's variables is created.

```
regressor = lm(formula = Salary~YearsExperience, data = training_set)
```

Figure 1. Training set and test set

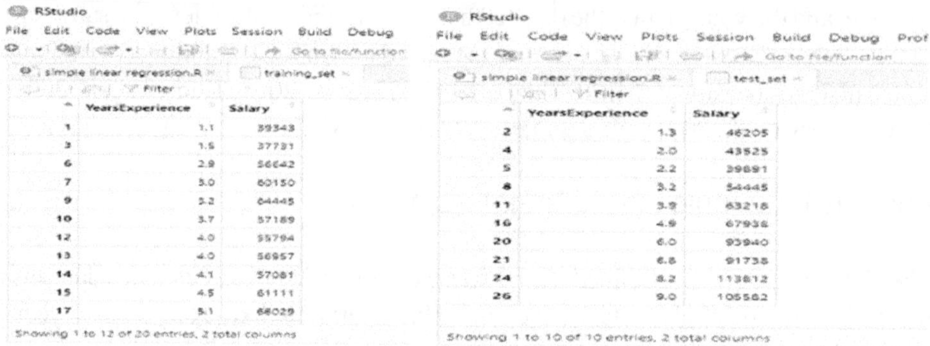

Making predictor

```
y_pred = predict(regressor, newdata = test_set)
```

Visualization of the Training Set

The information provided is then visualized using the “ggplot2” package. This package makes it easier to create graphical representations of the dataset that help with comprehension and interpretation.

```
install.packages(“ggplot2”)
library(‘ggplot2’)
```

```
ggplot()+geom_point(aes(x = training_set$YearsExperience, y = training_set$Salary), color = ‘red’)+ geom_line(aes(x = training_set$YearsExperience, y = predict(regressor, newdata = training_set)), color = ‘blue’)+ ggtitle(‘Salary VS Experience Training Set’)+ xlab(‘Experience’)+ylab(‘Salary’)
```

Visualization of Test Set

```
ggplot()+geom_point(aes(x = training_set$YearsExperience, y = training_set$Salary), color = ‘red’)+ geom_line(aes(x = test_set$YearsExperience, y = predict(regressor,newdata=test_set)),color=‘blue’)+ggtitle(‘Salary VS Experience Test Set’)+ xlab(‘Experience’)+ylab(‘Salary’)
```

Multiple Linear Regression

Multiple linear regression is a generalization of ordinary linear regression that models complicated interactions between a dependent variable and many independent variables. It provides light on the complicated structure of datasets. The dependent variable y, independent variables $x_1+x_2+x_3+\ldots+x_n$, y-intercept β_0, coefficients $\beta_1, \beta_2, \beta_3, \ldots, \beta_n$, and the error term ε are represented by the general formula

$$y = \beta_0 + \beta_1 x_1 + \beta_2 x_2 + \ldots + \beta_n x_n + \varepsilon$$

Figure 2. Visualization of the training set

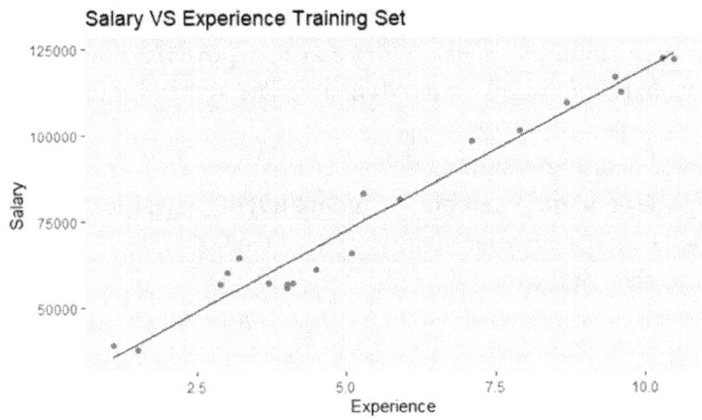

Figure 3. Visualization of the test set

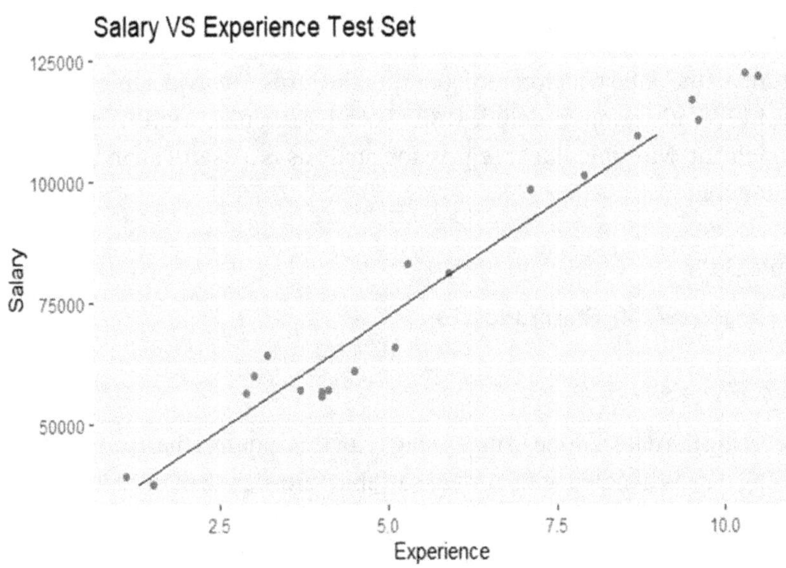

The use of coefficient estimation reduces the discrepancies between predicted and observed values. It has broad applications; in economics, it helps with product pricing, and in medical research, it improves comprehension of health consequences. Linearity, error independence, homoscedasticity, and normality are among the presumptions. When one unit of an independent variable changes while others stay constant, the dependent variable changes as well, as shown by coefficients. Model fit is evaluated using the coefficient of determination R2, "hich shows the proportion of explained variance. Research topics, particularly in ecology and biology, are guided by practical considerations; hence, the approach requires careful examination of assumptions about linearity, uniformity, error independence, and normality. All things considered, multiple linear regression is a powerful tool for interpreting intricate variable relationships across domains. The syntax for this algorithm is

```
#Fit a multiple linear regression model
model = lm(dependent_variable ~ independent_variable1+ independent_
    variable2+…, data = your_data)
#Print the summary of the model
summary(model)
```

The dependent variable is the expected variable, the different predictors are the independent_variables1, independent_variables2, ..., and the dataset containing these variables is your data. A thorough summary of the regression model, including coefficients and statistical measures of fit, is provided by the summary function.

Analysis for Multiple Linear Regression

The features of the data, which came from Kaggle (https://www.kaggle.com/datasets/abhishek14398/50startups), include R&D Spend, Administration, Marketing Spend, State, and Profit. Multiple linear regression analysis is a useful analytical technique in this situation.

Read the Data

```
dataset = read.csv("50_Startups.csv")
```

Data Pre-Processing

Pre-processing the data is done in many stages for this inquiry: the dataset is imported; any missing data is handled; categorical variables are encoded; the dataset is divided into training and testing subsets, and features are scaled during these steps. Each of these processes contributes to preparing the dataset for additional examination.

Throughout the procedure, the function "str()" will also be used to display the underlying structure of objects, such as arrays, lists, matrices, factors, or data frames.

```
str(dataset$State)
dataset$State = factor(dataset$State, levels = c("New York", "California", "Florida"),
      labels = c(1, 2, 3))
```

Split the Data Into Test and Training Set

The dataset is divided into training and testing sets at a predetermined ratio. This initial division is crucial for assessing the algorithm's performance on a smaller selection of data. The technique might subsequently be used for larger-scale data forecasting if it yields suitable results. The "caTools" module is used in the data-splitting process, and a specified seed set is employed to ensure consistent results between runs. Different training and test sets are generated for additional analysis during this process.

```
install.packages("caTools")
library("caTools")
set.seed(123)
split = sample.split(dataset$Profit, SplitRatio = 0.8)
training_set = subset(dataset, split==TRUE)
test_set = subset(dataset, split==FALSE)
```

Figure 4. Training set and test set

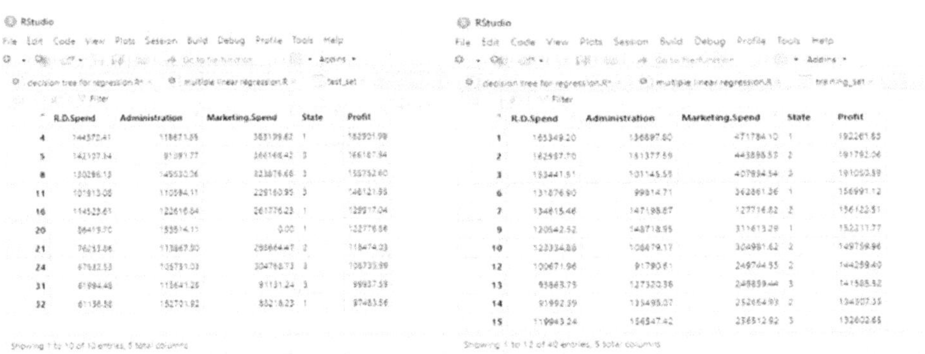

Making the Regressor

The "lm()" function, which is used to construct a regressor, represents the linear model after the dataset has been divided into training and testing sets. This function is used to develop a model that establishes a linear relationship between the variables in the training set. The "summary()" method is used in this situation to give a thorough summary of the data frame.

```
regressor = lm(formula = Profit~R.D.Spend+Administration+Marketing.
    Spend+State, data = training_set)
summary(regressor)
Making predictor
y_pred = predict(regressor, newdata = test_set)
```

The procedure of choosing regressors for multivariate linear regression entails choosing just those qualities that have a substantial influence on the data (Cohen et al., 2013; Fox, 2015; Gelman & Hill, 2006; Hair et al., 2019; Kutner et al., 2005; Montgomery et al., 2021; Rencher & Schaalje, 2008).

Polynomial Regression

A flexible method in statistics and machine learning, polynomial regression models complicated correlations between independent and dependent variables. The approach extends linear regression by inserting an nth-degree polynomial, where y is the dependent variable, x is the independent variable, and $\beta 0, \beta 1, \beta 2, \ldots, \beta n$ are coefficients. Applications come from a variety of disciplines, including finance for long-term stock price analysis and physics for projectile routes and nonlinear systems. Although it is flexible, care must be taken to avoid overfitting, particularly when working with high-degree polynomials. When a model closely fits training data but performs badly with fresh data, this is known as overfitting. Regularisation strategies and careful model evaluation are necessary to strike a balance between complexity and generalization. The use of scatter plots, especially in graphic analysis, facilitates the identification of curvilinear trends. Determining the polynomial degree requires striking a balance between averting overfitting and capturing crucial nonlinear information. Techniques like cross-validation aid in selecting the optimal degree, ensuring consistency across datasets. In a variety of fields, polynomial regression is useful for modelling nonlinear patterns and analyzing complex relationships because it performs well in situations with peaks, troughs, or complicated bends. The syntax for polynomial regression is

```
#Fit a polynomial linear regression model
model = lm(dependent_variable ~ poly(independent_variable, degree), data =
    your_data)
#Print the summary of the model
summary(model)
```

The independent_variable is the predictor, the predicted variable is the dependent_variable, the degree of the polynomial is the degree, and the dataset containing these variables is your_data. A thorough summary of the regression model, including coefficients and statistical measures of fit, is provided by the summary function (Hastie et al., 2009; James et al., 2013).

Analysis for Polynomial Regression

The data, which was obtained from Kaggle, (https://www.kaggle.com/datasets/mariospirito/position-salariescsv) includes characteristics like position, level, and salary. The dataset gives information about the salaries of different positions at different levels and we aim to find the expected salary of an employee at level 6.5. In this case, simple linear regression might give an inappropriate value. So, we employ a much better analytical approach, which is polynomial regression.

Read the Data

```
dataset = read.csv("Position_Salaries.csv")
dataset=dataset[,2:3]
```

We use polynomial regression when the data increases continuously and exponentially. If we closely observe the data, salary increases exponentially with an increase in the level. To perform this regression, we first create the higher-order values of the level, that is, we take the square, cube, and fourth power of the level.

```
dataset$Level2=dataset$Level^2
dataset$Level3=dataset$Level^3
dataset$Level4=dataset$Level^4
```

Making the Regressor

After constructing these levels, we build the polynomial regression model using the "lm" function. Using this, the relationship between the independent variable (level) and the dependent variable (salary) is modelled as an nth-degree polynomial.

```
poly_reg=lm(formula = Salary~.,data = dataset)
summary(poly_reg)
```

We now predict the expected salary for an employee whose level is given as 6.5. For this, we employ the "predict" function

```
y_predpoly=predict(poly_reg,newdata = data.frame(Level=6.5, Level2=6.5^2,
    Level3=6.5^3, Level4=6.5^4))
y_predpoly
```

The output of the analysis is obtained as Expected salary= 158862.5.

The polynomial regression model is then visualized using the "ggplot2" package. This package makes it easier to create graphical representations of the dataset that help with comprehension and interpretation.

```
install.packages("ggplot2")
library('ggplot2')
```

```
ggplot()+geom_point(aes(x=dataset$Level,y=dataset$Salary),color='red')+ geom_
line(aes(x=dataset$Level,y=predict(poly_reg,newdata = dataset)),color='blue')+
ggtitle('Salary vs Level')+xlab('Level')+ylab('Salary')
```

Figure 5. Visualization

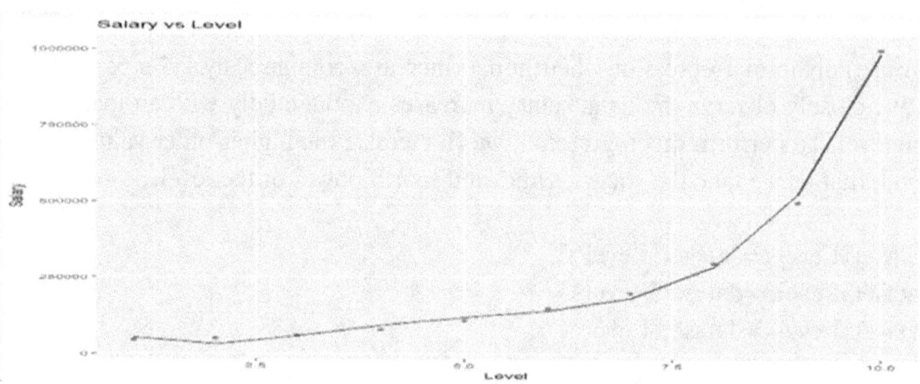

Decision Tree Regression

A popular and useful machine learning method for predictive modeling in regression contexts is decision tree regression. To find complicated associations in datasets, it uses graphical models called decision trees to do non-parametric supervised learning. Nodes, branches, and leaves make up the fundamental structure. Internal nodes reflect decisions made based on certain criteria, branching shows the results of decisions, and leaves hold estimated values. Recurrent data partitioning utilizing optimum splits that minimize the sum of squared differences between actual and forecast values is a step in the creative process. Decision tree regression works well with complicated datasets where linear regression models might not perform well since they can handle complex variable interactions and nonlinear correlations. Its decision-making process is visually shown, which improves interpretability and helps users discover important variables. It is advised to change the minimum number of samples per leaf to reduce overfitting. To sum up, decision tree regression is a flexible, interpretable, and successful method for capturing complicated relationships that work with a variety of datasets. The syntax for this algorithm is

```
#Fit a decision tree regression model
library(rpart)
model=rpart(formula=dependent_variable~independent_variable1+independent_
    variable2+…, data = your_data)
#Print the predict values
predictions = predict(model, newdata = new_data)
```

The code uses the 'rpart' library to fit a decision tree regression model in R, predicts values for a dependent variable based on given independent variables, and outputs the predictions (Breiman, 2017; Hastie et al., 2009; Loh, 2011; Quinlan, 2014).

Analysis for Decision Tree Regression

The dataset "Position_Salaries.csv" contains attributes like Position, Level, and Salary (https://www.kaggle.com/datasets/mariospirito/position-salariescsv). An implementation of the decision tree classification model is recommended for this dataset.

Read the Dataset

```
dataset = read.csv("Position_Salaries.csv")
```

Preparing the data for this inquiry requires several stages. These consist of splitting the dataset into training and testing subsets, scaling features, encoding categorical variables, loading the dataset, and completing any data gaps. To make sure that the dataset is ready for further analysis, all of these processes are essential.

```
dataset = dataset[,2:3]
```

Fitting Decision Tree Model in Training Set and Predicting

The Decision Tree model approach is used to classify the model using the training set after the data preparation stage. It is enabled by using the "rpart" library. The trained DT model is then used to create predictions.

```
install.packages("rpart")
regressor = rpart(formula = Salary~., data = dataset, control = rpart.control(minsplit
    = 1))
y_pred = predict(regressor, newdata = data.frame(Level = 6.5))
```

Visualization for the Result

The data is visualized using the "ggplot2" package, which facilitates the creation of graphical representations of data for simpler comprehension and analysis. This time, the x_grid is created using the "seq()" method and a regression line is displayed using the random forest approach.

Figure 6. Visualization

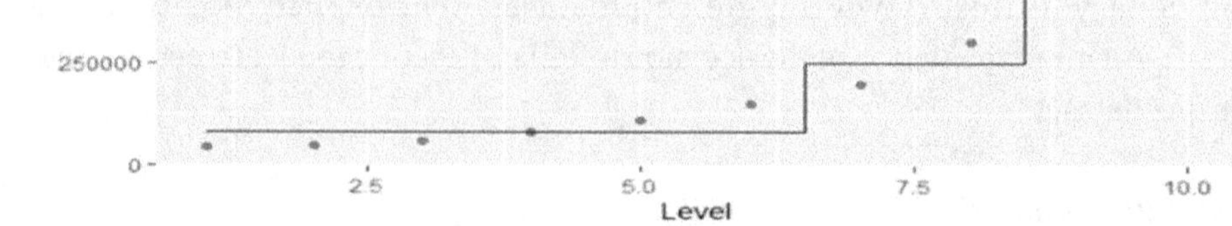

Random Forest Regression

Building on the ideas of decision tree regression, Random Forest Regression is a well-liked ensemble learning method in machine learning that is dependable and flexible. It introduces important kinds of randomness by using feature randomization and bootstrap sampling, which overcome the disadvantages of individual decision trees. By using replacement random sampling to create subgroups, bootstrap sampling allows for independent decision tree training. By ensuring that different subsets of features are used while building trees, feature randomization improves the general durability of the model and decorrelates predictions. When predictions from individual trees are combined in an ensemble method, a reliable and accurate regression model that can handle complicated relationships but is sensitive to overfitting is created. Because of its flexibility and ability to handle complex datasets well, Random Forest is a good fit in situations when other models are insufficient. Its ensemble technique offers insights into feature relevance and makes generalization to fresh data easier. A dataset's appropriateness is determined by variables such as its size, the existence of outliers, its nonlinearity, and its complexity. With moderate to large datasets, resistance against outliers, and the capacity to handle both categorical and numerical features, Random Forest Regression performs exceptionally well. By striking this balance, algorithm performance in regression tasks is ensured, providing accurate forecasts that satisfy interpretability requirements. In conclusion, Random Forest Regression is a useful tool that can be used in a variety of regression scenarios and offers speed, flexibility, and resilience when working with complicated data structures. The syntax for this algorithm is

```
#Fit a decision tree regression model
library(randomForest)
model = randomForest(formula = dependent_variable ~ independent_
    variable1+independent_variable2+..., data = your_data, ntree = number_
    of_trees)
#Print the predict values
predictions = predict(model, newdata = new_data)
```

The code fits a random forest regression model by providing predictors and response variables using the R randomForest library. Afterwards, it applies the trained model to forecast values for new data (Breiman, 2001; Cutler et al., 2007; Geurts et al., 2006; Hastie et al., 2009; Kursa & Rudnicki, 2010; Liaw & Wiener, 2002).

Analysis for Random Forest Regression

Position, Level, and Salary are among the attributes included in the Kaggle dataset (https://www.kaggle.com/datasets/mariospirito/position-salariescsv). It is advised to use a random forest regression model as an analytical technique for the examination of this data.

Read the Data

```
dataset = read.csv("Position_Salaries.csv")
```

Data Pre-Processing

For this investigation, many phases of data pre-processing are necessary. These include importing the dataset, addressing any data gaps, encoding categorical variables, dividing the dataset into training and testing subsets, and scaling features. Each of these steps contributes to ensuring that the dataset is prepared for additional analysis.

```
dataset = dataset[,2:3]
```

Making Regressor

The randomForest library will be called after the preparatory stages are finished. To build a regressor, use this library. To guarantee consistent outcomes each time the code is run, it is crucial to specify a seed before continuing.

```
install.packages("randomForest")
library('randomForest')
set.seed(1234)
regressor = randomForest(x = dataset[-2], y = dataset$Salary, ntree = 500)
```

Making Predictor

```
y_pred = predict(regressor, newdata = data.frame(Level = 6.5))
```

Visualization for the Result

The "ggplot2" package, which makes it easier to create graphical representations of data for easier understanding and interpretation, is used to visualize the data. This time, the "seq()" function is used to create the x_grid, which is then used to use the random forest technique to show a regression line.

```
install.packages("ggplot2")
```

```
library(ggplot2)
x_grid = seq(min(dataset$Level), max(dataset$Level), 0.01)

ggplot()+geom_point(aes(x = dataset$Level, y = dataset$Salary), colour = 'red')+
geom_line(aes(x = x_grid, y = predict(regressor, newdata = data.frame(Level =
x_grid))), color = 'blue')+ ggtitle('Truth or Bluff(Random Forest Regression')+
xlab('Level')+ ylab('Salary')
```

Figure 7. Visualization

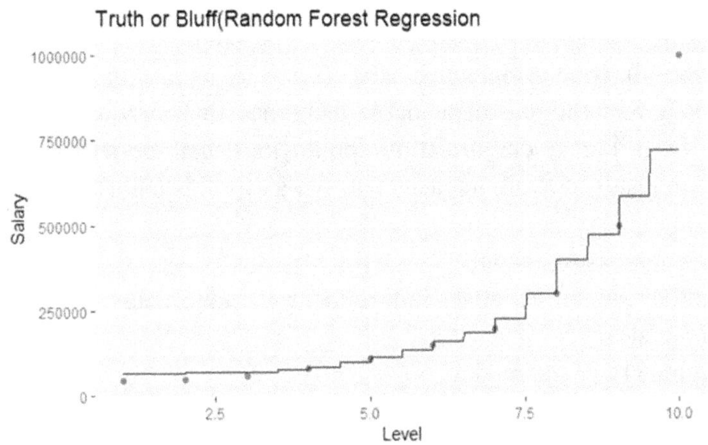

Classification Algorithm

In machine learning, classification is the process of teaching an algorithm to classify input data into labels or classes that have already been established. A collection of labelled training samples, where each input instance is connected to a particular class or category, is used to teach the algorithm. Enabling the algorithm to generalize its learning to properly forecast the class of new, unknown examples is the aim of classification. The method modifies its parameters during training to reduce the discrepancy between the training data's actual labels and its anticipated class labels. The classification model may be used to categorize fresh data into one of the established classes after it has been trained. The goal of classification, a basic machine learning problem, is to automatically assign data to discrete groups based on its attributes. It is utilized in many different applications, including spam detection, picture recognition, and medical diagnosis.

Logistic Regression

A popular statistical method in machine learning, logistic regression estimates the likelihood that an event will fall into one of two classes and is mostly used for binary classification problems. The sigmoid function, an S-shaped curve that converts real-valued integers into a binary range of 0 to 1, is the fundamental component of logistic regression. Based on the log-likelihood of an event, the logistic regression model theoretically implies a linear relationship between the independent variables. You need to avoid multicollinearity, handle categorical variables carefully, and have a large enough sample size. It might not be the best choice for datasets with a lot of variables or highly nonlinear interactions, even though it works well for binary outcomes. More complicated models, such as decision trees, could be better in some situations. In conclusion, when used effectively in machine learning, logistic regression is a versatile and dependable technique that provides simplicity and interpretability in binary classification applications, making it a great option in scenarios with results that are unclear. The syntax for this algorithm is

```
#Fit a logistic regression model
model = glm(dependent_variable ~ independent_variable, data = your_data, family
    = "binomial")
#Print the summary of the model
summary(model)
```

The code fits a logistic regression model with given dependent and independent variables by using a binomial family and the R glm function. Next, for significance and performance analysis, it makes use of the summary function to offer thorough insights into the model's coefficients, standard errors, z-values, p-values, and goodness-of-fit statistics (Agresti, 2012; Bishop & Nasrabadi, 2006; Hastie et al., 2009; Hosmer et al., 2013).

Analysis for Logistic Regression

Kaggle gathered the information, which included attributes like User ID, Gender, Age, Estimated Salary, and Purchased (https://www.kaggle.com/datasets/rakeshrau/social-network-ads). An application of the logistic regression model is suggested as an analytical method for this data.

Read the Data

```
data=read.csv("Social_Network_Ads.csv")
```

Data Pre-Processing

This research requires many stages of data pre-processing. These consist of loading the dataset, scaling features, encoding categorical variables, completing any gaps in the data, and splitting the dataset into training and testing subsets. All of these actions are required to guarantee that the dataset is ready for further examination.

```
data=data[,2:5]
data$Gender=factor(data$Gender, levels = c("Male","Female"), labels = c(1,0))
```

Split the Data Into Test and Training Set

The dataset is divided into training and testing sets using a predetermined ratio. This initial division is crucial for assessing the algorithm's performance on a smaller amount of data. The technique might subsequently be used for predictions of bigger amounts of data if it yields satisfactory results. The "caTools" module is used in the data-splitting process, and a predefined seed set is used to ensure consistent results between runs. The data needs to carry out feature scaling to achieve even better results. For additional analysis, several training and test sets are generated throughout this process.

```
library("caTools")
set.seed(123)
split = sample.split(data$Purchased, SplitRatio = 0.75)
training_set= subset(data, split == TRUE)
test_set = subset(data, split == FALSE)
training_set[,2:3] =scale(training_set[,2:3])
test_set[,2:3] = scale(test_set[,2:3])
```

Figure 8. Training and test set

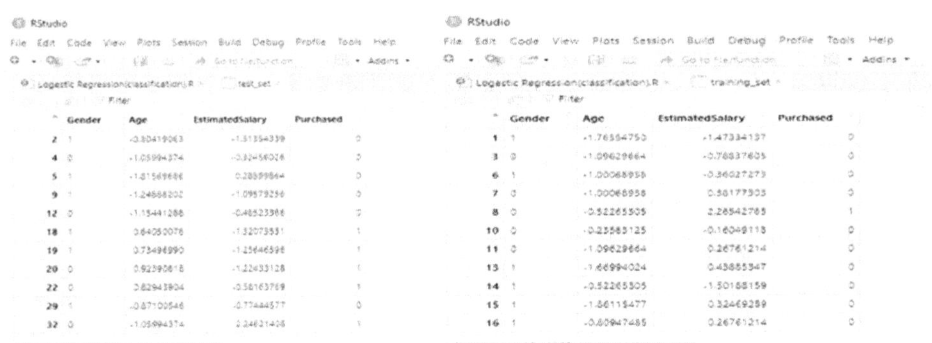

Making Classifier and Predictor

The "glm()" method is used to build the classifier. The "predict()" method is then used to create a probability predictor. Finally, the "if-else ()" method is used to generate a predictor. There can be issues with the prediction function during compilation because of the nature of the data.

```
classifier = glm(formula = Purchased~., family = binomial, data = training_set)
prob_pred = predict(classifier,newdata = test_set[-4])
y_pred = ifelse(prob_pred>0.5,1,0)
```

Making Confusion Matrix

To create a confusion matrix, the "table()" function must be utilized. The model's inaccurate predictions are measured using this matrix. To put it simply, it's a table that classifies the values in the dataset according to the model's projected and actual values.

```
cm = table(y_pred,test_set[,4])
```

Table 1. Confusion matrix

y_pred	0	1
0	58	14
1	6	22

Naive Bayes

A well-liked machine learning classification method for applications like text categorization, spam filtering, and sentiment analysis is called Naive Bayes. Assuming conditional independence of characteristics, it is based on the Bayes theorem. It is effective because of its simplicity, particularly in feature settings with many facets. Theorem

$$P\left(A|B\right) = \frac{P\left(B|A\right)*P\left(A\right)}{P\left(B\right)}$$

Updates hypothesis probabilities depending on fresh evidence. When it comes to classification, Naive Bayes works well with plenty of information and class labels. Among its variations are Gaussian Naïve Bayes for continuous features with a Gaussian distribution, Multinomial Naïve Bayes for discrete data (such as word counts), and Bernoulli Naïve Bayes for binary features. The decision is based on the properties of the data. Naive Bayes is very useful for text-related problems, where classes stand for subjects or moods and features stand for word occurrences. Its efficacy is demonstrated in sentiment analysis, spam filtering, and other areas. Because of the method's adaptability, users may select the best option depending on assumptions about distribution and data type. Naive Bayes is a popular categorization method in many different sectors because of its ease of use and efficiency. The syntax for this algorithm is

```
#Fit a naïve bayes model
library(e1071)
model = naiveBayes(class ~ ., data = your_data)
#Print the summary of the model
summary(model)
```

Using the response variable "class" and predictor variables from the dataset "your_data," the code fits a Naïve Bayes classification model in R using the e1071 library. The model is then summarised (Hastie et al., 2009; Lewis, 1998; Manning et al., 2008).

Analysis for Naive Bayes

The dataset from Kaggle, "Churn-Modelling.csv", consists of attributes like CredictScore, age, tenure, balance, active member, estimated salary, and excited. We aim to perform classification on the response variable "Excited" using Naïve-Bayes classification.

Read the Data

```
Dataset=read.csv("Churn_Modelling.csv")
Dataset=dataset[,-c(1,2,3,5,6)]
```

Numerous stages of data pre-processing are required for this inquiry. These consist of splitting the dataset into training and testing subsets, scaling features, fixing any data gaps, and importing the dataset. Each procedure helps guarantee that the dataset is ready for more examination.

Data Pre-Processing

The dataset is divided into training and testing sets at a predetermined ratio. This first division is crucial for assessing the algorithm's performance on a smaller subset of data. The technique could subsequently be applied to larger-scale data forecasting if it yields suitable results. The "caTools" module is used in the data-splitting process, and a specified seed set is employed to ensure consistent results between runs. Different training and test sets are generated for additional analysis during this process.

```
install.packages("caTools")
library('caTools')
set.seed(123)
split=sample.spli(dataset$Exited,SplitRatio = 0.75)
training_set=subset(dataset.split==TRUE)
test_set=subset(dataset.spli==FALSE)
training_set[,1:8]=scale(training_set[,1:8])
test_set[,1:8]=scale(test_set[,1:8])
```

Figure 9. Training and test set

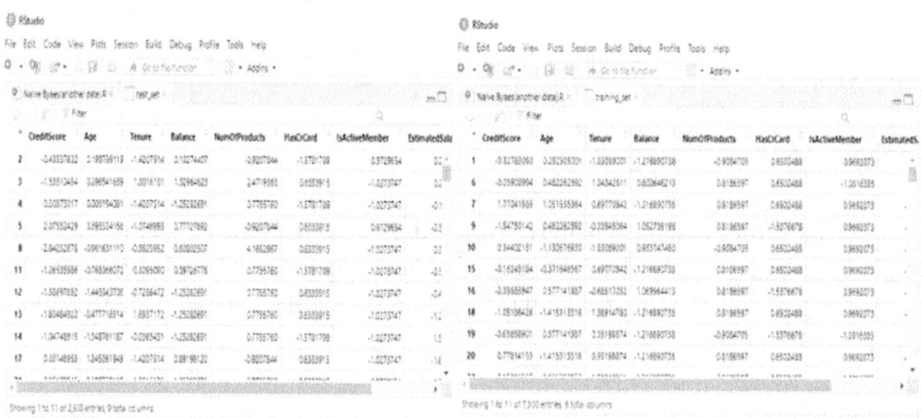

The Naïve-Bayes approach is used to classify the model using the training set after the data preparation stage. Naïve-Bayes is enables by using the "e1071" library. The trained Naïve-Bayes model is then used to create predictions.

```
library('e1071')
```

```
classifier=naiveBayes(x=training_set[,-9], y=training_set$Exited)
```

Prediction of Test Set

```
y_pred=predict(classifer,newdata=test_set[,-9])
```

Making Confusion Matrix

To create a confusion matrix, the "table()" function must be utilised. The model's inaccurate predictions are measues using this matrix. To put it simply, it's a table that classifies the values in the dataset according to the model's projected and actual values.

```
cm=table(y_pred,test_set[,9])
```

Table 2. Confusion matrix

y_pred	0	1
0	1957	394
1	34	115

K-Nearest Neighbors

A flexible supervised machine learning method that may be used for both regression and classification applications is K-Nearest Neighbours (KNN). The "k" parameter determines how many neighbors are taken into account for predicting or classifying new data points based on how close they are to pre-existing occurrences in the feature space. The algorithm's performance is heavily influenced by the ideal k-value selection, which achieves a balance between noise sensitivity and smooth decision boundaries. Cross-validation techniques are frequently used to determine the appropriate k value. It is important to use the right distance metric, such as Manhattan distance or Euclidean distance, especially when features have different sizes. KNN is particularly good at identifying regional trends and making predictions based on common features across data points. KNN leverages user preferences as features for recommendation systems, making relevant item suggestions based on comparable user behavior. To guarantee the algorithm's efficacy for a particular dataset, careful consideration of feature scaling and distance metrics is necessary. KNN addresses difficulties in feature space and improves predictive skills, making it a useful tool across a variety of applications due to its simplicity and versatility. The syntax for this algorithm is

```
#Train the model
library(class)
model = knn(train = your_train_data, test = your_test_data, cl = your_class_label,
    k = number_of_neighbors)
#Print the predicted values of the regression
predictions = predict(model, your_test_data)
```

Using predefined training data and class labels, the code trains a model using the k-nearest neighbours (KNN) algorithm from the R "class" library. The trained KNN model with a given number of neighbours (k) is then used to predict values for the test data, and the results are stored in the 'predictions' variable (Cover & Hart, 1967; Dua & Graff, 2017; Han et al., 2022; Hastie et al., 2009).

Analysis for K-Nearest Neighbors

The dataset, which was collected by Kaggle (https://www.kaggle.com/datasets/rakeshrau/social-network-ads), includes features like User ID, Gender, Age, EstimatedSalary, and Purchased. For this data, an implementation of the random forest model is recommended as an analytical technique.

Read the Data

```
dataset = read.csv("Social_Network_Ads.csv")
```

Data Pre-Processing

This investigation necessitates many phases of data pre-processing. They include loading the dataset, filling in any data gaps, encoding categorical variables, dividing the dataset into training and testing subsets, and scaling features. These steps are all necessary to ensure that the dataset is prepared for additional analysis.

```
dataset = dataset[,2:5]
dataset$Gender=factor(dataset$Gender, levels = c("Male","Female"), labels =
    c(1,0))
```

Split the Data Into Test and Training Set

A predefined ratio is used to separate the dataset into training and testing sets. For evaluating the algorithm's performance on a smaller set of data, this first division is essential. If the method produces acceptable results, it may then be used for larger-scale data predictions. The data-splitting procedure uses the "caTools" module, and to guarantee consistent outcomes between runs, a predetermined seed set is utilized. To obtain even better outcomes, feature scaling is carried out by the data requirements. During this procedure, several training and test sets are created for further analysis.

```
library("caTools")
set.seed(123)
split = sample.split(dataset$Purchased, SplitRatio = 0.8)
training_set = subset(dataset,split==TRUE)
test_set = subset(dataset, split==FALSE)
training_set[,2:3] = scale(training_set[,2:3])
test_set[,2:3] = scale(test_set[,2:3])
```

Figure 10. Training and test set

Fitting KNN in the Training Set and Predicting

The k-nearest neighbors (KNN) approach is used to fit the model to the training set after the data preparation stage. KNN is enabled by using the "class" library. The trained KNN model is then used to create predictions.

```
library("class")
y_pred = knn(train = training_set[,-4], test = test_set[,-4], cl = training_set[,4], k
    = 5, prob = TRUE)
```

Making Confusion Matrix

The "table()" function must be used to produce a confusion matrix. This matrix is used to quantify the erroneous predictions made by the model. In simple terms, it is a table that groups the dataset's values based on both the actual and predicted values by the model.

```
cm = table(y_pred, test_set[,4])
```

Table 3. Confusion matrix

y_pred	0	1
0	45	3
1	6	26

Support Vector Machine

Strong supervised learning method Support Vector Machine (SVM) finds applications in biotechnology, picture recognition, and text classification. It performs well in both classification and regression problems. SVM, which operates in a high-dimensional space, looks for the best hyperplane to divide data points into discrete groups while giving priority to maximising class margin and reducing classification errors. By maximizing the margin—a measure of the distance between the hyperplane and the nearest data points from each class—the selected hyperplane is optimal. The support vectors that are nearest to the hyperplane are essential in altering the decision boundary. Users still need to be aware of computing needs and parameter modifications notwithstanding stability and efficacy. SVM works effectively when a perfect hyperplane is essential in high-dimensional domains, and it performs best in datasets with a lot of features and matching class labels. Its uses include managing non-linear separations in text classification tasks like sentiment analysis, accurately classifying images in image recognition datasets, and comprehending gene expression patterns in bioinformatics datasets. SVM performs best when parameters and feature scaling are carefully considered, demonstrating its adaptability and significance in handling challenging classification issues. The syntax for this algorithm is

```
#Train the model
library(e1071)
```

```
model = svm(formula = dependent_variable ~ ., data = your_data, type = "C",
      kernel = "radial", cost = cost_value, gamma = gamma_value)
#Print the predicted values of the regression
predictions = predict(model, newdata = new_data)
```

Using the R e1071 library, the code trains a Support Vector Machine (SVM) regression model. It lays out the dependent variable's formula, the data, and SVM parameters like gamma and cost. It makes values predictions for new data after training and stores them in the "predictions" variable (Bishop & Nasrabadi, 2006; Cortes & Vapnik, 1995).

Analysis for Support Vector Machine

Position, Level, and Salary are among the attributes included in the "Position_ Salaries.csv" dataset (https://www.kaggle.com/datasets/mariospirito/position-salari escsv).For this dataset, the decision tree classification model should be implemented.

Read the Data

```
dataset = read.csv("Position_Salaries.csv")
```

Data Pre-Processing

For this investigation, many phases of data pre-processing are necessary. These include importing the dataset, addressing any data gaps, encoding categorical variables, dividing the dataset into training and testing subsets, and scaling features. Each of these steps contributes to ensuring that the dataset is prepared for additional analysis.

```
dataset = dataset[, 2:3]
```

Following the data preparation phase, the model is classified using the training set and the Support Vector Machine technique. Using the "e1071" library allows support vector machines. The next step involves making predictions using the learned Support Vector Machine model.

```
library('e1071')
regressor = svm(formula = Salary~., data = dataset, type = 'eps-regression')
y_pred = predict(regressor, newdata = data.frame(Level = 6.5))
```

Visualization of the training set

The “ggplot2” software is then used to visualize the given data. With the aid of this software, it is simpler to produce graphical representations of the dataset that facilitate understanding and interpretation.

library(ggplot2)

ggplot()+geom_point(aes(x = dataset$Level, y = dataset$Salary), color = ‘red’)+ geom_line(aes(x = dataset$Level, y = predict(regressor, newdata = dataset)), color = ‘blue’)+ ggtitle(‘SVM Bluff or Truth’)+ xlab(‘Level’)+ ylab(‘Salary’)

Figure 11. Visualization

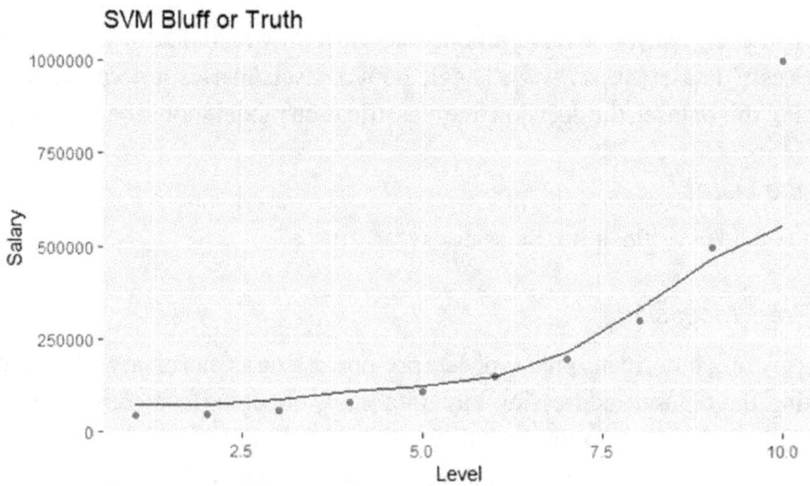

Decision Tree

Recursively dividing datasets according to important qualities, Decision Trees are a flexible machine-learning technique for regression and classification that result in a tree-like structure with nodes reflecting judgments. Iterative dataset partitioning is used to create these trees; it can stop at a certain depth, with a minimum number of leaf samples, or when the impurity stops getting better, preventing overfitting. Decision trees are transparent and easy to use, but to avoid overfitting, hyperparameters must be carefully considered. Multiple Decision Trees are used in ensemble methods such as Random Forests and Gradient Boosted Trees to improve the overall performance and generalization of the model. Decision Trees are used in marketing to discover distinct client groups by segmenting clients based on their online behavior, historical purchases, and demographics. These illustrations highlight Decision Trees' adaptability to a variety of classification and regression tasks in various fields. The syntax for this algorithm is

```
#Train the model
library(rpart)
model = rpart(dependent_variable ~ ., data = your_data)
#Print the predicted values of the regression
predictions = predict(model, newdata = new_data)
```

Regression tree model (model) is trained on your_data dataset by the code using R's rpart library to predict the dependent variable based on other variables. When new data (new_data) is applied to the trained model, the regression tree model is used to produce predictions (predictions) for the dependent variable (Breiman, 2017; Hastie et al., 2009; Quinlan, 1986).

Analysis for Decision Tree

The dataset, gathered by Kaggle (https://www.kaggle.com/datasets/rakeshrau/social-network-ads), comprises attributes such as Age, Gender, User ID, Purchased, and Estimated Salary. An application of the random forest model is suggested as an analytical method for this data.

Read the Dataset

```
dataset = read.csv("Socal_Network_Ads.csv")
```

Preparing the data for this inquiry requires several stages. These consist of splitting the dataset into training and testing subsets, scaling features, encoding categorical variables, loading the dataset, and completing any data gaps. To make sure that the dataset is ready for further analysis, all of these processes are essential.

```
dataset=dataset[,3:5]
dataset$Purchased = factor(dataset$Purchased, levels = c(0,1))
```

Splitting the Dataset

The dataset is divided into training and testing sets according to a preset ratio. This first division is crucial to assessing the algorithm's performance on a smaller batch of data. Larger-scale data forecasts could subsequently be made using the technology if it yields satisfactory results. A predefined seed set is used in the data-splitting process, which makes use of the "caTools" module to ensure consistent results between runs. Features are scaled according to the requirements of the data in order to maximize results. Several test and training sets are generated during this process for additional analysis.

```
library('caTools')
set.seed(123)
split=sample.split(dataset$Purchased,SplitRatio = 0.75)
training_set=subset(dataset,split==TRUE)
test_set=subset(dataset,split==FALSE)
training_set[,1:2]=scale(training_set[,1:2])
test_set[,1:2]=scale(test_set[,1:2])
```

Fitting Decision Tree Model in Training Set and Predicting

The Decision Tree model approach is used to classify the model using the training set after the data preparation stage. It is enabled by using the "rpart" library. The trained DT model is then used to create predictions.

```
library("rpart")
classifier=rpart(formula = Purchased~ ., data = training_set)
y_pred=predict(classifier,newdata = test_set[-3],type='class')
```

Making Confusion Matrix

The "table()" function must be used to produce a confusion matrix. This matrix is used to quantify the erroneous predictions made by the model. In simple terms, it is a table that groups the dataset's values based on both the actual and predicted values by the model.

```
cm=table(y_pred,test_set[,3])
```

Table 4. Confusion matrix

y_pred	0	1
0	53	6
1	11	30

Random Forest

An ensemble machine-learning technique called Random Forest is well known for its accuracy and robustness when it comes to solving problems with regression and classification. By merging the predictions of several models, it overcomes the shortcomings of each one and produces a more trustworthy and precise predictive model. Random Forest is based on Decision Trees, which iteratively separate datasets into discrete attributes. Its advantage is that it makes use of obtained samples. Several Decision Trees are trained using these data, which are produced via random sampling with replacement to reduce noise and overfitting. By decorrelating the features, the random subset of features taken into account at each split in the trees increases variety and decreases overfitting biases. The number of Decision Trees and other hyperparameters control overall performance and computational cost, while each tree's depth controls complex relationships. The quantity of samples needed to split an internal node is restricted to avoid overfitting. Random Forest is a recommended option in machine learning due to its constant prediction accuracy, resistance to overfitting, and flexibility. It performs exceptionally well on complicated datasets in a variety of domains, including bioinformatics (predicting protein structure), finance (credit scoring models), marketing (analyzing consumer behavior data, especially in customer turnover prediction), and finance (credit scoring models). These illustrations highlight Random Forest's adaptability in offering accurate and dependable predictions for problems involving regression and classification across a range of industries. The syntax for this algorithm is

```
#Train the model
library(randomForest)
model = randomForest(formula = dependent_variable ~ ., data = your_data, ntree
      = number_of_trees)
#Print the predicted values of the regression
predictions = predict(model, newdata = new_data)
```

The code trains a random forest regression model, which associates a dependent variable with other variables in the given data, by utilising the "randomForest" library in R. It fits the model, determines the number of trees in the forest, and forecasts values for new data, saving the outcomes in the 'predictions' variable (Breiman, 2001; Hastie et al., 2009; Liaw & Wiener, 2002).

Analysis for Random Forest

Features like User ID, Gender, Age, EstimatedSalary, and Purchased are all included in the dataset (https://www.kaggle.com/datasets/rakeshrau/social-network-ads), which was obtained from Kaggle. A random forest model implementation is a suggested analytical method for this data.

Read the Data

```
dataset = read.csv("Social_Network_Ads.csv")
```

Data Pre-Processing

Several stages of data pre-processing are required for this study. These consist of importing the dataset, handling any gaps in the data, encoding categorical variables, splitting the dataset into subsets for training and testing, and feature scaling. Every one of these procedures helps to guarantee that the dataset is ready for further examination.

```
dataset = dataset[, 3:5]
dataset$Purchased = factor(dataset$Purchased, levels = c(0,1))
str(dataset)
summary(dataset)
```

Split the Data Into Test and Training Set

The dataset is divided into training and testing sets at a predetermined ratio. This initial division is crucial for assessing the algorithm's performance on a smaller selection of data. The technique might subsequently be used for larger-scale data forecasting if it yields suitable results. The "caTools" module is used in the data-splitting process, and a specified seed set is employed to ensure consistent results between runs. And as per the requirement of the data feature scaling is done to get more better results. Different training and test sets are generated for additional analysis during this process.

```
install.packages("caTools")
library('caTools')
set.seed(123)
split = sample.split(dataset$Purchased, SplitRatio = 0.8)
training_set = subset(dataset, split==TRUE)
test_set = subset(dataset, split==FALSE)
training_set[,1:2] = scale(training_set[, 1:2])
```

```
test_set[,1:2] = scale(test_set[, 1:2])
```

Figure 12. Training and test set

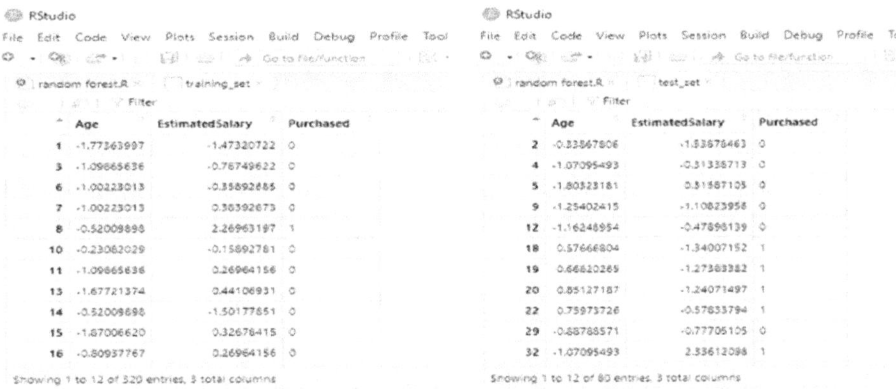

Making the Classifier

The "randomForest()" method is used to build the random forest classifier once the dataset has been split into training and testing sets. This function is essential to creating the classifier for further analysis, and it requires the "randomForest" library.

```
install.packages("randomForest")
library('randomForest')
classifier = randomForest(x = training_set[-3], y = training_set$Purchased, ntree
    = 10)
```

Making Predictor

```
y_pred = predict(classifier, newdata = test_set[-3])
```

Making Confusion Matrix

Utilizing the "table()" function is necessary to generate a confusion matrix. The model's inaccurate predictions are quantified using this matrix. Essentially, it is a table that classifies the values in the dataset according to the model's predictions and the actual values.

```
cm = table(y_pred, test_set[, 3])
```

Table 5. Confusion matrix

y_pred	0	1
0	45	4
1	6	25

Neural Network

Inspired by the architecture of the human brain, a neural network is a powerful machine-learning tool made up of layers of artificial neurons linked to one another. Neural networks have applications in picture and audio identification, natural language processing, and pattern recognition. They are composed of input layers that reflect the features of the data, hidden layers that allow for complex representations, and output layers that generate final predictions or classifications. By modifying the weights and biases associated with neural connections, the network gains knowledge about patterns and correlations throughout training. Information is transformed in feedforward neural networks, including activation functions for each neuron, weight multiplication, and bias addition. Sigmoid, hyperbolic tangent (tanh), and rectified linear units (ReLU) are examples of common activation functions that introduce non-linearity and help the network learn complicated connections. As a training method, backpropagation compares predicted and actual results, propagates mistakes backward, and optimizes by modifying weights and biases using strategies like stochastic gradient descent to minimize errors. Neural networks, which are essential to machine learning, can solve complex problems in a wide range of domains. Neural networks' adaptability in processing a wide range of data sources and resolving intricate issues is demonstrated by particular datasets, such as MNIST for image recognition, sentiment analysis datasets for natural language processing, and healthcare datasets for illness prediction. The syntax for this algorithm is

```
#Define the network structure
library(neuralnet)
net = neuralnet(formula = dependent_variable ~ ., data = your_data, hidden
    = c(number_of_nodes_in_hidden_layer1, number_of_nodes_in_hidden_
    layer2,...))
#Train the model
net = train(net, your_data)
#Print the predicted values of the regression
predictions = predict(model, newdata = new_data)
```

A neural network for regression is defined and trained by the code using the R neuralnet library. Using the supplied data, it trains the model and describes the network structure with hidden layers. The trained neural network is then used to print predicted values for a new dataset (Goodfellow et al., 2016; LeCun et al., 2015; Quinlan, 1986; Schmidhuber, 2015).

Analysis for Neural Network

The dataset from Kaggle, "Churn-Modelling.csv", consists of attributes like CredictScore, age, tenure, balance, active member, estimated salary, and excited. For this data, an implementation of the Artificial Neural Networks is recommended as an analytical technique.

Read the Dataset

```
Dataset = read.csv("Churn_Modelling.csv")
```

This investigation needs the data to be prepared in multiple steps. These include dividing the dataset into subgroups for testing and training, scaling features, loading the dataset, encoding categorical variables, and filling in any gaps in the data. Every one of these procedures is necessary to guarantee that the dataset is prepared for additional examination.

```
dataset=dataset[4:14]
```

Encoding the Categorical Variables

```
dataset$Geography=as.numeric(factor(dataset$Geography, levels = c('France',
    'Spain', 'Germany'), labels=c(1,2,3)))
dataset$Gender=as.numeric(factor(dataset$Gender, levels = c('Male','Female'),
    labels=c(1,0)))
set.seed(123)
```

Splitting the Dataset into Test and Training Sets

A preset ratio is used to separate the dataset into training and testing sets. To evaluate the algorithm's performance on a smaller batch of data, this first division is essential. If the system produces satisfactory results, then larger-scale data projections could be made in the future. The data-splitting procedure uses a specified seed set and the "caTools" package to guarantee consistent results between runs. To maximize outcomes, features are scaled in accordance with the data needs. In the process, many training and test sets are produced for further analysis.

```
library('caTools')
split=sample.split(dataset$Exited, SplitRatio = 0.8)
training_set = subset(dataset,split==TRUE)
test_set = subset(dataset,split==FALSE)
training_set[,1:10]=scale(training_set[,1:10])
test_set[,1:10]=scale(test_set[,1:10])
```

Figure 13. Training and test set

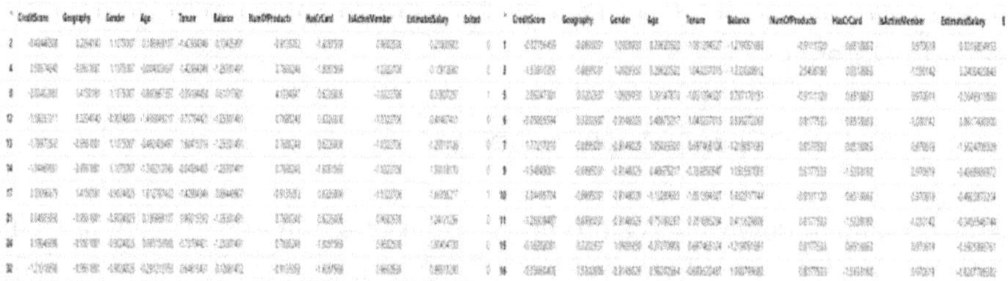

For performing unsupervised machine learning, we employ the "h2o" package under the artificial neural network. The h2o package provides an open-source software platform that is particularly well-suited for handling large datasets and performing distributed computing. It supports a variety of machine learning algorithms, including deep learning, which is a class of techniques that includes artificial neural networks.

```
library('h2o')
```

The h2o.init function is used to initialize an H2O cluster and nthreads argument specifies the number of threads to use on each node of the cluster. Setting nthreads = -1 in h2o.init means that H2O will attempt to use all available CPU threads on each node of the cluster.

```
h2o.init(nthreads= -1)
```

Defining the Variable

```
NN=h2o.deeplearning(y='Exited', training_frame=as.h2o(training_set),
    activation='Rectifier', hidden=c(5,5), epochs=100, train_samples_per_
    iteration=-2)
```

Using the predict function in h2o

```
y_pred=h2o.predict(NN, newdata = as.h2o(test_set[-11]))
y_pred=(y_pred>0.5)
y_pred=as.vector(y_pred)
```

Making the Confusion Matrix

To create a confusion matrix, the "table()" function is utilised. The model's inaccurate predictions are measured using this matrix. To put it simply, it's a table that classifies the values in the dataset according to the model's projected and actual values.

```
cm=table(test_set[,11],y_pred)
```

Table 6. Confusion matrix

y_pred	0	1
0	1533	60
1	222	185

```
h2o.shutdown()
```

After performing the operations in h2o, we have to close it since it was once initiated. For this we use the shutdown() function of h2o.

Advantages

Machine learning has many applications across several fields. It streamlines operating procedures and gets rid of the requirement for specialized programming by automating complicated tasks. Its ability to find patterns in big datasets enhances the precision of predictive analytics and decision-making. Dynamic environments are ideal for machine learning, as it is adaptable and keeps getting better via encounters. It predicts problems and creates customized treatment programs in the healthcare industry. It strengthens security in finance by providing thorough risk evaluations and fraud detection. Sentiment analysis, language translation, and smooth conversations with chatbots are all made possible by natural language processing. Most importantly, machine learning accelerates developments in machine learning, making precise object identification and instantaneous decision-making possible. Its scalable expansion fosters adaptability and creativity across a variety of sectors, processing huge amounts of data and producing complex solutions for a wide range of use cases (Bishop, 2006; Domingos, 2012; Géron, 2022; Nielsen, 2015).

Disadvantages

Machine learning drawbacks pose difficult problems. Reliance on extensive, high-quality datasets puts models in danger of being prejudiced or having issues with the data. Interpretability problems impede the comprehension of decision-making systems, particularly in complicated models such as deep neural networks. Overfitting is a prevalent issue that occurs when models perform well on training data but poorly on fresh data, requiring demanding validation methods. Moral dilemmas arise when training data reinforces pre-existing prejudices, producing unfavourable results. Significant computing resources are needed for advanced machine learning, which presents problems with energy usage. Security flaws are challenging because they can lead to adversarial attacks that manipulate input data. Black-box models' confidentiality problems give rise to questions about responsibility and regulations. System administration is made more difficult by the dynamic nature of machine learning, which needs constant monitoring and updates for continuing maintenance (Biggio & Roli, 2018; Lipton, 2018; Molnar, 2020; Ng, 2017; Selbst et al., 2019).

Practical Usage

By preparing for illnesses and customizing treatments, machine learning enhances healthcare diagnostics and demonstrates its adaptability across sectors. It supports intricate risk evaluations in finance and strengthens security with strong fraud detection, particularly in algorithmic trading. Machine learning helps natural language processing in sentiment analysis, language translation, and chatbot development, which improves human-computer interactions. Most importantly, machine learning makes a substantial contribution to autonomous systems by making it easier for self-driving cars to identify objects and make decisions in real-time. It customizes user experiences in e-commerce through dynamic pricing, focused marketing, and personalized recommendations. It also helps with process optimization, quality control, and predictive maintenance in manufacturing. These uses demonstrate how important machine learning is to productivity, automation, and creativity (Fletcher, 2012; Hapke et al., 2019; Ricci et al., 2010; Shanmugamani, 2018).

CONCLUSION

To sum up, the supervised machine learning techniques that have been discussed provide a wide range of tools for predictive modeling. Each approach, such as polynomial and linear regression, gradient boosting, decision trees, random forests, k-nearest neighbors, and support vector machines, has a specific function. This template's adaptable syntax makes it suitable for a range of datasets and modeling requirements. Both linear and non-linear connections are well-suited for linear or polynomial regression; decision trees offer clear models; and support vector machines and k-nearest neighbors perform well in classification. Sequential boosting maximizes model performance, whereas random forests use ensemble learning to improve prediction accuracy. The grammar of neural networks enables flexibility in both classification and regression. These methods, which are written in the R programming language, enable users to create dependable models for a range of applications, promoting data-driven insights and well-informed choices.

REFERENCES

Agresti, A. (2012). *Categorical data analysis* (Vol. 792). John Wiley & Sons.

Biggio, B., & Roli, F. (2018, October). Wild patterns: Ten years after the rise of adversarial machine learning. In *Proceedings of the 2018 ACM SIGSAC Conference on Computer and Communications Security* (pp. 2154-2156). 10.1145/3243734.3264418

Bishop, C. M. (2006). *Pattern Recognition and Machine Learning*. Springer Science+ Business Media, LLC.

Bishop, C. M., & Nasrabadi, N. M. (2006). *Pattern recognition and machine learning* (Vol. 4, No. 4). New York: Springer.

Breiman, L. (2001). Random forests. *Machine Learning*, *45*(1), 5–32. doi:10.1023/A:1010933404324

Breiman, L. (2017). *Classification and regression trees*. Routledge. doi:10.1201/9781315139470

Chang, C. C., & Lin, C. J. (2011). LIBSVM: A library for support vector machines. *ACM Transactions on Intelligent Systems and Technology*, *2*(3), 1–27. doi:10.1145/1961189.1961199

Cohen, J., Cohen, P., West, S. G., & Aiken, L. S. (2013). *Applied multiple regression/correlation analysis for the behavioral sciences*. Routledge. doi:10.4324/9780203774441

Cortes, C., & Vapnik, V. (1995). Support-vector networks. *Machine Learning*, *20*(3), 273–297. doi:10.1007/BF00994018

Cover, T., & Hart, P. (1967). Nearest neighbor pattern classification. *IEEE Transactions on Information Theory*, *13*(1), 21–27. doi:10.1109/TIT.1967.1053964

Cutler, D. R., Edwards, T. C. Jr, Beard, K. H., Cutler, A., Hess, K. T., Gibson, J., & Lawler, J. J. (2007). Random forests for classification in ecology. *Ecology*, *88*(11), 2783–2792. doi:10.1890/07-0539.1 PMID:18051647

Dietterich, T. G. (2000, June). Ensemble methods in machine learning. In *International workshop on multiple classifier systems* (pp. 1-15). Springer Berlin Heidelberg.

Domingos, P. (2012). A few useful things to know about machine learning. *Communications of the ACM*, *55*(10), 78–87. doi:10.1145/2347736.2347755

Dua, D., & Graff, C. (2017). *UCI machine learning repository*. Academic Press.

Fletcher, T. S. (2012). *Machine learning for financial market prediction* [Doctoral dissertation]. UCL (University College London).

Fox, J. (2015). *Applied regression analysis and generalized linear models*. Sage Publications.

Gelman, A., & Hill, J. (2006). *Data analysis using regression and multilevel/hierarchical models*. Cambridge university press. doi:10.1017/CBO9780511790942

Géron, A. (2022). *Hands-on machine learning with Scikit-Learn, Keras, and TensorFlow*. O'Reilly Media, Inc.

Geurts, P., Ernst, D., & Wehenkel, L. (2006). Extremely randomized trees. *Machine Learning*, *63*(1), 3–42. doi:10.1007/s10994-006-6226-1

Goodfellow, I., Bengio, Y., & Courville, A. (2016). Convolutional networks. In *Deep learning* (Vol. 2016, pp. 330–372). MIT Press.

Hair, J. F., Black, W. C., Babin, B. J., & Anderson, R. E. (2019). *Multivariate data analysis*. Cengage Learning.

Han, J., Pei, J., & Tong, H. (2022). *Data mining: concepts and techniques*. Morgan kaufmann.

Hapke, H., Howard, C., & Lane, H. (2019). *Natural Language Processing in Action: Understanding, analyzing, and generating text with Python*. Simon and Schuster.

Hastie, T., Tibshirani, R., Friedman, J. H., & Friedman, J. H. (2009). The elements of statistical learning: data mining, inference, and prediction (Vol. 2). New York: Springer.

Heaton, J. (2018). Ian Goodfellow, Yoshua Bengio, and Aaron Courville: Deep learning: The MIT Press, 2016, 800 pp, ISBN: 0262035618. *Genetic Programming and Evolvable Machines*, *19*(1-2), 305–307. doi:10.1007/s10710-017-9314-z

Hosmer, D. W. Jr, Lemeshow, S., & Sturdivant, R. X. (2013). *Applied logistic regression* (Vol. 398). John Wiley & Sons. doi:10.1002/9781118548387

James, G., Witten, D., Hastie, T., & Tibshirani, R. (2013). *An introduction to statistical learning* (Vol. 112). New York: Springer.

Krizhevsky, A., Sutskever, I., & Hinton, G. E. (2012). Imagenet classification with deep convolutional neural networks. *Advances in Neural Information Processing Systems*, 25.

Kursa, M. B., & Rudnicki, W. R. (2010). Feature selection with the Boruta package. *Journal of Statistical Software*, *36*(11), 1–13. doi:10.18637/jss.v036.i11

Kutner, M. H., Nachtsheim, C. J., Neter, J., & Li, W. (2005). *Applied linear statistical models*. McGraw-Hill.

LeCun, Y., Bengio, Y., & Hinton, G. (2015). Deep learning. *Nature, 521*(7553), 436-444.

Lewis, D. D. (1998, April). Naive (Bayes) at forty: The independence assumption in information retrieval. In *European conference on machine learning* (pp. 4-15). Springer Berlin Heidelberg. 10.1007/BFb0026666

Liaw, A., & Wiener, M. (2002). Classification and regression by random forest. *R News*, *2*(3), 18–22.

Lipton, Z. C. (2018). The mythos of model interpretability: In machine learning, the concept of interpretability is both important and slippery. *ACM Queue; Tomorrow's Computing Today*, *16*(3), 31–57. doi:10.1145/3236386.3241340

Loh, W. Y. (2011). Classification and regression trees. *Wiley Interdisciplinary Reviews. Data Mining and Knowledge Discovery*, *1*(1), 14–23. doi:10.1002/widm.8

Manning, C. D., Raghavan, P., & Schütze, H. (2008). *Xml retrieval*. Introduction to Information Retrieval.

Molnar, C. (2020). *Interpretable machine learning*. Lulu.com.

Montgomery, D. C., Peck, E. A., & Vining, G. G. (2021). *Introduction to linear regression analysis*. John Wiley & Sons.

Murphy, K. P. (2012). *Machine learning: a probabilistic perspective*. MIT Press.

Ng, A. (2017). *Machine learning yearning*. http://www. mlyearning. org/(96)

Nielsen, M. A. (2015). *Neural networks and deep learning* (Vol. 25). Determination press.

Quinlan, J. R. (1986). Induction of decision trees. *Machine Learning*, *1*(1), 81–106. doi:10.1007/BF00116251

Quinlan, J. R. (2014). *C4. 5: programs for machine learning*. Elsevier.

Rencher, A. C., & Schaalje, G. B. (2008). *Linear models in statistics*. John Wiley & Sons.

Ricci, F., Rokach, L., & Shapira, B. (2010). Introduction to recommender systems handbook. In Recommender systems handbook (pp. 1-35). Springer US.

Rumelhart, D. E., Hinton, G. E., & Williams, R. J. (1986). Learning representations by back-propagating errors. *Nature, 323*(6088), 533-536.

Samuel, A. L. (2000). Some studies in machine learning using the game of checkers. *IBM Journal of Research and Development, 44*(1.2), 206-226.

Schmidhuber, J. (2015). Deep learning in neural networks: An overview. *Neural Networks*, *61*, 85–117. doi:10.1016/j.neunet.2014.09.003 PMID:25462637

Selbst, A. D., Boyd, D., Friedler, S. A., Venkatasubramanian, S., & Vertesi, J. (2019, January). Fairness and abstraction in sociotechnical systems. In *Proceedings of the conference on fairness, accountability, and transparency* (pp. 59-68). 10.1145/3287560.3287598

Shanmugamani, R. (2018). *Deep Learning for Computer Vision: Expert techniques to train advanced neural networks using TensorFlow and Keras*. Packt Publishing Ltd.

Silver, D., Huang, A., Maddison, C. J., Guez, A., Sifre, L., Van Den Driessche, G., ... Hassabis, D. (2016). Mastering the game of Go with deep neural networks and tree search. *Nature, 529*(7587), 484-489.

Sutton, R. S., & Barto, A. G. (2018). *Reinforcement learning: An introduction*. MIT Press.

Vapnik, V. (1999). *The nature of statistical learning theory*. Springer science & business media.

Wasserman, W., & Kutner, M. H. (1985). *Applied linear statistical models: regression, analysis of variance, and experimental designs*. RD Irwin.

Chapter 6
Developing a Data Lakehouse for a South African Government-Sector Training Authority:
Implementing Quality Control for Incremental Extract-Load-Transform Pipelines in the Ingestion Layer

Priyanka Govender
Durban University of Technology, South Africa

Nalindren Naicker
Durban University of Technology, South Africa

Sulaiman Saleem Patel
https://orcid.org/0000-0003-3557-3645
Durban University of Technology, South Africa

Seena Joseph
Durban University of Technology, South Africa

Devraj Moonsamy
https://orcid.org/0000-0002-9690-5546
Durban University of Technology, South Africa

Ayotuyi Tosin Akinola
Durban University of Technology, South Africa

Lavanya Madamshetty
Durban University of Technology, South Africa

Thamotharan Prinavin Govender
https://orcid.org/0000-0003-3795-1179
Durban University of Technology, South Africa

DOI: 10.4018/978-1-6684-9716-6.ch006

ABSTRACT

The Durban University of Technology is undertaking a project to develop a data lakehouse system for a South African government-sector training authority. This system is considered critical to enhance the monitoring and evaluation capabilities of the training authority and ensure service delivery. Ensuring the quality of data ingested into the lakehouse is critical, as poor data quality deteriorates the efficiency of the lakehouse solution. This chapter studies quality control for ingestion-layer pipelines to propose a data quality framework. Metrics considered for data quality were completeness, accuracy, integrity, correctness, and timeliness. The framework was evaluated by practically applying it to a sample semi-structured dataset to gauge its effectiveness. Recommendations for future work include expanded integration, such as incorporating data from more varied sources and implementing incremental data ingestion triggers.

BACKGROUND TO THE STUDY

In South Africa, Sector Education and Training Authorities (SETAs) are fundamentally government-established groups that handle skills development and training in specific parts of the economy. These are known as Government-Sector Training Authorities (GTAs), holding significant importance for the country's strategy to enhance skills and training in different industries. The Durban University of Technology (DUT) has collaborated with one of these South African GTAs for an ongoing project to upgrade the approach that the GTA utilise to manage data. This is accomplished while aiding DUT students develop additional skills. To make the GTA proficient in managing data, the GTA acknowledged a necessity for a full system that stores data and automate reports. After discussing the matter, the DUT team proposed utilising Microsoft Azure services to create a data warehousing solution. Further background to the project is provided by Mthembu et al. (2024). This chapter focuses on creating a Data Lakehouse for a South African Government-Sector Training Authority. An essential facet involves exploring methods to guarantee the high quality of data flowing through the system, especially during Incremental Extract-Load-Transform Pipelines in the Ingestion Layer using Data Orchestration.

INTRODUCTION

In the era of Big Data, where the abundance of information presents both opportunities and obstacles, proficiently managing and leveraging data has become crucial for organisational triumph. The extensive array of data types, encompassing structured, semi-structured, and unstructured formats, necessitates an advanced strategy for data manipulation (Azad et al., 2020). Central to this effort is the Extract, Load, Transform (ELT) framework, a flexible tool recognised for its effectiveness in navigating the intricacies of modern data environments (Singhal & Aggarwal, 2022). Nevertheless, as data pipelines progress in size and complexity, ensuring the integrity of data quality (DQ) has risen to a central position of importance.

Notably, the rise of big data led to the necessity of DLH as Harby and Zulkernine (2022) insinuated that new challenges were presented to Data Warehouses (DWs) due to the big data era. The surge in heterogeneous data volumes resulting from digital transformation poses a challenge to conventional DW solutions within organisations (Čuš & Golec, 2022; Giebler et al., 2021). In addition, Barika et al. (2019) bring to light that researchers are grappling with how to orchestrate, manage and execute big data workflows due to their distinct nature from traditional ones. Once this data undergoes transformation and is loaded into the DW, the initial filtered information is no longer preserved (Figueira, 2018). Conventional, Nambiar and Mundra (2022) highlights that methods like the ETL process are not efficient enough for these data management needs.

A Data Lake (DL) functions as a unified storage and exploration system designed to handle vast quantities of diverse data, has gained prominence as the recommended approach for processing and storing heterogenous data (Begoli et al., 2021). A separate study conducted by the DUT team highlight the importance of data governance as it establishes control over data utilisation and decision-making by incorporating procedures, rules, organisational structures, and responsibilities (Mthembu et al., 2024). Without regular maintenance of a DL, managing data becomes a costly and challenging task. Inadequate implementation of data governance in DL systems may lead to the development of a disorderly "Data Swamp," compromising the value of information in knowledge management and analytical systems due to challenging-to-process and analyse data.

Thus, DLH became a revolutionary idea combining the advantages of DL with the advantages of DW, allowing organisations to manage, analyse and store massive amounts of data in a flexible and cost effective manner. Harby and Zulkernine (2022) further mentions that this aims to accelerate the process of effective knowledge extraction.

The aim of this study is to create a framework for data orchestration and ingestion of data in a Data Lakehouse (DLH) to ensure data quality (DQ). Aligned to the aim the following objectives are outlined for the study:

- Identify key factors and DQ control for data orchestration and ingestion by analyzing existing literature.

- Design and develop a framework using the key factors and DQ control identified for data orchestration and ingestion for a DLH system.
- To evaluate the effectiveness of the developed framework and make recommendations for data quality control of data orchestration and ingestion for a DLH system.

By providing more research data on utilising Azure Data Factory (ADF) for data orchestration and ingestion of data into a data lake. This contributes to the body of knowledge to aid in future research in data orchestration and ingestion utilising Azure Services whistle identifying the constraints of developing a pipeline for data orchestration and ingestion. In addition, providing feedback for future research in this field contributes to the significance of this study.

The research delves into data orchestration, a critical field at the intersection of data management and quality control (Barika et al., 2019). It focuses on applying quality control protocols in incremental ELT pipelines within the Ingestion Layer of a Data Warehouse (DW). The study identifies the challenges of using semi-structured data and acknowledges the need for specialised methodologies to ensure high DQ and integrity. The research output presents the development of a pipeline designed and framework to ingest data from SharePoint into a designated container within the data lake (DL) infrastructure. The pipeline incorporates critical stages for transforming semi-structured data into a structured format and implements data orchestration techniques to assist with the accuracy, completeness, and consistency of the ingested data.

Section 1 explicitly unravels the rise that brought forth the gap and proposes a robust solution depicted by the aims and motivated by presenting both an insight into the contribution to the area of study and the expected research outcome. The mentions of the objectives as well as the scope and delimitations of the study paints a clear picture of what this study entails. The methodology, datasets, matrices and depicts the tools and platforms that shall be utilised in conducting the experiment are outlined in Section 2. This allows for ample preparation for Chapter Four that follows. Section 3 illustrates the outcome of conducting the experiment and evaluate the effectiveness of the developed artifacts. Additionally, Section 3 mention the limitations and provide feedback on conducting the experiment. In accordance with the nature of experimenting, Section 4 communicates the results obtained from conducting the experiments whilst delivering the verdict of the overall performance of the developed artifacts created.

LITERATURE REVIEW

According to Figueira (2018), the main aim of big data as a field, is to provide a way to handle enormous volumes of data with the intent to develop insights and knowledge. Gupta (2023) reveals that big data initially began with the 3V's which comprised of: volume, the quantity of data (Liu & Zhang, 2020; Pratsri & Nilsook, 2020); variety, a wide range of data types and data sources, such as structured, semi-structured and unstructured data (Liu & Zhang, 2020) ; and velocity, the rate of which new data is created and moved around (Khan et al., 2019; Liu & Zhang, 2020; Quasim et al., 2019). This later evolved to the 5V's which additionally included the following to the 3V's: veracity, the most crucial aspect in the generation of Big Data, as maintaining correct data without duplication of the information is perhaps the most difficult and time-consuming task (Pratsri & Nilsook, 2020); value, pertains to valuable data that holds significance for business applications, encompassing analysis for summarisation and strategic planning, with the goal of augmenting product value and strengthening competitiveness within the target market. Figure 1 by Sandhu (2021) depicts examples of the 5V's.

Figure 1. Representation of the 5V's

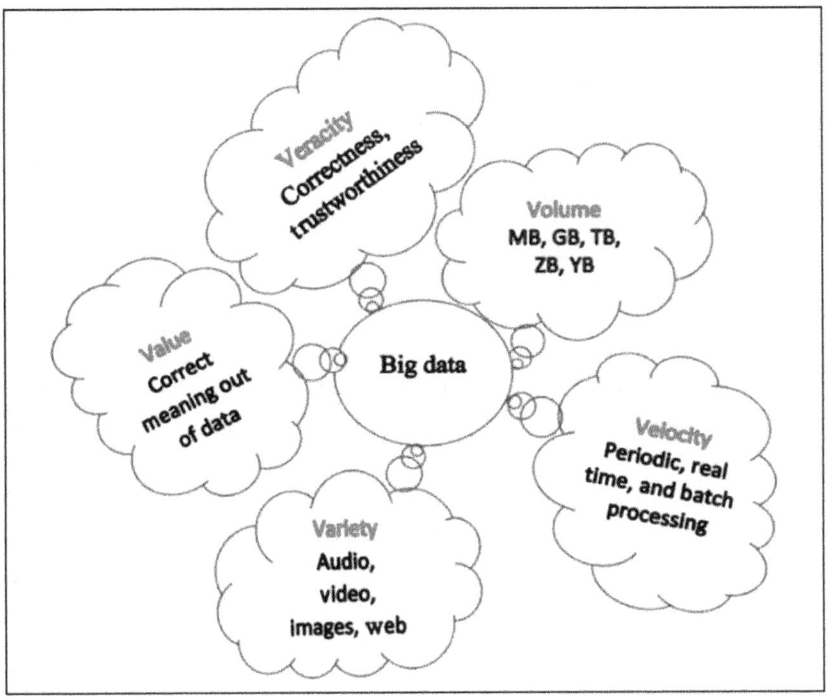

There are three types of content format sources which are namely structured data, semi-structured data, and unstructured data. Structured data refers to data that is organised in a particular ranked format and when data is stored in this format, it is easier for search engines to display and understand it (Sambrekar et al., 2018). Semi-structured data, on the other hand, has an irregular and implicit structure, lacking a defined data model. In this form of database, there is no obvious boundary between data and schema (Bjeladinovic, 2018). On the contrary to structured data, unstructured data serves as the opposite. This is due to the lack of structure, thus making the analysis of data time-consuming (Sambrekar et al., 2018).

Semi-structured data posts the most challenging to deal with as it does not adhere to a predefined data model and lacks a fixed schema (Sambrekar et al., 2018). This is due to its irregular and implicit structure (Dickson & Asagba, 2020). Durner *et al.* (2021); Nadal *et al.* (2022); Schäfer (2023) pointed out reasons why semi-structured data might be difficult to deal with when ingesting into a pipeline which includes schema flexibility posing challenges in establishing a uniform schema for processing, as it may need to accommodate diverse data instances.

Raj et al. (2020) states that ETL and ELT are the two main categories of data pipelines. DLs utilises the ELT (Extract, Load, and Transform) approach, where "raw data" is first loaded and then subsequently transformed (Cherradi & El Haddadi, 2022). Contrary to the ETL process, the ELT approach adheres to a similar foundational principle but diverges in sequence. Rather than executing transformation prior to loading, the data is initially loaded and subsequently transformed. Unlike data integration, which primarily focuses on consolidating data for reporting, data orchestration has a broader scope, encompassing activities such as resource allocation, monitoring, data discovery, preparation, integration, processing, and linking enriched data across diverse landscapes (Dinh & Nguyen, 2022; Kevin & Ginger, 2021). Kevin and Ginger (2021) emphasise its goal to process and merge data flexibly, thereby enhancing or creating business processes.

Data ingestion typically forms the preliminary layer in the architecture (Figueira, 2018; Liu et al., 2021; Yu et al., 2019). The ingestion layer's role is to bring in data from diverse sources into the DL system. Cherradi and El Haddadi (2022); Liu et al. (2021) reported that in the ingestion layer, depending on the source and destination, data ingested could be conducted in the following manner: batches, real-time or an amalgamation of both. Isah et al. (2019) points out that stream processing, as opposed to batch processing, includes the processing of continuous or dynamic data. Stream processing, enabling real-time data analysis without using long-term storage and becoming notably significant in social media platforms, like Twitter and Facebook, is heavily influenced by the incoming data rate (Isah et al., 2019; Nambiar & Mundra, 2022). Stream processing is adept at managing data of significant velocity and volume and can be easily scalable (Hlupić & Puniš, 2021). In addition to batch and stream processing, Nambiar and Mundra (2022) shed light on an additional processing technique which merges both batch and stream processing approaches to ensure greater accuracy while minimising processing time which is referred to as hybrid processing.

Table 1. DQ attributes and sources

DQ Attribute:	Source					
	Olson (2003)	Cheong and Chang (2007)	Peng et al. (2015)	Koltay (2020)	Lien et al. (2020)	Anastasova and Yanev (2021)
Correctness		X	X	X		
Validity			X		X	X
Data integrity/ Referential integrity		X	X			X
Consistency		X	X	X	X	
Accuracy	X		X			X
Trustworthiness	X			X		
Easy to understand	X			X	X	
Complete-ness	X	X		X	X	X
Concise				X	X	
Currentness/ Freshness		X		X		
Availability						X
Partition tolerance						X
Applicable/ Relevance	X					X
Timeliness	X				X	X
Business rules conformance		X				
Uniqueness		X				
Domain		X				
Data type		X				
Generalis-ability					X	
Traceability					X	

Table 1 shows the various types of DQ attributes which are depicted in literature. Koltay (2020) mention that DQ attributes are often clustered differently which insinuates that the attributes may have a different naming convention. Thus, when presenting the DQ attributes in Table 1, clustering of terms is done. The DQ framework presented in this chapter is based on the most widely adopted attributes from literature. Figure 2 presents a summary of the number of times each DQ attribute occurred in literature. To develop the framework, only attributes that appeared in at least three of the six (50%) of the in-scope articles were used. These are indicated by darkened bars in Figure 2.

Figure 2. DQ attribute occurrences

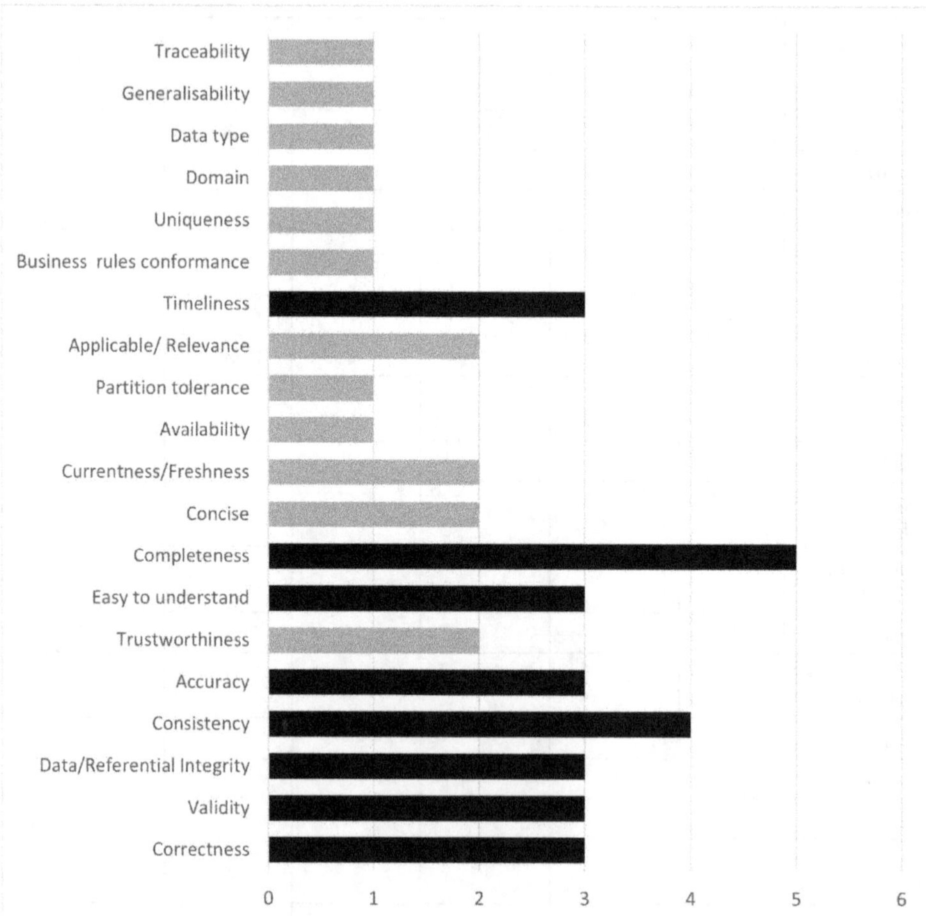

The following DQ attributes were selected: correctness, validity, data integrity, accuracy, completeness, and timeliness. Despite meeting the threshold criteria, evaluating consistency for ingestion-layer pipelines was deemed unnecessary. Consistency ensures that data is presented uniformly, aligns with other data, and remains free from contradiction. This was deemed more relevant to source systems and transformation-based pipelines. Similarly, determining whether data is easy to understand is most relevant to systems-level governance rather than being a focus at ingestion layer.

A data integrity check at the point of ingestion is fundamental for maintaining data reliability and ensuring data remains uncorrupted during transfer between providers and repositories (Anastasova & Yanev, 2021). According to Anastasova and Yanev (2021), validity evaluates whether data values meet predefined conditions, and any deviation indicates potential problems in the data collection process. However, Peng et al. (2015) mention that the validity of data refers to data integrity, which is the consistency and accuracy of data throughout its lifecycle. Accuracy in data means that the information correctly represents its intended subject or process (Anastasova & Yanev, 2021). Completeness ensures that data encompasses all expected attributes and related instances, defining the breadth of the information (Koltay, 2020). Timeliness reflects the data's age and is crucial in industrial systems managing continuous production; delays or gaps can result in flawed management decisions (Anastasova & Yanev, 2021; Koltay, 2020).

Notably, Gabarro and Stewart (2021) highlight that the efficacy of an orchestration's reliability can be evaluated through two distinct metrics. Firstly, by scrutinising its behavioural completeness, quantified by the count of its computed outcomes. Secondly, by examining its temporal efficiency, denoted by its execution duration (timeliness).

METHODOLOGY

Research Paradigm and Approach

This study utilized Design Science Research (DSR) as the paradigm as Vom Brocke et al. (2020) evokes that essentially DSR is a paradigm of problem solving. Referring to Figure 3 below, illustrates the DSR paradigm created by Ellis and Levy (2010).

The activities depicted in Figure 3 are adapted to this study as follows in Table 2:

By utilizing Mixed Method Research (MMR), this study uses qualitative methods to complement the quantitative results by giving more meaning to the results. This enriched data shall allow this study to produce meaningful results that will contribute to the body of research (Enosh et al., 2015; Plano Clark, 2017; Strijker et al., 2020).

Figure 3. DSR paradigm

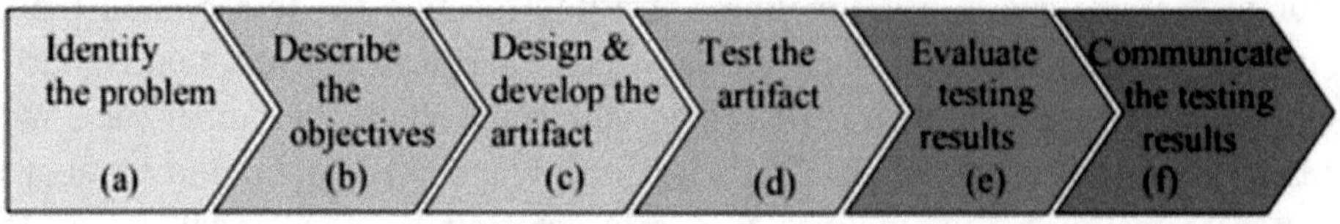

Table 2. DSR paradigm research adaptation

Activity	Study Adaptation
Identification of problem	Semi-structured data possess as a challenge for data ingestion
Description of objectives	Due to the flexible nature of semi-structured data, there is a need for a robust pipeline which can ensure that DQ is not compromised, when ingesting semi-structured data from the source to the destination.
Design and development of artifacts	The artifact designed in this study is the DQ frameworks and the data orchestration pipeline.
Testing of artifacts	The artifacts are tested by utilising a mock dataset obtained. The pipeline is developed and tested by transforming the source semi-structured data to structured data and stored in a SQL database table. The DQ framework are utilised to verify the completeness, accuracy, integrity, correctness, and timeliness.
Evaluation of testing results	The evaluation of the effectiveness of the artifacts are evaluated against the DQ framework created.
Communication of testing results	The results of the DQ and data orchestration frameworks are documented and discussed.

Dataset

The sample CSV dataset utilised contains employee details that was obtained from datablist.com (Datablist, n.d.). This selected dataset encompasses information such as User ID, First Name, Last Name, Date of Birth, and Job Title across 100 records. For the purposes of this experiment, only the first 80 records will undergo ingestion. The subsequent 20 records are reserved for testing data ingestion after the initial phase. Data entries are separated by semi-colons, which will be removed during the conversion from CSV to SQL database table. It is essential to acknowledge that the first row of the CSV indicates the column headers.

Dataflow Process

Figure 4 illustrates the flow of data from the source, which is depicted by SharePoint. The dataset which is being transfers is depicted by the CSV file, which represents semi-structed data. Arrows represents the pipeline which will be utilised for transferring the data. Notably, Azure Data Factory will be utilised for this process. From the source, the data will be transferred to the DL, where it will be copied in a container called "Raw". The data that resides in this container will remain in its raw form, allowing no modification to be performed on it. New instances are tracked by using data timestamp which displays the currentness of data. Thereafter, the data from the Raw container will be copied and converted to an Azure SQL database table, which will make it easier to apply data orchestration. Two additional columns will be added, namely hashing and date timestamp. Hashing will create a unique hash which will be used to identify a record, this will prevent duplication of records. The date timestamp will track when the data was added or updated. Thereafter the structured data will be stored in the DL in a container called "Curated". However, this research shall focus on testing the function of the data orchestration for curated data.

Data orchestration will be implemented to avoid records that were previously added to be added once again. This will prevent data from being duplicated due to hashing. If an existing record has changes to the data, it will be updated. In addition, to allow incremental ingestion of data, a trigger function will be implemented, which will automatically run the pipeline after a specified duration.

Figure 4. Pipeline dataflow

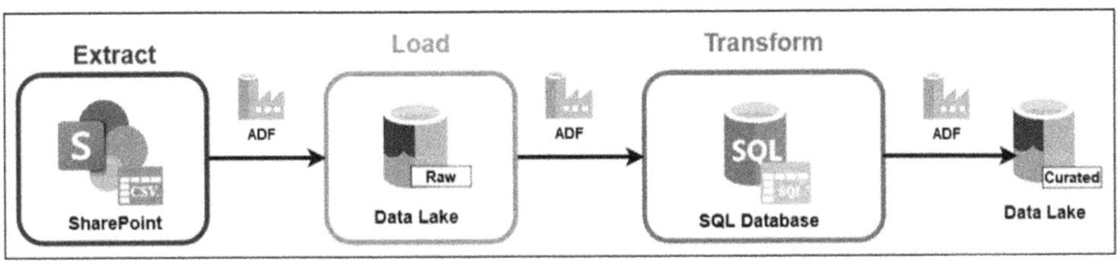

Data Quality Framework

The metrices illustrated in Figure 5 was created based off the results from Table 1 in Section 1. After taking the nature of integrity and validity depicted by Peng et al. (2015) into consideration, the DQ attributes integrity and validity are considered as one.

Figure 5. DQ framework

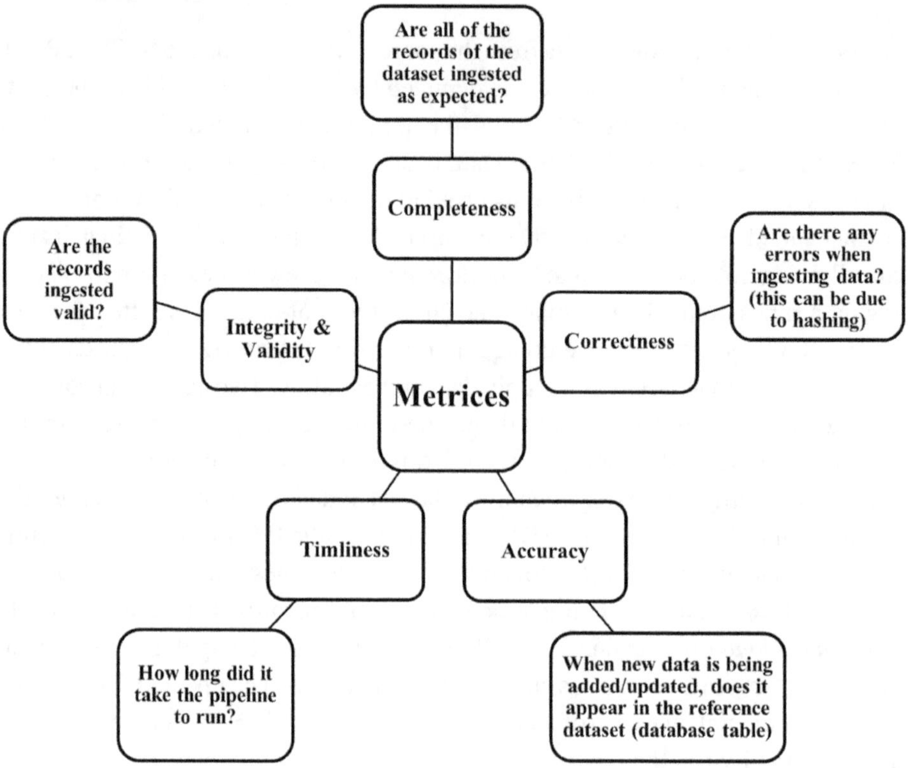

Calculation of Metrics

In this research, the term reference dataset refers to the expected number of records that should be captured in the dataset (Mahanti, 2019). The expected number of records is referred to the correct number of records anticipated as the result whereas the actual number of records is the result presented after executing the experiment. Often, a "benchmark" dataset is utilised as a standard for comparison. This benchmark is viewed as a comprehensive representation of the subject in question. The benchmark is an estimate of the expected number of records to evaluate the completeness of the dataset in question.

Completeness

Completeness refers to the extent to which the entire set of expected records is captured. The ratio of the actual number of records in the dataset to the total expected number of records is calculated to evaluate completeness. Completeness outcome would either be depicted by a percentage or N/A. The success criterion of the outcome is 100%.

The follow depicts what the symbols represents in the equation:

- *Comp%*: The rate of completeness of the dataset.
- *Arecords*: The actual number of records presented in the dataset.
- *Erecords*: The expected number of records in dataset.

$$Comp\% = \left(\frac{Arecords}{Erecords} \right) \times 100 \quad (1)$$

If:

Arecords > *Erecords*; *Comp%* = N/A

No data ingested then; *Acc%* = N/A

Correctness

Data correctness refers to its complete absence of errors; it follows a concept of data is deemed either right or wrong (binary), with no in-between. While accuracy can exist on a spectrum, any data that aspires to be labelled as accurate must first and foremost be correct. Correctness is an all-or-nothing principle for data, whereas accuracy measures the depth of that correctness in representing reality. But, for any data to be recognised as accurate, its base correctness is non-negotiable. The outcome of accuracy is depicted by either a Y or N or N/A. The success criterion of the outcome is 0.

The follow depicts what the symbols represents in the equation:

- *Corr*: The rate of completeness of the dataset.
- *Arecords*: The total number of actual records presented in the dataset.
- *Erecords*: The total number of expected records in the dataset.

$$Corr = |Erecord - Arecords| \quad (2)$$

Where:

Corr > 0; indicates an error in the correctness of the dataset.

Corr = 0; indicates that the ingestion of the dataset is correct.

No data ingested then; *Corr* = N/A

Accuracy

Evaluating accuracy at the data record level involves validating each record in a dataset by contrasting it with a reliable "reference dataset". To facilitate this, specific criteria or "rules" are established to determine what qualifies as an accurate record. These guidelines are instrumental in guiding the comparison of data points between the dataset in question and the "reference dataset". Notably, if a single vital record does not align with the "reference dataset" or is absent, that referred to as inaccurate. Following these predetermined rules, each record is then meticulously checked against the reference. In essence, this reveals the complete magnitude of the dataset and provides a clear insight into its accuracy quotient. Alternatively, this will verify the number of accurate records in the dataset ingested. The outcome of accuracy is depicted by either a percentage or N/A. The success criterion of the outcome is 100%.

The following depicts what the symbols represents in the equation:

- *Acc%*: The rate of accuracy of the dataset.
- *Trecords*: The total number of records presented in the dataset.
- *Tacc*: The number of accurate records in the dataset.
- *Arecords*: The total number of actual records presented in the dataset.
- *Erecords*: The total number of expected records in the dataset.

$$Acc\% = \left(\frac{Tacc}{Arecords}\right) \times 100 \tag{3}$$

If:

$Arecords \neq Erecords$ then; $Tacc = Erecords$
$Arecords = Erecords$ then; $Tacc = Arecords$
No data ingested then; $Acc\ \% =$ N/A

Validity and Integrity

A record would be deemed valid if the hashing is correct. In essence, this depicts the overall valid records in the actual number of records ingested. The outcome of validity and data integrity would either be depicted by a percentage or N/A. The success criterion of the outcome is 100%.

The follow depicts what the symbols represents in the equation:

- *Vi%*: The rate of the integrity records of the dataset.
- *Tvalid*: The total number of valid records presented in the dataset.
- *Arecords*: The total number of records presented in the dataset.
- *Tinacc*: The total number of inaccurate records presented in the dataset.

$$Tvalid = Arecords - Tinacc \tag{4}$$

$$Vi\% = \left(\frac{Tvaild}{Arecords}\right) \times 100 \tag{5}$$

If:

No data ingested then; *Vi%* = N/A

Timeliness

Timeliness, with reference to data management, refers to the speed at which data is delivered or made accessible to business users. Essentially, it evaluates the gap between the moment a piece of data originates and when it is presented to the end user. A crucial element of timeliness is the "Occurrence Time" which pinpoints the exact moment a real-world event, represented by the data, took place. It also signifies the point in time when a particular attribute or value related to an entity first materialised. Basically "Occurrence Time" refers to the start time. To measure this, the difference between the data delivery time (end time) compared to the start time and communicated via seconds. The success criterion of the outcome must be within 120s. Notably, some applications provide the duration of the execution.

The following depicts what the symbols represents in the equation:

- *Time(s)*: The rate of time it takes to ingest the dataset in seconds.
- *ST*: The Start Time (Occurrence time) of the dataset.
- *ET*: The End Time (Data delivery time) of the dataset.

$$Time(s) = ET - ST \tag{6}$$

If:

Time(s) < 120s; then valid.
Time(s) > 120s; then not valid.

Scenarios Case

Defining the scenario and its success criteria aids in defining the expected outcome and the expected results. Referring to Table 3 below, n represents the scenario number, the aim defines the main purpose of the scenario, the description outlines the processes involved and success criteria defines the criteria to determine whether the desired results were achieved.

Table 3. Scenario case

Scenario n	
Aim	**Ingestion of New records**
Description	• Describe the process which will take place
Success criteria	• Define what will deem the results a success

Test Case

Test cases offers a systematic approach to assess data based on the DQ attributes identified prior. Within this framework, users can note the starting data, any modifications or additions made during the process, and the anticipated results. It also has a section to monitor various test attempts, determine if they were successful or not, and make additional annotations. The concluding section provides a summary of the overall success of the test case.

In the test case, the header depicts information about the test case and scenario. The test number is represented by <number>, along with the scenario number depicted by n and the title, represented by <title>. Below the header resides the number of records belonging to the dataset. Input represents the initial row count, represents the current number of rows in the dataset, process depicts the number of additional rows that will be ingested into the dataset. Finally, the outcome depicts the expected outcome from the ingestion.

The next section captures the test results, whereby the calculation of the matrices is conducted, thus depicting the effectiveness of the pipeline for that scenario. Thereafter, based on the success criteria, the success is determined. This is represented by either yes (Y) or no (N). Additional notes / comments for each matric can be captured in addition, if required.

The overall results are the last section in the test case which communicates whether the experiment was successful or not. The number of successful outcomes is captured, the rate of success is calculated. Lastly the final verdict is determined if the experiment was overall a success or failure, based on the success criteria mentioned below.

Success Rate Calculation

The success criterion of the success rate outcome is 100%, thus the verdict will be Success, otherwise the verdict is Fail.

The follow depicts what the symbols represents in the equation:

- *Srate* represents the Success rate.
- *Tsuccess* represents the total number of metrics that met the success criteria.
- *Tmetrices* represents the total number of metrics.

$$Srate = \left(\frac{Tsuccess}{Tmetrices}\right) \times 100 \tag{7}$$

If:

Srate = 100%; success
Srate < 100%; fail.

Data Orchestration Framework

Figure 6 is the framework which will assist in the data orchestration evaluation. First, the scenario cases must be completed. The next step involves recording the initial row count, process, and outcome details in the test case. Once the preceding steps are conducted, the next step is to run the pipeline and lastly document the results in the test case and evaluate the overall outcome of the experiment.

Figure 6. Data orchestration framework

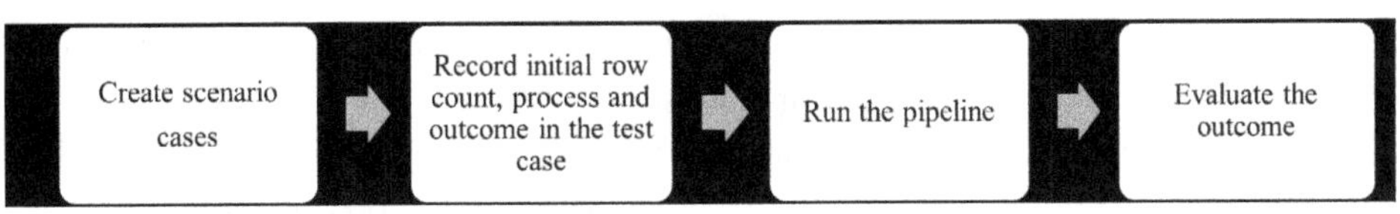

Steps to Create the Pipeline using Azure Services

Step 1: Create Azure Account

To utilise Azure Services, an Azure account must first be created to access the Azure portal. Additionally, credits are required to use certain services by which one will be charged based on the type of services created and used.

Step 2: Creating the Environment

First create a resource group to store all resources to be used. Notably, where applicable, the resource group that will be selected henceforth must be the resource created. The next step is creating a storage account to store to store the source data. Once deployment is successful, create container and thereafter create a folder within that container and upload the required files into the folder. For testing purposes blob storage was utilised. Next create an Azure SQL Server to store the Azure Database. Notably, this research utilises SQL authentication as the Authentication method which will prompt the user to login with a password to access the contents of the database server. Afterwards create an Azure SQL Database. This serves as the destination as this is where the semi-structured data (CSV file) is transformed into structured data and stored in a table. Notably, there are cost implications when creating a database, whereas this is absent when creating the database server. Configuration of the database is based on the required performance and purpose of the database. The cost summary will calculate the monthly cost based on the database configurations selected. The creation of the Azure Data Factory (ADF) instance follows the creation the database and once deployment is completed, launch the ADF studio.

Step 3: Copy CSV to Database Table

In ADF, create linked services for the source and sink. Create blob storage link service, the CSV is stored in a blob for this research. The second linked service is an Azure SQL Database which is linked to the database and then create a new pipeline and select the dataflow activity. A new data flow is required to be created in succession and set as the data flow of the data flow activity. Thereafter create datasets for the linked services, respectively. Next, create a new pipeline and select the copy activity. Set the source to the dataset with the CSV and set the sink to the dataset with the SQL database and table option was to auto create table as the table does not exist within the database. Afterwards, validate the pipeline and debug.

Step 4: Creating the Data Orchestration Pipeline

Create a new data flow then create a new pipeline and use the data flow activity. Thereafter, set data flow to the data flow created. Create two sources, the first source imports data from the blob storage, this source will be compared to the reference source which imports data from the database. Notably, the data flow debug is required to be activated as it allowed the data flow to run.

Create Connect a derived column transformation to the first source and create a column for hashing and another for the date timestamp. Since two new columns are being introduced, new columns are required to be created in the database. Notably, the data types of the column, the expression returns, in the "Dataflow expression builder" and the database must match.

Next, a Lookup transformation is required to be connected, to verify if records are pre-existing or deemed a new record. This is achievable by setting the lookup stream to the reference source. Lookup condition is utilised to set the condition for comparing both the sources to one another. To determine what will happen to the record once it is compared, a conditional split transformation was connected the to the dataflow. In this research there are three possible streams which are: new record, update, no action. The condition of each stream is set in its corresponding condition "Dataflow expression builder". Based on which condition is met, the process will follow its corresponding stream and eventually to the sink. The new record stream is connected to the sink whereas the update stream requires an additional transformation in comparison. The update stream requires an alter row transformation to be connected to allow a record to be updated.

Lastly the sink sets the destination of the records to the destination dataset. The update method differs between the new record stream as the insert option is only selected whereas, the insert and update options are selected for the update stream. Thereafter the columns in the data flow must be respectively mapped to the columns in the destination dataset.

Step 5: Execute the Pipeline

To execute the pipeline, select the pipeline created thereafter, validate the pipeline for error. If no errors were found, run the pipeline by selecting debug. To view the number of rows written, select output and thereafter select data flow details.

FRAMEWORK EVALUATION

Prior to obtaining and utilising the ADF environment, this study utilised a theoretical approach to conducting the experiment of testing the effectiveness of the artifacts created. This theoretical evaluation included both success and failure results for each scenario. The same scenarios were evaluated theoretically and practically.

Evaluation of Results

The first scenario evaluated the initial ingestion of data by ingesting eighty records. Notably, there were no prior records presented in the reference dataset. The new records ingested were compared to the reference dataset to verify if any records were pre-existing (this was utilised for all scenarios). Additionally, records ingested would receive a date timestamp and hashing performed on the ingested data. However, the data timestamp did not appear. As a result, 80 records were ingested which was the expected outcome. Completeness, accuracy, and validity/integrity yielded 100%, while correctness produced 0 (Y). Therefore, Scenario 1 was successful.

The ingestion of new records was evaluated in Scenario 2. This was accomplished by ingesting ten new records. Notably, there 80 records presented in the reference dataset. As a result, 10 records were ingested, resulting in a total of 90 records ingested (which was the expected outcome). Completeness, accuracy, and validity/integrity yielded 100%, while correctness produced 0 (Y). Therefore, Scenario 2 was successful.

Scenario three involved updating existing records. This was assessed by ingesting fifteen new records, whereby ten records were new while five records were pre-existing. The success criteria involved no new records ingested and five existing records are updated. Completeness and accuracy, yielded 100%, whereas validity/integrity yielded 95%, while correctness produced 0 (Y). Validity/integrity was compromised which insinuated that there was a flaw with the pipeline created, as the quality of data must be upheld in a real-world scenario. A flaw in data could deem a company's system as unreliable and possibly could have financially implications. Upon inspection, the new records were added, however, there were no records updated. Notably, as a result, a total of 100 records were ingested. Therefore, Scenario 3 was not successful.

The final scenario (Scenario 4) assessed the ingestion of existing records. The initial number of records ingested were 100 and 10 pre-existing records were utilised to test this scenario. The expected result involved no ingestion of records. Completeness, accuracy, and validity/integrity yielded 100%, while correctness produced 0 (Y). Therefore, Scenario 4 was successful.

Figure 6 illustrates the duration required for the pipeline to run and provide results. The execution of pipeline did not exceed 120 seconds, depicting that all scenarios yielded successful outcomes. Scenario 3 acquired the most time to complete the run and produce results. This scenario involved inserting and updating data. Notably, each time the pipeline was run, the execution time was reduced; however due to the first run for Scenario 3 being successful, this time was captured.

Figure 7. Timeliness evaluation

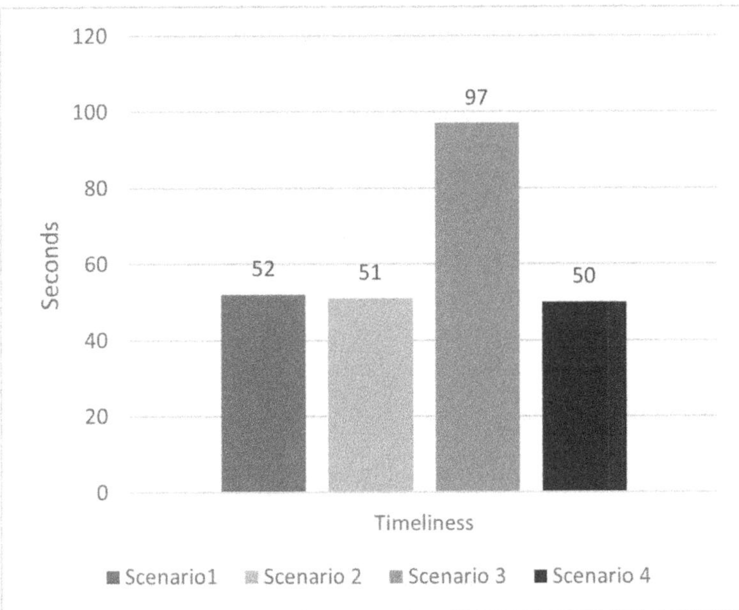

Overall Performance

After the experiment was concluded, the statistics states that the overall success rate of 84% succeeds the fail rate of 16% with success to fail ratio of 5:1 (84:16 = 5,25:1 ⇒ 5:1). According to the stats, this yielded a successful outcome. However, based on the requirements of DQ, data is required to be correct. Therefore, this experiment is deemed unsuccessful due to this nature as the pipeline failed to update records. The pie chart in Figure 7, illustrates the overall performance rate.

Figure 8. Overall performance

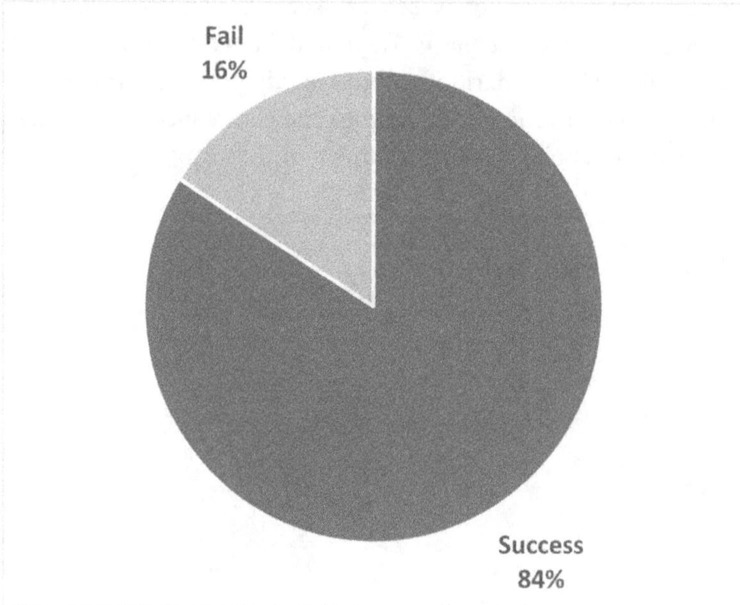

Challenges

The main challenge of the practical implementation of the experiment was obtaining credit to utilise resources in the Azure environment. the credit balance was limited, therefore restricting the amount of resources that could be created (such as creating another "SQL Database"). Additionally, the Azure credits required monitoring when creating the data flow, as running the debug had cost implication based on the amount of time it is utilised.

The update stream did not function as expected, leading to unreliable data. Attempts were made to revolve this conundrum; however, the desired outcome was still not met. This could possibly be due to the hashing not matching and if none of the conditions were not met, no records wills be affected. Additionally, the date timestamp was successfully executed in the "Azure SQL Database" query editor, yet the pipeline failed to include a datetime stamp to records ingested.

Discussion

After conducting the experiment, it was noted that utilizing the copy activity at the start of the process was not good practice. This is due to data being copied directly from the source to the sink without verifying whether any records were duplicated.

Even though this research does not address data cleaning, this is a factor to consider. A better method of coping records and obtaining the schema for the sink shall be noted for future research.

The intention of utilising blob storage as the source, instead of utilising other sources such as SharePoint, stemmed from the desire to iron out any creases. Problems did arise therefore it was easier to understand and trace back to the point of the error. This approach allowed for better understanding, which could potentially be utilised as a guidance for future implementation utilising other sources.

The sink was not set to a DL, as this task will be undertaken in future research. The sink was set to the "Azure SQL Database", which made it easier to visualise the transformation of the data from semi-structured to structured data. However, future research will set the data sink to the DL.

The framework proved effective in documenting the results of each scenario case. The design was appropriate however, it requires to be revised as flaws were discovered during the experiment. Additionally, it was observed that the comment section was not required yet this can be deemed as based off preference.

CONCLUSION

The objectives of this were achieved by identifying key factors and DQ control existing literature. Several DQ attributes were identified which led to further analysis of the occurrence and relevance. Notably, the DQ attributes selected for this research were required to ensure the quality of data during ingestion. Following the achievement of the first research object, the identified DQ attributes led to the metrics used in the design and development of the framework for data orchestration and ingestion. The effectiveness of the developed framework evaluated by executing the data orchestration and observing the outcome of the experiment. Thus, the last research objective was achieved.

The effectiveness of the frameworks developed were first evaluated theoretically and later practically. The theoretical evaluation alone would have not fully aligned with real-world scenarios however it did aid in understanding the success and fail scenario of utilising the DQ framework. Fully comprehending the effectiveness of the artifacts of this study, required the practical application of the pipeline. The practical implementation of the experiment brought to light that timeliness requires to be evaluated based on the expected quality that will be ingested.

The statistics presented in Section 3, reported that the experiment carried out was successful due to the success rate yielding 84% whereas the failure rate yielded 16%. Even though, the results depict success, given the requirements of DQ, this experiment has been deemed unsuccessful. To ensure DQ, the experiment required to yield a 100% success rate. The artifacts created in this study did show a degree of effectiveness, although the results suggest that it needs to be further refined to take full advantage of its potential and increase its efficiency. Notably, another important result of this experiment included the learning curves. It allowed for understanding and experiencing the complexity around creating and implementing pipelines and understanding the operations of data orchestration first hand.

Working with cloud technologies is extremely costly. The main limitation of this research pertains to access to limited credit. Experimenting with the data orchestration aspects were reduced due to the cost implications of debugging. However, despite the limitations of this research has improved the understanding of DQ maintenance and data orchestration. By proposing a set of guidelines for the design and implementation of data orchestration systems, it adds substantial value to the existing body of literature. Moreover, it furnishes practical insights for the development of a data orchestration pipeline. Future studies are encouraged to build upon these findings by examining how to adapt the data source and destination between SharePoint and DL, taking full advantage of the methodological framework and empirical insights provided by this study. It would also be interesting to determine if the results of this study would be the same in other cloud platforms such as Amazon Web Services and Oracle.

Future implementations should focus on integrating the study's findings with the DL and enhancing data extraction from SharePoint. Subsequent research is recommended to prioritise the development of a resilient metadata activity management system. Additionally, creating a trigger function is crucial to facilitate incremental data ingestion from the source. It is also imperative to conduct comprehensive testing to ascertain the framework's effectiveness in data orchestration. Notably, future research should address the shortcomings identified in this research. This includes attempting to refine the DQ metrics, test case, as well as resolve problem pertaining to updating data. It was also identified that an improved method should be explored when initially copying data from the source to the sink. This method should focus on only importing the schema utilised from the source the to sink as the method utilised copied the records without verifying if there were any duplications.

Future work should also include not overwriting the records that were updated as history should be maintained in a DLH. Instead, new records should be inserted and should be easily identified as the new variation of the existing record. The data timestamp could be utilised in developing this solution in the future. Referring to Table 1, currentness was amongst the identified DQ attribute apparent in literature. Therefore, an additional DQ attribute should explored in future research. Additionally, the various type of changes should be a focus area in future work as there can be a variety of changes occurring over time. Notably, slowly changing dimensions should also be considered.

Lastly, there is still a lot to be desired and considered as this research is but the tip of the iceberg of the capabilities data orchestration possess. Therefore, future research shall dive into more intricate levels of data modifications with this field.

REFERENCES

Anastasova, Y., & Yanev, N. (2021). Models and data quality in information systems applicable in the mining industry. E3S Web of Conferences, Sofia, Bulgaria.

Azad, P., Navimipour, N. J., Rahmani, A. M., & Sharifi, A. (2020). The role of structured and unstructured data managing mechanisms in the Internet of things. *Cluster Computing*, *23*(2), 1185–1198. doi:10.1007/s10586-019-02986-2

Barika, M., Garg, S., Zomaya, A. Y., Wang, L., Moorsel, A. V., & Ranjan, R. (2019). Orchestrating big data analysis workflows in the cloud: Research challenges, survey, and future directions. *ACM Computing Surveys*, *52*(5), 1–41. doi:10.1145/3332301

Begoli, E., Goethert, I., & Knight, K. (2021). *A lakehouse architecture for the management and analysis of heterogeneous data for biomedical research and mega-biobanks*. 2021 IEEE International Conference on Big Data (Big Data), Orlando, FL, USA

Bjeladinovic, S. (2018). A fresh approach for hybrid SQL/NoSQL database design based on data structuredness. *Enterprise Information Systems*, *12*(8-9), 1202–1220. doi:10.1080/17517575.2018.1446102

Cherradi, M., & El Haddadi, A. (2022). A Scalable framework for data lakes ingestion. *Procedia Computer Science*, *215*, 809–814. doi:10.1016/j.procs.2022.12.083

Čuš, B., & Golec, D. (2022). Data Lakehouse: Benefits in small and medium enterprises. *Mednarodno inovativno poslovanje= Journal of Innovative Business and Management, 14*(2), 1-10.

Datablist. (n.d.). *Download Sample CSV Files for free*. https://www.datablist.com/learn/csv/download-sample-csv-files

Dickson, M. S., & Asagba, P. (2020). The Semi-Structured Data Model and Implementation Issues for Semi-Structured Data. *International Journal of Innovation and Sustainability*, *3*, 47–51.

Dinh, V.-N., & Nguyen, H.-A. (2022). *Data Process Approach by Traditional and Cloud Services Methodologies*. Academic Press.

Ellis, T. J., & Levy, Y. (2010). A guide for novice researchers: Design and development research methods. Proceedings of Informing Science & IT Education Conference (InSITE).

Enosh, G., Tzafrir, S. S., & Stolovy, T. (2015). The development of client violence questionnaire (CVQ). *Journal of Mixed Methods Research, 9*(3), 273–290. doi:10.1177/1558689814525263

Figueira, R. B. (2018). *A framework for dataflow orchestration in lambda architectures*. Universidade do Porto.

Gabarro, J., & Stewart, A. (2021). Modelling web-service uncertainty: The angel/daemon approach. *Computer Science Review, 39*, 100355. doi:10.1016/j.cosrev.2020.100355

Giebler, C., Gröger, C., Hoos, E., Eichler, R., Schwarz, H., & Mitschang, B. (2021). The data lake architecture framework. *BTW 2021*.

Gupta, P. M. (2023). The Role of Big Data in Smart Healthcare. *International Journal of Internet of Things*. Advance online publication.

Harby, A. A., & Zulkernine, F. (2022). *From Data Warehouse to Lakehouse: A Comparative Review*. 2022 IEEE International Conference on Big Data (Big Data), Osaka, Japan.

Hlupić, T., & Puniš, J. (2021). An Overview of Current Trends in Data Ingestion and Integration. *2021 44th International Convention on Information, Communication and Electronic Technology (MIPRO)*.

Kevin, P., & Ginger, G. (2021). *Managing Data Orchestration and Integration at Scale*. O. R. Media.

Khan, N., Naim, A., Hussain, M. R., Naveed, Q. N., Ahmad, N., & Qamar, S. (2019). The 51 v's of big data: survey, technologies, characteristics, opportunities, issues and challenges. *Proceedings of the international conference on omni-layer intelligent systems*. 10.1145/3312614.3312623

Koltay, T. (2020). Quality of open research data: Values, convergences and governance. *Information (Basel), 11*(4), 175. doi:10.3390/info11040175

Liu, P., Loudcher, S., Darmont, J., & Noûs, C. (2021). Archaeodal: A data lake for archaeological data management and analytics. *Proceedings of the 25th International Database Engineering & Applications Symposium*. 10.1145/3472163.3472266

Liu, Z., & Zhang, A. (2020). Sampling for big data profiling: A survey. *IEEE Access : Practical Innovations, Open Solutions*, *8*, 72713–72726. doi:10.1109/ACCESS.2020.2988120

Mahanti, R. (2019). *Data Quality: Dimensions, Measurement, Strategy, Management, and Governance*. ASQ Quality Press.

Mthembu, Z. K., Patel, S. S., Naicker, N., Joseph, S., Madamshetty, L., Moonsamy, D., Akinola, A. T., & Govender, P. (2024). Developing a Data Lakehouse for a South African Government-Sector Training Authority: Governance Framework Design through Systematic Literature Review and Meta-Analysis. In O. S. Ogunleye (Ed.), *Machine Learning and Data Science Techniques for Effective Government Service Delivery*. IGI Global.

Nambiar, A., & Mundra, D. (2022). An Overview of Data Warehouse and Data Lake in Modern Enterprise Data Management. *Big Data and Cognitive Computing*, *6*(4), 132. doi:10.3390/bdcc6040132

Peng, G., Privette, J. L., Kearns, E. J., Ritchey, N. A., & Ansari, S. (2015). A unified framework for measuring stewardship practices applied to digital environmental datasets. *Data Science Journal*, *13*(0), 231–253. doi:10.2481/dsj.14-049

Plano Clark, V. L. (2017). Mixed methods research. *The Journal of Positive Psychology*, *12*(3), 305–306. doi:10.1080/17439760.2016.1262619

Pratsri, S., & Nilsook, P. (2020). Design on Big Data Platform-Based in Higher Education Institute. *Higher Education Studies*, *10*(4), 36–43. doi:10.5539/hes.v10n4p36

Quasim, M. T., Johri, P., Meraj, M., & Haider, S. (2019). 5V's of big data via cloud computing: Uses and importance. *Science International (Lahore)*, *31*(3), 367–371.

Raj, A., Bosch, J., Olsson, H. H., & Wang, T. J. (2020). *Modelling data pipelines*. 2020 46th Euromicro conference on software engineering and advanced applications (SEAA), Portoroz, Slovenia.

Sambrekar, K., Rajpurohit, V. S., & Joshi, J. (2018). A proposed technique for conversion of unstructured Agro-data to semi-structured or structured data. *2018 Fourth International Conference on Computing Communication Control and Automation (ICCUBEA)*, Pune, India. 10.1109/ICCUBEA.2018.8697432

Sandhu, A. K. (2021). Big data with cloud computing: Discussions and challenges. *Big Data Mining and Analytics*, *5*(1), 32–40. doi:10.26599/BDMA.2021.9020016

Singhal, B., & Aggarwal, A. (2022). *ETL, ELT and Reverse ETL: A business case Study. 2022 Second International Conference on Advanced Technologies in Intelligent Control, Environment, Computing & Communication Engineering (ICATIECE)*, Bangalore, India 10.1109/ICATIECE56365.2022.10046997

Strijker, D., Bosworth, G., & Bouter, G. (2020). Research methods in rural studies: Qualitative, quantitative and mixed methods. *Journal of Rural Studies*, *78*, 262–270. doi:10.1016/j.jrurstud.2020.06.007

Vom Brocke, J., Hevner, A., & Maedche, A. (2020). Introduction to design science research. *Design science research. Cases*, 1-13.

Yu, W., Dillon, T., Mostafa, F., Rahayu, W., & Liu, Y. (2019). A global manufacturing big data ecosystem for fault detection in predictive maintenance. *IEEE Transactions on Industrial Informatics*, *16*(1), 183–192. doi:10.1109/TII.2019.2915846

KEY TERMS AND DEFINITIONS

Data Ingestion: The process of collecting and importing information from a variety of sources into an archive, e.g. the Data Lakehouse, so that it can be made available for analysis.

Data Lakehouse: A unified data management architecture that enables organizations to store and analyse structured and unstructured data on a single platform, combining the benefits of Data Lakes and Data Warehouses.

Data Orchestration: This is to ensure efficient data flows and integration into a system, often facilitated through automated working processes, by coordinating and managing different processing tasks.

Data Quality: The degree to which data are accurate, complete, timely, and consistent, providing reliable and meaningful information for decision making.

Semi-Structured Data: Data which has an irregular and implicit structure that lacks a defined data model.

Chapter 7
Developing a Data Lakehouse for a South African Government-Sector Training Authority:
Governance Framework Design Through Systematic Literature Review

Zamani Khulekani Mthembu
Durban University of Technology, South Africa

Lavanya Madamshetty
Durban University of Technology, South Africa

Sulaiman Saleem Patel
https://orcid.org/0000-0003-3557-3645
Durban University of Technology, South Africa

Devraj Moonsamy
https://orcid.org/0000-0002-9690-5546
Durban University of Technology, South Africa

Nalindren Naicker
Durban University of Technology, South Africa

Ayotuyi Tosin Akinola
Durban University of Technology, South Africa

Seena Joseph
Durban University of Technology, South Africa

Thamotharan Prinavin Govender
https://orcid.org/0000-0003-3795-1179
Durban University of Technology, South Africa

DOI: 10.4018/978-1-6684-9716-6.ch007

ABSTRACT

The Durban University of Technology is undertaking a project to develop a data lakehouse system for a South African government-sector training authority. This system is considered critical to enhance the monitoring and evaluation capabilities of the training authority and ensure service delivery. Key to the successful deployment of the data lakehouse is the implementation of suitable data governance for the system. This chapter identifies the key components of data governance relevant to the system through a systematic literature review process. Thereafter, the components of data governance are mapped against the technical architecture of the data lakehouse and the governance mechanisms are for all lakehouse system components are defined. A practitioner expert evaluation is presented to assess the data governance mechanisms. Overall, the data governance framework and resulting mechanisms were found to be sufficient, except regarding ensuring data quality. The need for separate studies focused on ensuring data quality for the data lakehouse system was identified as future work.

BACKGROUND TO THE STUDY

In South Africa, Sector Education and Training Authorities are organizations established by government to facilitate skills development and training within specific sectors of the economy. These Government-Sector Training Authorities (GTAs) are a critical component of the country's National Skills Development Strategy and play a pivotal role in addressing the skills gap and training needs within various industries. This study is part of an ongoing project between the Durban University of Technology (DUT) and a South African GTA. The aim of this project is to modernize the knowledge management capabilities of the GTA, while simultaneously developing skill and capacity among DUT students.

To improve the knowledge management capabilities of the GTA, it was identified that an end-to-end data warehousing and automated reporting system was needed. Through scoping discussions and consultation between GTA stakeholders and the DUT design team, it was decided that the data warehousing solution would be developed on the Microsoft Azure technology stack.

The study presented in this chapter was conducted as part of the aforementioned project and focuses on the data governance and management considerations that are needed alongside the technical development of the data warehousing system.

While Microsoft Azure cloud services provide a robust platform for building DLHs, the development of a data governance framework (DGF) tailored to the unique needs of South African GTAs remains a crucial yet understudied area (Al-Ruithe et al., 2019). Existing literature on data governance in DLH predominantly focuses on generic frameworks and fails to address the challenges faced by GTAs such as:

- Privacy and confidentiality: GTAs deal with sensitive personal information of individuals participating in training programs. Ensuring data privacy and confidentiality is crucial to comply with data protection regulations and maintain trust (Amo et al., 2021).
- Data quality and integrity: Accurate and reliable data is vital for decision-making and policy formulation. GTAs may face challenges in maintaining data quality and integrity, such as data inconsistencies, duplicates, and data integration issues from various sources (Abraham et al., 2019).
- Data security and access control: Protecting data from unauthorized access, breaches, and cyber threats is a critical concern. GTAs need robust security measures and access controls to safeguard sensitive information and ensure compliance with security standards (Gupta et al., 2022).
- Compliance with regulations: GTAs must comply with specific regulations and legislation related to data management and protection. These can include laws like the Protection of Personal Information Act, 2013 (POPIA) or sector-specific regulations that impose additional requirements on data handling.

The aim of this study is thus to develop a data governance framework for the data warehousing solution being developed for the South African GTA. In the following sections of the chapter, an introduction to modern data warehousing and data governance is first provided. Thereafter, an overview of the data warehousing solution designed by the DUT project team is provided. This establishes an understanding of the technical system that the governance framework is being designed to support. With that understanding in mind, the third section of the chapter presents a systematic literature review that identifies the key elements of data governance that are most relevant to government-sector organizations. Using these elements, the bespoke governance framework is designed for the system under study, and evaluated through consultation with an industry expert practitioner. The final section of the chapter presents conclusions and findings arising from the study, and suggests directs for future research efforts.

INTRODUCTION

A modern data warehouse is a "subject-oriented, nonvolatile, integrated, time-variant collection of data in support of management decisions" (Nambiar & Mundra, 2022). Traditionally, data warehouses were developed for database systems that represented data in highly structured formats. However, these systems are outdated – modern organizations utilize diverse types of data, beyond the traditional data records in structured databases. The latest evolution of data warehousing, the data lakehouse (DLH), has emerged as a new architectural paradigm that allows for a wide variety of structured, semi-structured and unstructured data (Azeroual et al., 2022; Nambiar & Mundra, 2022; Oreščanin & Hlupić, 2021). The key technology that differentiates a DLH from a traditional data warehouse is the inclusion of a data lake, which is essentially a storage container that holds data in its native file formats (Miloslavskaya & Tolstoy, 2016)

Although the phrases "Data Lakes" and "Data Warehouses" are sometimes used interchangeably, they are not the same. Data lakes hold raw or unprocessed data, whereas DWs store data that has been processed and filtered. The schema in the data lake is defined by source systems and unprocessed file types, whereas the schema in a data warehouse is defined by the design of the warehouse. Data from the DW that has been cleaned is used for analysis. Instead, in a data lake, data is picked and arranged as and when they are required (Nambiar & Mundra, 2022)

Data lakes retain massive volumes of data in their unprocessed forms; hence the implementation of data management processes is a crucial requirement for a successful DLH system (Abraham et al., 2019; Hlupić et al., 2022). This is especially true for DLHs developed in environments that are subject to strict regulatory requirements and procedures, such as government-sector entities (Marcucci et al., 2023). The Data Management Association defines data governance as "the exercise of authority, control, and shared decision making over the management of data assets" (Al-Ruithe et al., 2019). Data governance offers a mechanism for controlling data use and decision-making, including procedures, rules, organizational structures, and responsibilities (Karkošková, 2023). Failure to implement proper data governance for DLH systems can result in the data lake becoming a collection of noisy data that is difficult to process and analyze, which is referred to as a "Data Swamp"(Paschalidi, 2015). In general, noisiness diminishes the value of data in knowledge management and analytical systems, and is highly undesirable.

DATA LAKEHOUSE SYSTEM OVERVIEW

The data lakehouse designed by the DUT project team is presented in Figure 1, which has been presented in an abstracted manner to respect the privacy and sensitivity of government-sector data systems.

Due to existing cloud infrastructure agreements in place with the GTA, the DLH was designed for the Microsoft Azure cloud technology stack. The system design was based on a four-layer, two-tier architecture (Armbrust et al., 2021; Harby &

Table 1. Summary of resources to implement data lakehouse

Data Lakehouse Component	Cloud Resources and Development Interfaces
Data lake storage	Azure Storage Account – Data Lake Generation 2
Data pipelines and data orchestration	Azure Data Factory
Data transformations within the data lake	Azure Databricks
Database storage	Azure SQL Server (and SQL Server Management Studio)
Data cube analytics engine	Azure Analytics Services (and Visual Studio)
Automated reporting and analytics	Microsoft Power BI

Figure 1. Illustration of data lakehouse system

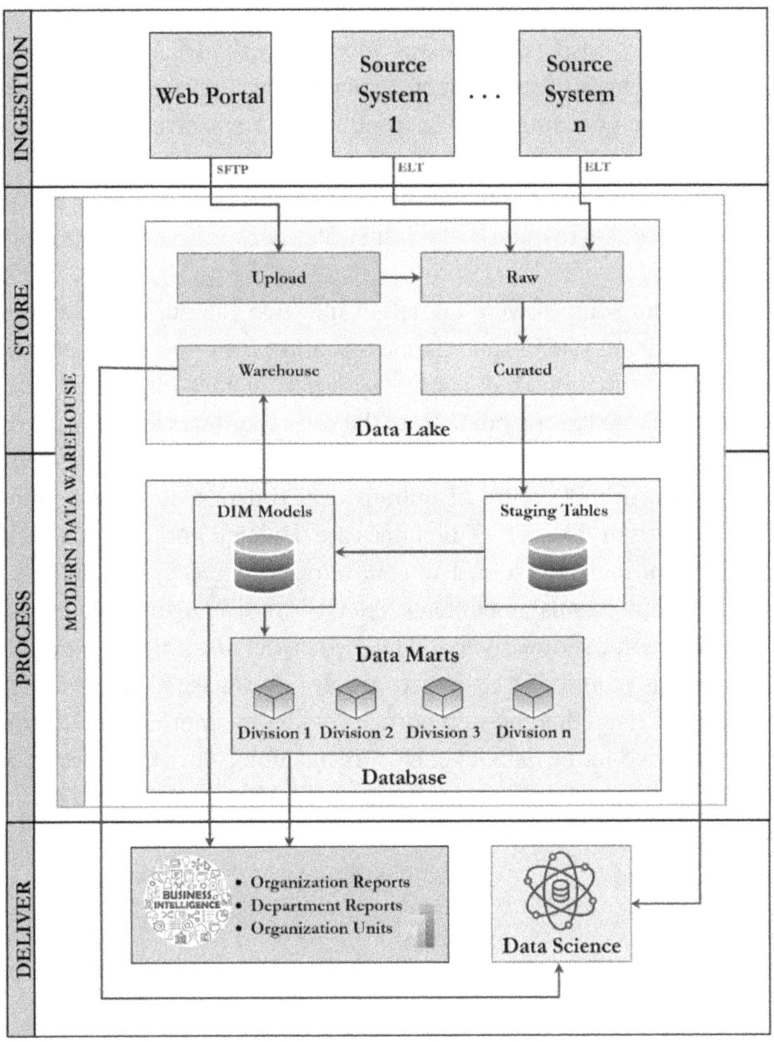

Zulkernine, 2022). The four layers defined for the system were: Ingestion, Store, Process and Deliver. Within these layers, there are two tiers: (i) the data lake tier, which stores data files organized in a hierarchical namespace, and (ii) the database tier, which stores data units in structured records. The Microsoft Azure resources deployed to implement this data lakehouse are detailed in Table 1.

The Ingestion Layer

The first layer of the DLH system is responsible for ingesting data from various source systems and landing them into the data lake. This is referred to as the Ingestion Layer.

To meet the data warehousing needs of the South African GTA, the DUT project team conducted an extensive requirements gathering and analysis process in consultation with GTA stakeholders. Arising from this process, it was identified that some of the key business processes adopted by the GTA were performed in a paper-based and email-based manner. Management reporting on these activities was found to be time-consuming and susceptible to human error. Stakeholders from the GTA have embarked on automation and process digitization projects to address these challenges. However, for the purpose of the DLH system, it was identified that a secure mechanism to upload individual files pertaining to business processes was needed.

As a result, data sources were classified into two categories: data originating from digitized source systems, and data originating from manual documents. For data originating from digitized source systems, extract-load-transform (ELT) pipelines were designed to copy data from the source systems and sink the data into a designated container within the data lake. This was declared the Raw container, and was designed to hold copies of untransformed data that could be reconciled with the source system. These ELT pipelines are depicted in Figure 1, which shows the ingestion from Source System 1 to an arbitrary Source System n. To cater for data originating from manual documents, the DUT project team designed a secured web portal that interfaces directly to the DLH. The details of the web portal design and development is reported in a separate article – for this study, it is sufficient for the reader to understand that the web portal provides an interface for documents to be securely uploaded to the data lake. Documents uploaded via the web portal are transmitted using Secure File Transfer Protocol (SFTP) and are landed in a separate Upload container within the data lake.

The Storage Layer

Within the DLH, the Storage Layer is primarily concerned with storing data in the data lake. A zonal architecture (Sawadogo & Darmont, 2021) that utilizes discrete containers, each with its own set of directories and namespaces, was chosen.

The Upload container was designed to act as a pseudo-source system, hence an ELT pipeline was created to ingest from the Upload container and sink to the Raw container.

Data contained in the Raw container is then transformed, cleaned and prepared for downstream processing. This included converting unstructured and semi-structured data into structured formats that are conducive to online analytical processing (OLAP). This is primarily achieved through the use of Azure Databricks, a cloud analytics service based on Apache Spark which runs within the Microsoft Azure ecosystem (Etaati, 2019). The resulting cleaned data is stored in the Curated container. Transformations are done within an extract-transform-load (ETL) pipeline between the Raw and Curated containers. In the Curated container, new data that has been ingested into the data lake was appended to historic data.

Data from the Curated container is transferred to the database tier of the DLH, for further processing that will be described in the next subsection. The resulting output from the Process Layer is fed back to the Storage Layer and housed in the Warehouse container.

The Process Layer

The Process Layer of the designed data lakehouse consists of a database server and analytics engine. In this layer of the architecture, the cleaned and processed data from the Curated container of the data lake is first staged in structured, SQL-based tables. These tables are used as the basis for generating multi-dimensional OLAP data cubes, wherein measurable data points are aggregated across each of the dimensions (Djiroun et al., 2019). The design of the data cubes was done using a star schema dimensional modelling paradigm, focusing on distinct business processes (Edastama et al., 2021; Kimball & Ross, 2013). The resulting cubes were packaged into data marts according to the business divisions within the GTA. The underlying business processes represented by each multi-dimensional model were used to assign data cubes to data marts. Figure 4 represents the data marts created for an arbitrary number of business divisions.

Additionally, the tables generated through the dimensional modelling process were exported to the data lake in flat file format. The Warehouse container within the data lake is used as a sink for this data.

The Deliver Layer

The Deliver Layer of the data lakehouse is the final layer of the architecture. At this layer, extraction queries were designed to access data for analytical purposes. At the Deliver Layer, end-users from the GTA engage with the data through the following mechanisms: (i) automated business intelligence reports for business units, which are driven by data from the data marts; (ii) ad-hoc extraction queries developed for business units, which are driven by data from the data marts; and (iii) direct access to datasets and data files for data science purposes, which are retrieved from the Curated and Warehouse containers of the data lake.

Typical tools deployed at the Deliver Layer are business intelligence and data analytics tools and packages. As shown in Table 1, the business intelligence tool chosen was Microsoft Power BI – however, the architecture is flexible enough to support other potential tools that the GTA may adopt in future. Query optimization at the Deliver Layer is planned for a future phase of the project.

IDENTIFYING COMPONENTS OF DATA GOVERNANCE

To identify the key components of data governance relevant to the DLH system, the Preferred Reporting Items for Systematic Reviews and Meta-Analyses (PRISMA) methodology was adopted (Page et al., 2021). The PRISMA methodology clearly indicates the systematic steps followed by the research team in sourcing, screening and critiquing literature. This provides transparency in the process that was followed, ensuring that the correct standards of academic rigor and thoroughness were applied. As part of the PRISMA methodology, the researchers explicitly present the sources of academic literature consulted to source articles for the review, as well as the criteria followed when screening articles to discern whether they should be included or excluded.

Search Strategy

The search strategy was carried out in adherence with the PRISMA reporting checklist (Page et al., 2021), and is depicted in Figure 2. Three sources of academic literature searched were considered for the search: IEEEXplore, Science Direct, and Google Scholar.

In the first phase of the search, the search keywords, and criteria for exclusion and inclusion of an article were defined. The major variables and keywords for the study were:

Figure 2. PRISMA search strategy

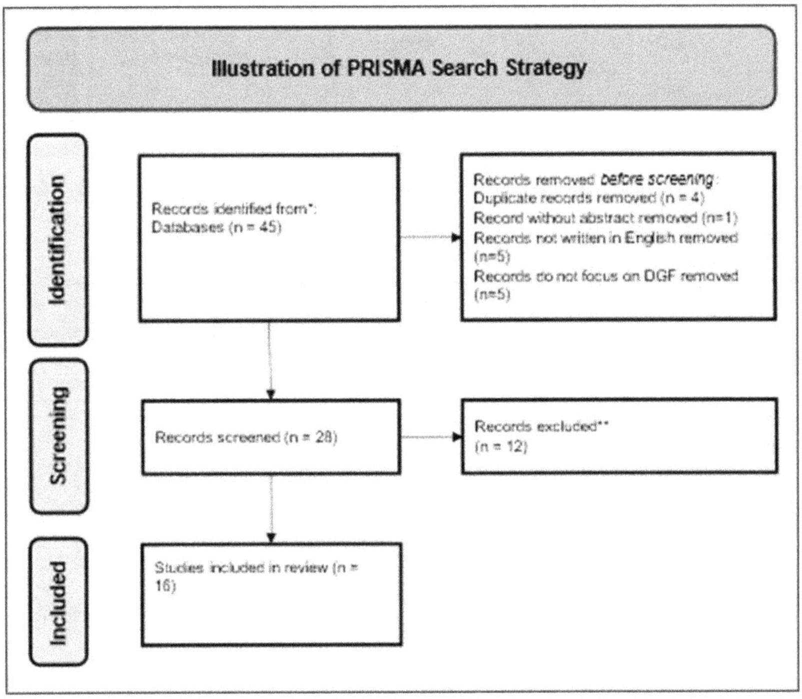

- modern data warehouse,
- data lakehouse,
- data governance,
- data governance framework,
- government cloud services, and
- cloud service.

The exclusion criteria applied to the search results were:

EC 1. Articles for which the full-text was unavailable.

EC 2. Articles which were indexed in multiple sources of academic literature (i.e. duplicated articles)

EC 3. Articles which were not written in the English language.

EC 4. Articles which did not have sufficient focus on data governance.

Furthermore, the following inclusion criteria was applied to ensure that only recent and up-to-date literature was considered:

IC 1. Articles which were published within the last five years (2019 to 2023).

IC 2. Articles that are published pre-prints are permitted.

Table 2. Articles identified from systematic literature review

Study ID	Title	Authors	Journal Name / Title of Conference Proceedings	Pub. Year
S1	Data governance: A conceptual framework, structured review, and research agenda	R. Abraham, J. Schneider and J. vom Brocke.	International Journal of Information Management	2019
S2	A systematic literature review of data governance and cloud data governance	M. Al-Ruithe, E. Benkhelifa and K. Hameed	Personal and Ubiquitous Computing	2019
S3	Data Governance Maturity Assessment: A Case Study in IT Bureau of Audit Board	D. H. Kurniawan, Y. Ruldeviyani, M. R. Adrian, S. Handayani, M. R. Pohan and R. Khairunnisa T.	2019 International Conference on Information Management and Technology (ICIMTech)	2019
S4	Improving Data Security, Interoperability, and Veracity using Blockchain for One Data Governance, Case Study of Local Tax Big Data	S. Wibowo and T. Sandikapura	2019 International Conference on ICT for Smart Society (ICISS)	2019
S5	Government data governance framework based on a data middle platform	Z Mao, J. Wu, Y. Qiao and H Yao	Aslib Journal of Information Management	2022
S6	Use of big data governance in several corporate sectors	M.A. Rasheed, H.Z. Ahmad, H.A. Tanweer, H. Murtaza, M.A. Rasheed, and M. Ahmed	VFAST Transactions on Software Engineering	2022
S7	Using Semantic Technologies to Manage a Data Lake: Data Catalog, Provenance and Access Control	H. Dibowski, S. Schmid, Y. Svetashova, C. Henson, and T. Tran	SSWS@ ISWC	2020
S8	Bringing in the technological, ethical, educational, and social-structural for a new education data governance	V. Hillman	Learning, Media, and Technology	2023
S9	Strengthening data governance in Africa	S. Osakwe and A. P. Adeniran	Centre for the Study of economies of Africa	2021
S10	Mapping and Comparing Data Governance Frameworks: A benchmarking exercise to inform global data governance deliberations	S. Marcucci, N. G. Alarcón, S. G. Verhulst and E. Wüllhorst	arXiv preprint arXiv:2302.13731	2023

Table 2. Continued

Study ID	Title	Authors	Journal Name / Title of Conference Proceedings	Pub. Year
S11	Data governance functions to support responsible data stewardship in pediatric radiology research studies using artificial intelligence	S. R. Monah, M. W. Wagner, A. Biswas, F. Khalvati, L. E. Erdman, A. Amirabadi, L. Vidarsson, M. D. McCradden and B. B. Ertl-Wagner.	Pediatric Radiology	2022
S12	Overlooked Aspects of Data Governance: Workflow Framework for Enterprise Data Deduplication	O. Azeroual, A. Nikiforova and K. Sha	2023 International Conference on Intelligent Computing, Communication, Networking and Services (ICCNS)	2023
S13	CEBA: A Data Lake for Data Sharing and Environmental Monitoring	D. Sarramia, A. Claude, F. Ogereau, J. Mezhoud and G. Mailhot	CEBA: A Data Lake for Data Sharing and Environmental Monitoring	2022
S14	Modeling metadata in data lakes—A generic model	R. Eichler, C. Giebler, C. Gröger, H. Schwarz, and B. Mitschang	Data & Knowledge Engineering	2021
S15	The Danish National Energy Data Lake: Requirements, Technical Architecture, and Tool Selection	H. B. Hamadou, T. Bach Pedersen and C. Thomsen	2020 IEEE International Conference on Big Data (Big Data)	2020

As shown in Figure 2, a total of 45 articles were identified through executing the search through the identified databases. Prior to screening the contents of the articles, 15 articles were removed at the identification phase. As there were some articles that were duplicated more than once, this resulted in a total of 28 articles considered at the screening phase.

During the screening phase, the research team analyzed the content of the articles and the technical rigor applied by the researchers. It was concluded that 12 articles were not relevant to the scope of this literature review. Some of the rationales applied at this stage included: (i) incomparable contexts, where the literature was deeply embedded in an organizational context that was disparate from the context of the South African GTA; and (ii) insufficient rigor, where the methodology adopted in the literature was found to have deficiencies.

Table 2 presents the final set of 15 articles that were identified (Abraham et al., 2019; Al-Ruithe et al., 2019; Azeroual et al., 2023; Dibowski et al., 2020; Eichler et al., 2021; Hamadou et al., 2020; Hillman, 2023; Kurniawan et al., 2019; Mao et al., 2022; Marcucci et al., 2023; Monah et al., 2022; Osakwe & Adeniran, 2021; Rasheed et al., 2022; Sarramia et al., 2022; Wibowo & Sandikapura, 2019).

The analysis of the articles identified was conducted in two stages – the first stage involved clustering the articles identified to establish groupings for further analysis. Thereafter, in the second stage, a more in-depth qualitative analysis was performed on the article content to identify the final set to data governance components relevant to this study.

Article Clustering and Relevance of Articles

The 15 articles identified through the PRISMA search strategy were analyzed and clustered into four categories. The first category consisted of Conceptual Studies, which were research articles that focused on understanding fundamental nuances of data governance. The second category focused on research articles of a technical nature, where the study proposed a new technical framework, method or tool to facilitate data governance practices. The third category focused on case studies, which considered data governance frameworks applied to specific contexts. The final category considered studies that amalgamated the results of other literature, i.e. review papers and comparative studies. Table 3 presents the categorization of the articles and the cumulative number of articles identified per category.

Thereafter, Figure 3 presents a breakdown of the number of articles per category over time. Figure 3 shows that all conceptual studies that were considered in this paper were published from 2021 onwards. This highlights the recency of the articles informing the literature review at a conceptual level. The review papers and comparative studies, on the other hand, were mostly published in 2019 (n=2). This corresponds with studies S1 and S2, which were expansive review articles on data governance practices that were published in high-impact journals – S1 was based on a study of 145 articles published between 2001 and 2019, while S2 covered 52 articles published between 2005 to 2017. Thus, it was deduced that S1 and S2 adequately summarize the salient details from literature published prior to the scope of the study in this chapter; and that their results are sufficient to inform this study.

Table 3.Categorization of articles

Category	Study IDs	No. of Articles in Category
Conceptual Studies	S5, S8, S9, S11, S14	5
Technical Framework or Method	S7, S12	3
Case Study	S3, S4, S6, S13, S15	5
Review Papers and Comparative Studies	S1, S2, S10	3

Figure 3. Cumulative number of articles per year by category

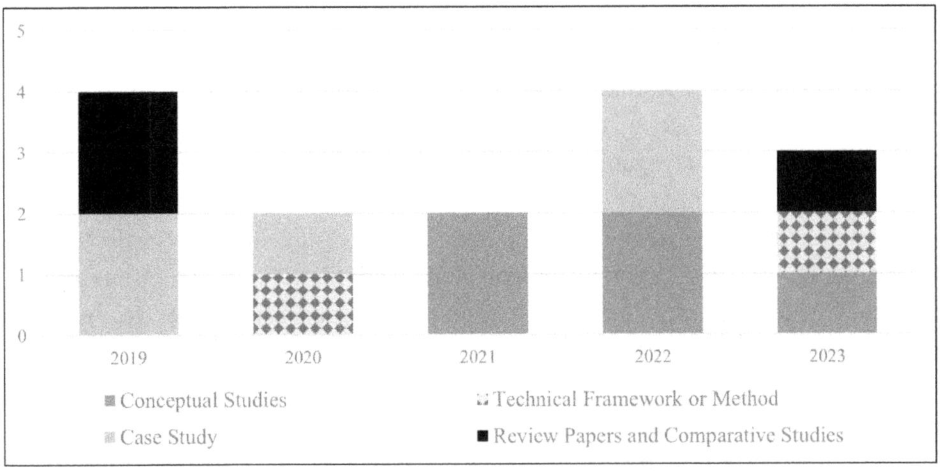

The last article in this category was published in 2023 (*n*=1), which is deemed to adequately cover research published more recently than S1 and S2.

It is also evident from Figure 3 that the case studies articles deemed in-scope for this review were published in 2019 (*n*=2), 2020 (*n*=1) and 2022 (*n*=2) respectively. Similarly, the research articles that present new technical methods or frameworks were published in 2020 (*n*=1) and 2023 (*n*=1). Hence, it is inferred that within the five-year period, all case studies and technical research articles are suitably recent to inform this review.

Review, Meta-Analysis and Discussion of In-Scope Literature

The review of in-scope literature focuses on synthesizing the information presented in articles S1-S15, and presenting the relevant discourse for this chapter.

A key guiding principle in understanding data governance in the context of this chapter is the conceptual framework developed by Abraham et al. (2019) in Study S1. The conceptual framework consisted of six core elements, as presented in Figure 4. At the core of this framework are Governance Mechanisms, which refer to the structural, procedural and relational mechanisms deployed within an organization. Structural mechanisms focus on individuals, committees and other structures within the organization, and relate to defining their roles and responsibilities, chains of command, reporting structures and decision-making authorities. Procedural mechanisms are more action-oriented, and focus on defining how data governance is implemented in the organization. This is done by defining policies, processes, procedures, strategies and other such guiding artefacts. Finally, relational mechanisms relate to collaborative efforts that align different organizational units. The key elements within relational mechanisms are communication, training and the co-ordination of decision-making efforts (Abraham et al., 2019).

As depicted in Figure 4, there are three scopes that impact governance mechanisms – the organizational scope, the data scope and the domain scope. Each scope defines elements of an organization's data landscape that require governing. The organizational scope focuses on the organization as a business entity, and relates to areas such as project management, progress tracking, legislative compliance and inter-organization data sharing protocols and standards. The data scope explicitly describes which data points and data systems governance is applied to. In many instances, this varies within an organization, as data of different levels of sensitivity require different levels of governance. Finally, the domain scope focuses on the data decision domain. Within this scope, the manner in which data is used to address business needs and drive decision-making is explicated (Abraham et al., 2019).

The conceptual framework further presents the antecedents of data governance, which are external or internal driving forces that impact data governance considerations. Typical examples of external antecedents include regulatory requirements, while internal antecedents may include the organizational strategies around digital transformation and cloud technology adoption, among others. Many examples of external antecedents are presented in study S9, which expounds the role of data governance at international level in facilitating the digitization of trade in Africa (Osakwe & Adeniran, 2021). The idea of considering antecedents to data governance is coherent with the findings of study S8, wherein Hillman (2023) argues for the consideration of multiple stakeholder perspectives in the design of a data governance framework (specifically in the context of education). Obverse to antecedents are consequences, which describe the results of applying data governance. These are classed into immediate performance management and risk management (Abraham et al., 2019).

The researchers have determined that the detail provided by the Abraham conceptual framework is superior and more comprehensive than the other conceptual frameworks identified from in-scope literature. Indeed, in Study S11, the conceptual framework presented covers only data stewardship, ownership, policies and standards (Monah et al., 2022), which are all encompassed in the organizational scope of data governance per the Abraham Framework. Similarly, the 'data middle platform' approach of data governance for government entities presented in Study S5 (Mao et al., 2022) also falls within the organizational scope of the Abraham Framework.

In the context of this chapter, the scoping definitions provided by the Abraham Framework were critical to understand the boundaries of the DGF being designed in this chapter. Especially for a government-sector institution, understanding the antecedents from national strategy and policy were crucial to ensure the suitability

Figure 4. Illustration of the Abraham conceptual framework of data governance

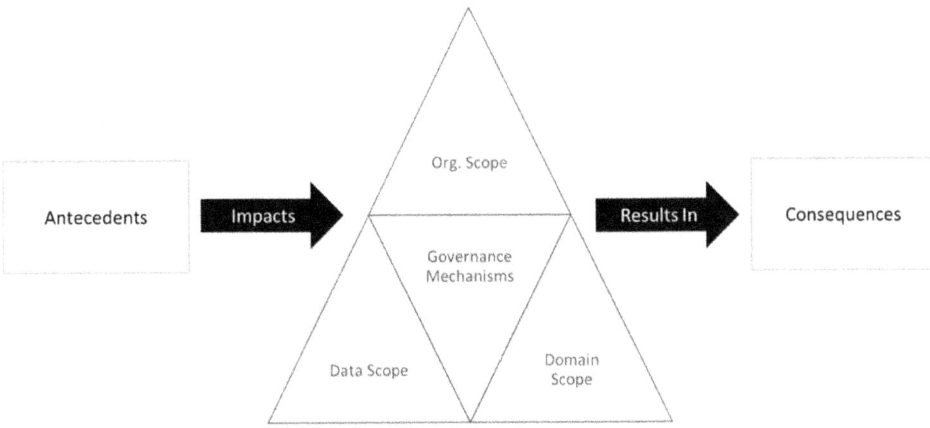

of the DLH system design. The aspect of data scope was identified as particularly crucial, as the DGF design was to be constrained to the DLH system which is integrated within the wider information technology ecosystem of the GTA and the data governance practices adopted by the GTA at an organizational level. It was also determined that the DUT project team could only make *recommendations* towards data governance mechanisms through the organizational scope, as the organizational responsibilities remained with the GTA stakeholders. It was thus determined that the majority of the framework design would be undertaken within the domain scope.

Critical factors to be considered in the design of the framework were identified by S2, which compared aspects of data governance between cloud-based and non-cloud systems. These factors included the need for creating new roles (or transitioning existing roles) within the organization due to many elements of information technology management being outsourced to cloud service providers (Al-Ruithe et al., 2019). This necessitates formal communication and collaboration between the organization and third parties. The resulting loss of control poses a risk to organizations. As a result, it is recommended that monitoring controls and activities be implemented to provide transparency and ensure that governance processes are implemented correctly. Another key point raised by Al-Ruithe et al. (2019) was that organizations may need to invest in training staff in the use of cloud technologies.

In S10, Marcucci et al. (2023) conducted a macro-level comparative analysis of 58 data governance frameworks from public institutions. The majority (64%) of these frameworks were proposed by intergovernmental organizations, such as the United Nations Children's Education Fund (UNICEF). During their analysis, Marcucci et al. (2023) indicated that the most important principles in data governance for the frameworks reviewed were related to: (i) confidentiality, security and privacy, (ii)

Table 4. Components of data governance identified from case studies

Data Governance Component	Study IDs
Access Control and Security	S3, S4, S6, S13, S15
Data Quality	S3, S4, S13
Data Ownership, Stewardship and Stakeholder Engagement	S3
Metadata Management	S3, S4, S6, S13, S15
Regulatory Compliance	S6

accountability and transparency and (iii) the use of data for defined and legitimate purposes. These represent important considerations when designing the DGF for the South African GTA, as the responsibilities that state organizations have towards citizens of the state is an antecedent to data governance mechanisms.

Informed by the findings of S1, S2 and S10, the researchers next reviewed the case study articles. In the analysis of the case studies, the overall objective was to discern the key elements and peculiarities of data governance for government-sector entities that relate to a cloud-based data lakehouse. Through a process of content analysis and thematic rearrangement, the researchers have mapped the findings from the case study articles to five core data governance components, as presented in Table 4. Further discussion on each of these components is provided in the next section of this chapter.

The implementation of each of these components of data governance requires significant effort. Studies such as S14 (Eichler et al., 2021) focused only on metadata management, while others such as S7 (Azeroual et al., 2023) focused on data quality.

CORE COMPONENTS OF DATA GOVERNANCE

Access Control and Security

Effective data governance starts with solid data collection, integration, processing, and access control procedures. Due to the diverse nature of data sources, accessing data from different sources has become increasingly difficult. Kayes et al. (2020) suggests that it is especially significant in terms of picking necessary data and information from many sources and giving an integrated data picture via information fusion (e.g., by considering who can access what data under what conditions).

- Access Control: Define clear access control policies and procedures to safeguard data privacy and security. Implement Role-Based Access Control

(RBAC) to ensure that individuals and teams only access data relevant to their roles and responsibilities. Regularly review and audit access permissions to prevent unauthorized data access. Maintain an access log for accountability and traceability.

- Data Gathering: Establish standardized procedures for data collection from various sources, ensuring data is collected in a structured and consistent manner. Define data acquisition protocols, data formats, and data acquisition tools. Implement data validation checks during the data gathering phase to identify and rectify any discrepancies or errors at the source.
- Data Integration: Develop a data integration strategy that harmonizes data from diverse sources. Implement data integration tools and techniques that enable the seamless blending of data from different systems and formats. Ensure data mapping and transformation processes are well-documented and regularly updated to reflect changes in data sources.
- Data Processing: Employ efficient data processing pipelines that cleanse, transform, and enrich data to make it suitable for analysis and reporting. Implement data processing workflows that adhere to data quality standards, ensuring that data anomalies are addressed promptly. Monitor data processing pipelines to detect and mitigate bottlenecks or failures.
- Interoperability Framework: Develop an interoperability framework that allows for seamless data exchange and integration between different systems, including external data sources and government agencies.

Data Quality

Data quality is a paramount concern within GTAs, given the criticality of accurate data for training programs and decision-making. Dark data is their largest drive and greatest difficulty at the same time, and data quality plays a specific role in it (Azeroual et al., 2023). Drawing from best practices identified in the literature, the DGF design includes a robust data quality framework. This framework incorporates data validation, cleansing, and monitoring mechanisms to ensure the reliability of data within the DLH.

Maintaining data quality, accuracy, and reliability is essential for trustworthy and dependable data.

- Data Quality Standards: Establish comprehensive data quality standards that define the criteria for data accuracy, completeness, consistency, and timeliness. Regularly assess data against these standards and implement data quality checks to identify and rectify data anomalies.

- Data Accuracy: Implement data validation and verification processes to ensure the accuracy of data. Utilize data profiling tools to identify inaccuracies, outliers, and anomalies in the data. Develop data cleansing routines to correct inaccuracies as part of data processing.
- Data Reliability: Monitor data sources for reliability and establish data lineage to track the origin and transformations of data. Implement data version control to ensure that historical data is preserved accurately. Regularly validate and audit data to maintain reliability over time.
- Data Deduplication: Develop data deduplication routines that remove duplicate data records from data repositories. Ensure that data deduplication processes adhere to data governance standards and do not compromise data reliability.

Data Ownership, Stewardship and Stakeholder Engagement

- Stakeholder Engagement: Actively engage stakeholders from various divisions and teams within the GTA. Encourage feedback and input from stakeholders to shape data governance practices that meet their specific needs and objectives.
- Executive Sponsorship: Identify a dedicated executive sponsor within the GTA responsible for driving data governance efforts and ensuring high-level support.
- Data Governance Committee: Establish a GTA-specific committee responsible for overseeing data governance initiatives. Define the roles and responsibilities of committee members within the GTA context. Making sure that the necessary roles and duties are handled throughout the organization at the appropriate organizational levels requires careful consideration when designing the DGF (Al-Ruithe et al., 2019).
    - Chief Steward: whose responsibility it is to put the control mechanisms in place and specify the conditions for the DGF implementation (Azeroual et al., 2023).
    - Business Data Steward: whose task it is to describe, from a business viewpoint, the DGF for the area of responsibility (Azeroual et al., 2023).
    - Technical Data Steward: whose job it is to develop technical standards and specifications for individual components as well as to technically characterize systems and data flows between systems (Azeroual et al., 2023).
- Data Stewards: Designate data stewards for various GTA training data domains. Describe how they will manage and guarantee the integrity, quality, and compliance of the data. As a way to formally establish accountability for

managing information assets on behalf of and in the best interests of others, think about data stewardship (Janssen et al., 2020).

 - Data Quality Steward: Responsible for ensuring data quality, accuracy, and reliability.
 - Compliance Steward: Ensures data compliance with regulatory requirements.
 - Access Control Steward: Manages access control mechanisms and permissions.
 - Metadata Steward: Oversees metadata management, including data lineage and provenance tracking.

- Data Owners: Assign data owners within the GTA, outlining their responsibilities in governing specific datasets related to training programs and services. Data owners can encrypt their files and define an access policy to ensure that only approved users can decode them (Xue et al., 2018).
- Data Custodians: Define the roles and responsibilities of custodians responsible for the technical aspects of data management, focusing on GTA training data.
- Data Customers: Highlight the roles of data consumers within the GTA who rely on data-driven insights for decision-making regarding training programs and services.
- Data Governance Charter: Develop a GTA-specific Data Governance Charter that outlines the organization's commitment to data governance and its alignment with the GTA's mission and goals.

Metadata Management

Comprehensive metadata management is essential for enhancing data discovery and accessibility. The issue of metadata management has been a core focus area for studies such as S7 (Dibowski et al., 2020). The core data governance mechanisms that relate to metadata management are:

- Data Lineage and Provenance: Implement metadata management tools that capture data lineage and provenance information. Maintain a detailed record of how data is sourced, transformed, and used. Ensure that data lineage and provenance are readily accessible to stakeholders for transparency.
- Metadata Catalog: Develop a metadata catalog that catalogs all data assets within the GTA. Provide detailed descriptions, classifications, and tagging for data assets, making it easier for users to discover and understand the available data resources.

- Metadata Annotation: Implement metadata governance tools that allow for data annotation and tagging during the data ingestion process. Annotate data information such as data sources, data owner, data quality, and access permissions.

Provenance Tracking: Continuously track data provenance using metadata to provide a clear history of data lineage and transformations. Provenance information enhances data traceability and auditability.

Regulatory Compliance

The importance of adhering to data management and regulatory obligations cannot be overstated. The government is making a positive effort to protect the privacy, security, and confidentiality of data subjects' personal information, as well as to ensure that such data is handled legitimately and responsibly, under the Protection of Personal Information Act (POPIA) No.4 of 2013. It ensures that the individual whose data is being processed is participating in the process. The National Integrated Information and Communication Technology Policy White Paper, a thorough study that considers cutting-edge technologies like cloud computing and the internet of things, was issued by the Department of Telecommunications and Postal Services. Even if the White Paper does not go into depth on new technologies, it does show that the government is aware of them (Mohlameane & Ruxwana, 2020).

- Data Consolidation: Address the challenge of data consolidation by implementing a data consolidation strategy that integrates data from various sources while adhering to data governance principles. Ensure that data consolidation processes do not compromise data quality or security.
- Data Retention: Develop data retention policies that align with regulatory requirements and industry best practices. Clearly define data retention periods and implement data archiving and purging mechanisms accordingly.
- Regulatory Compliance: Stay abreast of relevant data protection and privacy regulations, such as the Protection of Personal Information Act (POPIA) in South Africa. Implement data governance practices that ensure compliance with these regulations, including data encryption, consent management, and data subject rights management.

APPLICATION OF FRAMEWORK FOR DATA LAKEHOUSE SYSTEM

A graphical polyglot representation of the data lakehouse system is presented in Figure 5.

Technology Stack

As mentioned earlier in the chapter, the South African GTA expressed a preference for the Microsoft Azure technology stack for the implementation of the data lakehouse. An overview of the key cloud resources deployed in the application of the DGF is provided below:

Figure 5. Polyglot representation of data lakehouse system

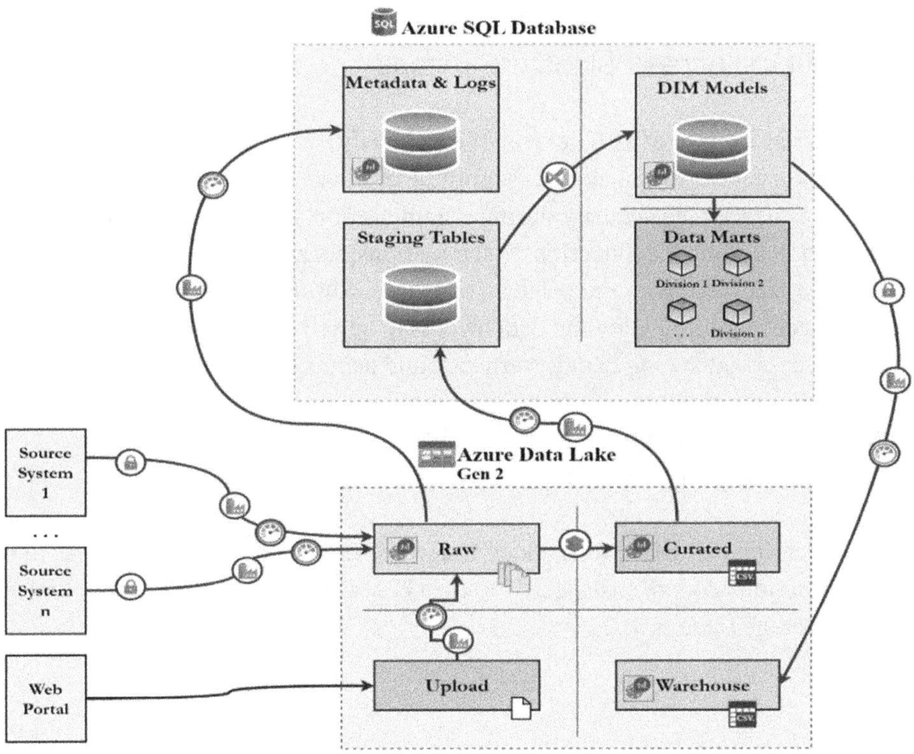

Microsoft Purview

Microsoft Purview is a comprehensive data governance and metadata management platform that aligns well with the design principles of the DGF. It offers robust metadata capture, data lineage tracking, data cataloging capabilities. Its integration with other Microsoft services ensures seamless data governance within a Microsoft-centric environment. Key features of Microsoft Purview include: (i) a centralized data catalog for comprehensive data asset management, including descriptions, classifications and tagging; (ii) advanced metadata tracking, including data lineage and provenance, and (iii) ease of integration with other Microsoft Azure services, which facilitates scalability, and ensures security.

Azure Monitor

Azure Monitor is a critical tool for continuous monitoring and oversight of activities within the DLH architecture. It was chosen to ensure data security and compliance by providing real-time insights into system performance and security. Azure Monitor also provides alerting mechanisms to notify administrators or relevant personnel in the event of suspicious activities or potential data breaches, ensuring swift responses to security incidents.

Azure Shared Access Signature Tokens

Shared Access Signature (SAS) tokens are employed to secure data source connections and data transfers between sources and the Data Lake within the DLH. They are chosen to enhance data security during data ingestion and movement. SAS tokens ensure that data source connections and data transfers are secure, reducing the risk of unauthorized access to data during transit. Additionally, SAS tokens provide granular access control, allowing data owners to define permissions and conditions for data access, enhancing data governance and access control.

Implementing Data Governance for Components of the Data Lakehouse

In implementing the data governance framework and determining guidelines to be followed, various documents specific to the GTA were analyzed. These documents are tabulated in Table 5.

Table 5. Organizational documents analyzed

Document Name	Relevance
Organization Staff Organogram	The organization staff organogram provided an overview of the management structures, business divisions and key personnel within the organization. This was important to inform guidelines related to Data Ownership, Stewardship and Stakeholder Engagement.
Organization Regular Performance Reports from Business Divisions	The regular performance reports highlighted key business performance indicators used by the organization. This helped to define the data scope for the data lakehouse system, and hence the governance framework.
Digital Strategy	The data governance framework must be aligned to the overall digital strategy of the organization.
Business Process Automation Plan Documented Business Processes and Procedures (As-Is and To-Be)	The data governance framework must consider changes to existing business processes, especially those that will be automated. The automation of business processes introduce new data points for the data lakehouse system.
Transactional System Database Schema	Understanding the schema of the database underlying the transactional systems of the organization facilitates an understanding of the data points available for ingestion.

Data Ingestion Pipelines

Data Pipelines are "complex chains of activities that manipulate data where the output of one component becomes the input to the other, thereby allowing smooth, automated flow of data from source to destination", (Raj et al., 2020). Microsoft Azure Monitor was employed to diligently track and oversee the activities within the ingestion pipelines, providing real-time monitoring and alerting capabilities.

SAS (Shared Access Signature) tokens were used to provide time-limited, fine-grained access control to resources within the DLH. Specifically, during the data ingestion process, SAS tokens were utilized to securely connect the data sources, including Source System 1, Source System n, and the Web Portal, to the Data Lake. By granting access only to authorized users and for specific time periods, SAS tokens significantly enhance security.

Furthermore, data encryption was rigorously implemented to safeguard data within the DLH. Azure's robust encryption capabilities ensure that data remains protected both transit and while at rest. During data ingestion, Transport Layer Security (TLS) encryption was applied to secure data in transit, preventing unauthorized access during transmission. Data stored in the Raw Container on Azure Data Lake Gen2 was encrypted at rest, adding an additional layer of protection to sensitive data assets.

Role-Based Access Control (RBAC) is of equal importance. Figure 6, adapted from Microsoft Azure Documentation, which illustrates the authentication flow for RBAC. This RBAC framework was applied in the Web Portal particularly, which is

Figure 6. RBAC authentication flow

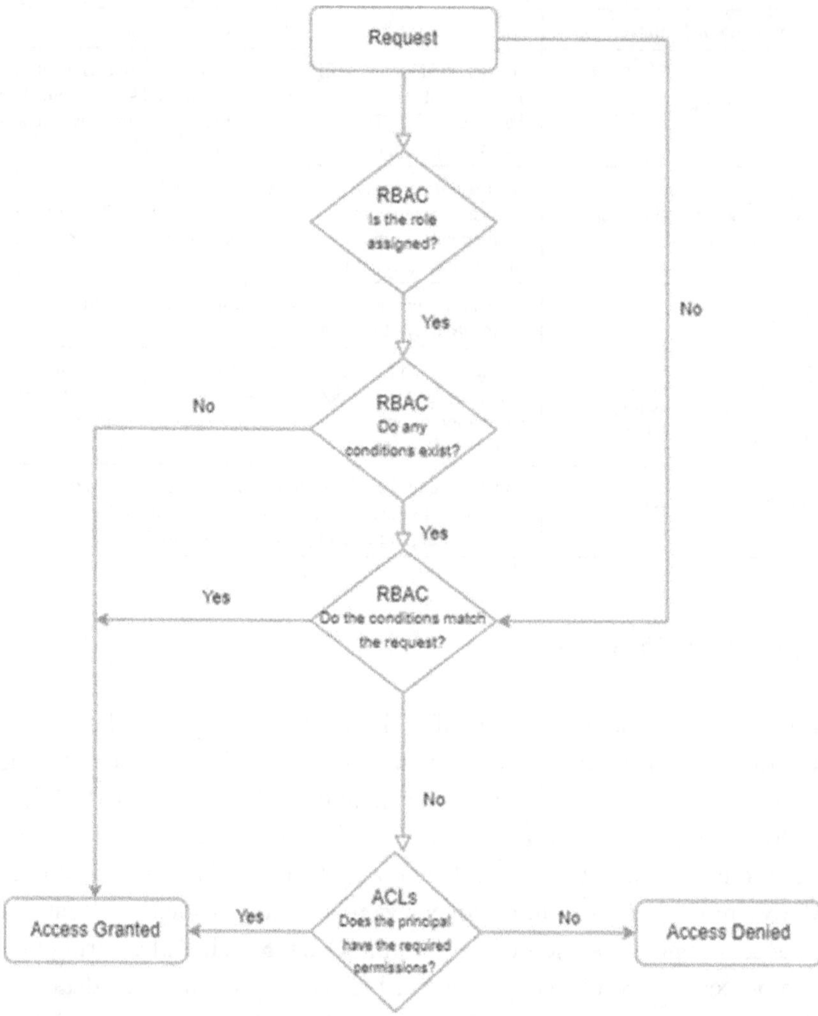

one of the key data sources. RBAC grants users' specific permissions based on their roles, ensuring that access to data is strictly controlled. For example, data upload privileges were granted only to authorized personnel, limiting access to those who require it. This not only aligns with the DGF principles but also provides a highly secure and well-structured approach to managing data access within the DLH. The following are the Data Ingestion guidelines for the DGF.

- Clearly define the types of data to be logged during the data ingestion process, including source data, metadata, and pipeline-related information.

- Utilize Microsoft Azure Data Factory to develop ELT pipelines that facilitate the automated flow of data from source systems to the DLH.
- Log critical pipeline run details, including start time, result, and end time for each data ingestion operation.
- Ensure that timestamps are consistently recovered to provide a timeline of data ingestion events.
- Ingestion of data from multiple sources, including Source System 1, Source System n, and the secured Web Portal.
- Log metadata information for each pipeline run, such as the name of the pipeline, version, and description.
- Include pipeline run status, whether it was successful or encountered issues, to provide a quick overview of the pipeline's performance.
- Orchestration of transformation pipelines using Microsoft Azure Data Factory, enabling data manipulation, and maintaining data quality as per the Data Quality Framework.
- Log details related to data transformation processes, including data quality checks, data enrichment, and any data masking or anonymization applied.
- Record data transformations that occur during the data ingestion process for traceability and audit purposes.
- Implement data masking techniques to protect sensitive information during logging.

Ensure that sensitive data is not exposed in logs, using methods such as,

- Replacing sensitive data with masked values.
- Logging only the necessary portions of sensitive data, if required.
- Ensuring that access to masked data is restricted to authorized personnel.
    - Implement SAS tokens to fortify security. These tokens provide time-limited, fine-grained access control to resources within the DLH.
    - Use of SAS tokens to securely connect data sources to the Data Lake. Access to be granted only to authorized users and specify time periods for access, enhancing security.
    - Rigorous application of data encryption to safeguard data. Utilization of Azure's encryption capabilities to ensure data remains protected during transit and at rest.
    - Implement TLS encryption during data ingestion to secure data in transit, preventing unauthorized access during transmission.
    - Implement RBAC, particularly in the Web Portal, to control data access based on users' roles. Specific permissions to be granted to authorized

personnel, aligning with the DGF principles, and ensuring a well-structured approach to data access management.

Transformation Pipelines

In the Transformation Pipelines, the DLH architecture ensures the seamless and secure flow of data by building upon the robust security measures established during Data Ingestion Pipelines (as previously discussed). Microsoft Azure Data Factory orchestrates these pipelines, facilitating data manipulation and ensuring data quality. As part of the implementation, Azure Purview metadata management was leveraged to track and document metadata related transformation activities, enhancing data governance. In terms of security, SAS tokens continued to be employed to secure data source connections, while data remained encrypted during transit using TLS. RBAC was meticulously applied, ensuring only authorized personnel could access and modify transformation pipelines, aligning with the DLH's stringent data governance and security standards. These measures collectively ensured that data was not only efficiently transformed but also maintained securely and in accordance with data governance principles. The following are the Transformation Pipeline guidelines for the DGF:

- Ensure the transformation pipelines allow the seamless and secure flow of data, building upon the security measures established during Data Ingestion Pipelines.
- Clearly define the types of data to be logged during the transformation process, including source data, metadata, and pipeline-related information.
- Log details related to data transformation processes, including data quality checks, data enrichment, and any data masking or anonymization applied.
- Record data transformations that occur during the data ingestion process for traceability and audit purposes.
- Implement data masking techniques to protect sensitive information during logging.

Ensure that sensitive data is not exposed in logs, using methods such as,

- Replacing sensitive data with masked values.
- Logging only the necessary portions of sensitive data, if required.
- Ensuring that access to masked data is restricted to authorized personnel.
    - Orchestration of transformation pipelines using Microsoft Azure Data Factory, enabling data manipulation, and maintaining data quality as per the Data Quality Framework.

- Include pipeline run status, whether it was successful or encountered issues, to provide a quick overview of the pipeline's performance.
- Leverage Azure Purview metadata management to track and document metadata related to transformation activities. This enhances data governance and ensures comprehensive documentation of data transformations.
- Continue the utilization of SAS tokens to secure data source connections during transformation pipelines. Implement fine-grained access control to maintain data security.
- Apply encryption to data during transit using TLS, ensuring data remains protected during transmission and adheres to security standards.
- Implement RBAC to control access and modifications within the transformation pipelines. Only authorized personnel should have access, aligning with the DLH's data governance and security standards.

Extraction Queries

Extraction Queries represent a critical phase for retrieving and extracting data from the curated container. These queries were essential for generating meaningful insights and reports. To implement this phase effectively, Azure services like Azure Databricks or Azure SQL Database were employed to execute extraction queries. The data governance principles established in the previous sections are consistently applied, ensuring that data access was controlled, data was classified appropriately, and metadata was meticulously managed. Access to the extraction queries were regulated through RBAC to align with predefined roles and permissions, maintaining data security and adherence to governance standards. This phase was pivotal in delivering actionable insights and ensuring that data is extracted and used responsibly within the DLH architecture. The following are the Extraction Query guidelines for the DGF:

- Utilization of Azure Services such as Azure Databricks or Azure SQL Database to execute extraction queries effectively.
- Application of data governance principles consistently in this phase. Ensure that data access is controlled, data is appropriately classified, and metadata is meticulously managed.
- Regulation of access to extraction queries through RBAC to align with redefined roles and permissions. This ensures that only authorized individuals can access and extract data, maintaining data security.

- Emphasize the responsible use of extracted data. Define roles and responsibilities for individuals involved in data extraction to ensure accountability and compliance with data governance standards.
- Prioritize data classification to ensure that sensitive information is handled appropriately. Clearly define data categories and access permissions.
- Continue to manage metadata diligently, including data lineage and provenance tracking. Well-documented metadata enhances the understanding of data assets and their usage.
- Recognize the pivotal role of the extraction phase in delivering actionable insights. Ensure that the data is extracted, processed, and used responsibly within the DLH architecture, contributing to the organization's objectives.

Data Storage

Within the DLH architecture, data storage is a fundamental component, serving as the repository for various data assets and contributing to the overall DGF. The storage components encompass SQL Server Databases, Azure Data Lake Gen2, and Data Marts, each playing a unique role in the data lifecycle. Here is an overview of how these storage elements are implemented in alignment with the established data governance principles.

SQL Server Database

SQL Server Databases within the DLH architecture serve as a structured repository for data, providing a platform for data transformation, integration, and data modeling. Data is securely stored and organized within these databases, ensuring its availability for further analysis and reporting. To maintain data governance, access control was meticulously managed through RBAC, ensuring that only authorized individuals have access to specific data sets. Data classifications and metadata management were seamlessly integrated to categorize data based on its sensitivity and importance, allowing for precise access control policies in compliance with data governance standards. The following are the SQL Server Database Storage in the DLH's guidelines for the DGF:

- Utilize SQL Server Databases as a structured repository for data and metadata within the DLH architecture. These databases serve as a central hub for data transformation, integration, and modeling.
- Ensure data security by meticulously managing access through RBAC. Define roles and permissions to restrict access to specific data sets, aligning with the principle of least privilege.

- Implement data classification mechanisms to categorize data based on its sensitivity and importance. Clearly define data categories to guide access control policies, ensuring that only authorized users have access to specific data sets.
- Integrate metadata management practices within the SQL Server Database. Document data lineage, descriptions, and other metadata to enhance data discoverability and traceability.
- Prioritize data integrity and quality within the database. Implementation of data validation checks and filters to ensure that incoming data adheres to quality standards. Data that fails validation should not be ingested.
- Establish mechanisms for compliance and auditing within the database. Continuously monitor user interactions with the data to detect unauthorized actions or potential data breaches, ensuring compliance with data governance and security standards.
- Use of the SQL Server Database for data modeling and structuring. Organize data in a way that supports analysis, reporting, and other data-driven activities within the DLH.
- Implement data lifecycle management practices to ensure data is retained and disposed of in accordance with data governance policies and regulatory requirements.
- Establish a robust backup and recovery strategy to protect data assets. Regularly back up data to prevent loss and ensure data availability.
- Enable auditing and compliance mechanisms to track user interactions with the data. Regularly review audit logs to detect unauthorized actions or potential data breaches, ensuring compliance with data governance and security requirements.
- Plan for database scalability to accommodate growing data volumes and evolving data storage needs within the DLH.

Azure Data Lake Gen2

Azure Data Lake Gen2 acts as a versatile and scalable repository for a wide range of data, both structured and unstructured. It is important in the DLH architecture by storing raw and curated data. Data classification, encryption, and access control mechanisms are consistently applied to data stored in Azure Data Lake Gen2 to enforce data governance principles. The metadata management capabilities ensure that data lineage, descriptions, and classifications are well-documented, contributing to data discoverability and traceability. The DLH's security measures, such as SAS tokens for secure data source connections and data encryption in transit and at rest, continued to be rigorously maintained within Azure Data Lake Gen2, enforcing data security. The following are the Azure Data Lake Gen2 guidelines for the DGF:

- Utilize Azure Data Lake Gen2 as a versatile and scalable repository for storing raw and curated data within the DLH architecture.
- Implement data classification mechanisms to categorize data based on its sensitivity and importance. Clearly define data categories to guide access control policies and ensure that data is handled appropriately.
- Enforce data encryption both in transit and at rest within Azure Data Lake Gen2. Utilization of TLS encryption during data ingestion to secure data in transit. Ensure that data stored in the repository is encrypted at rest to protect sensitive data assets.
- Apply access control mechanisms to restrict data access based on RBAC principles. Define roles and permissions to ensure that only authorized individuals or roles can interact with specific data sets.
- Implement comprehensive metadata management practices within Azure Data Lake Gen2. Document data lineage, descriptions, classifications, and other metadata details to enhance data discoverability and traceability.
- Establish data retention and disposal policies to manage the lifecycle of data stored in Azure Data Lake Gen2. Define procedures for data retention and ensure that data is disposed of in compliance with regulatory requirements.
- Implement data quality checks and validation mechanisms to ensure that data ingested into the repository adheres to defined quality standards. Data that fails validation should not be stored.
- Enable auditing and compliance mechanisms to track user interactions with the data. Regularly review audit logs to detect unauthorized actions or potential data breaches, ensuring compliance with data governance and security requirements.
- Plan for the scalability of Azure Data Lake Gen2 to accommodate growing data volumes and evolving data storage needs within the DLH.

Data Marts

Data Marts are tailored data repositories designed to support specific business functions or departments within the organization. These repositories were populated with data transformed and refined in alignment with the DLH's data governance standards. Metadata management plays a critical role in documenting the contents and purpose of each Data Mart, ensuring clarity and ease of access. RBAC is employed to restrict access to Data Marts based on user roles, adhering to the principle of least privilege. Data classification and security measures extend to Data Marts, contributing to the overall data governance and ensuring that users access only the data pertinent to their roles and responsibilities. The following are the guidelines for Data Marts in the DGF:

- Each Data Mart should align with a specific business function's data need.
- Populate Data Marts with data that has been transformed and refined in accordance with DLH data governance standards. Ensure that data quality and accuracy are maintained during the transformation process.
- Implement robust metadata management practices for Data Marts. Document the contents and purpose of each Data Mart, including data lineage, descriptions, classifications, and any other relevant metadata. This documentation enhances data discoverability and clarity.
- Apply RBAC to restrict access to Data Marts. Define roles and permissions that align with specific user responsibilities, adhering to the principle of least privilege. Ensure that users can only access the data relevant to their roles.
- Enforce data security measures within Data Marts to protect the confidentiality and integrity of the data. Implement data encryption for data at rest and transit, ensuring that sensitive information remains secure.
- Extension data classification mechanisms to Data Marts. Classify data within these repositories based on sensitivity and importance. This classification should guide access control and data handling within Data Marts.
- Define data retention and disposal policies specific to each Data Mart. These policies should align with regulatory requirements and ensure that data is managed throughout its lifecycle.
- Implement data quality assurance processes within Data Marts. Regularly monitor and validate data to maintain high data quality standards. Data that fails validation should not be included.
- Ensure that metadata consistency is maintained across Data Marts. Consistent metadata practices make it easier for users to understand and work with data from different repositories.
- Enable auditing and compliance mechanisms for Data Marts to track user interactions with the data. Regularly review audit logs to detect unauthorized actions or potential data breaches, ensuring compliance with data governance and security requirements.
- Plan for the scalability of Data Marts to accommodate growing data volumes and evolving data storage needs within the DLH.

Incorporating these storage components within the DLH architecture not only enables efficient data management but also enforces robust data governance practices. Data classifications, metadata management, access controls, and encryption collectively ensure that data is handled securely and in compliance with these established data governance principles.

Paper-Based Governance

Paper-based Governance is underpinned by the analysis of organizational documents presented in Table 5. This analysis delved into the organizational structure of the GTA, revealing a hierarchical structure with a Board at the helm, led by the CEO. The organizational structure also includes key positions such as the Board Secretary, Committee Secretary, Ethics & Governance Officer, and Admin. Moreover, the GTA houses a Legal and Compliance office, encompassing roles that extend throughout the organization.

The study's document analysis further uncovered that the GTA already has existing data policies and procedures in place for its source systems. This existing framework serves as a foundation upon which the Paper-based governance of the DLH can be built. It establishes a basis for aligning the DLH's data governance with the GTA's established data practices and regulations, ensuring consistency and compliance.

Key elements such as stakeholder engagement provide essential building blocks for paper-based governance within the DLH. These elements emphasize the importance of actively engaging stakeholders from various GTA divisions and teams. They encourage feedback and input to shape data governance practices that meet specific needs and objectives, ensuring that the DGF aligns with the GTA's mission and goals.

The concept of a Data Governance Committee, which includes roles like the Chief Steward, Business Data Steward, and Technical Data Steward, offers a framework for defining responsibilities and ensuring that the necessary roles and duties are distributed throughout the organization. The Chief Steward plays a critical role in setting control mechanisms and specifying conditions for the implementation of the DGF.

The assignment of Data Stewards, including Data Quality Steward, Compliance Steward, Access Control Steward, and Metadata Steward, outlines the accountability structure for managing information assets. These stewards are responsible for data security, quality, compliance with regulatory requirements, access control, and metadata management, ensuring that data is governed effectively within the DLH.

The designation of Data Owners, Data Custodians, and Data Customers defines the roles and responsibilities of individuals within the GTA who are essential for effective governance. Data Owners are responsible for governing specific data assets related to training programs and services. Data Custodians focus on the technical aspects of data management, while Data Customers rely on data driven insights for decision-making.

Procedure Documentation

Paper-based governance is an essential facet of the DGF, encompassing the creation, documentation, and maintenance of data governance policies, guidelines, and procedures in written form. These documents are integral to governing data handling, access controls and security within the DLH. Comprehensive data governance policies serve as the overarching framework, covering data classification, retention, access controls, and compliance requirements, all meticulously aligned with the specific DGF developed for the GTA.

Written procedures guide the lifecycle, from data ingestion to transformation, storage, extraction, and disposal, ensuring the consistent application of data governance standards. Access control guidelines were documented, specifying the implementation of RBAC within the DLH. These guidelines define role definitions, permissions, and access management procedures to enhance data security.

Data classification standards, documented in written form, categorize data based on sensitivity and importance, serving as a valuable reference for correct data asset classification. Best practices for metadata management, encompassing data lineage, descriptions, and metadata tagging, were documented to ensure data assets are well documented and easily discoverable.

To ensure adherence to regulatory and compliance requirements, compliance documentation outlines measures, audit trails, and data retention policies within the DLH. These paper-based governance documents collectively serve as a backbone of the DLH's DGF, providing clear, structured, and easily accessible reference for all stakeholders engaged in data management. They ensure the consistent application of data governance principles, align with the specific GTA DGF, and significantly contribute to the overall effectiveness and security of the DLH system. The following are the DGF guidelines for formal requesting of data and documents from the DLH.

- Formal data and document requests must be initiated in writing, either in electronic or hard copy format.
- Include the requester's name, department, and contact information to facilitate communication.
- Clearly state the purpose of the data or document request, explaining the need and intended use.
- Ensure that the request aligns with the organization's mission and objectives.
- Specify the type of data, documents, or reports required for the request.
- Provide detailed descriptions, including data elements, document titles, or report topics.
- Define the timeframe for data or document delivery, specifying deadlines or preferred delivery dates.

- Consider the urgency of the request and realistic processing timelines.
- If applicable, indicate the sensitivity level of the requested data and the corresponding data classification.
- Ensure compliance with data classification standards and access controls.
- Confirm that the data or document request adheres to legal and regulatory requirements, including privacy laws and data protection regulations.
- Clearly state any specific access or security requirements related to the requested data or documents.
- Specify if additional security measures, such as data masking or encryption, are necessary.
- Provide details about the intended recipient of the requested data or documents.
- Specify the recipient's role, responsibilities, and any access permissions required.
- Include an authorization section for the requester's supervisor or designated authority to review and approve the request.
- Ensure that only authorized personnel can make formal data and document requests.
- Ensure that the data request aligns with the established DGF and policies.
- Verify that the request complies with the documented data handling and access control guidelines.
- Maintain records of all formal data and document requests, including the request, approval, and fulfillment processes.
- Document any changes, discussions, or decisions related to the request.
- Acknowledge the receipt of the data or document request promptly and provide an estimated timeline for processing.
- Keep the requester informed of the request's progress and any delays.
- Implement quality checks to ensure the accuracy and completeness of the provided data, documents, or reports.
- Verify that the content meets the requester's specifications.
- Use secure and authorized channels for the delivery of requested data or documents, ensuring data security during transmission.
- Encourage the requester to provide feedback or suggestions for improvement after receiving the requested data or documents.
- Consider feedback for enhancing future data and document request processes.

FRAMEWORK EVALUATION

The evaluation of the data governance framework and guidelines developed was done by presenting the framework to an industry expert in data engineering and governance. The expert was asked to evaluate the results using the following four-point Likert scale: (1) Guidelines are insufficient or invalid, (2) Guidelines are valid, but lack sufficient detail, (3) Guidelines are valid, but there are gaps that need to be addressed, and (4) Guidelines are valid, and no gaps were identified. The expert was also given the opportunity to provide comments and suggestions to enhance the framework. Regulatory compliance was not assessed as part of this evaluation, as it was determined that stakeholders from the GTA would be required to assess and amend these guidelines.

The results of the expert evaluation are presented in Table 6.

Table 6. Expert evaluation results

Data Lake House Component	Access Control and Security	Metadata Management	Data Quality	Data Ownership and Stakeholder Engagement
Ingestion Pipelines	2	2	1	3
Transformation Pipelines	2	3	3	3
Extraction Queries	3	3	3	4
Azure SQL Database	4	4	4	4
Azure Data Lake Gen2	4	4	3	4
Data Marts	4	4	4	4
Paper-based Governance	4	4	4	4

From the results in Table 6, it is evident that the guidelines presented have deficiencies in ensuring data quality for both ingestion and transformation pipelines. This has resulted in the DUT team conducting separate studies into specific quality frameworks to address these deficiencies, which is future research that will be considered for publication.

Areas for enhancement identified by the industry expert included developing more sophisticated development management processes and considering the cost implications of unoptimized transformations. These areas affect the ongoing maintenance of the DLH and are dynamic areas that must be iteratively improved upon throughout the development and maintenance project lifecycle.

CONCLUDING REMARKS

This chapter presented a data governance framework designed for a data lakehouse system that is being developed for a South African Government-sector training authority. A rigorous systematic review was conducted using the PRISMA methodology. The systematic review identified 45 articles from literature, which were analyzed and distilled to a final set of 15 studies that were deemed most relevant. A meta-analysis was conducted to motivate the recency and validity of the final set of articles. Five key components of data governance relevant to the framework being developed were identified: (i) access control and security, (ii) data quality, (iii) data ownership, stewardship and stakeholder engagement, (iv) metadata management, and (v) regulatory compliance.

The theoretical elements of the data governance framework were then applied to the and described governance mechanisms for each component of the system; as well as paper-based and procedural elements of data governance for the overall system. An expert practitioner evaluation was conducted to verify the effectiveness of the governance mechanisms. Deficiencies were noted in terms of mechanisms to ensure data quality, which has been noted as an area for improvement in future work. Subsequent studies that specifically address data quality for the designed data lakehouse system are being conducted.

Other areas of interest for future work include a longitudinal study that evaluates the long-term effectiveness of the data governance mechanisms developed, and any subsequent enhancements made, as well as conducting and assessing the regulatory compliance of the system at a more detailed level.

REFERENCES

Abraham, R., Schneider, J., & vom Brocke, J. (2019). Data governance: A conceptual framework, structured review, and research agenda. *International Journal of Information Management*, *49*, 424–438. doi:10.1016/j.ijinfomgt.2019.07.008

Al-Ruithe, M., Benkhelifa, E., & Hameed, K. (2019). A systematic literature review of data governance and cloud data governance. *Personal and Ubiquitous Computing*, *23*(5), 839–859. doi:10.1007/s00779-017-1104-3

Amo, D., Gómez, P., Hernández-Ibáñez, L., & Fonseca, D. (2021). Educational Warehouse: Modular, Private and Secure Cloudable Architecture System for Educational Data Storage, Analysis and Access. *Applied Sciences (Basel, Switzerland)*, *11*(2), 806. doi:10.3390/app11020806

Armbrust, M., Ghodsi, A., Xin, R., & Zaharia, M. (2021). Lakehouse: a new generation of open platforms that unify data warehousing and advanced analytics. *11th Annual Conference on Innovative Data Systems Research (CIDR '21).*

Azeroual, O., Nikiforova, A., & Sha, K. (2023). *Overlooked Aspects of Data Governance: Workflow Framework For Enterprise Data Deduplication. 2023 International Conference on Intelligent Computing, Communication, Networking and Services (ICCNS)*, Valencia, Spain.

Azeroual, O., Schöpfel, J., Ivanovic, D., & Nikiforova, A. (2022). Combining Data Lake and Data Wrangling for Ensuring Data Quality in CRIS. *Procedia Computer Science, 211*, 3–16. doi:10.1016/j.procs.2022.10.171

Dibowski, H., Schmid, S., Svetashova, Y., Henson, C., & Tran, T. (2020). Using Semantic Technologies to Manage a Data Lake: Data Catalog, Provenance and Access Control. *Proceedings of the 13th International Workshop on Scalable Semantic Web Knowledge Base Systems (SSWS 2020).*

Djiroun, R., Boukhalfa, K., & Alimazighi, Z. (2019). Designing data cubes in OLAP systems: A decision makers' requirements-based approach. *Cluster Computing, 22*(3), 783–803. doi:10.1007/s10586-018-2883-7

Edastama, P., Dudhat, A., & Maulani, G. (2021). Use of Data Warehouse and Data Mining for Academic Data: A Case Study at a National University. *International Journal of Cyber and IT Service Management, 1*(2), 206–215. doi:10.34306/ijcitsm.v1i2.55

Eichler, R., Giebler, C., Gröger, C., Schwarz, H., & Mitschang, B. (2021). Modeling metadata in data lakes—A generic model. *Data & Knowledge Engineering, 136*, 101931. doi:10.1016/j.datak.2021.101931

Etaati, L. (2019). Azure Databricks. In L. Etaati (Ed.), *Machine Learning with Microsoft Technologies: Selecting the Right Architecture and Tools for Your Project* (pp. 159–171). Apress. doi:10.1007/978-1-4842-3658-1_10

Gupta, I., Singh, A. K., Lee, C. N., & Buyya, R. (2022). Secure Data Storage and Sharing Techniques for Data Protection in Cloud Environments: A Systematic Review, Analysis, and Future Directions. *IEEE Access : Practical Innovations, Open Solutions, 10*, 71247–71277. doi:10.1109/ACCESS.2022.3188110

Hamadou, H. B., Pedersen, T. B., & Thomsen, C. (2020). *The Danish National Energy Data Lake: Requirements, Technical Architecture, and Tool Selection.* 2020 IEEE International Conference on Big Data (Big Data), Atlanta, GA.

Harby, A. A., & Zulkernine, F. (2022). *From Data Warehouse to Lakehouse: A Comparative Review*. 2022 IEEE International Conference on Big Data (Big Data), Osaka, Japan.

Hillman, V. (2023). Bringing in the technological, ethical, educational and social-structural for a new education data governance. *Learning, Media and Technology*, *48*(1), 122–137. doi:10.1080/17439884.2022.2052313

Hlupić, T., Oreščanin, D., Ružak, D., & Baranović, M. (2022). *An Overview of Current Data Lake Architecture Models*. 2022 45th Jubilee International Convention on Information, Communication and Electronic Technology (MIPRO), Opatija, Croatia.

Janssen, M., Brous, P., Estevez, E., Barbosa, L. S., & Janowski, T. (2020). Data governance: Organizing data for trustworthy Artificial Intelligence. *Government Information Quarterly*, *37*(3), 101493. doi:10.1016/j.giq.2020.101493

Karkošková, S. (2023). Data Governance Model To Enhance Data Quality In Financial Institutions. *Information Systems Management*, *40*(1), 90–110. doi:10.1080/10580530.2022.2042628

Kayes, A. S. M., Rahayu, W., Watters, P., Alazab, M., Dillon, T., & Chang, E. (2020). Achieving security scalability and flexibility using Fog-Based Context-Aware Access Control. *Future Generation Computer Systems*, *107*, 307–323. doi:10.1016/j.future.2020.02.001

Kimball, R., & Ross, M. (2013). *The Data Warehouse Toolkit: The Definitive Guide to Dimensional Modeling*. Wiley. https://books.google.co.za/books?id=4rFXzk8wAB8C

Kurniawan, D. H., Ruldeviyani, Y., Adrian, M. R., Handayani, S., & Pohan, M. R., & R. K, T. (2019). *Data Governance Maturity Assessment: A Case Study in IT Bureau of Audit Board*. 2019 International Conference on Information Management and Technology (ICIMTech), Jakarta & Bali, Indonesia. 10.1109/ICIMTech.2019.8843742

Mao, Z., Wu, J., Qiao, Y., & Yao, H. (2022). Government data governance framework based on a data middle platform. *Aslib Journal of Information Management*, *74*(2), 289–310. doi:10.1108/AJIM-03-2021-0068

Marcucci, S., Alarcon, N. G., Verhulst, S. G., & Wullhorst, E. (2023). Mapping and Comparing Data Governance Frameworks: A benchmarking exercise to inform global data governance deliberations. *arXiv preprint arXiv:2302.13731*.

Miloslavskaya, N., & Tolstoy, A. (2016). Big Data, Fast Data and Data Lake Concepts. *Procedia Computer Science*, *88*, 300–305. doi:10.1016/j.procs.2016.07.439

Mohlameane, M., & Ruxwana, N. (2020). Exploring the impact of cloud computing on existing South African regulatory frameworks. *South African Journal of Information Management, 22*(1), 1–9. doi:10.4102/sajim.v22i1.1132

Monah, S. R., Wagner, M. W., Biswas, A., Khalvati, F., Erdman, L. E., Amirabadi, A., Vidarsson, L., McCradden, M. D., & Ertl-Wagner, B. B. (2022). Data governance functions to support responsible data stewardship in pediatric radiology research studies using artificial intelligence. *Pediatric Radiology, 52*(11), 2111–2119. doi:10.1007/s00247-022-05427-2 PMID:35790559

Nambiar, A., & Mundra, D. (2022). An Overview of Data Warehouse and Data Lake in Modern Enterprise Data Management. *Big Data and Cognitive Computing, 6*(4).

Oreščanin, D., & Hlupić, T. (2021). *Data Lakehouse - a Novel Step in Analytics Architecture*. 2021 44th International Convention on Information, Communication and Electronic Technology (MIPRO), Opatija, Croatia.

Osakwe, S., & Adeniran, A. P. (2021). *Strengthening Data Governance in Africa: Project Inception Report*. Centre for the Study of Economies of Africa.

Page, M. J., McKenzie, J. E., Bossuyt, P. M., Boutron, I., Hoffmann, T. C., Mulrow, C. D., Shamseer, L., Tetzlaff, J. M., Akl, E. A., Brennan, S. E., Chou, R., Glanville, J., Grimshaw, J. M., Hróbjartsson, A., Lalu, M. M., Li, T., Loder, E. W., Mayo-Wilson, E., McDonald, S., ... Moher, D. (2021). The PRISMA 2020 statement: An updated guideline for reporting systematic reviews. *Systematic Reviews, 10*(1), 89. doi:10.1186/s13643-021-01626-4 PMID:33781348

Paschalidi, C. (2015). *Data Governance: A conceptual framework in order to prevent your Data Lake from becoming a Data Swamp* [Master of Science in Information Security Thesis, Luleå University of Technology]. Digitala Vetenskapliga Arkivet (DiVA). https://www.diva-portal.org/smash/record.jsf?pid=diva2%3A1019917

Raj, A., Bosch, J., Olsson, H. H., & Wang, T. J. (2020). Modelling Data Pipelines. *2020 46th Euromicro Conference on Software Engineering and Advanced Applications (SEAA).*

Sarramia, D., Claude, A., Ogereau, F., Mezhoud, J., & Mailhot, G. (2022). CEBA: A Data Lake for Data Sharing and Environmental Monitoring. *Sensors (Basel), 22*(7), 2733. doi:10.3390/s22072733 PMID:35408347

Sawadogo, P., & Darmont, J. (2021). On data lake architectures and metadata management. *Journal of Intelligent Information Systems, 56*(1), 97–120. doi:10.1007/s10844-020-00608-7

Wibowo, S., & Sandikapura, T. (2019). *Improving Data Security, Interoperability, and Veracity using Blockchain for One Data Governance, Case Study of Local Tax Big Data*. 2019 International Conference on ICT for Smart Society (ICISS), Bandung, Indonesia.

Xue, K., Chen, W., Li, W., Hong, J., & Hong, P. (2018). Combining Data Owner-Side and Cloud-Side Access Control for Encrypted Cloud Storage. *IEEE Transactions on Information Forensics and Security*, *13*(8), 2062–2074. doi:10.1109/TIFS.2018.2809679

KEY TERMS AND DEFINITIONS

Data Governance Framework: A set of guiding principles that the exercise of authority, control, and shared decision making over the management of data assets.

Data Lakehouse: An enterprise information system that facilitates the analysis of structured, semi-structured or unstructured data by an organization.

Data Management: The operational and strategic management of data assets.

Chapter 8
Development, Monitoring, and Management Approaches of Machine Learning Implementations for the Effective Delivery of Government Services

Santosh Ramkrishna Durugkar
https://orcid.org/0000-0002-5079-2224
Independent Researcher, India

ABSTRACT

New age technologies like machine learning, artificial intelligence, and deep learning are playing a crucial role in many applications. The chapter focuses on development, monitoring, and management approaches to machine learning implementation for effective government service deliveries. Government forms different policies and aims to successfully pass them to the citizens. The government service deliveries include many sectors like healthcare system, education policies, foreign policies, infrastructure and construction policies, public transportation policies, etc. Machine learning (ML), deep learning (DL), and artificial intelligence (AI) provide many methods like time series analysis, regression, classification, reinforcement learning, clustering, dimensionality reduction, long short-term memory, etc. These methods help retrieving meaningful data from the large volume and predict the desired results. These technologies already revolutionized many sectors like automating the application processes, fetching the relevant and required data instantly, etc.

DOI: 10.4018/978-1-6684-9716-6.ch008

1. INTRODUCTION

This chapter gives brief introduction of machine learning techniques like classification, regression, time series analysis etc. These techniques are widely used in many applications for the better accuracy and results. Governments provide services to the citizens with the changing trend of digitization & it is necessary to convert the same into e-services (e-portals). Citizens can access these services from any location, upload required documents and track their requests (applications), administrators or the concerned authorities can have a '*dashboard*' to analyze, and process the submitted data. There are many benefits of applying the recent machine learning (ML) and artificial intelligence (AI) methods for the development of e-services. With the help of ML methods, one can develop e-portals, monitor and manage the developed e-services (e-portals) and contribute in effective delivery of these services to the citizens. With the digitization of services there are few risks associated with the data privacy, and cyber-attacks. Hence, stringent mechanisms can be integrated (as a security layer) in every services to prevent the cyber-attack and maintain the data privacy. *Actually, every e-service (e-portal) must be developed including a CIA security i.e. confidentiality, integrity and availability.* With the help of AI and ML techniques it is possible to cater various services to the citizens (large population) within minimum time and efforts. Hence, using recent AI and ML methods one can develop prescriptive, descriptive and decision making models. However, at the same time it is the responsibility of the governments to securely and ethically establish the proposed framework of policies.

As mentioned earlier, there are many sectors where new age technologies can help governments to effectively apply their polices are *managing the traffic flow, incident prevention* (unwanted incident), *cyber-attack prevention, providing world class healthcare facilities, automating task in many fields, linking various documents and representing them into a unique format* etc. Recently world has faced a pandemic situation like Covid-19, hence using such newly age technologies one can develop a model predicting if any pandemic situation could occur in the future? *There are many methods like regression and classification which can be used to predict the future values.* Even it is possible to analyze the historical climate related data & predictive model can be prepared forecasting the tentative temperature, rainfall etc.

Logistics, infrastructure and construction fields can be revolutionize with the help of these technologies. *It is also necessary to work on transportation i.e. by road, by rail and using by sea transportation.* It means smoothing the transportation by minimizing the accidents, connecting the maximum cities and once this phase successfully completes it benefits the import-export businesses. Such revolution automatically increases the gross domestic product (GDP) of the citizens. Once the GDP of citizens increases it positively affects (increases) the economy of the country. *As discussed these technologies can be used for infrastructure and civil construction, it enables government agencies to carefully observe if there are any illegal constructions or people are changing their properties & not paying the taxes. Autonomous computing* can be introduced in the small to large applications where a citizen can file any application from home (anywhere) and can track it further. *The most beautiful advantage of this digital automation is 'paperless' applications in many sectors. Therefore, paper and application cost significantly reduces and approval process becomes more transparent and easier.* However it must be noted, there are many challenges in application of these new age technologies. With the help of these technologies it is possible to store, process and make available the required data to the citizens at any time (access transparency). Even it is possible to develop a 'guide to citizen' (gov-bot) application guiding citizens about any queries. It can also guide the citizens in application process with all the necessary requirements. Decision support systems (DSS) are the best examples of these technologies and a good governance based on DSS can be develop to take better decision by evaluating large volume of data. *Knowledge management, predictive modeling, threat intelligence (cyber-attack prevention), automation and visualization etc. are the few approaches of machine learning which can be used in setting good governance.*

The ML methods are divided into supervised and unsupervised learning categories. One of the popular methods '*regression*' processes the integrated data and predicts the possible value. '*Classification*' a supervised learning ML method classifies the input data which is very useful for the government. With the help of 'classification' approach an e-service model for the government can classify the citizen data based on gender, income, tax liabilities, education etc. '*Dimensionality reduction*' method can be applied to reduce the data (dimensions). *PCA – principal component analysis* a dimensionality reduction method helps reducing the feature space and identifies important vectors only. '*Ensemble method*' can be developed by integrating ML models predicting with maximum accuracy. '*Random forest*' and '*Decision tree*' processes many datasets and improves the effectiveness of prediction. It is also possible to develop an e-service using 'reinforcement learning' method of ML focusing on the 'output' and based on the observed 'output' (results) takes next steps (actions). This process continues with the 'n' iterations and determines the step (action) was correct or incorrect.

2. REVIEW OF LITERATURE

The research study focuses on consumer's complaints (Chen, Y. et al. 2018) which is very important to improvise the businesses & services. It may be possible that, for a particular service or business 'n' people may lodge 'm' complaints or feedbacks.

It could be difficult tasks for human to differentiate them into various segments. Hence, authors have suggested with the help of machine learning (ML) methods like classification one can easily classify the 'm' complaints into different classes. Once the machine learning model adopted for this task finishes there are many chances to improvise the service or business. Based on the classification methods like *SVM, naïve Bayes* etc. classification becomes easier and it also enables the model to identify the consumer segment. Especially this approach is beneficial to the sales & marketing sector. There are many visualization methods exists to visualize the consumer segment, changes in the complaints, complaints raised and resolved. Hence, responsible authorities (like grievance officer) can have a dashboard on his system showing the complaints raised, complaints assigned to concern authorities and resolved etc. This approach also identifies the concerned person, authority responsible for specific task. Additionally, if the task have deadline then dashboard can shows the reasons behind delay.

Big Data is nothing but large volume of data and the research study (Alexopoulos, C., et al. 2019) discusses the generation, and processing of the big data. It is obvious that, e-service portals may receive 'm' feedbacks, 'n' applications and large volume of supporting data. Therefore, proposed models for e-services must be capable enough to process the large volume of data. However, important point discussed in this research work focuses on retrieving the hidden, meaningful information from the large volume with the help of existing machine learning techniques. Machine learning techniques are capable to process the large volume of data and helps in decision making process. Governments can explore different possible opportunities after processing the big data. This approach helps finding new ways catering the future services to the citizens. *Banking, logistics, real estate, defense etc. are the major government sectors which can be improve with the application of machine learning and artificial intelligence techniques.* The research work (Dana, R. D. et al. 2019) emphasizes on the health services provided to the citizens. Citizens expect good quality health-care services from the governments and governments are also responsible to provide the same. However, providing the health-care services to the large population is quite difficult. Classification and clustering based ML models groups the population in different *income groups* and provides the required services to the eligible citizens. Therefore, this research work discusses the 'satisfaction ratings' given by the patients (citizens) improvising the quality of health-care services. '*Satisfaction*' of the patients must be considered as an indicator to evaluate the performance of the service. Research study suggests with the help of clustering algorithm like k-means, C-means one can group the different satisfaction (ratings) given by the patients. Experiment conducted in this research work evaluates the algorithmic performance based on the grouping of 'n' satisfactions and concluded that k-means gave 96% accuracy whereas the C-means gave 76%. This research study showed that, machine learning (ML) methods (clustering) are very useful in grouping of different feedbacks, ratings of the citizens for the various services offered by the government. Authors (Veale & Brass 2019) have discussed a data analysis approach providing good quality e-services. e-services are the digitized transformation of government services enabling the access of e-service from any place. Citizens can access the e-service portals from remote location without visiting concerned offices which significantly reduces the efforts & cost. Authors have discussed the use of machine learning techniques in daily operations of the e-service portals. This research work focuses on the administrative reforms with data analytics approach. *New machine learning methods bridges the gap between citizens and the government.* The ultimate goal of such approach is providing better quality e-services to the citizens. Administration plays an important role in government, private sector and public sector enterprises. A good quality administration keenly observes the data, process that data and apply the reforms wherever applicable.

Author (Henman, 2020) have discussed advantages of applying the artificial intelligence (AI) techniques in multiple sectors. AI, ML and IoT applications are very popular and help improvising the existing applications especially in medical, public sector, and defense. AI, ML methods can be applied in better decision making process. Meaningful, required relevant information must be retrieved from the large volume of data. Being human it is usually difficult to process the large volume of data & requires intelligent machines and algorithms to process the same. Government provides various e-services to the citizens and requires proper administration to check whether the citizens are happy with the provided services. Therefore to have a good administration e-portal, there are few challenges like accuracy, bias and discrimination. Hence, machine learning techniques such as time series analysis, regression and classification etc. help improving the administration skills.

Authors (Balta et al. 2021) have discussed the advantages of applications of machine learning methods. Authors have discussed the importance of storing the large volume of data and processing it using recent ML techniques. Authors noted the advantage of keeping 'data' at central place. However, ML models can be developed processing the data without moving it to the central place. *This research work emphasizes on the legislative framework to process the data. Accountability, trustworthiness and privacy are the key factors which must be considered while processing the public and private data.* Recent technologies and the requirement of advanced machines (system configuration) were discussed in the research work (Yulu Pi, 2021) focusing on the rapidly increasing data size & the required computational power. It is necessary to process the data and take perfect decision accordingly. This research paper focuses on application of machine learning methods in government applications providing the e-services to the citizens. *Proper administration, processing the data and retrieving the relevant required information, and better decision making are the key aspects of the applications of AI and ML techniques.* Authors (Dreyling et al. 2021) have discussed the use of ML, AI applications in government portals. This research work gives *multi-dimensional view of ML and AI methods.* Authors have listed various key factors related to social, legal and technical aspects of the AI and ML methods. This research is related to the Estonian government services for their citizens and taking feedbacks from the citizens. Application of the recent machine learning methods improves the government services & ultimately bridges the gap between government and the citizens. An 'email' case study was discussed in this research work i.e. citizens emailing to the various government offices, concerned authorities etc. Citizens expect their queries must be resolved on an earlier basis by the concerned officials. However as per the population size the 'emails' could be more than expected and government officials, employees has to deal with such large volume of emails. This process consumes more time because it adds one more step in this process i.e. after reading the email, government officials and employees forwards the same to the concerned departments. With the application of AI and ML techniques a 'decision engine' dealing with these emails can be developed helps forwarding them automatically to the respective departments. This approach saves more time in 'email handling' with better decision making.

Authors (Mengesha & Ayanso 2021) have discussed e-government key aspects & initiatives taken to improvise the same. In this research work, authors have mentioned the UN e-government development index structure used to calculate the weight of various services provided to the citizens. Government offers 'n' online services, telecom services, infra services, and health services etc. to the citizens. *It is necessary for the governments to measure the effectiveness of all the provided services.* Hence, appropriate measurements must be applied to calculate the effectiveness of these services. It shows efforts taken by the government over the specific time period and helps improving in the weaker sections. Authors have presented the research work of the policies adopted by the nations over the time. This research work concludes with the implications of the proposed approach and resulted insights obtained. Author (Wei, 2022) have discussed the contributing factors in the effective e-government. It consists of socio-economic factors which must be carefully studied to improve the e-services. The research work proposed by the author uses machine learning algorithms and performs data analysis. Research work presents an intelligent analysis model for the effective e-governance. Author executed a cloud computing based simulation of the "e-government model" in order to show its effectiveness. Authors (AlDhaheri et al. 2022) have discussed the importance of digital revolution in many sectors. Everyone understood the necessity of the digitized services in many sectors such as banking and finance, medical, infra, and other government services. The research work proposed by the authors identifies the relation between machine learning based digitization and the services offered by the UAE government. Researchers, academician, government authorities etc. understood the importance of digitization. Governments are responsible for catering various services to its citizens. With the help of digitization, new ways of innovation are possible and use of digitized services always intends to provide quality services. Research work concludes with the discussion of digital revolution and its various implications. Authors (Duan et al. 2023) have represented a research study to help identifying accountability in endowment of services to the citizens. This research study also helps administrators in better decision making. Research work is based on "text mining" methods and machine learning algorithms applied on social media data i.e. Twitter data. The proposed research work also classifies the integrated data with the help of naïve Bayes, Random forest, and XGBoost algorithms. Other advantage of the research work is handling the imbalanced data distribution and extracting opinions/feedbacks. With the help of proposed research work authors have differentiated two social media platforms. The observed values of different social media platforms can be used to improve the effectiveness of government services.

Authors (Samuel, P. et al. 2023) discussed effective delivery of the E-government. E-services are developed in order to give multiple benefits to the citizens. The aim of applying e-services is to improve the living standards of the citizens. Authors have also discussed the big data analytics approach used to effective deliver the e-services. This research study focuses on the various aspects involved in the big data computing.

Authors (Ibrahim, I. K. et al. 2023) discussed the threat of cybercrime and the need of stringent security measures to avoid the same. Authors have mentioned though e-governance applications are gaining popularity among the citizens but there is threat to the data's privacy and security. E-services transmit data from one machine to another and hence there is need to secure it using strong 'encryption' methods. Research study presented a framework identifying the various 'threats' to the internet traffic. Pre-processing, correlating and selecting the best results are the few steps involved in the proposed research work. Authors have discussed machine learning (ML) methods to distinguish the 'internet traffic' into normal traffic and suspicious traffic. Application of support vector machine (SVM) achieved great accuracy with 99.16%. The objective of this research work is to 'protect the data' during transmission from one machine to another. Authors (Duggar, D. et al. 2023) handling complex big data using recent techniques. Big data could be structured, semi-structured and unstructured and size of the data is increasing rapidly. Authors have discussed e-government services have dealing with big data & it must analyze big data properly for better insights. Research study reveals how big data must be analyzed in e-governance using different big analytics techniques by designing a framework for the same. Authors (Gkikas, D. C. et al. 2023) proposed a chapter based on the use of artificial intelligence (AI) in agriculture sector. AI and ML methods can be used to develop smart applications for different sectors. This chapter discussed how various nations are investing in smart technologies to improvise the citizen's lives. The main advantage of smart technologies is there is always a scope to modify, improve the application. The research study (Ali, M. 2023) focused on digital transformation in e-governance. These e-services should be citizen centric and must process the data efficiently and effectively. It is expected, citizens must participate in developing e-services by giving proper feedbacks, responses, and ratings for the various e-services offered by the governments.

This research study devises a new concept e-democracy enabling more participation of the citizens in decision making models. Author (Khouya, M. 2023) explained how information and communication technology (ICT) have uplifted the society. Especially, public governance benefitted using different ICT applications. Author have discussed ICT strengthen the e-governance and benefit the society. The proposed research study focused on various aspects of ICT in government's e-services. This paper also enlists challenges and other aspects of AI and ML in e-governance. The main concern in this regard is data's privacy and security. To handle and solve technical issues in e-services it is necessary to have skillful employees.

3. MACHINE LEARNING APPROACHES FOR E-SERVICES

3. 1 Time Series Analysis and Visualization

As its name indicates '*time series analysis*' is related with the historical data & based on a series of data points noted over the specific period (interval). It processes the historical data in order to extract the meaningful and relevant information. Following Table 1 (data is assumed & stock wise data can be downloaded from the respective stock exchanges) & Figure 1 illustrates the time series analysis & visualization of the historical data. *This analysis is very useful in stock market prediction, population analysis, banking and finance sector, healthcare etc*. However, time series analysis requires '*perfect visualization*' so that user can understand the trends. Proper visualization gives better insights and helps extracting meaningful information within less time.

A **time series data** can be used as a set of measurement processing the independent and dependent variables. Time series data can measure the following (examples)

- ***Energy consumption by the residents and industries***
- ***Calculating the energy/power requirement hourly and daily basis***
- ***Sales data of industries***
- ***Profits of the organizations***

Table 1. Time series data

Date	Open	High	Low	Close	Stock	Volume
11/1/2023	40	44	39	42	abc	350000
11/2/2023	42	45	38	43	def	430000
11/3/2023	40	44	37	36	ghi	380000
11/4/2023	46	48	42	45	jkl	370000
11/5/2023	39	43	38	36	mno	440000
11/6/2023	40	43	38	43	pqr	420000

Figure 1. Line plot for time series data

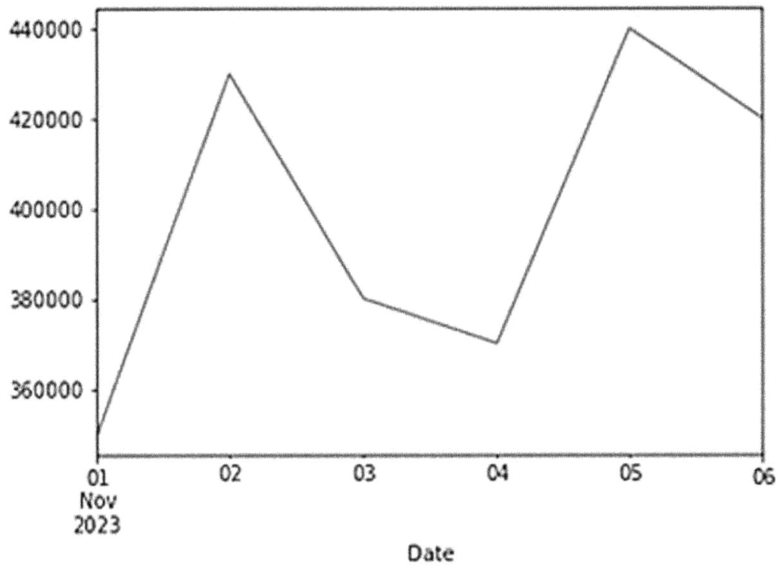

- ***Population of the country***
- ***Annual rainfall***
- ***Industrial growth***
- ***Climate change data***
- ***GDP (Gross domestic product) etc.***

Figure 2 illustrates the cumulative plot of all the features & Figure 3 indicates the minimum and maximum values from the datasets.

Figure 2. Cumulative plot of all the features

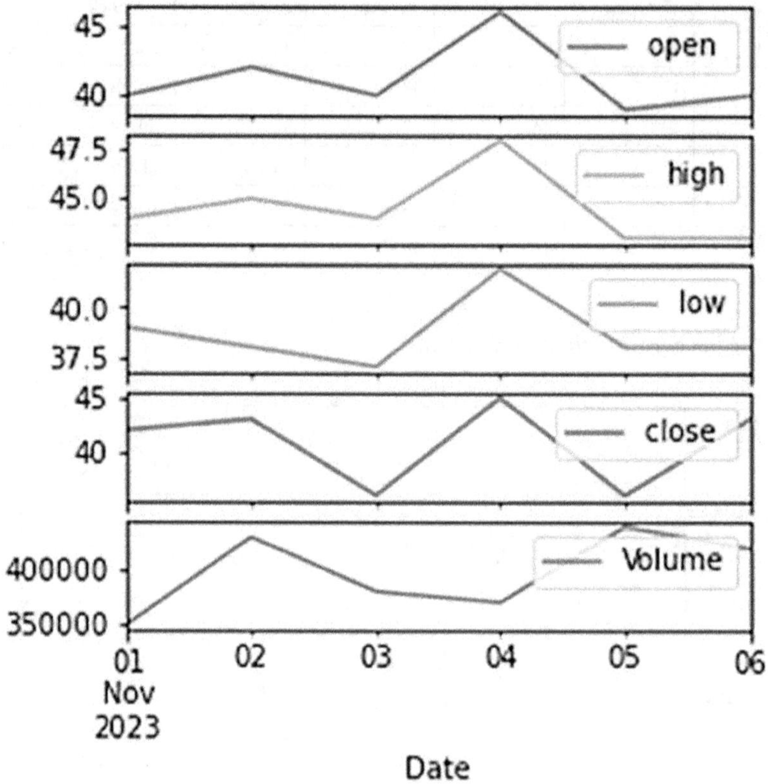

3.2 Classification

Classification is a supervised learning method used in machine learning (ML). It predicts the possible classes with labels. It trains the data and uses it to test the remaining predicting the classes.

Governments can develop e-services based on classification methods classifying the input data received from the citizens. E-service portal classifies the data into different classes like education, income, gender wise population analysis, industrial growth etc. Classification in machine learning can be categorized in few types like binary classification, multi-class classification, multi-label classification and imbalanced classification. *Types of classification algorithms available in machine learning are logistic regression, naïve Bayes, K-nearest neighbor, decision tree, random forest, and support vector machine (SVM).*

Figure 3. Min-max values from the datasets

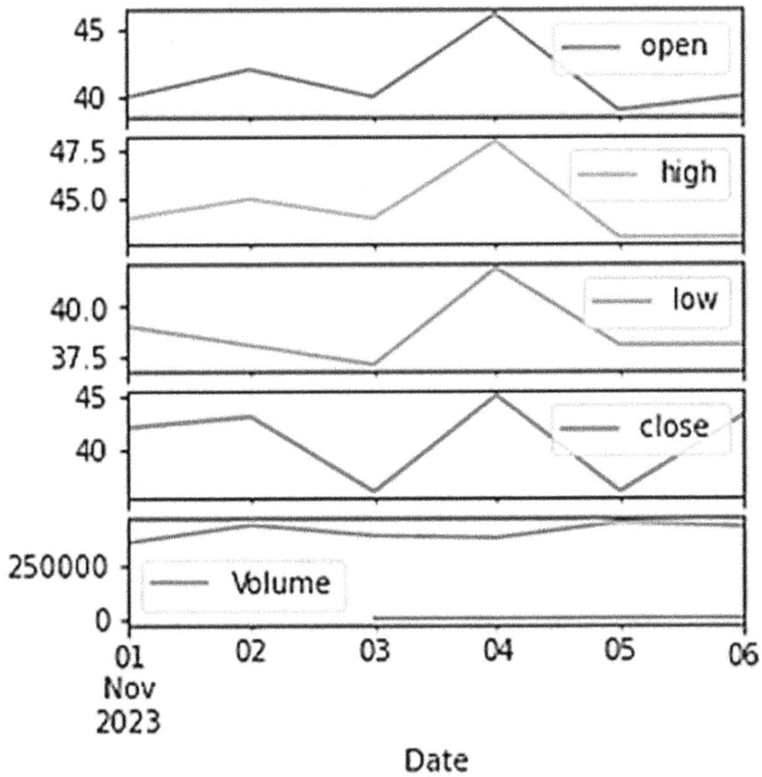

Applications of Classification Method in E-Services Are as Follows

- **Healthcare**: Recently world has faced Covid-19 pandemic situation. Many researchers, academician and health-care professionals have developed a machine learning models identifying whether a person is having Covid-19 symptoms or not? These ML models also help categorizing the patients as per the different comorbidities (high blood pressure, diabetes, obesity etc.). ML models processes the historical data and predicts whether any similar situation is arising in the near future.
- **Education**: e-learning trends is very popular since last few years and it consists of audio, video, and text data. It might be possible that, it could be in unstructured format and hence needs appropriate classification. NLP- natural language processing processes this data and converts it into structured format

to find the relevant and required information. LMS – learning management systems is the best example of the e-education service. Even the classification based ML models can distinguish the feedbacks/opinions received from the instructors, students and other stakeholders.

- **Logistics**: There are many sectors playing crucial role in the country's economy. Logistics plays an important role for every industry and with the help of machine learning and deep learning methods develop ML models to ease the process of logistics.

Almost in every metro city there is huge traffic and everyone rushes to the home, offices and wishes to pass the distance within less time. Advanced logistics ML and AI models can predict the 'possible traffic' on the specific path and suggest alternative path within less time. It significantly reduces the clogging and save more time. The major problem logistics face is the weather condition. Monsoon or other geographical issues (conditions) can be predicted either prior scheduling the logistic operation or e-logistic service must be intelligent enough dealing with such abnormal conditions during the logistic operations.

- **Future precision agriculture practices**: With the application of IoT and ML methods best precision model can be developed for the agriculture. Sensors like temperature and humidity, soil moisture sensors, pH sensors, and TDS sensor etc. can be used to get the real time values and transmit them to the system (application) e.g. via microcontrollers.

Due to water scarcity it has been observed that crop yield decreases and many times available ground water is utilized for the agriculture. Therefore, optimum use of the 'available ground water' can be scheduled using machine learning based methods.

These AI and ML based models helps calculating the 'evapotranspiration rate' and schedule the irrigation accordingly. With the help of such advanced AI and ML algorithms one can identify the applied irrigation weekly, monthly etc. It helps calculating the 'water requirement' by the crops. As all of we know every 'drop' of water is precious and it must be utilized in a proper way. Using 'drone' or by designing a 'probe' of the soil moisture sensors these AI and ML models fetches 'real time' soil moisture values and passes them to the system. System upon receiving these 'moisture' values can schedule the 'irrigation' on priority basis.

As shown in the above Figure 4 with the help of machine learning, IoT, and artificial intelligence (AI) methods government can develop an e-agri. Model helping the farmers. Nowadays, farming is highly dependent on 'monsoon' and due to water scarcity crop yield is decreased. A machine learning based e-agri. Model can help the farmers in multiple ways to increase the crop yield and utilize

Figure 4. E-agri ML-based model

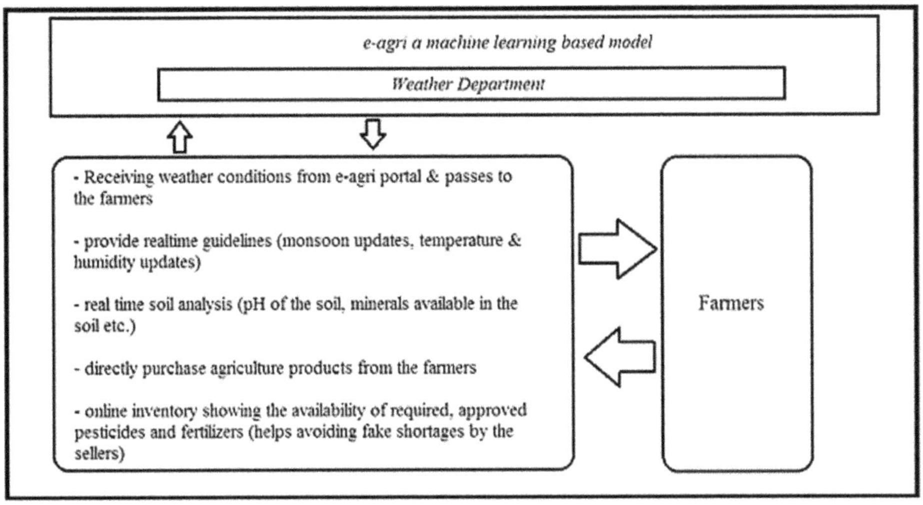

the available resources such as pesticides, fertilizers, ground water, seeds etc. in an optimum way. ML, AI and IoT based applications can be develop with the help of sensors, and microcontrollers. These applications require less human intervention and increase the yield. As shown in the above figure, real time updates, guidelines and queries of the farmers can be solved within less time. Weather department can give real time update to the farmers.

3.3 Regression

Regression methods categorized as supervised machine learning. It helps predicting a numerical value based on the existing data. It is widely used in many applications such as calculating an asset's price, estimating the required resources by the people such as energy consumption etc. Regression analysis can be added as an integral part forecasting or predictive model. Regression is classified under the supervised machine learning methods. It requires labeled input and output training data (as shown in the Table 2 and predicted values in Table 3 –these values are assumed). ML regression model understands the relationship between variables and accurately labels the training data. *There are different types of regression methods like linear regression, logistic regression, polynomial regression, and ridge regression etc.*

Use of machine learning regression models in e-Governance are as follows:

- Forecasting the possible real estate prices & imposing the tax duties accordingly.

- Government can make sure the effectiveness of the delivery of the e-services to the citizens. It is possible by getting the feedbacks, opinions, and ratings from the citizens and processing those to calculate the effectiveness of the e-service.
- Regression can be incorporated in the time series analysis i.e. e-service predicting the rainfall, gender wise population, income levels of the citizens etc.
- Once the income levels of the citizens determined, government e-service portal can calculate the tax liabilities automatically.

Table 2. Sample data

Years' Experience	Salary
1	40000
1.3	46500
1.5	47000
2	43525
2.5	40000
3	56642
3	60150
3.3	54445
3.4	64445
3.7	57189
3.9	63218
4.3	56000
4	56957
4.1	57081
4.5	62000
4.9	67938
5.1	66029
5.3	83088
5.9	81363
6	93940
6.8	91738
7.1	98273
7.9	101302
8.2	113812

Table 2 consists of years' experience & the appropriate salary of the employee. Once the model processes the dataset given input data is divided into the training and testing data as shown in the Figure 5 and Figure 6. Table 3 enlists the predicted values for the given data.

Regression analysis is a supervised learning method and processes the independent & dependent variables. Recently world has encountered a pandemic situation & many people with various comorbidities lost their lives. E.g. people with diabetes, blood pressure, obesity, lungs problems etc. infected more with Covid-19. Hence, e-healthcare model based on regression method can be provided to the healthcare infra to keep track on future pandemic issue. These models will help tracking the patients with 'n' comorbidities and 'x' disease. So that immediate remedial action can be taken by the government to avoid future pandemic situations.

Regression based ML model can process historical data like rainfall data of last few years i.e. 50 years or 100 years. This historical data has all the values i.e. min, max rainfall statistics and these values can be compared with the rising temperature. Hence, *e-weather department service* keeps track on temperature, humidity, evapotranspiration rate, and can guide farmers in their regular farming practices. This service can be added as an integral part of e-agriculture service.

Similarly, education department can keep track on 'higher education' offered to the citizens. With the rising population it is the responsibility of the government to

Figure 5. Training set

Figure 6. Testing set

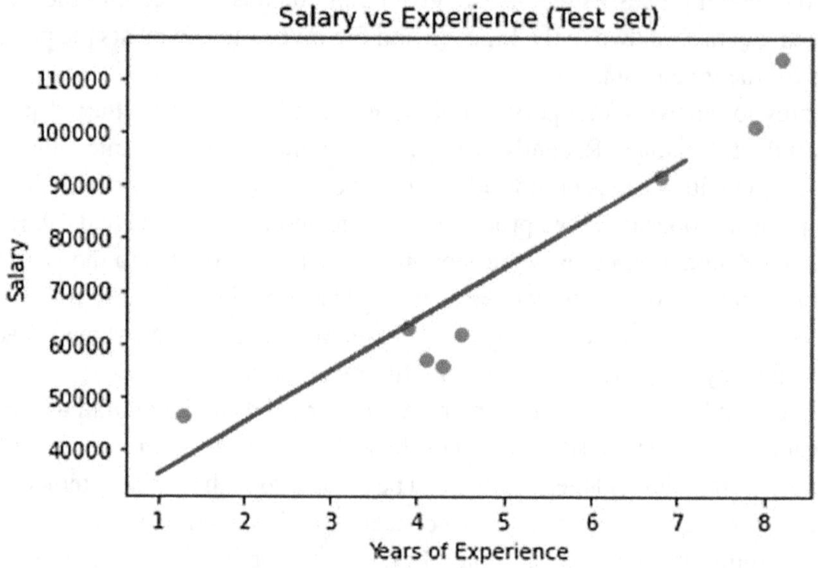

Table 3. Predicted values

67511.3
63612.9
102597
69460.6
91876.6
38273
65562.1
105521

uplift the society. *e-education service* with necessary skills e.g. vocational, medical, paramedical, engineering etc. can be provided to the citizens. Institutes providing such education can be established as per the trend. Regression based e-education model helps identifying the variables like education, people's age, people's income etc.

3.4 Clustering

Clustering is an unsupervised learning method dividing the data points into a number of groups (clusters). Based on the similarity (after applying the threshold) the data points are grouped and to do this task one can set the 'threshold' or 'boundary value'.

It is basically a collection of objects on the basis of similarity and presents the dissimilarity between them. Following table 4 consist of gender, age, annual income and the spending of the citizens. Such approach groups the citizens based on age groups, income groups and gender.

Figure 7 illustrates the formation of clusters using Elbow method for the data given in Table 4.

Clustering plays very important role in many areas like -

Table 4. Sample data for clustering

Citizen	Gender	Age	Annual Income ($)	Spending Score (1-100)
1	Male	19	15000	39
2	Male	21	15000	81
3	Female	20	16000	6
4	Female	23	16000	77
5	Female	31	17000	40
6	Female	22	17000	76
7	Female	35	18000	6
8	Female	23	18000	94
9	Male	64	19000	3
10	Female	30	19000	72
11	Male	67	19200	14
12	Female	35	19000	99
13	Female	58	20000	15
14	Female	24	20000	77
15	Male	37	20000	13
16	Male	22	20000	79
17	Female	35	21000	35
18	Male	20	21000	66
19	Male	52	23000	29

Figure 7. Clustering using elbow method

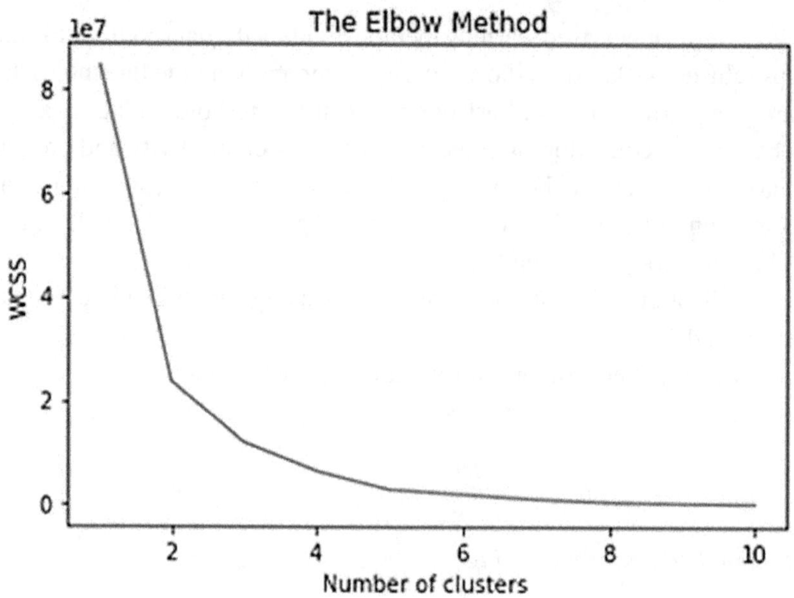

Figure 8. Formation of clusters

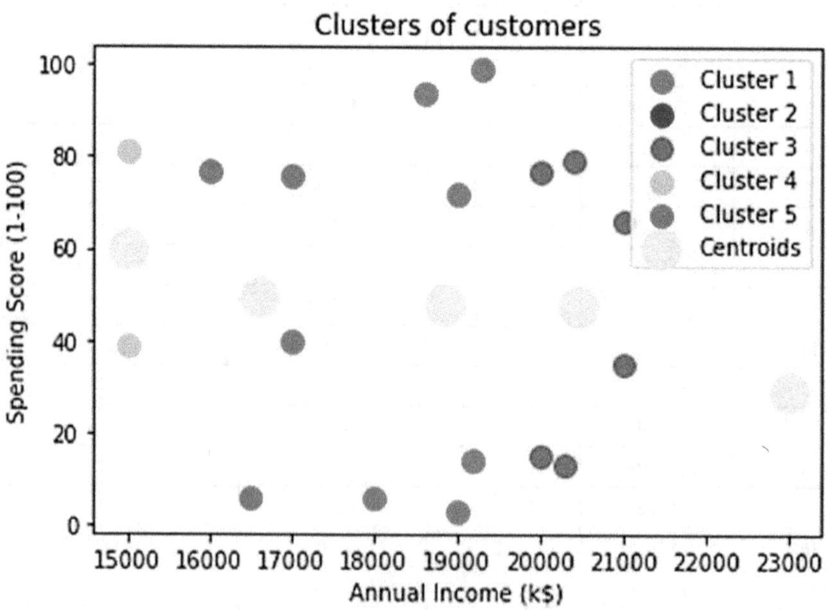

- City planning (e-town service): e-town planning service can be developed assisting the corporate authorities, institutes and residents. e-town service will provide different zones of the city according to the 'population density' and future infrastructure plans. The main of this e-town service is visualizing the future with different parameters like population density, roads, and other necessary infrastructures.

e-town service must focus on avoiding 'congestion of future traffic' and design the 'roads', 'government offices', and other infrastructures. Regression, clustering and time series analysis etc. methods of machine learning can be very useful in these applications.

- e-disaster management: with the help of IoT, and machine learning methods like 'clustering' e-disaster management service can be designed to divide the city, state and country in mild to moderate danger zones. Geographical areas can be divided into level 0 to level 5 (low to high) risks zones and helps avoiding future casualties. This e-disaster management service can be integrated as a part of e-town service.
- e-traffic management: nowadays, values i.e. time for handling the traffic is fixed. However, machine learning model can be generated to handle the 'real traffic' by considering parameters like peak hours, different routes, etc. The main aim of this e-traffic management is to handle the 'congestion' or 'high traffic'.

The main objective of e-traffic management is to handle 'real time traffic' i.e. if there is any traffic congestion then 'alternate, feasible and shortest route' must be suggested by the e-traffic service.

3.5 Reinforcement Learning

Reinforcement learning (RL) is very popular method of the Machine Learning & aims to gain maximum reward with best possible results. Many decision making applications can be developed using reinforcement learning. Iterative approach ('n' steps) results in maximum rewards. With 'n' iterations and learning capability of the proposed model increase i.e. one can say it is a '*trial and error*' method. Iterative approach adopts 'adaptive learning' strategy. Proposed model learns and takes decision (action) at the end of 'n' iterations by studying the 'outcomes' (results). Model decides which action to take in the next step and determines if the selection was correct or incorrect. Once successfully implemented, it automates the tasks with

Table 5. e-services accessed by the citizens

E-Service 1	E-Service 2	E-Service 3	E-Service 4	E-Service 5	E-Service 6	E-Service 7	E-Service 8	E-Service 9	E-Service 10
1	0	0	0	1	0	0	0	1	0
0	0	0	0	0	0	0	0	1	0
0	0	0	0	0	0	0	0	0	0
0	1	0	0	0	0	0	1	0	0
0	0	0	0	0	0	0	0	0	0
1	1	0	0	0	0	0	0	0	0
0	0	0	1	0	0	0	0	0	0
1	1	0	0	1	0	0	0	0	0
0	0	0	0	0	0	0	0	0	0
0	0	1	0	0	0	0	0	0	0
0	0	0	0	0	0	0	0	0	0
0	0	0	0	0	0	0	0	0	0
0	0	0	1	0	0	0	0	0	0
0	0	0	0	0	0	0	0	1	0
0	0	0	0	0	0	0	1	0	0
0	0	0	0	1	0	0	1	0	0
0	0	0	0	0	0	0	0	0	0
0	0	0	0	0	0	0	0	0	0
0	0	0	0	0	0	0	1	0	0
0	0	0	0	0	0	0	0	1	0
0	1	0	0	0	0	0	1	0	0
0	0	0	0	1	0	0	0	0	1
0	0	0	0	0	0	0	0	0	0
0	0	0	0	0	0	0	1	1	0
0	0	0	0	1	0	1	1	0	0
0	0	0	0	0	0	0	0	0	0
0	1	0	0	1	0	0	1	0	0
0	1	0	1	0	0	0	0	0	0
0	0	0	0	0	0	0	0	0	0
0	0	0	0	1	0	0	1	1	0
1	0	0	0	1	0	0	0	0	0
0	0	0	0	0	0	0	0	0	0
-	-	-	-	-	-	-	-	-	-
-	-	-	-	-	-	-	-	-	-
-	-	-	-	-	-	-	-	-	-

Figure 9. Histogram showing e-service accessed

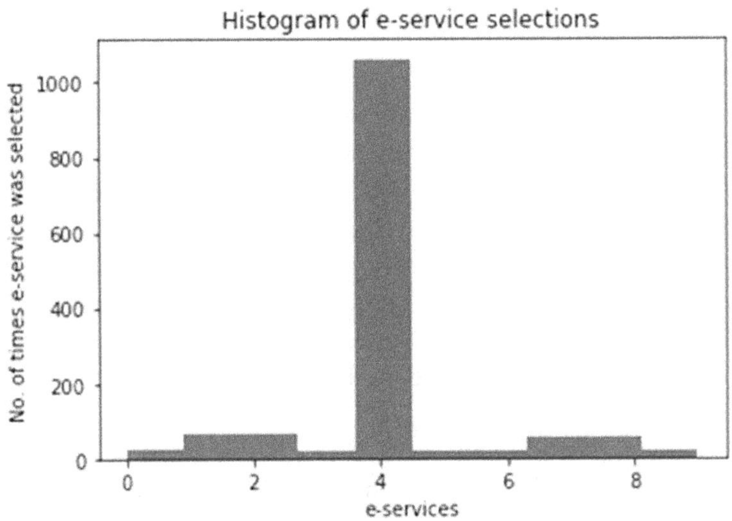

less human intervention. Idea behind the *learning by studying* in the reinforcement learning is to retrieve the best outcome.

Thompson sampling in Reinforcement learning:

There are many applications which can have 'reinforcement learning' as an integral part. One of the RL based application can be developed is 'e-grid management' – an energy management system (including hydro project, solar project) providing continuous energy supply. Geographical locations (state, country) can be divided into 'parts/zones/regions' etc. Using RL and the 'clustering' method of machine learning, governments can manage the grids. Grids are nothing the 'power supply' units (manufacturers) and operated from the 'central' location.

A 'dashboard' can be prepared showing all the 'grids' with the available energy, demand of energy from the industry and residents. Every grid can calculate the 'residual' energy. Dashboard can show the cumulative 'residual energy' and if required can fulfill real-time energy demand. Such approach automate the real-time decision making tasks, helps avoiding the energy outages, and also forecasts the energy requirement from specific region. This approach will revolutionize the power sector.

3.6 Long Short-Term Memory

Long Short-Term Memory (LSTM) is a recurrent neural network (RNN). As its name indicates it has a 'memory' and involves sequence of prediction of tasks. It consists of forget, input and output gates. *LSTM is widely used in many applications like modeling the languages, recognizing the speech, analyzing the video, detecting anomalies, etc.* As discussed earlier, it remembers the 'inputs' and updates the same in each step. *A 'predictive' model can be developed using LSTM using a series of gates (forget, input and output). These gates allow information to be flow in the network. It is widely used in 'forecasting' applications like stock value forecasting.*

Image captioning and image generation are the best examples of LSTM. Hence, e-identity government service can be developed & integrated in different applications. e-identity service processes the images of the citizens with 'unique identities'. This service can be used in various other government e-services like passport validation, unique identity creation, immigration, giving government benefits to the specifics citizens, providing healthcare facilities to the beneficiaries etc.

A perfect e-identity government service can be implemented using CNN (convolutional neural network and LSTM) to process the image, and video. Even it is possible to develop an application processing the *multi-modalities like image, audio and video.* e-identity service can also help minimizing the crime rate by accurately identifying the criminals, can process the real time video and process it by dividing it into the 'n' frames (images). More advanced versions can be used to process the blur images, removing unnecessary background, improving the illumination, working on different color intensities etc.

3.7 Natural Language Processing

ML and AI based models are developed to process the 'big data' integrated from variety of sources which could be heterogeneous in nature. *A 'chat-bot' module can be integrated in every e-government service as an integral part to assist the citizens.* This approach requires less human intervention and eases the interaction between e-services and the citizens. A chat-bot will assist the citizen using natural language processing (NLP) by answering the queries of citizens. Every *e-service* must have a natural language processing (NLP) based chat-bot i.e. Gov.-bot guiding the citizens in accessing the particular e-service. It should assist the citizens in applications, step by step submitting the application, uploading the necessary documents, and finally keep tracking their applications. This approach will revolutionize the government services, requires less human interaction, can be accessible from any place etc. Addition to this use of NLP will improvise the e-services by processing the feedbacks, responses and ratings received from the citizens. Based on the feedbacks e-service can be improved significantly. NLP processes the feedbacks (texts) by dividing it into the words, calculating the frequencies of each word within the document and from other available documents. It is known as term frequency (TF) and inverse

*Table 6. TF*IDF values*

(0, 7) 0.3535533905932738
(0, 7) 0.3535533905932738
(0, 8) 0.3535533905932738
(0, 11) 0.3535533905932738
(0, 2) 0.3535533905932738
(0, 9) 0.3535533905932738
(0, 1) 0.3535533905932738
(0, 10) 0.3535533905932738
(0, 4) 0.3535533905932738
(1, 5) 0.7071067811865476
(1, 6) 0.7071067811865476
(2, 0) 0.7071067811865476
(2, 3) 0.7071067811865476

document frequency (IDF) and prepares a TF*IDF matrix. Following example illustrates the working of TF*IDF matrix –

Suppose there are 03 documents

d0 = 'Development, Monitoring, and Management Approaches of Machine Learning'
d1 = 'IGI Global'
d2 = 'December 2023'
Result –
Word indexes:
{'development': 4, 'monitoring': 10, 'and': 1, 'management': 9, 'approaches': 2, 'of': 11, 'machine': 8, 'learning': 7, 'igi': 6, 'global': 5, 'december': 3, '2023': 0}

3.8 Boosting

Boosting is very popular method to integrate the weak classifiers into one strong classifier. Initially a single model is executed & verified for any error. If here is nay error then 2nd model is built to minimize the same. This process continues if there are any errors & predicts the results accurately. *Adaboost algorithm is the best example of boosting method which built a strong classifier. Boosting adopts the 'ensemble learning' strategy & integrates different models to get the final output. Gradient boosting method (GBM) is widely used in machine learning applications. There are many advantages of GBM are – it reduces the bias errors in machine learning applications, resolves issues related to regression & classification.*

Advantages of Gradient Boosting

- It is based on ensemble method & can handle data easily.
- Ensemble method increases accuracy and helps in better prediction.
- Can process the large datasets easily.
- Easily handles the over-fitting issues during processing of the datasets.

3.9 Dimensionality Reduction

Many machine learning applications processes large datasets and variables included in the dataset represents its dimensionality. However to minimize the efforts & time machine learning models needs to focus on 'necessary variables' only. Dimensionality reduction (DM) works on reducing the variables i.e. focusing on the required and ignoring the remaining variables. If the proposed machine learning model considers all the variables then performance and accuracy could be degrades. Hence, a simple model can be developed to consider required variables. DM can be known as data preparation method and applied after the data cleaning. With this DM one can have a good predictive model by focusing on the important variable only.

DM has different techniques autoencoder, feature selection, manifold learning and matrix factorization etc.

Applications of dimensionality reduction:

- ◦ **Hence, dimensionality reduction (DM) method can be added as an integral part of the various e-government service portals. It can be added into the e-identity to process the images & video.**
- ◦ **DM can be used in e-surveillance to monitor the speeches given by political leaders, influencers, motivators etc.**
- ◦ **DM can also be included with NLP to process the texts (social media) to analyze the tweets, posts etc.**
- ◦ **DM can be added into the 'time series' analysis to correctly forecast the desired results.**

3.10 Challenges in Application of Machine Learning (ML)

- *Quality data*
- *Underfitting issues*

- *Overfitting issues*
- *Training required to apply the ML methods*
- *Privacy of the user data*
- *Security of the user data*
- *Scalability of the ML models with rising data size*

3.11 Advantages of Machine Learning in E-Governance

- *Automating the tasks*
- *Less human intervention*
- *Reducing the cost*
- *Identification of trends & patterns*
- *Users can have better insights & prediction*
- *Improves the accuracy*
- *Can be integrated in any application & e-government service portal*
- *Scope for improvement*
- *Ease of handling large & heterogeneous data*
- *Highly scalable application can be developed*

CONCLUSION

This chapter enlists and explains the various aspects of machine learning (ML) in different government services. Following figure illustrates the use of artificial intelligence (AI) & ML in e-services.

The machine learning methods classification, regression, reinforcement learning, natural language processing, clustering, LSTM, convolutional neural network etc. are discussed using various government service (e-portals). The ultimate goal of applying the ML methods is ease the accessibility, improving the interaction between government, government's services & the citizens. There is continuous scope for improvising the e-portals as there is maximum interaction between citizens & the e-services. The major benefit of the implementation of e-services is reducing 'corruption' significantly. Citizen empowerment is the advantage of government's e-services. As e-services can be accessible from any place and reduces corruption, it will surely increase the 'revenue' for the government. Digitized version of e-services reduces less hierarchic structure i.e. no. of employees can be very less. With the integration of e-service (unique identification) governments can successfully implement public distribution system (PDS) i.e. providing necessary food, grains etc. to the eligible citizens. Transparency & accountability is another benefit of the e-governance.

Figure 10. Proposed architecture of e-services

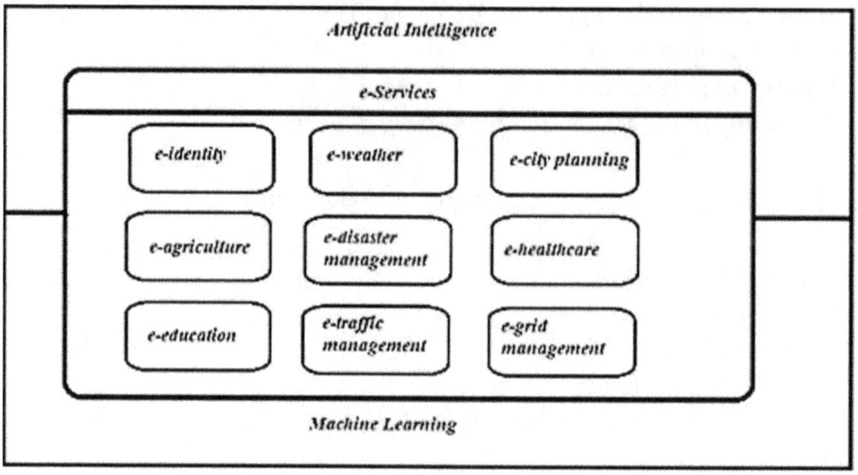

REFERENCES

AlDhaheri, R. A., Sulaiman, I. F., & Matrooshi, H. A. A. (2022, April). The Relationship Between Digital Transformation and Quality of UAE Government Services Through Machine Learning. In *International Conference on Advanced Machine Learning Technologies and Applications* (pp. 412-421). Cham: Springer International Publishing. 10.1007/978-3-031-03918-8_35

Alexopoulos, C., Lachana, Z., Androutsopoulou, A., Diamantopoulou, V., Charalabidis, Y., & Loutsaris, M. A. (2019, April). How machine learning is changing e-government. In *Proceedings of the 12th international conference on theory and practice of electronic governance* (pp. 354-363). 10.1145/3326365.3326412

AliM. (2023). E-governance and E-democracy: a Digital Revolution. *Available at* SSRN 4623414.

Balta, D., Sellami, M., Kuhn, P., Schöpp, U., Buchinger, M., Baracaldo, N., ... Altakrouri, B. (2021). Accountable federated machine learning in government: engineering and management insights. *Electronic Participation: 13th IFIP WG 8.5 International Conference, ePart 2021, Granada, Spain, September 7–9, 2021 Proceedings*, *13*, 125–138.

Chen, Y., Wang, J., & Cai, Z. (2018, July). Study on the application of machine learning in government service: take consumer protection service as an example. In *2018 15th International Conference on Service Systems and Service Management (ICSSSM)* (pp. 1-5). IEEE. 10.1109/ICSSSM.2018.8465040

Dana, R. D., Dikananda, A. R., Sudrajat, D., Wanto, A., & Fasya, F. (2019, October). Measurement of health service performance through machine learning using clustering techniques. *Journal of Physics: Conference Series, 1360*(1), 012017. doi:10.1088/1742-6596/1360/1/012017

Dreyling, R., Jackson, E. B., Tammet, T., Labanava, A., & Pappel, I. (2021, April). Social, Legal, and Technical Considerations for Machine Learning and Artificial Intelligence Systems in Government. ICEIS, (1), 701-708.

Duan, H. K., Vasarhelyi, M. A., Codesso, M., & Alzamil, Z. (2023). Enhancing the government accounting information systems using social media information: An application of text mining and machine learning. *International Journal of Accounting Information Systems, 48*, 100600. doi:10.1016/j.accinf.2022.100600

Duggar, D., Bang, S. M., & Tripathy, B. K. (2023). Big Data Analytics in E-Governance and Other Aspects of Society. In *Encyclopedia of Data Science and Machine Learning* (pp. 116–128). IGI Global.

Gkikas, D. C., Theodoridis, P. K., & Gkikas, M. C. (2023). Artificial Intelligence (AI) Use for e-Governance in Agriculture: Exploring the Bioeconomy Landscape. In *Recent Advances in Data and Algorithms for e-Government* (pp. 141–172). Springer International Publishing. doi:10.1007/978-3-031-22408-9_7

Henman, P. (2020). Improving public services using artificial intelligence: Possibilities, pitfalls, governance. *Asia Pacific Journal of Public Administration, 42*(4), 209–221. doi:10.1080/23276665.2020.1816188

Ibrahim, I. K., Elmorsy, S. A., Kashef, N. M., & Al-Borai, M. M. M. (2023). Securing E-Governance Services Based on Two Level Classification Algorithms. *Mathematical Modelling of Engineering Problems, 10*(2).

Khouya, M. (2023). E-Governance: Origin, challenges, and prospects in the era of ICTs and artificial intelligence. *American Scientific Journal, 3*(18), 884–884.

Mengesha, N., & Ayanso, A. (2021). Examining the Evolution of E-Government Development of Nations Through Machine Learning Techniques. In *Handbook of Research on Applied Data Science and Artificial Intelligence in Business and Industry* (pp. 85–107). IGI Global. doi:10.4018/978-1-7998-6985-6.ch004

Pi, Y. (2021). Machine learning in governments: Benefits, challenges and future directions. *JeDEM-eJournal of eDemocracy and Open Government, 13*(1), 203-219.

Samuel, P., Reshmy, A. K., Rajesh, S., Kanipriya, M., & Karthika, R. A. (2023). AI-Based Big Data Algorithms and Machine Learning Techniques for Managing Data in E-Governance. In AI, IoT, and Blockchain Breakthroughs in E-Governance (pp. 19-35). IGI Global. doi:10.4018/978-1-6684-7697-0.ch002

Veale, M., & Brass, I. (2019). Administration by algorithm? Public management meets public sector machine learning. *Public Management Meets Public Sector Machine Learning*.

Wei, L. (2022). Intelligent analysis of e-government influence factors based on improved machine learning. *Neural Computing & Applications*, *34*(15), 12241–12256. doi:10.1007/s00521-021-06657-5

KEY TERMS AND DEFINITIONS

Artificial Intelligence (AI): Ability of the computer systems, machines to automate the tasks intelligently with less human intervention.

Autoencoder: It is a combination of encoder & decoder. It processes by extracting the valuable information from the given input.

Big Data: Big data means max. Volume of data with characteristics like volume, variety and veracity, etc.

Classification: A supervised learning method from machine learning classifying the input data.

Dimension Reduction: It minimizes the dimensions and represents only the necessary variables, features in feature vector space.

Feature: An input variable in model is known as 'features'.

Feature Extraction: A process to retrieve the features with the help of proposed machine learning model.

Gradient Boosting: Iteratively trains the models & integrate them to have a strong model.

Machine Learning: It is a branch of artificial intelligence (AI) trains the machines to automatically train and tests the data, learns from the past experiences with less human intervention.

Overfitting: It occurs when model can process the training data but fails to process the testing data.

Regression: A method from machine learning predicting the relationship between independent and dependent variables.

Reinforcement Learning (RL): Model learns by studying the outcome of the iteration. It helps in better decision making and get most possible output i.e. maximum reward.

Underfitting: It is expected that machine learning model learn from the training data and analyze the patterns. However, if the ML model doesn't work as expected then underfitting occurs.

Chapter 9
The Role of Data Science and Volunteered Geographic Information in Enhancing Government Service Delivery:
Opportunities and Challenges

Munir Ahmad
https://orcid.org/0000-0003-4836-6151
Survey of Pakistan, Pakistan

ABSTRACT

This chapter explored the transformative impact of data science and VGI on public service provision. VGI, as user-generated content, has played a significant role in democratizing geographic information, empowering users to actively participate in data generation and curation. The integration of VGI into government operations has presented new opportunities for improving service delivery across various domains like education, health, transportation, and waste management. Additionally, data science has complemented VGI by utilizing advanced techniques such as AI, IoT, big data, and blockchain, thereby revolutionizing the entire landscape of government service delivery. However, the successful utilization of VGI in public sector delivery requires addressing critical challenges, including data quality, security, inclusivity, technological infrastructure, and specialized skill sets. Collaborative efforts involving governments, volunteers, and academia can enhance the quality of VGI data.

DOI: 10.4018/978-1-6684-9716-6.ch009

INTRODUCTION

The delivery of public services has been transformed in recent years by the incorporation of technology and data-driven strategies. The application of Volunteered Geographic Information (VGI) with Data Science is a noteworthy development in this field. VGI is the term used to describe location-based data that people voluntarily share on different digital platforms (Goodchild, 2007), such as social media, mobile apps, and crowdsourcing projects. Whereas, data science refers to the procedures and strategies for extracting conclusions and information from huge datasets (Brodie, 2019; Provost & Fawcett, 2013).

Due to a number of reasons, the use of VGI and data science in the delivery of public services has significantly increased. Firstly, there is an unprecedented amount of location-based data being collected and disseminated because of the expanding availability of mobile devices and the Internet availability (Huang et al., 2021). Nowadays, citizens can contribute to the creation of geographic data, offering important insights into their needs, preferences, and experiences (Goodchild, 2007). Secondly, traditional data collection techniques are expensive and time-consuming. VGI, in comparison, provides a real-time, cost-effective substitute that enables public sector organizations to acquire reliable information for decision-making procedures (Ahmad et al., 2022).

Informed and data-driven policy formation is made possible by the effective analysis and interpretation of large datasets available by the combination of VGI and data science (Arnaboldi & Azzone, 2020; Provost & Fawcett, 2013; Wong & C. Hinnant, 2022). As a result, public service providers can strengthen resource allocation, increase the effectiveness of their services, and cater to the unique requirements of the communities they serve. For example, poverty at the village level can be assessed by combining various data sources, including high-resolution imagery (HRI), point-of-interest (POI), OpenStreetMap (OSM), and digital surface model (DSM) data (Hu et al., 2022). Similarly, Ma et al., (2022) proposed a rationality evaluation approach for the spatial distribution of public toilets in urban functional areas by using POI big data and OSM. Whereas, KUCUKALI et al., (2022) utilized open-source geospatial data, including OSM, to evaluate pedestrian accessibility to essential public services and facilities and Abdulkarim et al., (2014) developed a VGI application using Google Street View to invite people to contribute to the classification of roof materials to support energy efficiency initiatives.

To this effect, the primary objective of this chapter is to present to examine the use of volunteered geographic information and data science in the context of providing public services. It will explore the possible advantages and difficulties of integrating these two elements in different spheres of the public sphere. To achieve this objective, the chapter is structured as follows: Section two provides an in-depth exploration of VGI with a particular focus on its impact on public service delivery. Similarly, section three delves into the concept of data science and its potential in enhancing government services. In section four, the synergistic integration of VGI and data science across four key government sectors is examined. Section five is dedicated to addressing the challenges that arise in this context. Finally, the last section serves as the concluding remarks of the chapter, accompanied by future directions for further research.

VOLUNTEERED GEOGRAPHIC INFORMATION

VGI can be viewed as a type of user-generated content that includes a variety of location-specific data, including geotagged images, check-ins, reviews, and other contributions that are made from a particular area (Haklay, 2013; Kitchin et al., 2018). As people interact with their surroundings, they freely gather and exchange these data points. VGI is generally created by citizens through location-aware devices like smartphones, where they collect geographic data in the form of geo-tagged text, photos, or videos (Honarparvar et al., 2019). This information is then shared through various online social media platforms, such as Twitter, contributing to the creation of VGI. Established in 2004, OpenStreetMap (OSM) is a global endeavor aimed at creating and maintaining an open, editable database and map of the entire world (Grinberger et al., 2022). Renowned as a prime example of VGI, it stands out for its extensive volunteer community and the vast repository of spatial data it has generated.

The fundamental idea behind VGI is the democratization of geographic information, where users have an active role in data development and curation rather than merely passively receiving government datasets (Goodchild, 2007). New digital platforms have surfaced, providing opportunities for individuals to collaboratively contribute geographic information, leading to the co-construction of digital representations and conceptualizations of nature (Calcagni et al., 2019). These platforms facilitate interactions between users, enabling them to collectively shape and imagine geographical aspects within the digital realm.

In urban environments, the incidence of catastrophes, such as intense flooding, yields severe repercussions, impacting not only the human population but also critical infrastructures like road networks, which hold paramount significance for daily life and, notably, emergency response mechanisms. VGI can offer real-time data updates, enabling prompt responses to circumstances or events that are evolving very quickly. This is especially helpful in disaster management activities. In times of emergencies, the valuable geo-located information offered by affectee communities can prove to be highly advantageous and instrumental (Tzavella et al., 2018).

VGI can improve the recommendation process of Recommender Systems (RS) by adding contextual information (Honarparvar et al., 2019). Users can freely contribute useful geographical data to RS by integrating VGI, providing insights into their preferences and interests in relation to particular locations and areas of interest. The use of VGI can enhance the precision and applicability of location-based suggestions offered by RS. For instance, RS can use VGI to make recommendations for nearby healthcare facilities, educational institutions, or social welfare services, Additionally, VGI can add to the dynamic nature of suggestions by reflecting changes in user preferences and interactions with their surroundings in real-time (Honarparvar et al., 2019). Thus VGI can help in improving the personalization and currency of RS recommendations.

Government departments can better comprehend the existing land use patterns in urban areas using land cover maps. However, these maps need to be validated to make sure the data is accurate and trustworthy, which is essential for urban planning and development. VGI can be used to support the land cover validation processes (Antoniou et al., 2016; Fonte et al., 2015; Olteanu-Raimond et al., 2020). Validated land cover maps can be used by public service organizations to pinpoint ideal places for new infrastructure initiatives, neighbourhoods, business districts, and public amenities. This improves the quality of life for residents by facilitating the orderly growth of cities and assisting in the efficient use of resources.

Benefits of VGI for Government Service Delivery

VGI has become a useful tool for governments and public service organizations The main benefits of VGI in terms of public services are summarized in Figure 1 and presented below.

Citizen Engagement

Citizen engagement fosters a sense of empowerment among the public, as they become active participants in shaping public services. Government organizations can get important insights into the actual needs and preferences of the community by incorporating citizens in the planning, design, and assessment of services. VGI can serve as an important tool to engage citizens in public services (Güiza & Stuart, 2018; Sangiambut & Sieber, 2016). Through this involvement, it can be sure that services are designed to satisfy the unique needs of citizens, hence increasing overall satisfaction and efficiency.

Real-Time Data Updates

The capacity of VGI to give real-time data updates is one of its most important advantages. Through smartphones and other devices, users engage with their environment and voluntarily contribute location-specific data, making the data instantaneously accessible for analysis and decision-making. This real-time feature of VGI in public services might be especially helpful for emergency services, traffic management, and disaster response, enabling quick actions and well-informed decisions (Annis & Nardi, 2019; Chen et al., 2016).

Better Decision-Making

VGI provides a variety of geospatial data that can help various government sectors make better decisions. Public service organizations can acquire insightful information on residents' preferences, requirements, and challenges regarding certain places and services by using VGI data. Governments can create more citizen-centric policies and efficiently distribute resources thanks to this data-driven decision-making strategy (Dias et al., 2019; Malik & Shaikh, 2019)

Targeted Service Delivery

VGI data can be used to locate areas that have particular requirements or that don't have enough public services. Governments can identify underserved neighbourhoods and focus their efforts on enhancing service delivery in those regions by analyzing VGI data. For instance, the creation of new facilities and services can be facilitated by using VGI to identify locations with insufficient access to healthcare or educational resources (Kihumbe, 2019; Sezer et al., 2018).

Cost-Effectiveness

Conventional data collection techniques can be costly and time-consuming. On the other hand, VGI makes use of the group efforts of residents, drastically lowering the expenses of data collection. Gathering geospatial data has been made more affordable by the accessibility of large-scale, crowdsourced data through VGI platforms like OpenStreetMap (OSM) (Grinberger et al., 2022).

Updated Information

When compared to typical government datasets, VGI datasets are frequently more current and dynamic. Since data from citizens is always being added, the information is always up-to-date and accurate. Because VGI data is dynamic, public service organizations may always access the most up-to-date information, enabling quick reactions to changing circumstances (Honarparvar et al., 2019).

Social Sustainability

By taking into account the requirements of many communities, the inclusiveness of VGI initiatives fosters social sustainability. Marginalized and underrepresented groups can express their concerns and participate in the planning and design of public services through VGI. As a result, more inclusive and equitable services can be created (Bittner et al., 2016; Muzaffar et al., 2017).

Visual Reporting

Geo-tagged images and videos are specialized forms of VGI. Visual reporting uses geo-tagged images and videos captured with contemporary cellphones and cameras to provide important on-the-ground data. Drones with cameras can help rescue workers in their efforts and improve the evaluation of damage in catastrophe scenarios. Delivery of products and services is made more effective with geotagged photographs (To et al., 2015; Tsou et al., 2017).

Insightful Planning and Delivery

Public sector organizations can use location data to learn more about the spatial distribution of different services and resources. Policymakers can properly distribute resources by using this data to inform their judgements. It assists in locating places that have particular requirements for things like healthcare facilities, educational facilities, transportation infrastructure, and more (Ahmad BinTouq, 2015).

Transparency and Accountability

Governments can use VGI to show transparency by making data available to the general public. Additionally, data science can help to ensure data quality, validate information, and avoid data exploitation, improving accountability in government services (Georgiadou et al., 2014).

Figure 1. Benefits of VGI for government service delivery

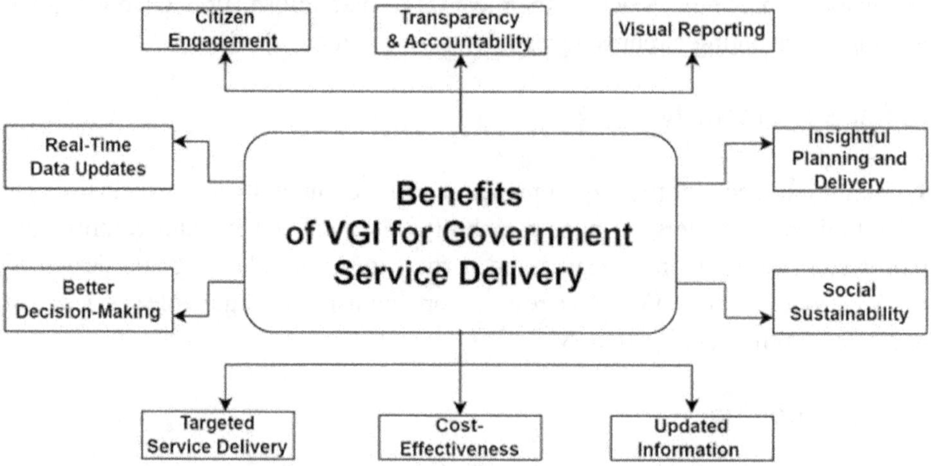

DATA SCIENCE

Data science is an interdisciplinary field, that involves extracting significant knowledge and insights from enormous and varied data sources (Subrahmanya et al., 2022). It includes a range of methods for handling, analyzing, and interpreting data, such as data mining, machine learning, statistical analysis, and data visualization to support decision-making (Asamoah et al., 2020). Data science can be used to supply public services by combining data from various sources, including administrative boundaries, surveys, social media, and VGI, to develop a deeper understanding of societal trends and citizen needs. By allowing governmental organizations to extract useful insight from raw data, data science can facilitate the development of well-informed policies and the use of evidence-based decision-making (Gunapati, 2011). Governments and organizations can better able to address problems in a proactive manner, anticipate citizens' needs, and allocate resources efficiently for maximum impact when data analytics are integrated into public services (Maffei et al., 2020).

In the realm of governance, the advent of data science technologies such as artificial intelligence (AI), the Internet of Things (IoT), big data and behavioral/predictive analytics, and blockchain is on the brink of ushering in a transformative era. These cutting-edge technologies can revolutionize government service delivery through data-driven innovations (Engin & Treleaven, 2019; Mikhaylov et al., 2018). They can be utilized in various domains, such as public health development (R & B, 2022), provision of public agricultural extension services (Namyenya et al., 2022), raising awareness regarding climate change (Appelgren & Jönsson, 2021), establishing policy innovation labs for digital governance of education (Williamson, 2015), and facilitating the planning and implementation of public transport (Keller et al., 2022).

Data science has sparked a revolutionary wave in the public sector, driving economic growth and presenting tremendous opportunities for enhancing the quality of public service delivery (Manikam et al., 2019). Through big data analysis, data science can set a benchmark for public service quality, enabling the improvement of citizen-centric services (Manikam et al., 2019). Data intelligence and analytics emerge as pivotal tools in the public sector, empowering decision-makers to make informed choices and achieve greater efficiency, and fostering better outcomes in the public sector (Di Vaio et al., 2022). The profound impact of big data analytics on public organizations' performance and efficiency is evident, underscoring its transformative potential (Rogge et al., 2017; Wahdain et al., 2019).

In the public sector, data analytics can be harnessed by auditors to uphold accountability and ensure responsible management of state finances (Novita & Indrany Nanda Ayu Anissa, 2022). This utilization of data analytics can fosters transparency and strengthens financial oversight within government entities. The transformation brought about by data science development will significantly influence the future roles and responsibilities of public sector organizations across various functional domains (Gamage, 2016).

Data Science Applications for Government Service Delivery

A wide range of data science applications can be utilized in the public sector. Below, are a few of these applications briefed in Figure 2 and presented below.

Predictive Analytics for Resource Planning

Predictive analytics for resource planning is a prominent use of data science in the public sector. Governmental organizations can predict future demand for a variety of services, including healthcare, education, and public safety, by examining previous data and patterns. For instance, the Singaporean government makes use of predictive analytics to plan for and distribute resources in accordance with the healthcare demands of the aging population (Liming et al., 2015; Rangaswamy et al., 2021). With this proactive strategy, resources can be distributed more effectively, improving service delivery and reducing costs.

Sentiment Analysis for Citizen Feedback

Huge amounts of citizen comments gathered through multiple means, including social media, surveys, and feedback forms, can be analyzed for sentiment using data science. Governments can measure public contentment, pinpoint areas for improvement, and quickly address public concerns by analyzing the sentiment of citizens' ideas and feelings (Muneeb & Chandler, 2021).

Network Analysis for Transportation Optimization

Using data science techniques, network analysis is essential for improving urban transport networks. Government organizations can pinpoint areas of high traffic congestion, improve public transit routes, and schedule infrastructure construction by analyzing traffic data. For instance, PTV Visum, a software provided by PTV Group, is utilized by the Barcelona Metropolitan Transport Authority (ATM) to perform demand modeling and analyze various scenarios pertaining to the supply of public transport services (Gomes, 2021).

Anomaly Detection for Fraud Prevention

Data science is essential for spotting irregularities and fraud in government transactions. Government agencies can spot strange patterns and possible fraud attempts by analyzing financial data and transaction records. The Internal Revenue Service is embracing cutting-edge technologies to enhance its ability to identify tax fraud, undisclosed assets, money laundering, identity theft, and other forms of noncompliance more effectively (Aprio, 2019; stahlesq.com, 2018).

Figure 2. Data science applications for government service delivery

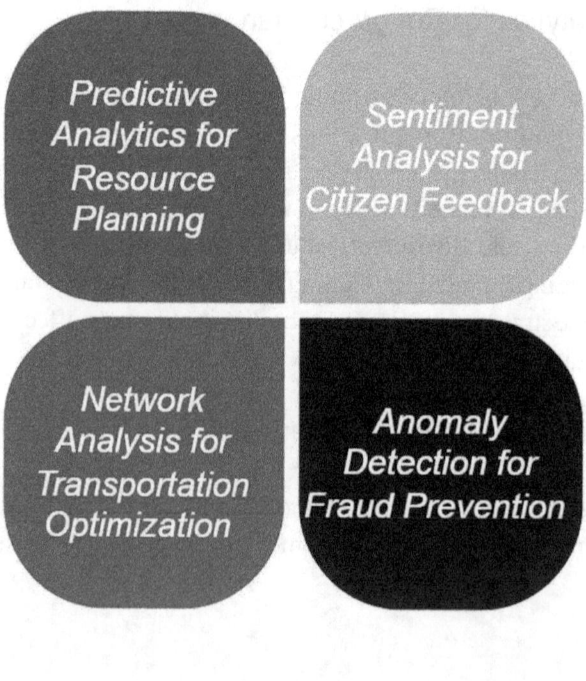

VGI AND DATA SCIENCE SYNERGY: ENHANCING GOVERNMENT SERVICES

Data science and VGI hold significant potential to enhance government services through various means. Selected potential applications of VGI and data science techniques are summarized in Figure 3 and elaborated upon in detail below.

Health

Disease Surveillance

VGI data can help by giving real-time information on symptoms and locations to track the spread of diseases. This data can be analyzed using data science approaches to forecast disease outbreaks, identify high-risk locations, analyze disease impact, and allocate healthcare resources appropriately. Accurate maps that show where homes are located in a region provide several advantages in a variety of fields. Public health initiatives that concentrate on providing services at the household level, like indoor residual pesticide spraying to treat malaria, are one of the essential areas where such maps prove beneficial. Sturrock et al., (2018) demonstrated the potential of ensemble machine learning approaches to improve the accuracy of building categorization in VGI datasets, providing valuable insights for targeted public health interventions and other applications such as planning fumigation campaigns. Similarly, Solís et al., (2018) illustrated the process of mapping building and road infrastructure in Mozambique and Kenya using VGI to support an insecticide spray campaign aimed at malaria prevention and safeguarding public health.

Rodriguez et al., (2021) evaluated the impact of the Covid-19 pandemic on hospital services in major cities of Ecuador by assessing the distribution and area of effect of hospitals equipped to treat Covid-19 patients using cutting-edge computational methods, data from OSM. Qi et al., (2018) introduced a novel approach for detecting and mapping foodborne diseases using VGI datasets. Diggle, (2005) highlighted how businesses and governments can leverage data to improve healthcare services for marginalized communities, ensuring equitable access to high-quality healthcare.

Healthcare Access and Planning

VGI data can be utilized to pinpoint healthcare facilities, concerns with accessibility, and service gaps. These data can be analyzed using data science to better position healthcare facilities and increase access to healthcare for marginalized communities. For instance, Kihumbe (2019) demonstrates VGI's utility in mapping HIV hotspot areas, while Mooney et al. (2013) assessed OSM's potential for pervasive health computing applications. Additionally, Malik & Shaikh (2019) investigated VGI data's effectiveness in studying the spatial distribution of healthcare facilities in Pakistan.

In the delivery of healthcare services, ambulance services are essential. It is impossible to stress the importance of successfully managing and operating ambulances since it guarantees that these expensive and valuable resources are used to their full potential. Ambulance services play a vital role in the delivery of healthcare services. The significance of effectively managing and operating ambulances cannot be overstated, as it ensures that these expensive and valuable resources are used to their full potential. (Okyere et al., 2022) developed an ambulance management system based on VGI in Ghana.

In public health practices, community asset mapping is indispensable because it recognizes a community's assets, requirements, and effective urban health intervention strategies. Kolak et al., (2020) presented an innovative participatory asset mapping infrastructure utilizing VGI in the context of urban health. Air quality has long been a critical factor influencing public health. To effectively combat air pollution in urban regions, it is essential to have precise and reliable air quality exposure data. Gupta et al., (2018) introduced valuable insights into the organized implementation of VGI air quality sensors to develop accurate air quality maps for urban monitoring purposes.

Health Awareness Campaigns

VGI data can help in identifying the population's information requirements and concerns around their health. Data science can be used to find trends and create focused health awareness programmes to successfully address particular health conditions. As noted by Noveck et al., (2017) the effectiveness of control measures against mosquito-borne diseases (MBDs) is significantly hindered by a lack of public awareness and misconceptions. Myths, rumors, and misinformation create higher risks of disease transmission within communities and impede the successful mobilization of the public for prevention efforts. Social media is a big source of VGI and Social media platforms play a crucial role in closing the information gaps between communities by fostering information exchange and awareness (Crowley et al., 2012). Noveck et al., (2017) suggested that sentiment analysis and network analysis of social media data collected through crowdsourcing can be utilized to assess public opinions regarding the spread of a specific disease, the effectiveness of outreach activities, and opportunities for improvement.

Education

School Planning and Allocation

VGI data can be used to pinpoint regions with dense populations and few educational resources. By utilizing spatial data analysis, regions with limited access to high-quality educational opportunities can be identified, enabling governments and businesses to establish and enhance educational services for marginalized communities. In order to ensure equal access to high-quality education, data science approaches can analyze this data to identify the best locations for new schools or redistribute existing resources. As noted by Xie et al., (2019) VGI data can be used for urban planning in the areas where insufficient official building data exist. These initiatives can contribute to social sustainability by narrowing educational disparities and empowering communities through education (Muzaffar et al., 2017).

Transportation and Accessibility

To comprehend students' transport demands, VGI data can be employed. To ensure that students can get to their schools easily, data science can be used to develop effective school bus routes, detect regions lacking safe pedestrian pathways, and optimize transportation services. For instance, Sezer et al., (2018) conducted an analysis that combined OSM data with population data to assess school accessibility.

Educational Resource Mapping

VGI may assist in the creation of extensive databases by crowdsourcing data about educational resources and facilities across the globe. In order to generate resource maps that help policymakers and educators make data-driven decisions regarding resource allocation and improvement plans, data science can analyze this information. Filho et al., (2013) conducted a test involving the mapping of towns within cartography disciplines, and the results established the effectiveness of OSM in enhancing the learning process. Through the utilization of "local knowledge," participants were motivated to engage in problem-oriented learning by addressing real-life issues in their neighborhoods. This approach demonstrated how OSM can be a valuable tool in incorporating practical and relevant tasks into the learning experience.

Transportation

Traffic Management

VGI data can offer up-to-the-minute details on accidents, blocked roads, and traffic congestion. These data can be analyzed using data science approaches to forecast traffic patterns, improve signal timings, and suggest other routes for improved traffic flow. OpenStreetMap has demonstrated its worth as a valuable data resource for traffic simulations, providing information comparable to, and in certain cases, even surpassing proprietary network models offered by governmental authorities (Rieck et al., 2015; Zilske et al., 2011).

Planning for Public Transport

Public transportation plays a crucial role in the transportation system, serving as a vital component for urban mobility. However, rapid expansion and urban growth have led to a substantial rise in the demand for public transportation. Easy and quick access to both public and private services, including schools, parks, and shops, is a crucial factor in determining the quality of life in urban areas. VGI data can provide information on the demand for public transport and the most well-liked transit routes. Using data science, public transport networks may be planned and optimized, including the most effective routes and high-traffic locations.

To assess urban accessibility for transportation planning, Steiniger et al., (2016) created a web-based platform. The results showed that OSM data can be utilized to evaluate urban accessibility, however, its completeness may vary across different areas. Tran et al., (2013) introduced a framework to synchronize transport data between OSM and a transit GTFS dataset. This made it simple for public transport agencies to post GTFS data to OSM and receive useful crowdsourced data in return. This framework is useful to modify and improve bus stop placements and amenities using the current GTFS data as a guide by employing online communities.

Carpooling and Ride-Sharing

VGI data can be used to promote and enhance programmes for ride- and carpooling. Data science can be used to create user-friendly tools to make carpooling arrangements and analyze commuter patterns to find prospective matches. According to Hariz et al., (2021), VGI has the potential to enhance transportation systems by optimizing riders' satisfaction through real-time data exchange among the regional manager, public buses, car ride-sharing services, and the riders themselves. Chao & Wang, (2018) developed a model to assess bicycle circulation by determining the best sites for docking stations using geographic information comprising highways, sidewalks, bicycle lanes, and well-known locations from OSM in Taipei City.

Waste Management

Waste Collection Routing

Information about waste-generating patterns and the locations of waste collection points can be found in VGI data. Data science can improve waste collection routes, minimizing the environmental impact and consuming less energy. Dias et al., (2019) integrated VGI into garbage collection routes, to enhance citizen involvement, improve recyclable waste collection rates, and lower logistics costs. Similarly, Dowd et al., (2020) demonstrated the use of OpenStreetMap and Google OR-Tools to optimize waste management collection routes, addressing mixed fleet routing problems. Additionally, Felício et al., (2022) introduced an architecture utilizing OSM for route planning in the context of solid waste collection.

Recycling and Disposal Centers

VGI data can be used to map recycling and disposal facilities and pinpoint regions with insufficient waste management facilities. In order to situate recycling facilities in the best possible locations and increase waste diversion rates, data analysis using data science can help. Improper planning has resulted in a substantial amount of waste disposal, giving rise to both economic and environmental issues. Addressing this concern, Thompson et al., (2013) offered a solution for the allocation and relocation of waste bins, integrating recyclable waste into the same bins and establishing direct communication channels between citizens and waste management authorities. Similarly, Mavakala et al., (2017) proposed the exploration of crowdsourcing as a potential mechanism for identifying, locating, and characterizing solid waste landfills.

Environmental Impact Assessment

Insights into unlawful dumping and pollution hotspots can be gained from VGI data. This data can be analyzed using data science to determine the environmental effects of improper waste management and to guide targeted activities to reduce environmental risks. Spatial data can promote sustainable waste reduction and management practices while enhancing waste management policies (A. Singh, 2019). Singh et al., (2016) developed a WebGIS-based platform for the citizen reporting, monitoring, and visualization of solid waste in urban areas. To discover

Figure 3. Opportunities offered by VGI and data science

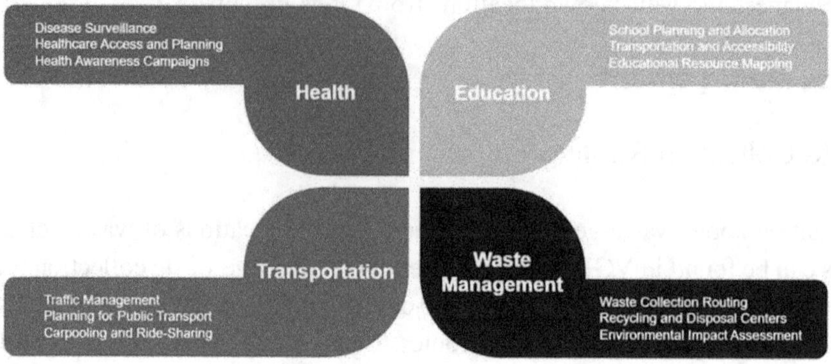

the locations of the facility to end-users for reporting and lodging complaints, etc., a Geo-locator tool is built.

CHALLENGES

In the context of public sector service delivery, VGI presents numerous advantages, but it also poses certain challenges that necessitate careful consideration. This section explores some significant VGI-related issues, as highlighted and illustrated in Figure 4.

Data Quality and Validation

The quality of VGI and crowdsourced data, including factors like accuracy, consistency, and completeness, can vary significantly, making validation and verification procedures essential to assess its reliability. In the realm of public sector delivery, relying on inaccurate information may hinder effective resource allocation and decision-making (Ray & Bala, 2020). Poor data quality can lead to inefficient use of limited resources and delays in providing support to communities in need. Thus, accurate and validated data is paramount for well-informed decision-making and prompt response actions.

To mitigate the spread of false information and potential data misuse, robust quality control procedures and data validation methods are indispensable. This includes implementing data cleaning, filtering, and cross-validation techniques. Collaborations with academic institutions, organizations, and volunteers can be established to ensure data accuracy and reliability in various public service scenarios.

Additionally, Machine Learning techniques can be employed to differentiate between false and authentic information and automate the detection and removal of inaccurate data (Ray & Bala, 2020).

Data Security and Privacy

In the context of public sector service delivery, VGI raises concerns regarding data security and privacy. As more community members contribute data, it becomes essential to safeguard their privacy and obtain explicit consent (Yingwei et al., 2020). Inadequate data security and privacy controls can lead to the disclosure of personal information, eroding public confidence and deterring citizen engagement. Protecting privacy is crucial to preserve VGI's core principles of opportunism, data-centricity, disruption, and inclusivity (B. T. Haworth et al., 2018).

Privacy challenges may deter individuals from providing critical information, hindering the efficiency of public sector activities. To ensure data security and privacy, stringent procedures and regulations must be established. Implementing data encryption methods and secure data storage practices can safeguard sensitive information (Muthi Reddy et al., 2018). Furthermore, individuals involved in VGI collection should be educated about secure data handling procedures.

Participation and Inclusivity

Encouraging active participation from diverse community members in VGI initiatives can be challenging. Technological accessibility, literacy levels, linguistic barriers, and power imbalances within communities may constrain the inclusivity of VGI efforts (B. T. Haworth et al., 2018). Incomplete or biased data may result from limited involvement, overlooking the needs and perspectives of vulnerable populations (B. T. Haworth et al., 2018). Inclusive involvement enhances the accuracy and relevance of VGI data, contributing to more effective decision-making and targeted interventions.

Efforts should be made to bridge these gaps and ensure that marginalized perspectives are heard and represented in community-led processes (Bittner et al., 2016). Outreach campaigns can be organized to raise awareness and interest in VGI initiatives, particularly among marginalized communities (B. Haworth et al., 2016). Providing training and support to individuals who may not be technologically savvy or digitally literate can further enhance their participation in VGI efforts.

Technological Infrastructure

In the context of public sector service delivery, the full potential of VGI may be hindered by limited access to technology (Li & Ulaganathan, 2017). Certain communities may face challenges in accessing and utilizing the necessary platforms and tools for data submission and analysis (Crawford & Finn, 2015). The gathering and utilization of VGI and data science techniques may be constrained by insufficient technological infrastructure, leading to delays in real-time monitoring, data exchange, and decision-making. Critical information gathering may be impeded, hampering the coordination of effective response teams.

To overcome these obstacles, it is essential to ensure the availability of the required infrastructure and equitable access to technology and the Internet, especially in underprivileged areas. Developing user-friendly, multilingual software and platforms that are compatible with various hardware and networks can help mitigate the impact of limited technological infrastructure. Data science approaches can also play a role in optimizing data transmission, storage, and processing to ensure seamless information flow in public sector operations.

Specialized Skillset

The absence of digital literacy and specific skill sets among participants can hinder the full utilization of VGI in public sector delivery (Li & Ulaganathan, 2017). Without the necessary abilities and knowledge, individuals may struggle to effectively participate in data collection, analysis, and interpretation (Sboui & Aissi, 2022). This constraint can compromise the accuracy and usability of the generated information. Moreover, the thoroughness and reliability of VGI can be limited by the lack of specialized knowledge and digital literacy, leading to the collection of erroneous or incomplete data. Additionally, the analysis and interpretation of data can become challenging, impeding valuable insights and informed decision-making during public sector activities.

To address this challenge, comprehensive training, and technical support must be provided to individuals and communities engaged in VGI activities (B. Haworth et al., 2016). Capacity-building programs can enhance data-gathering methods, data analysis methodologies, and digital literacy skills. Furthermore, user-friendly tools and platforms must be developed, taking into consideration the diverse backgrounds and abilities of potential VGI contributors. Data science can contribute to data analysis tools, automating data processing, and generating actionable insights for decision-makers in the public sector.

CONCLUSION

Data science and VGI have become revolutionary forces in the provision of public services. By enabling users to actively participate in data generation and curation,

Figure 4. Challenges of VGI

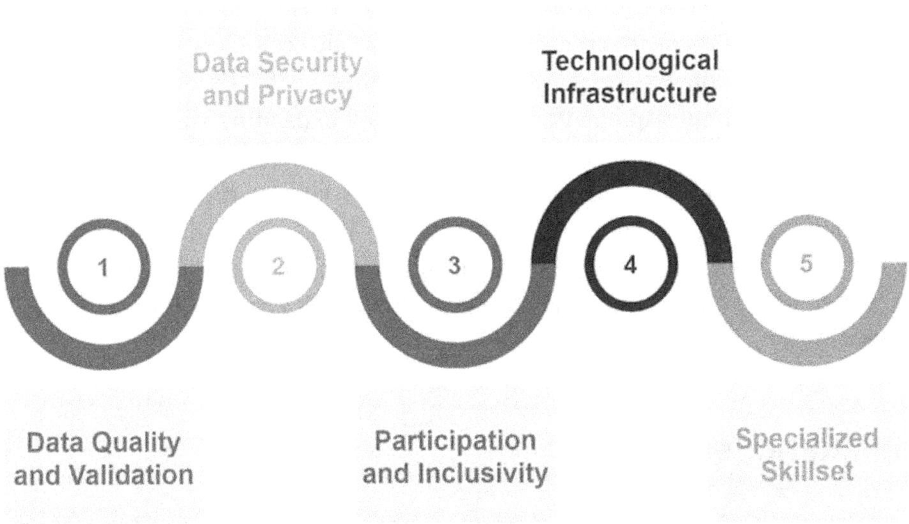

VGI, a type of user-generated content, democratizes geographic information. The incorporation of VGI into public sector operations can create new opportunities for improving government services across a range of areas. By gleaning valuable insights from a wide range of data sources, such as administrative boundaries, surveys, social media, and VGI itself, data science can complement VGI. Data science supports data-driven policy development and evidence-based decision-making by using data mining, machine learning, and statistical analysis. In addition, modern technologies like AI, IoT, big data analytics, and blockchain have the potential to completely change how government services are provided.

VGI can offer real-time disease surveillance in the context of health, enhancing emergency response capabilities. Data science can improve location-based recommendations for citizens by integrating VGI into recommender systems, which optimizes the provision of public services. A better allocation of resources and the development of infrastructure are also made possible by VGI's help for urban planning and land use validation. Additionally, VGI's citizen involvement programme encourages empowerment and co-creation of public services, ensuring that they are in line with the community's genuine needs and preferences. To properly utilize the promise of VGI in public sector delivery, however, issues including data quality, security, inclusivity, technological infrastructure, and specialized skill sets must be addressed.

Future initiatives should concentrate on improving data quality control and validation procedures for VGI in order to further improve government services.

Broader and more inclusive citizen participation will be made possible by creating user-friendly tools and platforms to reduce technological accessibility gaps and by boosting digital literacy. In cases involving the public sector, cooperation between organizations, volunteers, and academia can improve VGI's dependability and accuracy. Additionally, to handle the continuously expanding volume of data and offer real-time insights for quick decision-making, data science methodologies need to be continually improved. To expand public service delivery, increase transparency, and tighten financial monitoring, governments should invest in data intelligence and analytics. Utilizing data science will promote efficiency, sustainability, and resource optimization in industries like education, health transportation, and waste management.

REFERENCES

Abdulkarim, B., Kamberov, R., & Hay, G. J. (2014). Supporting Urban Energy Efficiency with Volunteered Roof Information and the Google Maps API. *Remote Sensing (Basel)*, *6*(10), 9691–9711. Advance online publication. doi:10.3390/rs6109691

Ahmad, M., Khayal, M. S. H., & Tahir, A. (2022). Analysis of Factors Affecting Adoption of Volunteered Geographic Information in the Context of National Spatial Data Infrastructure. *ISPRS International Journal of Geo-Information*, *11*(2), 120. Advance online publication. doi:10.3390/ijgi11020120

Ahmad BinTouq. (2015). The UAE Federal Government's E-Participation Roadmap: Developments in UAE Empowerment Initiatives With VGI/PGIS and Location Based Services (LBS). *Canadian Social Science*, *11*(5). Advance online publication. doi:10.3968/6919

Annis, A., & Nardi, F. (2019). Integrating VGI and 2D hydraulic models into a data assimilation framework for real time flood forecasting and mapping. *Geo-Spatial Information Science*, *22*(4), 223–236. Advance online publication. doi:10.1080/10095020.2019.1626135

Antoniou, V., Fonte, C. C., See, L., Estima, J., Arsanjani, J. J., Lupia, F., Minghini, M., Foody, G., & Fritz, S. (2016). Investigating the feasibility of geo-Tagged photographs as sources of land cover input data. *ISPRS International Journal of Geo-Information*, *5*(5), 64. Advance online publication. doi:10.3390/ijgi5050064

Appelgren, E., & Jönsson, A. M. (2021). Engaging Citizens for Climate Change—Challenges for Journalism. *Digital Journalism (Abingdon, England)*, *9*(6), 755–772. Advance online publication. doi:10.1080/21670811.2020.1827965

Aprio. (2019). *Artificial Intelligence to Help Resource-Strapped IRS More Efficiently Identify Tax Crimes.* https://www.aprio.com/artificial-intelligence-to-help-resource-strapped-irs-more-efficiency/

Arnaboldi, M., & Azzone, G. (2020). Data science in the design of public policies: Dispelling the obscurity in matching policy demand and data offer. *Heliyon*, *6*(6), e04300. Advance online publication. doi:10.1016/j.heliyon.2020.e04300 PMID:32637693

Asamoah, D. A., Doran, D., & Schiller, S. (2020). Interdisciplinarity in Data Science Pedagogy: A Foundational Design. *Journal of Computer Information Systems*, *60*(4), 370–377. Advance online publication. doi:10.1080/08874417.2018.1496803

Bittner, C., Michel, B., & Turk, C. (2016). Turning the spotlight on the crowd: Examining the participatory ethics and practices of crisis mapping. *ACME, 15*(1).

Brodie, M. L. (2019). What Is Data Science? In Applied Data Science: Lessons Learned for the Data-Driven Business. doi:10.1007/978-3-030-11821-1_8

Calcagni, F., Amorim Maia, A. T., Connolly, J. J. T., & Langemeyer, J. (2019). Digital co-construction of relational values: Understanding the role of social media for sustainability. *Sustainability Science*, *14*(5), 1309–1321. Advance online publication. doi:10.1007/s11625-019-00672-1

Chao, C. Y., & Wang, S. (2018). Using OpenStreetMap data for the location analysis on public bicycle stations – A case study on the Youbike system in downtown Taipei city. *Proceedings - 39th Asian Conference on Remote Sensing: Remote Sensing Enabling Prosperity, ACRS 2018.*

Chen, X., Elmes, G., Ye, X., & Chang, J. (2016). Implementing a Real-Time Twitter-Based System for Resource Dispatch in Disaster Management. *GeoJournal*, *81*(6), 863–873. Advance online publication. doi:10.1007/s10708-016-9745-8

Crawford, K., & Finn, M. (2015). The limits of crisis data: Analytical and ethical challenges of using social and mobile data to understand disasters. *GeoJournal*, *80*(4), 491–502. Advance online publication. doi:10.1007/s10708-014-9597-z

Crowley, D. N., Breslin, J. G., Corcoran, P., & Young, K. (2012). Gamification of citizen sensing through mobile social reporting. *4th International IEEE Consumer Electronic Society - Games Innovation Conference, IGiC 2012*. 10.1109/IGIC.2012.6329849

Di Vaio, A., Hassan, R., & Alavoine, C. (2022). Data intelligence and analytics: A bibliometric analysis of human–Artificial intelligence in public sector decision-making effectiveness. *Technological Forecasting and Social Change*, *174*, 121201. Advance online publication. doi:10.1016/j.techfore.2021.121201

Dias, V. E. C., Sperandio, V. G., & Lisboa-Filho, J. (2019). Routes generation for selective collection of urban waste using volunteered geographic information. *Iberian Conference on Information Systems and Technologies, CISTI, 2019-June*. 10.23919/CISTI.2019.8760773

Diggle, P. (2005). Applied Spatial Statistics for Public Health Data. *Journal of the American Statistical Association*, *100*(470), 702–703. Advance online publication. doi:10.1198/jasa.2005.s15

Dowd, M., Dixon, A., & Kinsella, B. (2020). Optimizing waste management collection routes in Urban Haiti: A collaboration between DataKind and SOIL. *ArXiv, 2012*.

Engin, Z., & Treleaven, P. (2019). Algorithmic Government: Automating Public Services and Supporting Civil Servants in using Data Science Technologies. *The Computer Journal*, *62*(3), 448–460. Advance online publication. doi:10.1093/comjnl/bxy082

Felício, S., Hora, J., Ferreira, M. C., Abrantes, D., Costa, P. D., Dangelo, C., Silva, J., & Galvão, T. (2022). Handling OpenStreetMap georeferenced data for route planning. *Transportation Research Procedia*, *62*, 189–196. Advance online publication. doi:10.1016/j.trpro.2022.02.024

Filho, H. F., Leite, B. P., Pompermayer, G. A., Werneck, M. G., & Leyh, W. (2013). Teaching VGI as a strategy to promote the production of urban digital cartographic databases. *Joint Urban Remote Sensing Event 2013. JURSE, 2013*. Advance online publication. doi:10.1109/JURSE#.2013.6550705

Fonte, C. C., Bastin, L., See, L., Foody, G., & Lupia, F. (2015). Usability of VGI for validation of land cover maps. *International Journal of Geographical Information Science*, *29*(May), 1–23. doi:10.1080/13658816.2015.1018266

Gamage, P. (2016). New development: Leveraging 'big data' analytics in the public sector. *Public Money & Management*, *36*(5), 385–390. Advance online publication. doi:10.1080/09540962.2016.1194087

Georgiadou, Y., Lungo, J. H., & Richter, C. (2014). Citizen sensors or extreme publics? Transparency and accountability interventions on the mobile geoweb. *International Journal of Digital Earth*, *7*(7), 516–533. Advance online publication. doi:10.1080/17538947.2013.782073

Gomes, M. (2021). Barcelona improves public transport with modelling technology. *PTV Blog*. https://blog.ptvgroup.com/en/city-and-mobility/barcelona-improve-public-transport-modelling/

Goodchild, M. F. (2007). Citizens as sensors: The world of volunteered geography. GeoJournal. doi:10.1007/s10708-007-9111-y

Grinberger, A. Y., Minghini, M., Juhász, L., Yeboah, G., & Mooney, P. (2022). OSM Science—The Academic Study of the OpenStreetMap Project, Data, Contributors, Community, and Applications. In ISPRS International Journal of Geo-Information (Vol. 11, Issue 4). doi:10.3390/ijgi11040230

Güiza, F., & Stuart, N. (2018). When citizens choose not to participate in volunteering geographic information to e-governance: a case study from Mexico. GeoJournal. doi:10.1007/s10708-017-9820-9

Gunapati, S. (2011). Key Features for Designing a Dashboard. *Government Finance Review, 27.*

Gupta, S., Pebesma, E., Degbelo, A., & Costa, A. C. (2018). Optimising citizen-driven air quality monitoring networks for cities. *ISPRS International Journal of Geo-Information*, *7*(12), 468. Advance online publication. doi:10.3390/ijgi7120468

Haklay, M. (2013). Citizen science and volunteered geographic information: Overview and typology of participation. In Crowdsourcing Geographic Knowledge: Volunteered Geographic Information (VGI) in Theory and Practice. doi:10.1007/978-94-007-4587-2_7

Hariz, M. (2021). A dynamic mobility traffic model based on two modes of transport in smart cities. *Smart Cities*, *4*(1), 253–270. Advance online publication. doi:10.3390/smartcities4010016

Haworth, B., Whittaker, J., & Bruce, E. (2016). Assessing the application and value of participatory mapping for community bushfire preparation. *Applied Geography (Sevenoaks, England)*, *76*, 115–127. Advance online publication. doi:10.1016/j.apgeog.2016.09.019

Haworth, B. T., Bruce, E., Whittaker, J., & Read, R. (2018). The good, the bad, and the uncertain: Contributions of volunteered geographic information to community disaster resilience. In Frontiers in Earth Science (Vol. 6). doi:10.3389/feart.2018.00183

Honarparvar, S., Forouzandeh Jonaghani, R., Alesheikh, A. A., & Atazadeh, B. (2019). Improvement of a location-aware recommender system using volunteered geographic information. *Geocarto International*, *34*(13), 1496–1513. Advance online publication. doi:10.1080/10106049.2018.1493155

Hu, S., Ge, Y., Liu, M., Ren, Z., & Zhang, X. (2022). Village-level poverty identification using machine learning, high-resolution images, and geospatial data. *International Journal of Applied Earth Observation and Geoinformation*, *107*, 102694. Advance online publication. doi:10.1016/j.jag.2022.102694

Huang, H., Yao, X. A., Krisp, J. M., & Jiang, B. (2021). Analytics of location-based big data for smart cities: Opportunities, challenges, and future directions. *Computers, Environment and Urban Systems*, *90*, 101712. Advance online publication. doi:10.1016/j.compenvurbsys.2021.101712

Keller, C., Glück, F., Gerlach, C. F., & Schlegel, T. (2022). Investigating the Potential of Data Science Methods for Sustainable Public Transport. *Sustainability (Basel)*, *14*(7), 4211. Advance online publication. doi:10.3390/su14074211

Kihumbe. (2019). *Kihumbe- Survey Digitization and Mapping for HIV Monitoring*. Academic Press.

Kitchin, R., Lauriault, T. P., & Wilson, M. W. (2018). Understanding Spatial Media. In Understanding Spatial Media. doi:10.4135/9781526425850.n1

Kolak, M., Steptoe, M., Manprisio, H., Azu-Popow, L., Hinchy, M., Malana, G., & Maciejewski, R. (2020). *Extending Volunteered Geographic Information (VGI) with Geospatial Software as a Service: Participatory Asset Mapping Infrastructures for Urban Health*. doi:10.1007/978-3-030-19573-1_11

Kucukali, A., Pjeternikaj, R., Zeka, E., & Hysa, A. (2022). Evaluating the pedestrian accessibility to public services using open-source geospatial data and QGIS software. *Nova Geodesia*, *2*(2), 42. Advance online publication. doi:10.55779/ng2242

Li, L., & Ulaganathan, M. N. (2017). Design and development of a crowdsourcing mobile app for disaster response. *International Conference on Geoinformatics*. 10.1109/GEOINFORMATICS.2017.8090943

Liming, B., Gavino, A. I., Lee, P., Jungyoon, K., Na, L., Pink Pi, T. H., Xian, T. H., Buay, T. L., Xiaoping, T., Valera, A., Jia, E. Y., Wu, A., & Fox, M. S. (2015). SHINESeniors: Personalized services for active ageing-in-place. *2015 IEEE 1st International Smart Cities Conference, ISC2 2015*. 10.1109/ISC2.2015.7366181

Ma, Q., Wang, L., Gong, X., & Li, K. (2022). Research on the Rationality of Public Toilets Spatial Layout based on the POI Data from the Perspective of Urban Functional Area. *Journal of Geo-Information Science*, *24*(1). Advance online publication. doi:10.12082/dqxxkx.2022.210331

Maffei, S., Leoni, F., & Villari, B. (2020). Data-driven anticipatory governance. Emerging scenarios in data for policy practices. *Policy Design and Practice*, *3*(2), 123–134. Advance online publication. doi:10.1080/25741292.2020.1763896

Malik, N. A., & Shaikh, M. A. (2019). Spatial distribution and accessibility to public sector tertiary care teaching hospitals: Case study from Pakistan. *Eastern Mediterranean Health Journal*, *25*(6), 431–434. Advance online publication. doi:10.26719/emhj.18.049 PMID:31469163

Manikam, S., Sahibudin, S., & Kasinathan, V. (2019). Business intelligence addressing service quality for big data analytics in public sector. *Indonesian Journal of Electrical Engineering and Computer Science*, *16*(1), 491. Advance online publication. doi:10.11591/ijeecs.v16.i1.pp491-499

Mavakala, B., Mulaji, C., Mpiana, P., Elongo, V., Otamonga, J.-P., Biey, E., Wildi, W., & Pote-Wembonyama, J. (2017). Citizen Sensing of Solid Waste Disposals : Crowdsourcing As Tool Supporting Waste Management in a. *Proceedings Sardinia 2017 / Sixteenth International Waste Management and Landfill Symposium*. https://doi.org/https://archive-ouverte.unige.ch/unige:97650

Mikhaylov, S. J., Esteve, M., & Campion, A. (2018). Artificial intelligence for the public sector: Opportunities and challenges of cross-sector collaboration. *Philosophical Transactions. Series A, Mathematical, Physical, and Engineering Sciences*, *376*(2128), 20170357. Advance online publication. doi:10.1098/rsta.2017.0357 PMID:30082303

Muneeb, S., & Chandler, T. W. (2021). *Sentiment Analysis for COVID-19 National Vaccination Policy*. https://pide.org.pk/blog/sentiment-analysis-for-cov

Muthi Reddy, P., Manjula, S. H., & Venugopal, K. R. (2018). Secured Privacy Data using Multi Key Encryption in Cloud Storage. *Proceedings of 5th International Conference on Emerging Applications of Information Technology, EAIT 2018*. 10.1109/EAIT.2018.8470399

Muzaffar, H. M., Tahir, A., Ali, A., Ahmad, M., & McArdle, G. (2017). Quality assessment of volunteered geographic information for educational planning. In *Volunteered Geographic Information and the Future of Geospatial Data*. IGI Global. doi:10.4018/978-1-5225-2446-5.ch005

Namyenya, A., Daum, T., Rwamigisa, P. B., & Birner, R. (2022). E-diary: A digital tool for strengthening accountability in agricultural extension. *Information Technology for Development, 28*(2), 319–345. Advance online publication. doi:10.1080/02681102.2021.1875186

Noveck, B. S., Ayoub, R., Hermosilla, M., Marks, J., & Suwondo, P. (2017). *Smarter Crowdsourcing for Zika and Other Mosquito-Borne Diseases*. Academic Press.

Novita, N., & Indrany Nanda Ayu Anissa, A. (2022). The role of data analytics for detecting indications of fraud in the public sector. *International Journal of Research in Business and Social Science, 11*(7). doi:10.20525/ijrbs.v11i7.2113

Okyere, F., Minnich, T., Sproll, M., Mensah, E., Amartey, L., Otoo-Kwofie, C., & Brunn, A. (2022). Implementation of a low-cost Ambulance Management System. *Dgpf, 30*.

Olteanu-Raimond, A. M., See, L., Schultz, M., Foody, G., Riffler, M., Gasber, T., Jolivet, L., le Bris, A., Meneroux, Y., Liu, L., Poupée, M., & Gombert, M. (2020). Use of automated change detection and VGI sources for identifying and validating urban land use change. *Remote Sensing (Basel), 12*(7), 1186. Advance online publication. doi:10.3390/rs12071186

Provost, F., & Fawcett, T. (2013). Data Science and its Relationship to Big Data and Data-Driven Decision Making. *Big Data, 1*(1), 51–59. Advance online publication. doi:10.1089/big.2013.1508 PMID:27447038

Qi, Y., Guo, K., Zhang, C., Guo, D., & Zhi, Z. (2018). A VGI-based Foodborn Disease Report and Forecast System. *Proceedings of the 4th ACM SIGSPATIAL International Workshop on Safety and Resilience, EM-GIS 2018*. 10.1145/3284103.3284124

R, J., & B, S. (2022). Social Impacts of Data Science in Food, Housing And Medical Attention Linked to Public Service. *Technoarete Transactions on Advances in Data Science and Analytics, 1*(1). doi:10.36647/TTADSA/01.01.A004

Rangaswamy, E., Periyasamy, G., & Nawaz, N. (2021). A study on singapore's ageing population in the context of eldercare initiatives using machine learning algorithms. *Big Data and Cognitive Computing, 5*(4), 51. Advance online publication. doi:10.3390/bdcc5040051

Ray, A., & Bala, P. K. (2020). Social media for improved process management in organizations during disasters. *Knowledge and Process Management, 27*(1), 63–74. Advance online publication. doi:10.1002/kpm.1623

Rieck, D., Schünemann, B., & Radusch, I. (2015). Advanced Traffic Light Information in OpenStreetMap for Traffic Simulations. Lecture Notes in Mobility. doi:10.1007/978-3-319-15024-6_2

Rodriguez, G., Torres, H., Fajardo, M., & Medina, J. (2021). Covid-19 in Ecuador: Radiography of Hospital Distribution Using Data Science. *ETCM 2021 - 5th Ecuador Technical Chapters Meeting*. 10.1109/ETCM53643.2021.9590641

Rogge, N., Agasisti, T., & De Witte, K. (2017). Big data and the measurement of public organizations' performance and efficiency: The state-of-the-art. *Public Policy and Administration*, *32*(4), 263–281. Advance online publication. doi:10.1177/0952076716687355

Sangiambut, S., & Sieber, R. (2016). The V in VGI: Citizens or Civic Data Sources. *Urban Planning*, *1*(2), 141–154. doi:10.17645/up.v1i2.644

Sboui, T., & Aissi, S. (2022). *A Risk-based Approach for Enhancing the Fitness of use of VGI*. IEEE., doi:10.1109/ACCESS.2022.3201022

Sezer, A., Deniz, M., & Topuz, M. (2018). Analysis of Accessibility of Schools in Usak City via Geographical Information Systems (GIS). *Tarih Kultur ve Sanat Arastirmalari Dergisi-Journal of History Culture and Art Research*, *7*(5).

Singh, A. (2019). Remote sensing and GIS applications for municipal waste management. *Journal of Environmental Management*, *243*, 22–29. Advance online publication. doi:10.1016/j.jenvman.2019.05.017 PMID:31077867

Singh, Y. P., Singh, A. K., & Singh, R. P. (2016). *Web GIS based Framework for Citizen Reporting on Collection of Solid Waste and Mapping in GIS for Allahabad City. SAMRIDDHI : A Journal of Physical Sciences*, Engineering and Technology. doi:10.18090/samriddhi.v8i1.11405

Solís, P., McCusker, B., Menkiti, N., Cowan, N., & Blevins, C. (2018). Engaging global youth in participatory spatial data creation for the UN sustainable development goals: The case of open mapping for malaria prevention. *Applied Geography (Sevenoaks, England)*, *98*, 143–155. Advance online publication. doi:10.1016/j.apgeog.2018.07.013

stahlesq.com. (2018). *How the IRS Uses Artificial Intelligence to Detect Tax Evaders*. https://stahlesq.com/criminal-defense-law-blog/how-the-irs-uses-artificial-intelligence-to-detect-tax-evaders/

Steiniger, S., Poorazizi, M. E., Scott, D. R., Fuentes, C., & Crespo, R. (2016). Can we use OpenStreetMap POIs for the Evaluation of Urban Accessibility? *International Conference on GIScience Short Paper Proceedings, 1*. 10.21433/B31167F0678P

Sturrock, H. J. W., Woolheater, K., Bennett, A. F., Andrade-Pacheco, R., & Midekisa, A. (2018). Predicting residential structures from open source remotely enumerated data using machine learning. *PLoS One, 13*(9), e0204399. Advance online publication. doi:10.1371/journal.pone.0204399 PMID:30240429

Subrahmanya, S. V. G., Shetty, D. K., Patil, V., Hameed, B. M. Z., Paul, R., Smriti, K., Naik, N., & Somani, B. K. (2022). The role of data science in healthcare advancements: applications, benefits, and future prospects. In Irish Journal of Medical Science (Vol. 191, Issue 4). doi:10.1007/s11845-021-02730-z

Thompson, A. F., Afolayan, A. H., & Ibidunmoye, E. O. (2013). Application of geographic information system to solid waste management. *2013 Pan African International Conference on Information Science, Computing and Telecommunications, PACT 2013*. 10.1109/SCAT.2013.7055110

To, H., Kim, S. H., & Shahabi, C. (2015). Effectively crowdsourcing the acquisition and analysis of visual data for disaster response. *Proceedings - 2015 IEEE International Conference on Big Data, IEEE Big Data 2015*. 10.1109/BigData.2015.7363814

Tran, K., Barbeau, S., Hillsman, E., & Labrador, M. A. (2013). GO_Sync - A Framework to Synchronize Crowd-Sourced Mapping Contributors from Online Communities and Transit Agency Bus Stop Inventories. *International Journal of Intelligent Transportation Systems Research, 11*(2), 54–64. Advance online publication. doi:10.1007/s13177-013-0056-x

Tsou, M. H., Jung, C. Te, Allen, C., Yang, J. A., Han, S. Y., Spitzberg, B. H., & Dozier, J. (2017). Building a real-time geo-targeted event observation (Geo) viewer for disaster management and situation awareness. *Lecture Notes in Geoinformation and Cartography*. doi:10.1007/978-3-319-57336-6_7

Tzavella, K., Fekete, A., & Fiedrich, F. (2018). Opportunities provided by geographic information systems and volunteered geographic information for a timely emergency response during flood events in Cologne, Germany. *Natural Hazards, 91*. Advance online publication. doi:10.1007/s11069-017-3102-1

Wahdain, E. A., Baharudin, A. S., & Ahmad, M. N. (2019). Big data analytics in the malaysian public sector: The determinants of value creation. *Advances in Intelligent Systems and Computing, 843*, 139–150. Advance online publication. doi:10.1007/978-3-319-99007-1_14

Williamson, B. (2015). Governing methods: Policy innovation labs, design and data science in the digital governance of education. *Journal of Educational Administration and History*, *47*(3), 251–271. Advance online publication. doi:10.1080/00220620.2015.1038693

Wong, W., & Hinnant, C. C. (2022). Competing perspectives on the Big Data revolution: A typology of applications in public policy. *Journal of Economic Policy Reform*. Advance online publication. doi:10.1080/17487870.2022.2103701

Xie, X., Zhou, Y., Xu, Y., Hu, Y., & Wu, C. (2019). OpenStreetMap Data Quality Assessment via Deep Learning and Remote Sensing Imagery. *IEEE Access : Practical Innovations, Open Solutions*, *7*, 176884–176895. Advance online publication. doi:10.1109/ACCESS.2019.2957825

Yingwei, Y., Dawei, M., & Hongchao, F. (2020). A research framework for the application of volunteered geographic information in post-disaster recovery monitoring. *Tropical Geography*, *40*(2). Advance online publication. doi:10.13284/j.cnki.rddl.003239

Zilske, M., Neumann, A., & Nagel, K. (2011). OpenStreetMap For Traffic Simulation. *Proceedings of the 1st European State of the Map – OpenStreetMap Conference*.

Compilation of References

Abdulkarim, B., Kamberov, R., & Hay, G. J. (2014). Supporting Urban Energy Efficiency with Volunteered Roof Information and the Google Maps API. *Remote Sensing (Basel)*, *6*(10), 9691–9711. Advance online publication. doi:10.3390/rs6109691

Abraham, R., Schneider, J., & vom Brocke, J. (2019). Data governance: A conceptual framework, structured review, and research agenda. *International Journal of Information Management*, *49*, 424–438. doi:10.1016/j.ijinfomgt.2019.07.008

Accenture. (2016). *Why Artificial Intelligence is the Future of Growth*. Author.

Adhytia, B., Kurnia, Sh., Dilnutt, R., & Hidayanto, A. (2023). *Investigating the Role of Enterprise Architecture in Big Data Analytics Implementation: A Case Study in a Large Public Sector Organization. ACIS 2023 Proceedings Australasian*. ACIS.

Agievich, V. (2014). *Mathematical model and multi-criteria analysis of designing large-scale enterprise roadmap*. PhD thesis.

Agresti, A. (2012). *Categorical data analysis* (Vol. 792). John Wiley & Sons.

Ahmad BinTouq. (2015). The UAE Federal Government's E-Participation Roadmap: Developments in UAE Empowerment Initiatives With VGI/PGIS and Location Based Services (LBS). *Canadian Social Science*, *11*(5). Advance online publication. doi:10.3968/6919

Ahmad, G. (2010). *Domain-Oriented Modeling of Indian Education System Through UML*. IUP.

Ahmad, H., Asghar, M. U., Khan, A., & Mosavi, A. H. (2021). A Hybrid Deep Learning Technique for Personality Trait Classification from Text. *IEEE Access : Practical Innovations, Open Solutions*, *9*, 146214–146232. doi:10.1109/ACCESS.2021.3121791

Ahmad, M., Khayal, M. S. H., & Tahir, A. (2022). Analysis of Factors Affecting Adoption of Volunteered Geographic Information in the Context of National Spatial Data Infrastructure. *ISPRS International Journal of Geo-Information*, *11*(2), 120. Advance online publication. doi:10.3390/ijgi11020120

AlDhaheri, R. A., Sulaiman, I. F., & Matrooshi, H. A. A. (2022, April). The Relationship Between Digital Transformation and Quality of UAE Government Services Through Machine Learning. In *International Conference on Advanced Machine Learning Technologies and Applications* (pp. 412-421). Cham: Springer International Publishing. 10.1007/978-3-031-03918-8_35

Aletras, N., Tsarapatsanis, D., Preotuic-Pietro, D., & Lampos, V. (2016). Predicting judicial decisions of the European Court of Human Rights: A Natural language Processing Perspective. *PeerJ. Computer Science*, *2*, 93–99. doi:10.7717/peerj-cs.93

Alexopoulos, C., Lachana, Z., Androutsopoulou, A., Diamantopoulou, V., Charalabidis, Y., & Loutsaris, M. A. (2019, April). How machine learning is changing e-government. In *Proceedings of the 12th international conference on theory and practice of electronic governance* (pp. 354-363). 10.1145/3326365.3326412

Alford, J., & Hughes, O. (2008). Public Value Pragmatism as the Next Phase of Public Management. *American Review of Public Administration*, *38*(2), 130–148. doi:10.1177/0275074008314203

Alghazzawi, D., Bamasag, O., Albeshri, A., Sana, I., Ullah, H., & Asghar, M. Z. (2022). Efficient prediction of court judgments using an LSTM+ CNN neural network model with an optimal feature set. *Mathematics*, *10*(5), 683. doi:10.3390/math10050683

Ali, R. (2020). *Predictive Modeling: Types, Benefits, and Algorithms*. Retrieved from Oracle Netsuite: https://www. netsuite. com/portal/resource/articles/financial-management/predictive-modeling. shtml

AliM. (2023). E-governance and E-democracy: a Digital Revolution. *Available at* SSRN 4623414.

Al-Ruithe, M., Benkhelifa, E., & Hameed, K. (2019). A systematic literature review of data governance and cloud data governance. *Personal and Ubiquitous Computing*, *23*(5), 839–859. doi:10.1007/s00779-017-1104-3

Amo, D., Gómez, P., Hernández-Ibáñez, L., & Fonseca, D. (2021). Educational Warehouse: Modular, Private and Secure Cloudable Architecture System for Educational Data Storage, Analysis and Access. *Applied Sciences (Basel, Switzerland)*, *11*(2), 806. doi:10.3390/app11020806

Anastasova, Y., & Yanev, N. (2021). Models and data quality in information systems applicable in the mining industry. E3S Web of Conferences, Sofia, Bulgaria.

Annis, A., & Nardi, F. (2019). Integrating VGI and 2D hydraulic models into a data assimilation framework for real time flood forecasting and mapping. *Geo-Spatial Information Science*, *22*(4), 223–236. Advance online publication. doi:10.1080/10095020.2019.1626135

Anthopoulos, L. (2017). Understanding Smart Cities: A Tool for Smart Government or an Industrial Trick? *Public Administration Review*.

Antoniou, V., Fonte, C. C., See, L., Estima, J., Arsanjani, J. J., Lupia, F., Minghini, M., Foody, G., & Fritz, S. (2016). Investigating the feasibility of geo-Tagged photographs as sources of land cover input data. *ISPRS International Journal of Geo-Information*, *5*(5), 64. Advance online publication. doi:10.3390/ijgi5050064

Appelgren, E., & Jönsson, A. M. (2021). Engaging Citizens for Climate Change—Challenges for Journalism. *Digital Journalism (Abingdon, England)*, *9*(6), 755–772. Advance online publication. doi:10.1080/21670811.2020.1827965

Aprio. (2019). *Artificial Intelligence to Help Resource-Strapped IRS More Efficiently Identify Tax Crimes*. https://www.aprio.com/artificial-intelligence-to-help-resource-strapped-irs-more-efficiency/

Armbrust, M., Ghodsi, A., Xin, R., & Zaharia, M. (2021). Lakehouse: a new generation of open platforms that unify data warehousing and advanced analytics. *11th Annual Conference on Innovative Data Systems Research (CIDR '21)*.

Arnaboldi, M., & Azzone, G. (2020). Data science in the design of public policies: Dispelling the obscurity in matching policy demand and data offer. *Heliyon*, *6*(6), e04300. Advance online publication. doi:10.1016/j.heliyon.2020.e04300 PMID:32637693

Asamoah, D. A., Doran, D., & Schiller, S. (2020). Interdisciplinarity in Data Science Pedagogy: A Foundational Design. *Journal of Computer Information Systems*, *60*(4), 370–377. Advance online publication. doi:10.1080/08874417.2018.1496803

Ashley, K. (2019). A Brief History of the changing roles of case prediction in AI and Law: Law in context. *Socio-Legal Journal*, *36*(1), 93–112. doi:10.26826/law-in-context.v36i1.88

Ashley, K., & Brüninghaus, S. (2009). Automatically classifying case texts and predicting outcomes. *Artificial Intelligence and Law*, *17*(2), 125–165. doi:10.1007/s10506-009-9077-9

Azad, P., Navimipour, N. J., Rahmani, A. M., & Sharifi, A. (2020). The role of structured and unstructured data managing mechanisms in the Internet of things. *Cluster Computing*, *23*(2), 1185–1198. doi:10.1007/s10586-019-02986-2

Azeroual, O., Nikiforova, A., & Sha, K. (2023). *Overlooked Aspects of Data Governance: Workflow Framework For Enterprise Data Deduplication. 2023 International Conference on Intelligent Computing, Communication, Networking and Services (ICCNS)*, Valencia, Spain.

Azeroual, O., Schöpfel, J., Ivanovic, D., & Nikiforova, A. (2022). Combining Data Lake and Data Wrangling for Ensuring Data Quality in CRIS. *Procedia Computer Science*, *211*, 3–16. doi:10.1016/j.procs.2022.10.171

Balta, D., Sellami, M., Kuhn, P., Schöpp, U., Buchinger, M., Baracaldo, N., ... Altakrouri, B. (2021). Accountable federated machine learning in government: engineering and management insights. *Electronic Participation: 13th IFIP WG 8.5 International Conference, ePart 2021, Granada, Spain, September 7–9, 2021 Proceedings*, *13*, 125–138.

Barika, M., Garg, S., Zomaya, A. Y., Wang, L., Moorsel, A. V., & Ranjan, R. (2019). Orchestrating big data analysis workflows in the cloud: Research challenges, survey, and future directions. *ACM Computing Surveys*, *52*(5), 1–41. doi:10.1145/3332301

Barocas, S., & Selbst, A. D. (2016). Big Data's Disparate Impact. *California Law Review*.

Begoli, E., Goethert, I., & Knight, K. (2021). *A lakehouse architecture for the management and analysis of heterogeneous data for biomedical research and mega-biobanks*. 2021 IEEE International Conference on Big Data (Big Data), Orlando, FL, USA

Bélanger, F., & Carter, L. (2008). Trust and Risk in E-Government Adoption. *The Journal of Strategic Information Systems*.

Bertot, J. C., Jaeger, P. T., & Grimes, J. M. (2010). Using ICTs to Create a Culture of Transparency: E-government and social media as openness and anti-corruption tools for societies. *Government Information Quarterly*, *27*(3), 264–271. doi:10.1016/j.giq.2010.03.001

Bevir, M. (2012). *Governance: A very short introduction*. Oxford University Press. doi:10.1093/actrade/9780199606412.001.0001

Bhilare, P., Parab, N., Soni, N., & Thakur, B. (2019). Predicting outcome of judicial cases and analysis using machine learning. *International Research Journal in Engineering Technology, 6*, 326-330. Retrieved from https://www.irjet.net/archives/V6/i3/IRJET-V6I362.pdf

Biggio, B., & Roli, F. (2018, October). Wild patterns: Ten years after the rise of adversarial machine learning. In *Proceedings of the 2018 ACM SIGSAC Conference on Computer and Communications Security* (pp. 2154-2156). 10.1145/3243734.3264418

Bishop, C. M. (2006). *Pattern Recognition and Machine Learning*. Springer Science+ Business Media, LLC.

Bishop, C. M., & Nasrabadi, N. M. (2006). *Pattern recognition and machine learning* (Vol. 4, No. 4). New York: Springer.

Bishop, C. M. (2006). *Pattern Recognition and Machine Learning*. Springer.

Bittner, C., Michel, B., & Turk, C. (2016). Turning the spotlight on the crowd: Examining the participatory ethics and practices of crisis mapping. *ACME, 15*(1).

Bjeladinovic, S. (2018). A fresh approach for hybrid SQL/NoSQL database design based on data structuredness. *Enterprise Information Systems*, *12*(8-9), 1202–1220. doi:10.1080/17517575.2018.1446102

Blackburn, R., & Rosen, B. (1993). Total quality and human resources management: lessons learned from Baldrige Award-winning companies. *Academy of Management Perspectives, 7*(3).

Bonsón, E., Torres, L., Royo, S., & Flores, F. (2012). Local E-Government 2.0: Social Media and Corporate Transparency in Municipalities. *Government Information Quarterly*, *29*(2), 123–132. doi:10.1016/j.giq.2011.10.001

Breiman, L. (2001). Random forests. *Machine Learning*, *45*(1), 5–32. doi:10.1023/A:1010933404324

Breiman, L. (2017). *Classification and regression trees*. Routledge. doi:10.1201/9781315139470

BRM. (2022). *Action Research*. Business Research Methodology. BRM.

Brodie, M. L. (2019). What Is Data Science? In Applied Data Science: Lessons Learned for the Data-Driven Business. doi:10.1007/978-3-030-11821-1_8

Buenfil, J., Arnold, R. D., Abruzzo, B., & Korpela, C. (2019). Artificial Intelligence Ethics: Governance through Social Media. *2019 IEEE International Symposium on Technologies for Homeland Security (HST).* 10.1109/HST47167.2019.9032907

Buolamwini, J., & Gebru, T. (2018). *Gender Shades: Intersectional Accuracy Disparities in Commercial Gender Classification*. Academic Press.

Calcagni, F., Amorim Maia, A. T., Connolly, J. J. T., & Langemeyer, J. (2019). Digital co-construction of relational values: Understanding the role of social media for sustainability. *Sustainability Science*, *14*(5), 1309–1321. Advance online publication. doi:10.1007/s11625-019-00672-1

Canada Immigration. (2019). *AI in Canadian Immigration Processing*. Author.

Carter, L., & Bélanger, F. (2005). The utilization of e-government services: Citizen trust, innovation and acceptance factors. *Information Systems Journal*, *15*(1), 5–25. doi:10.1111/j.1365-2575.2005.00183.x

Chalkidis, I., Androutsopoulos, I., & Aletras, N. 2019. Neural Legal Judgement Prediction In English. *Proceedings of the 57th Annual Meeting of the Association for Computational Linguistics*, 4317-4323. 10.18653/v1/P19-1424

Chang, C. C., & Lin, C. J. (2011). LIBSVM: A library for support vector machines. *ACM Transactions on Intelligent Systems and Technology*, *2*(3), 1–27. doi:10.1145/1961189.1961199

Chao, C. Y., & Wang, S. (2018). Using OpenStreetMap data for the location analysis on public bicycle stations – A case study on the Youbike system in downtown Taipei city. *Proceedings - 39th Asian Conference on Remote Sensing: Remote Sensing Enabling Prosperity, ACRS 2018.*

Chen, Y., Wang, J., & Cai, Z. (2018, July). Study on the application of machine learning in government service: take consumer protection service as an example. In *2018 15th International Conference on Service Systems and Service Management (ICSSSM)* (pp. 1-5). IEEE. 10.1109/ICSSSM.2018.8465040

Chen, X., Elmes, G., Ye, X., & Chang, J. (2016). Implementing a Real-Time Twitter-Based System for Resource Dispatch in Disaster Management. *GeoJournal*, *81*(6), 863–873. Advance online publication. doi:10.1007/s10708-016-9745-8

Cherradi, M., & El Haddadi, A. (2022). A Scalable framework for data lakes ingestion. *Procedia Computer Science*, *215*, 809–814. doi:10.1016/j.procs.2022.12.083

Chicago Data Portal. (2018). Predictive Analytics in Public Services.

Clark, W., Johnson, K., & Turner, C. (2004). *Cross-Functional Student Teams as a Teaching Tool for Enhanced Learning*. East Tennessee State University, Johnson City.

Cohen, J., Cohen, P., West, S. G., & Aiken, L. S. (2013). *Applied multiple regression/correlation analysis for the behavioral sciences*. Routledge. doi:10.4324/9780203774441

Cordella, A., & Bonina, C. M. (2012). A Public Values Perspective for ICT Enabled Public Sector Reforms: A Theoretical Reflection. *Government Information Quarterly*, *29*(4), 512–520. doi:10.1016/j.giq.2012.03.004

Cortes, C., & Vapnik, V. (1995). Support-vector networks. *Machine Learning*, *20*(3), 273–297. doi:10.1007/BF00994018

Cotellessa, A. (2018). In Pursuit of Polymaths: Understanding Renaissance Persons of the 21st Century. Department Human and Organizational Learning and International Affairs. The Faculty of The Graduate School of Education and Human Development of The George Washington University.

Cover, T., & Hart, P. (1967). Nearest neighbor pattern classification. *IEEE Transactions on Information Theory*, *13*(1), 21–27. doi:10.1109/TIT.1967.1053964

Crawford, K., & Finn, M. (2015). The limits of crisis data: Analytical and ethical challenges of using social and mobile data to understand disasters. *GeoJournal*, *80*(4), 491–502. Advance online publication. doi:10.1007/s10708-014-9597-z

Criado, J. I., Sandoval-Almazan, R., & Gil-Garcia, J. R. (2013). Government Innovation through Social Media. *Government Information Quarterly*, *30*(4), 319–326. doi:10.1016/j.giq.2013.10.003

Crittenden, V., & Wilson, E. (2006). An Exploratory Study of Cross-Functional Education in the Undergraduate Marketing Curriculum. *Journal of Marketing Education*, *28*(1), 81–86. doi:10.1177/0273475305284643

Crosley, N., Indrajit, R., & Dazki, E. (2023). TOGAF Framework For an AI-enabled Software House. *Sinkron: Jurnal dan Penelitian Teknik Informatika*, *8*(2). doi:10.33395/sinkron.v8i2.12390

Crowley, D. N., Breslin, J. G., Corcoran, P., & Young, K. (2012). Gamification of citizen sensing through mobile social reporting. *4th International IEEE Consumer Electronic Society - Games Innovation Conference, IGiC 2012*. 10.1109/IGIC.2012.6329849

Cui, J., Shen, X., Nie, F., Wang, Z., Wang, J., & Chen, Y. (2022). *A Survey on Legal Judgment Prediction: Datasets, Metrics, Models and Challenges*. https://doi.org//arXiv.2204.04859 doi:10.48550

Curtis, P., & Carey, M. (2012). *Committee of Sponsoring Organizations of the Treadway Commission-Risk Assessment in Practice*. Deloitte & Touche LLP.

Čuš, B., & Golec, D. (2022). Data Lakehouse: Benefits in small and medium enterprises. *Mednarodno inovativno poslovanje= Journal of Innovative Business and Management*, *14*(2), 1-10.

Cutler, D. R., Edwards, T. C. Jr, Beard, K. H., Cutler, A., Hess, K. T., Gibson, J., & Lawler, J. J. (2007). Random forests for classification in ecology. *Ecology*, *88*(11), 2783–2792. doi:10.1890/07-0539.1 PMID:18051647

Daellenbach, H., McNickle, D., & Dye, Sh. (2012). *Management Science. Decision-making through systems thinking* (2nd ed.). Plagrave Macmillian.

Dana, R. D., Dikananda, A. R., Sudrajat, D., Wanto, A., & Fasya, F. (2019, October). Measurement of health service performance through machine learning using clustering techniques. *Journal of Physics: Conference Series, 1360*(1), 012017. doi:10.1088/1742-6596/1360/1/012017

Datablist. (n.d.). *Download Sample CSV Files for free*. https://www.datablist.com/learn/csv/download-sample-csv-files

Dawes, S. S. (2008). The Evolution and Continuing Challenges of E-Governance. *Public Administration Review, 68*(s1). Advance online publication. doi:10.1111/j.1540-6210.2008.00981.x

Dawes, S. S. (2009). Governance in the digital age: A research and action framework for an uncertain future. *Government Information Quarterly, 26*(2), 257–264. doi:10.1016/j.giq.2008.12.003

de Oliveira, R. S., Reis, J. A., & Sperandio Nascimento, E. G. (2022). Predicting the number of days in court cases using artificial intelligence. *PLoS One, 17*(5), e0269008. doi:10.1371/journal.pone.0269008 PMID:35617285

Della Croce, F., & T'kindt, V. (2002). A recovering beam search algorithm for the one-machine dynamic total completion time scheduling problem. *The Journal of the Operational Research Society, 53*(11), 1275–1280. doi:10.1057/palgrave.jors.2601389

Di Vaio, A., Hassan, R., & Alavoine, C. (2022). Data intelligence and analytics: A bibliometric analysis of human–Artificial intelligence in public sector decision-making effectiveness. *Technological Forecasting and Social Change, 174*, 121201. Advance online publication. doi:10.1016/j.techfore.2021.121201

Dias, V. E. C., Sperandio, V. G., & Lisboa-Filho, J. (2019). Routes generation for selective collection of urban waste using volunteered geographic information. *Iberian Conference on Information Systems and Technologies, CISTI, 2019-June*. 10.23919/CISTI.2019.8760773

Dibowski, H., Schmid, S., Svetashova, Y., Henson, C., & Tran, T. (2020). Using Semantic Technologies to Manage a Data Lake: Data Catalog, Provenance and Access Control. *Proceedings of the 13th International Workshop on Scalable Semantic Web Knowledge Base Systems (SSWS 2020).*

Dickson, M. S., & Asagba, P. (2020). The Semi-Structured Data Model and Implementation Issues for Semi-Structured Data. *International Journal of Innovation and Sustainability, 3*, 47–51.

Dietterich, T. G. (2000, June). Ensemble methods in machine learning. In *International workshop on multiple classifier systems* (pp. 1-15). Springer Berlin Heidelberg.

Diggle, P. (2005). Applied Spatial Statistics for Public Health Data. *Journal of the American Statistical Association, 100*(470), 702–703. Advance online publication. doi:10.1198/jasa.2005.s15

Dinh, V.-N., & Nguyen, H.-A. (2022). *Data Process Approach by Traditional and Cloud Services Methodologies*. Academic Press.

Djiroun, R., Boukhalfa, K., & Alimazighi, Z. (2019). Designing data cubes in OLAP systems: A decision makers' requirements-based approach. *Cluster Computing*, *22*(3), 783–803. doi:10.1007/s10586-018-2883-7

Dogan, S., Çalgici, P., Arditi, D., & Gunaydin, H. (2015). *Critical success factors of partnering in the building design process. METU JFA 2015/2*. Department of Architecture, İzmir Institute of Technology.

Domingos, P. (2012). A few useful things to know about machine learning. *Communications of the ACM*, *55*(10), 78–87. doi:10.1145/2347736.2347755

Dornemann, J., Rückert, N., Fischer, K., & Taraz, A. (2020). *Artificial intelligence and operations research in maritime logistics. Econstor*. Leibniz Information Centre for Economics.

Dowd, M., Dixon, A., & Kinsella, B. (2020). Optimizing waste management collection routes in Urban Haiti: A collaboration between DataKind and SOIL. *ArXiv, 2012*.

Dreyling, R., Jackson, E. B., Tammet, T., Labanava, A., & Pappel, I. (2021, April). Social, Legal, and Technical Considerations for Machine Learning and Artificial Intelligence Systems in Government. ICEIS, (1), 701-708.

Dua, D., & Graff, C. (2017). *UCI machine learning repository*. Academic Press.

Duan, H. K., Vasarhelyi, M. A., Codesso, M., & Alzamil, Z. (2023). Enhancing the government accounting information systems using social media information: An application of text mining and machine learning. *International Journal of Accounting Information Systems*, *48*, 100600. doi:10.1016/j.accinf.2022.100600

Duggar, D., Bang, S. M., & Tripathy, B. K. (2023). Big Data Analytics in E-Governance and Other Aspects of Society. In *Encyclopedia of Data Science and Machine Learning* (pp. 116–128). IGI Global.

Dunleavy, P., Margetts, H., Bastow, S., & Tinkler, J. (2006). *Digital Era Governance: IT Corporations, the State, and e-Government*. Oxford University Press. doi:10.1093/acprof:oso/9780199296194.001.0001

Dwivedi, D. N., Mahanty, G., & Vemareddy, A. (2022). How Responsible Is AI?: Identification of Key Public Concerns Using Sentiment Analysis and Topic Modeling. *International Journal of Information Retrieval Research*, *12*(1), 1–14. doi:10.4018/IJIRR.298646

Dwivedi, D. N., Tadoori, G., & Batra, S. (2023). Impact of women leadership and ESG ratings and in organizations: A time series segmentation study. *Academy of Strategic Management Journal*, *22*(S3), 1–6.

Dwivedi, D., Batra, S., & Pathak, Y. K. (2023). A machine learning based approach to identify key drivers for improving corporate's esg ratings. *Journal of Law and Sustainable Development*, *11*(1), e0242. doi:10.37497/sdgs.v11i1.242

DWP. (2021). *Using Machine Learning to Detect Welfare Fraud. EU GDPR (2018)*. General Data Protection Regulation.

Easterbrook, S., Singer, J., Storey, M., & Damian, D. (2008). *Guide to Advanced Empirical Software Engineering-Selecting Empirical Methods for Software Engineering Research*. Springer.

Edastama, P., Dudhat, A., & Maulani, G. (2021). Use of Data Warehouse and Data Mining for Academic Data: A Case Study at a National University. *International Journal of Cyber and IT Service Management, 1*(2), 206–215. doi:10.34306/ijcitsm.v1i2.55

Eichler, R., Giebler, C., Gröger, C., Schwarz, H., & Mitschang, B. (2021). Modeling metadata in data lakes—A generic model. *Data & Knowledge Engineering, 136*, 101931. doi:10.1016/j.datak.2021.101931

Ellis, T. J., & Levy, Y. (2010). A guide for novice researchers: Design and development research methods. Proceedings of Informing Science & IT Education Conference (InSITE).

Engin, Z., & Treleaven, P. (2019). Algorithmic Government: Automating Public Services and Supporting Civil Servants in using Data Science Technologies. *The Computer Journal, 62*(3), 448–460. Advance online publication. doi:10.1093/comjnl/bxy082

Enosh, G., Tzafrir, S. S., & Stolovy, T. (2015). The development of client violence questionnaire (CVQ). *Journal of Mixed Methods Research, 9*(3), 273–290. doi:10.1177/1558689814525263

Erman, E., & Furendal, M. (2022). Artificial Intelligence and the Political Legitimacy of Global Governance. *Political Studies, 50*(4), 621–647. doi:10.1177/00323217221126665

Etaati, L. (2019). Azure Databricks. In L. Etaati (Ed.), *Machine Learning with Microsoft Technologies: Selecting the Right Architecture and Tools for Your Project* (pp. 159–171). Apress. doi:10.1007/978-1-4842-3658-1_10

European Union. (2018). *General Data Protection Regulation (GDPR)*. Author.

Felício, S., Hora, J., Ferreira, M. C., Abrantes, D., Costa, P. D., Dangelo, C., Silva, J., & Galvão, T. (2022). Handling OpenStreetMap georeferenced data for route planning. *Transportation Research Procedia, 62*, 189–196. Advance online publication. doi:10.1016/j.trpro.2022.02.024

Figueira, R. B. (2018). *A framework for dataflow orchestration in lambda architectures*. Universidade do Porto.

Filho, H. F., Leite, B. P., Pompermayer, G. A., Werneck, M. G., & Leyh, W. (2013). Teaching VGI as a strategy to promote the production of urban digital cartographic databases. *Joint Urban Remote Sensing Event 2013. JURSE, 2013*. Advance online publication. doi:10.1109/JURSE#.2013.6550705

Fletcher, T. S. (2012). *Machine learning for financial market prediction* [Doctoral dissertation]. UCL (University College London).

Floridi, L., Cowls, J., Beltrametti, M., Chatila, R., Chazerand, P., Dignum, V., & Schafer, B. (2018). *AI4People—An Ethical Framework for a Good AI Society: Opportunities, Risks, Principles, and Recommendations. Minds and Machines*. Academic Press.

Fonte, C. C., Bastin, L., See, L., Foody, G., & Lupia, F. (2015). Usability of VGI for validation of land cover maps. *International Journal of Geographical Information Science*, *29*(May), 1–23. doi:10.1080/13658816.2015.1018266

Fox, J. (2015). *Applied regression analysis and generalized linear models*. Sage Publications.

Gabarro, J., & Stewart, A. (2021). Modelling web-service uncertainty: The angel/daemon approach. *Computer Science Review*, *39*, 100355. doi:10.1016/j.cosrev.2020.100355

Gamage, P. (2016). New development: Leveraging 'big data' analytics in the public sector. *Public Money & Management*, *36*(5), 385–390. Advance online publication. doi:10.1080/09540962.2016.1194087

Gasser, U., & Almeida, V. A. F. (2017). A layered model for AI governance. *IEEE Internet Computing*, *21*(6), 58–62. doi:10.1109/MIC.2017.4180835

Gelman, A., & Hill, J. (2006). *Data analysis using regression and multilevel/hierarchical models*. Cambridge university press. doi:10.1017/CBO9780511790942

Georgiadou, Y., Lungo, J. H., & Richter, C. (2014). Citizen sensors or extreme publics? Transparency and accountability interventions on the mobile geoweb. *International Journal of Digital Earth*, *7*(7), 516–533. Advance online publication. doi:10.1080/17538947.2013.782073

Géron, A. (2022). *Hands-on machine learning with Scikit-Learn, Keras, and TensorFlow*. O'Reilly Media, Inc.

Geurts, P., Ernst, D., & Wehenkel, L. (2006). Extremely randomized trees. *Machine Learning*, *63*(1), 3–42. doi:10.1007/s10994-006-6226-1

Giebler, C., Gröger, C., Hoos, E., Eichler, R., Schwarz, H., & Mitschang, B. (2021). The data lake architecture framework. *BTW 2021*.

Gil-Garcia, J. R., Helbig, N., & Ojo, A. (2019). Smart Governance in the Context of Smart Cities: A Literature Review. *Information Polity*.

Gil-Garcia, J. R., & Pardo, T. A. (2005). E-government success factors: Mapping practical tools to theoretical foundations. *Government Information Quarterly*, *22*(2), 187–216. doi:10.1016/j.giq.2005.02.001

Gkikas, D. C., Theodoridis, P. K., & Gkikas, M. C. (2023). Artificial Intelligence (AI) Use for e-Governance in Agriculture: Exploring the Bioeconomy Landscape. In *Recent Advances in Data and Algorithms for e-Government* (pp. 141–172). Springer International Publishing. doi:10.1007/978-3-031-22408-9_7

Gomes, M. (2021). Barcelona improves public transport with modelling technology. *PTV Blog*. https://blog.ptvgroup.com/en/city-and-mobility/barcelona-improve-public-transport-modelling/

Goodchild, M. F. (2007). Citizens as sensors: The world of volunteered geography. GeoJournal. doi:10.1007/s10708-007-9111-y

Goodfellow, I., Bengio, Y., & Courville, A. (2016). Convolutional networks. In *Deep learning* (Vol. 2016, pp. 330–372). MIT Press.

Google Developers. (2021). *Get Started with OR-Tools for C#*. Google. https://developers.google.com/optimization/introduction/dotnet

Grinberger, A. Y., Minghini, M., Juhász, L., Yeboah, G., & Mooney, P. (2022). OSM Science—The Academic Study of the OpenStreetMap Project, Data, Contributors, Community, and Applications. In ISPRS International Journal of Geo-Information (Vol. 11, Issue 4). doi:10.3390/ijgi11040230

Güiza, F., & Stuart, N. (2018). When citizens choose not to participate in volunteering geographic information to e-governance: a case study from Mexico. GeoJournal. doi:10.1007/s10708-017-9820-9

Gunapati, S. (2011). Key Features for Designing a Dashboard. *Government Finance Review, 27*.

Gupta, A., Dwivedi, D. N., & Shah, J. (2023a). Overview of Money Laundering. In Artificial Intelligence Applications in Banking and Financial Services. Future of Business and Finance. Springer. doi:10.1007/978-981-99-2571-1_1

Gupta, A., Dwivedi, D. N., & Shah, J. (2023b). Financial Crimes Management and Control in Financial Institutions. In Artificial Intelligence Applications in Banking and Financial Services. Future of Business and Finance. Springer. doi:10.1007/978-981-99-2571-1_2

Gupta, A., Dwivedi, D. N., & Shah, J. (2023c). Overview of Technology Solutions. In Artificial Intelligence Applications in Banking and Financial Services. Future of Business and Finance. Springer. doi:10.1007/978-981-99-2571-1_3

Gupta, A., Dwivedi, D. N., & Shah, J. (2023d). Data Organization for an FCC Unit. In Artificial Intelligence Applications in Banking and Financial Services. Future of Business and Finance. Springer. doi:10.1007/978-981-99-2571-1_4

Gupta, A., Dwivedi, D. N., & Shah, J. (2023e). Planning for AI in Financial Crimes. In Artificial Intelligence Applications in Banking and Financial Services. Future of Business and Finance. Springer. doi:10.1007/978-981-99-2571-1_5

Gupta, A., Dwivedi, D. N., & Shah, J. (2023f). Applying Machine Learning for Effective Customer Risk Assessment. In Artificial Intelligence Applications in Banking and Financial Services. Future of Business and Finance. Springer. doi:10.1007/978-981-99-2571-1_6

Gupta, A., Dwivedi, D. N., & Shah, J. (2023g). Artificial Intelligence-Driven Effective Financial Transaction Monitoring. In Artificial Intelligence Applications in Banking and Financial Services. Future of Business and Finance. Springer. doi:10.1007/978-981-99-2571-1_7

Gupta, A., Dwivedi, D. N., & Shah, J. (2023h). Machine Learning-Driven Alert Optimization. In Artificial Intelligence Applications in Banking and Financial Services. Future of Business and Finance. Springer. doi:10.1007/978-981-99-2571-1_8

Gupta, A., Dwivedi, D. N., & Shah, J. (2023i). Applying Artificial Intelligence on Investigation. In Artificial Intelligence Applications in Banking and Financial Services. Future of Business and Finance. Springer. doi:10.1007/978-981-99-2571-1_9

Gupta, A., Dwivedi, D. N., & Shah, J. (2023j). Ethical Challenges for AI-Based Applications. In Artificial Intelligence Applications in Banking and Financial Services. Future of Business and Finance. Springer. doi:10.1007/978-981-99-2571-1_10

Gupta, A., Dwivedi, D. N., & Shah, J. (2023k). Setting up a Best-In-Class AI-Driven Financial Crime Control Unit (FCCU). In Artificial Intelligence Applications in Banking and Financial Services. Future of Business and Finance. Springer. doi:10.1007/978-981-99-2571-1_11

Gupta, I., Singh, A. K., Lee, C. N., & Buyya, R. (2022). Secure Data Storage and Sharing Techniques for Data Protection in Cloud Environments: A Systematic Review, Analysis, and Future Directions. *IEEE Access : Practical Innovations, Open Solutions*, *10*, 71247–71277. doi:10.1109/ACCESS.2022.3188110

Gupta, P. M. (2023). The Role of Big Data in Smart Healthcare. *International Journal of Internet of Things*. Advance online publication.

Gupta, S., Pebesma, E., Degbelo, A., & Costa, A. C. (2018). Optimising citizen-driven air quality monitoring networks for cities. *ISPRS International Journal of Geo-Information*, *7*(12), 468. Advance online publication. doi:10.3390/ijgi7120468

Hair, J. F., Black, W. C., Babin, B. J., & Anderson, R. E. (2019). *Multivariate data analysis*. Cengage Learning.

Haklay, M. (2013). Citizen science and volunteered geographic information: Overview and typology of participation. In Crowdsourcing Geographic Knowledge: Volunteered Geographic Information (VGI) in Theory and Practice. doi:10.1007/978-94-007-4587-2_7

Hamadou, H. B., Pedersen, T. B., & Thomsen, C. (2020). *The Danish National Energy Data Lake: Requirements, Technical Architecture, and Tool Selection.* 2020 IEEE International Conference on Big Data (Big Data), Atlanta, GA.

Han, J., Pei, J., & Tong, H. (2022). *Data mining: concepts and techniques*. Morgan kaufmann.

Hapke, H., Howard, C., & Lane, H. (2019). *Natural Language Processing in Action: Understanding, analyzing, and generating text with Python.* Simon and Schuster.

Harby, A. A., & Zulkernine, F. (2022). *From Data Warehouse to Lakehouse: A Comparative Review.* 2022 IEEE International Conference on Big Data (Big Data), Osaka, Japan.

Hariz, M. (2021). A dynamic mobility traffic model based on two modes of transport in smart cities. *Smart Cities*, *4*(1), 253–270. Advance online publication. doi:10.3390/smartcities4010016

Hastie, T., Tibshirani, R., Friedman, J. H., & Friedman, J. H. (2009). The elements of statistical learning: data mining, inference, and prediction (Vol. 2). New York: Springer.

Haworth, B. T., Bruce, E., Whittaker, J., & Read, R. (2018). The good, the bad, and the uncertain: Contributions of volunteered geographic information to community disaster resilience. In Frontiers in Earth Science (Vol. 6). doi:10.3389/feart.2018.00183

Haworth, B., Whittaker, J., & Bruce, E. (2016). Assessing the application and value of participatory mapping for community bushfire preparation. *Applied Geography (Sevenoaks, England), 76*, 115–127. Advance online publication. doi:10.1016/j.apgeog.2016.09.019

Heaton, J. (2018). Ian Goodfellow, Yoshua Bengio, and Aaron Courville: Deep learning: The MIT Press, 2016, 800 pp, ISBN: 0262035618. *Genetic Programming and Evolvable Machines, 19*(1-2), 305–307. doi:10.1007/s10710-017-9314-z

Heeks, R., & Bailur, S. (2007). Analyzing e-government research: Perspectives, philosophies, theories, methods, and practice. *Government Information Quarterly, 24*(2), 243–265. doi:10.1016/j.giq.2006.06.005

Henman, P. (2020). Improving public services using artificial intelligence: Possibilities, pitfalls, governance. *Asia Pacific Journal of Public Administration, 42*(4), 209–221. doi:10.1080/23276665.2020.1816188

Heywood, S., Hillar, R., & Turnbull, D. (2010). *Insights into organization-How do I manage the complexity in my organization? Organization Practice*. McKinsey & Company.

Hillman, V. (2023). Bringing in the technological, ethical, educational and social-structural for a new education data governance. *Learning, Media and Technology, 48*(1), 122–137. doi:10.1080/17439884.2022.2052313

Hine, G. S. C. (2013). The importance of action research in teacher education programs. In *Design, develop. evaluate: The core of the learning. environment. Proceedings of the 22nd Annual Teaching Learning Forum, 7-8 February 2013*. Murdoch University. http://ctl.curtin.edu.au/professional_development/conferences/tlf/tlf2013/refereed/hine.html

Hinkelmann, K. (2016). *Modelling in Enterprise Architecture. University of applied sciences northwest Switzerland*. Business School.

Hlupić, T., Oreščanin, D., Ružak, D., & Baranović, M. (2022). *An Overview of Current Data Lake Architecture Models*. 2022 45th Jubilee International Convention on Information, Communication and Electronic Technology (MIPRO), Opatija, Croatia.

Hlupić, T., & Puniš, J. (2021). An Overview of Current Trends in Data Ingestion and Integration. *2021 44th International Convention on Information, Communication and Electronic Technology (MIPRO)*.

Ho, A. T. (2002). Reinventing Local Governments and the E-Government Initiative. *Public Administration Review, 62*(4), 434–444. doi:10.1111/0033-3352.00197

Honarparvar, S., Forouzandeh Jonaghani, R., Alesheikh, A. A., & Atazadeh, B. (2019). Improvement of a location-aware recommender system using volunteered geographic information. *Geocarto International, 34*(13), 1496–1513. Advance online publication. doi:10.1080/10106049.2018.1493155

Hosiaisluoma, E. (2021). *ArchiMate Cookbook-Patterns & Examples*. Hosiaisluoma.

Hosmer, D. W. Jr, Lemeshow, S., & Sturdivant, R. X. (2013). *Applied logistic regression* (Vol. 398). John Wiley & Sons. doi:10.1002/9781118548387

Huang, H., Yao, X. A., Krisp, J. M., & Jiang, B. (2021). Analytics of location-based big data for smart cities: Opportunities, challenges, and future directions. *Computers, Environment and Urban Systems, 90*, 101712. Advance online publication. doi:10.1016/j.compenvurbsys.2021.101712

Hu, S., Ge, Y., Liu, M., Ren, Z., & Zhang, X. (2022). Village-level poverty identification using machine learning, high-resolution images, and geospatial data. *International Journal of Applied Earth Observation and Geoinformation, 107*, 102694. Advance online publication. doi:10.1016/j.jag.2022.102694

Hussain, O., Dillon, Th., Chang, E., & Hussain, F. (2010). Transactional risk-based decision making system in e-business interactions. *International Journal of ComputSystSci & Eng, 1*, 15-28.

Ibrahim, I. K., Elmorsy, S. A., Kashef, N. M., & Al-Borai, M. M. M. (2023). Securing E-Governance Services Based on Two Level Classification Algorithms. *Mathematical Modelling of Engineering Problems, 10*(2).

Jaeger, P. T. (2007). Deliberative Democracy and the Concept of E-Government. *Administration & Society*.

Jaeger, P. T., & Mattson, T. (2009). E-Government, the Information Society, and the Future of Public Administration. *Public Administration Review*.

James, G., Witten, D., Hastie, T., & Tibshirani, R. (2013). *An introduction to statistical learning* (Vol. 112). New York: Springer.

Janssen, M., Brous, P., Estevez, E., Barbosa, L. S., & Janowski, T. (2020). Data governance: Organizing data for trustworthy Artificial Intelligence. *Government Information Quarterly, 37*(3), 101493. doi:10.1016/j.giq.2020.101493

Janssen, M., Van der Voort, H., & Wahyudi, A. (2017). Factors influencing big data decision-making quality. *Journal of Business Research, 70*, 338–345. doi:10.1016/j.jbusres.2016.08.007

Janzen, D., & Saiedian, H. (2005). *Test-driven development concepts, taxonomy, and future direction. Computer, 38(9).*

Javatpoint. (2021). *Understanding SWOT Analysis*. Javatpoint. https://www.javatpoint.com/swot

Jia, H. (2020). Yi Zeng: Promoting good governance of artificial intelligence. *National Science Review, 7*(12), 1861–1862. doi:10.1093/nsr/nwaa255 PMID:34676086

Jin, D. (2019). *Reconstructing our orders: Artificial intelligence and human society, no. 99*. Springer Singapore.

Johnson, R., & Onwuegbuzie, A. (2004). *Mixed Methods Research: A Research Paradigm Whose Time Has Come*. Sage Journals.

Jonkers, H., Band, I., & Quartel, D. (2012a). *ArchiSurance Case Study*. The Open Group.

Kankanhalli, A., Charalabidis, Y., & Mellouli, S. (2019, April). IoT and AI for smart government: A research agenda. *Government Information Quarterly*, *36*(2), 304–309. doi:10.1016/j.giq.2019.02.003

Kapoor, A. (2021). *Artificial intelligence and machine learning: 5 trends to watch out for in 2021*. AI Zone. https://dzone.com/articles/artificial-intelligence-amp-machine-learning-5-dev

Karkošková, S. (2023). Data Governance Model To Enhance Data Quality In Financial Institutions. *Information Systems Management*, *40*(1), 90–110. doi:10.1080/10580530.2022.2042628

Kayes, A. S. M., Rahayu, W., Watters, P., Alazab, M., Dillon, T., & Chang, E. (2020). Achieving security scalability and flexibility using Fog-Based Context-Aware Access Control. *Future Generation Computer Systems*, *107*, 307–323. doi:10.1016/j.future.2020.02.001

Kelbert, F., Shirazi, F., Simo, H., Wüchner, T., Buchmann, J., Pretschner, A., & Waidner, M. (2012). State of online privacy: A technical perspective. In *Internet Privacy* (pp. 189–279). Springer. doi:10.1007/978-3-642-31943-3_4

Keller, C., Glück, F., Gerlach, C. F., & Schlegel, T. (2022). Investigating the Potential of Data Science Methods for Sustainable Public Transport. *Sustainability (Basel)*, *14*(7), 4211. Advance online publication. doi:10.3390/su14074211

Kevin, P., & Ginger, G. (2021). *Managing Data Orchestration and Integration at Scale*. O. R. Media.

Khan, N., Naim, A., Hussain, M. R., Naveed, Q. N., Ahmad, N., & Qamar, S. (2019). The 51 v's of big data: survey, technologies, characteristics, opportunities, issues and challenges. *Proceedings of the international conference on omni-layer intelligent systems*. 10.1145/3312614.3312623

Khouya, M. (2023). E-Governance: Origin, challenges, and prospects in the era of ICTs and artificial intelligence. *American Scientific Journal*, *3*(18), 884–884.

Kihumbe. (2019). *Kihumbe- Survey Digitization and Mapping for HIV Monitoring*. Academic Press.

Kimball, R., & Ross, M. (2013). *The Data Warehouse Toolkit: The Definitive Guide to Dimensional Modeling*. Wiley. https://books.google.co.za/books?id=4rFXzk8wAB8C

Kim, J., & Lennon, Sh. (2017). *Descriptive Content Analysis on E-Service Research. International Journal of Service Science, Management, Engineering, and Technology*. doi:10.4018/IJSSMET.2017010102

Kitchin, R., Lauriault, T. P., & Wilson, M. W. (2018). Understanding Spatial Media. In Understanding Spatial Media. doi:10.4135/9781526425850.n1

Klipfolio. (2022). *What is Cloud Business Intelligence?* https://www.klipfolio.com/resources/articles/what-is-cloud-business-intelligence

Kolak, M., Steptoe, M., Manprisio, H., Azu-Popow, L., Hinchy, M., Malana, G., & Maciejewski, R. (2020). *Extending Volunteered Geographic Information (VGI) with Geospatial Software as a Service: Participatory Asset Mapping Infrastructures for Urban Health.* doi:10.1007/978-3-030-19573-1_11

Koltay, T. (2020). Quality of open research data: Values, convergences and governance. *Information (Basel), 11*(4), 175. doi:10.3390/info11040175

Korjus, K. (2019). *Estonia's E-Residency Program Success Metrics.* E-Residency Blog.

Kort, F. (1957). Predicting Supreme Court decisions mathematically: A quantitative analysis of the" right to counsel cases. *The American Political Science Review, 51*(1), 1–12. doi:10.2307/1951767

Koudelia, N. (2011). *Acceptance test-driven development* [Master Thesis]. University of Jyväskylä.

Kovač, I. (2018). *At His Crossroad: Reflections on the Work of France Bucar.* His Crossroad Reflections Work Fr. Bucar. doi:10.1007/978-3-319-78331-4

Krizhevsky, A., Sutskever, I., & Hinton, G. E. (2012). Imagenet classification with deep convolutional neural networks. *Advances in Neural Information Processing Systems*, 25.

Kucukali, A., Pjeternikaj, R., Zeka, E., & Hysa, A. (2022). Evaluating the pedestrian accessibility to public services using open-source geospatial data and QGIS software. *Nova Geodesia, 2*(2), 42. Advance online publication. doi:10.55779/ng2242

Kumar, V., & Best, M. L. (2006). *Impact and Sustainability of E-Government Services in Developing Countries: Lessons Learned from Tamil Nadu.* The Information Society.

Kurniawan, D. H., Ruldeviyani, Y., Adrian, M. R., Handayani, S., & Pohan, M. R., & R. K, T. (2019). *Data Governance Maturity Assessment: A Case Study in IT Bureau of Audit Board.* 2019 International Conference on Information Management and Technology (ICIMTech), Jakarta & Bali, Indonesia. 10.1109/ICIMTech.2019.8843742

Kursa, M. B., & Rudnicki, W. R. (2010). Feature selection with the Boruta package. *Journal of Statistical Software, 36*(11), 1–13. doi:10.18637/jss.v036.i11

Kutner, M. H., Nachtsheim, C. J., Neter, J., & Li, W. (2005). *Applied linear statistical models.* McGraw-Hill.

Lage-Freitas, A., Allende-Cid, H., Santana, O., & Lıvia, O. (2022). Predicting Brazilian court decisions. *PeerJ. Computer Science, 8*, e904. doi:10.7717/peerj-cs.904 PMID:35494851

LAPD. (2019). *Predictive Policing Program Analysis.* Author.

Layne, K., & Lee, J. (2001). Developing fully functional E-government: A four stage model. *Government Information Quarterly, 18*(2), 122–136. doi:10.1016/S0740-624X(01)00066-1

LeCun, Y., Bengio, Y., & Hinton, G. (2015). Deep learning. *Nature, 521*(7553), 436-444.

Lewis, D. D. (1998, April). Naive (Bayes) at forty: The independence assumption in information retrieval. In *European conference on machine learning* (pp. 4-15). Springer Berlin Heidelberg. 10.1007/BFb0026666

Liaw, A., & Wiener, M. (2002). Classification and regression by random forest. *R News, 2*(3), 18–22.

Li, L., & Ulaganathan, M. N. (2017). Design and development of a crowdsourcing mobile app for disaster response. *International Conference on Geoinformatics.* 10.1109/GEOINFORMATICS.2017.8090943

Liming, B., Gavino, A. I., Lee, P., Jungyoon, K., Na, L., Pink Pi, T. H., Xian, T. H., Buay, T. L., Xiaoping, T., Valera, A., Jia, E. Y., Wu, A., & Fox, M. S. (2015). SHINESeniors: Personalized services for active ageing-in-place. *2015 IEEE 1st International Smart Cities Conference, ISC2 2015.* 10.1109/ISC2.2015.7366181

Linders, D. (2012). From E-Government to We-Government: Defining a Typology for Citizen Coproduction in the Age of Social Media. *Government Information Quarterly, 29*(4), 446–454. doi:10.1016/j.giq.2012.06.003

Lipton, Z. C. (2018). The mythos of model interpretability: In machine learning, the concept of interpretability is both important and slippery. *ACM Queue; Tomorrow's Computing Today, 16*(3), 31–57. doi:10.1145/3236386.3241340

LiuH. W.LinC. F.ChenY. J. (2018). Beyond State v. Loomis: Artificial Intelligence, Government Algorithmization, and Accountability. *International Journal of Law and Information Technology, 27*(2), 122-141. https://ssrn.com/abstract=3313916

Liu, P., Loudcher, S., Darmont, J., & Noûs, C. (2021). Archaeodal: A data lake for archaeological data management and analytics. *Proceedings of the 25th International Database Engineering & Applications Symposium.* 10.1145/3472163.3472266

Liu, Z., & Zhang, A. (2020). Sampling for big data profiling: A survey. *IEEE Access : Practical Innovations, Open Solutions, 8*, 72713–72726. doi:10.1109/ACCESS.2020.2988120

Loh, W. Y. (2011). Classification and regression trees. *Wiley Interdisciplinary Reviews. Data Mining and Knowledge Discovery, 1*(1), 14–23. doi:10.1002/widm.8

Loukis, E., Maragoudakis, M., & Kyriakou, N. (2019). Economic Crisis Policy Analytics Based on Artificial Intelligence (vol. 11685). Springer International Publishing.

Macintosh, A. (2004). Characterizing E-Participation in Policymaking. *Proceedings of the 37th Annual Hawaii International Conference on System Sciences.*

Maffei, S., Leoni, F., & Villari, B. (2020). Data-driven anticipatory governance. Emerging scenarios in data for policy practices. *Policy Design and Practice*, *3*(2), 123–134. Advance online publication. doi:10.1080/25741292.2020.1763896

Mahanti, R. (2019). *Data Quality: Dimensions, Measurement, Strategy, Management, and Governance*. ASQ Quality Press.

Malik, N. A., & Shaikh, M. A. (2019). Spatial distribution and accessibility to public sector tertiary care teaching hospitals: Case study from Pakistan. *Eastern Mediterranean Health Journal*, *25*(6), 431–434. Advance online publication. doi:10.26719/emhj.18.049 PMID:31469163

Manikam, S., Sahibudin, S., & Kasinathan, V. (2019). Business intelligence addressing service quality for big data analytics in public sector. *Indonesian Journal of Electrical Engineering and Computer Science*, *16*(1), 491. Advance online publication. doi:10.11591/ijeecs.v16.i1.pp491-499

Manning, C. D., Raghavan, P., & Schütze, H. (2008). *Xml retrieval*. Introduction to Information Retrieval.

Mao, Z., Wu, J., Qiao, Y., & Yao, H. (2022). Government data governance framework based on a data middle platform. *Aslib Journal of Information Management*, *74*(2), 289–310. doi:10.1108/AJIM-03-2021-0068

Ma, Q., Wang, L., Gong, X., & Li, K. (2022). Research on the Rationality of Public Toilets Spatial Layout based on the POI Data from the Perspective of Urban Functional Area. *Journal of Geo-Information Science*, *24*(1). Advance online publication. doi:10.12082/dqxxkx.2022.210331

Marcucci, S., Alarcon, N. G., Verhulst, S. G., & Wullhorst, E. (2023). Mapping and Comparing Data Governance Frameworks: A benchmarking exercise to inform global data governance deliberations. *arXiv preprint arXiv:2302.13731*.

Marda, V. (2018, November). Artificial intelligence policy in India: A framework for engaging the limits of data-driven decision-making. *Philos. Trans. R. Soc. A Math. Phys. Eng. Sci.*, *376*(2133), 1–19.

Markides, C. (2011, March). Crossing the Chasm: How to Convert Relevant Research Into Managerially Useful Research. *The Journal of Applied Behavioral Science*, *47*(1), 121–134. doi:10.1177/0021886310388162

Marković, M., & Gostojić, S. (2018). Open Judicial Data: A Comprehensive Analysis. *Social Science Computer Review*, *38*(3), 295–314. doi:10.1177/0894439318770744

Mavakala, B., Mulaji, C., Mpiana, P., Elongo, V., Otamonga, J.-P., Biey, E., Wildi, W., & Pote-Wembonyama, J. (2017). Citizen Sensing of Solid Waste Disposals : Crowdsourcing As Tool Supporting Waste Management in a. *Proceedings Sardinia 2017 / Sixteenth International Waste Management and Landfill Symposium*. https://doi.org/https://archive-ouverte.unige.ch/unige:97650

McKinsey Global Institute. (2018). *Notes from the AI Frontier: Modeling the Impact of AI on the World Economy*. Author.

Medvedeva, M., Vols, M., & Wieling, M. (2020). Using Machine Learning to predict decisions of the European Court of Human Rights. *Artificial Intelligence and Law*, *28*(2), 237–266. doi:10.1007/s10506-019-09255-y

Medvedeva, M., Wieling, M., & Vols, M. (2023). Rethinking the Field of Automatic Prediction of Court Decisions. *Artificial Intelligence and Law*, *31*(1), 195–212. doi:10.1007/s10506-021-09306-3

Meijer, A., & Thaens, M. (2018). Digital Government Transformation: A Structural Analysis of Digital Government's Impacts. *Public Administration Review*.

Mengesha, N., & Ayanso, A. (2021). Examining the Evolution of E-Government Development of Nations Through Machine Learning Techniques. In *Handbook of Research on Applied Data Science and Artificial Intelligence in Business and Industry* (pp. 85–107). IGI Global. doi:10.4018/978-1-7998-6985-6.ch004

Mergel, I. (2013). Social Media Adoption and Resulting Tactics in the U.S. Federal Government. *Government Information Quarterly*, *30*(2), 123–130. doi:10.1016/j.giq.2012.12.004

Mergel, I., Edelmann, N., & Haug, N. (2018). Defining digital transformation: Results from expert interviews. *Government Information Quarterly*.

Mikhaylov, S. J., Esteve, M., & Campion, A. (2018). Artificial intelligence for the public sector: Opportunities and challenges of cross-sector collaboration. *Philosophical Transactions. Series A, Mathematical, Physical, and Engineering Sciences*, *376*(2128), 20170357. Advance online publication. doi:10.1098/rsta.2017.0357 PMID:30082303

Miloslavskaya, N., & Tolstoy, A. (2016). Big Data, Fast Data and Data Lake Concepts. *Procedia Computer Science*, *88*, 300–305. doi:10.1016/j.procs.2016.07.439

Mobus, G., & Fisher, P. (1999). *Foraging Search at the Edge of Chaos*. Lawrence Erlbaum & Associates.

Mohlameane, M., & Ruxwana, N. (2020). Exploring the impact of cloud computing on existing South African regulatory frameworks. *South African Journal of Information Management*, *22*(1), 1–9. doi:10.4102/sajim.v22i1.1132

Molnar, C. (2020). *Interpretable machine learning*. Lulu.com.

Monah, S. R., Wagner, M. W., Biswas, A., Khalvati, F., Erdman, L. E., Amirabadi, A., Vidarsson, L., McCradden, M. D., & Ertl-Wagner, B. B. (2022). Data governance functions to support responsible data stewardship in pediatric radiology research studies using artificial intelligence. *Pediatric Radiology*, *52*(11), 2111–2119. doi:10.1007/s00247-022-05427-2 PMID:35790559

Montgomery, D. C., Peck, E. A., & Vining, G. G. (2021). *Introduction to linear regression analysis*. John Wiley & Sons.

Moon, M. (2023). Searching for Inclusive Artificial Intelligence for Social Good: Participatory Governance and Policy Recommendations for Making AI More Inclusive and Benign for Society. *Public Administration Review*, *83*(2), 366–378. doi:10.1111/puar.13648

Morse, M. (2020). *Making a Difference Through Collaboration: A Case Study Exploring Cross-Functional Collaboration Within an Urban High School in the Northeastern United States* [Doctoral thesis]. The College of Professional Studies of Northeastern University.

Mthembu, Z. K., Patel, S. S., Naicker, N., Joseph, S., Madamshetty, L., Moonsamy, D., Akinola, A. T., & Govender, P. (2024 under review). Developing a Data Lakehouse for a South African Government-Sector Training Authority: Governance Framework Design through Systematic Literature Review and Meta-Analysis. In O. S. Ogunleye (Ed.), *Machine Learning and Data Science Techniques for Effective Government Service Delivery*. IGI Global.

Muneeb, S., & Chandler, T. W. (2021). *Sentiment Analysis for COVID-19 National Vaccination Policy*. https://pide.org.pk/blog/sentiment-analysis-for-cov

Murphy, K. P. (2012). *Machine learning: a probabilistic perspective*. MIT Press.

Muthi Reddy, P., Manjula, S. H., & Venugopal, K. R. (2018). Secured Privacy Data using Multi Key Encryption in Cloud Storage. *Proceedings of 5th International Conference on Emerging Applications of Information Technology, EAIT 2018*. 10.1109/EAIT.2018.8470399

Muzaffar, H. M., Tahir, A., Ali, A., Ahmad, M., & McArdle, G. (2017). Quality assessment of volunteered geographic information for educational planning. In *Volunteered Geographic Information and the Future of Geospatial Data*. IGI Global. doi:10.4018/978-1-5225-2446-5.ch005

Nagel, S. (1960). Using simple calculations to predict judicial decisions. *The American Behavioral Scientist*, *4*(4), 24–28. doi:10.1177/000276426000400409

Nambiar, A., & Mundra, D. (2022). An Overview of Data Warehouse and Data Lake in Modern Enterprise Data Management. *Big Data and Cognitive Computing, 6*(4).

Nambiar, A., & Mundra, D. (2022). An Overview of Data Warehouse and Data Lake in Modern Enterprise Data Management. *Big Data and Cognitive Computing*, *6*(4), 132. doi:10.3390/bdcc6040132

Namyenya, A., Daum, T., Rwamigisa, P. B., & Birner, R. (2022). E-diary: A digital tool for strengthening accountability in agricultural extension. *Information Technology for Development*, *28*(2), 319–345. Advance online publication. doi:10.1080/02681102.2021.1875186

Naudé, W., & Dimitri, N. (2020). The race for an artificial general intelligence: Implications for public policy. *AI & Society*, *35*(2), 367–379. doi:10.1007/s00146-019-00887-x

Ng, A. (2017). *Machine learning yearning*. http://www. mlyearning. org/(96)

Ngcobo, N. H., Akinola, A. T., Madamshetty, L., Naicker, N., Patel, S. S., Joseph, S., Moonsamy, D., & Govender, P. (2023). An Efficient and Secure Web Portal System to Support a Microsoft Azure Data Lakehouse for a Government Sector Training Authority. *International Journal of Advanced Computer Science and Applications*.

Ngige, O. C., Ayankoya, F. Y., Balogun, J. A., Onuiri, E., Agbonkhese, C., & Sanusi, F. A. (2023). A dataset for predicting Supreme Court judgments in Nigeria. *Data in Brief, 50*. doi:10.1016/j.dib.2023.109483

NHS. (2021). *AI in Healthcare Delivery*. NHS.

Nielsen, M. A. (2015). *Neural networks and deep learning* (Vol. 25). Determination press.

Noveck, B. S., Ayoub, R., Hermosilla, M., Marks, J., & Suwondo, P. (2017). *Smarter Crowdsourcing for Zika and Other Mosquito-Borne Diseases*. Academic Press.

Novita, N., & Indrany Nanda Ayu Anissa, A. (2022). The role of data analytics for detecting indications of fraud in the public sector. *International Journal of Research in Business and Social Science, 11*(7). doi:10.20525/ijrbs.v11i7.2113

O'Neil, C. (2016). *Weapons of Math Destruction: How Big Data increases inequality and threatens democracy*. Crown Publishing Group.

Ogbu, O. (2006). *Modern Nigerian Legal System* (3rd ed.). AP Press.

Ojo, A., Janowski, T., & Estevez, E. (2018). Blockchain for Government and Public Services: A Systematic Literature Review. *Government Information Quarterly*.

Okeke, G. N. (2016). Judicial precedent in the Nigerian legal system and a case for its application under international law. *Nnamdi Azikiwe University Journal of International Law and Jurisprudence, 1*, 107–115.

Okyere, F., Minnich, T., Sproll, M., Mensah, E., Amartey, L., Otoo-Kwofie, C., & Brunn, A. (2022). Implementation of a low-cost Ambulance Management System. *Dgpf, 30*.

O'Leary. (2007). *Action Research-Research Methodologies Guide. A collection of resources describing research.* Academic Press.

Olteanu-Raimond, A. M., See, L., Schultz, M., Foody, G., Riffler, M., Gasber, T., Jolivet, L., le Bris, A., Meneroux, Y., Liu, L., Poupée, M., & Gombert, M. (2020). Use of automated change detection and VGI sources for identifying and validating urban land use change. *Remote Sensing (Basel), 12*(7), 1186. Advance online publication. doi:10.3390/rs12071186

OMG. (2022). *Decision model and notation (DMN)*. OMG. https://www.omg.org/dmn/

Orayer, O. (2023). *Is Polymath Thinking the Answer to Thriving in the AI Era?* Medium. https://medium.com/@opher.brayer/is-polymath-thinking-the-answer-to-thriving-in-the-ai-era-d269000163a3

Oreščanin, D., & Hlupić, T. (2021). *Data Lakehouse - a Novel Step in Analytics Architecture*. 2021 44th International Convention on Information, Communication and Electronic Technology (MIPRO), Opatija, Croatia.

Osakwe, S., & Adeniran, A. P. (2021). *Strengthening Data Governance in Africa: Project Inception Report*. Centre for the Study of Economies of Africa.

Page, M. J., McKenzie, J. E., Bossuyt, P. M., Boutron, I., Hoffmann, T. C., Mulrow, C. D., Shamseer, L., Tetzlaff, J. M., Akl, E. A., Brennan, S. E., Chou, R., Glanville, J., Grimshaw, J. M., Hróbjartsson, A., Lalu, M. M., Li, T., Loder, E. W., Mayo-Wilson, E., McDonald, S., ... Moher, D. (2021). The PRISMA 2020 statement: An updated guideline for reporting systematic reviews. *Systematic Reviews*, *10*(1), 89. doi:10.1186/s13643-021-01626-4 PMID:33781348

Panopoulou, E., Tambouris, E., Tarabanis, K. (2014). E-participation Initiatives: How is Europe Progressing? *European Journal of ePractice.*

Pardo, T. A., Gil-Garcia, J. R., & Burke, G. B. (2008). Governance Structures in E- Government: Are They Changing? *International Journal of Electronic Government Research.*

Pardo, T. A., Nam, T., & Burke, G. B. (2012). E-government interoperability: Interaction of policy, management, and technology dimensions. *Social Science Computer Review*, *30*(1), 7–23. doi:10.1177/0894439310392184

Park, S. (2020). Data Science in South Korea's COVID-19 Response. *Journal of Public Health Policy.*

Park, M., & Chai, S. (2021). AI Model for Predicting Legal Judgments to Improve Accuracy and Explainability of Online Privacy Invasion Cases. *Applied Sciences (Basel, Switzerland)*, *11*(23), 11080. doi:10.3390/app112311080

Paschalidi, C. (2015). *Data Governance: A conceptual framework in order to prevent your Data Lake from becoming a Data Swamp* [Master of Science in Information Security Thesis, Luleå University of Technology]. Digitala Vetenskapliga Arkivet (DiVA). https://www.diva-portal.org/smash/record.jsf?pid=diva2%3A1019917

Patni, S. (2017). *Pro RESTful APIs Design.* Build and Integrate with REST, JSON, XML and JAX-RS. doi:10.1007/978-1-4842-2665-0

Peng, G., Privette, J. L., Kearns, E. J., Ritchey, N. A., & Ansari, S. (2015). A unified framework for measuring stewardship practices applied to digital environmental datasets. *Data Science Journal*, *13*(0), 231–253. doi:10.2481/dsj.14-049

Pi, Y. (2021). Machine learning in governments: Benefits, challenges and future directions. *JeDEM-eJournal of eDemocracy and Open Government*, *13*(1), 203-219.

Pittman, J., Severino, L., DeCarlo-Tecce, M., & Kiosoglous, C. (2021). An action research case study: digital equity and educational inclusion during an emergent COVID-19 divide. *Journal for Multicultural Education.*

Plano Clark, V. L. (2017). Mixed methods research. *The Journal of Positive Psychology*, *12*(3), 305–306. doi:10.1080/17439760.2016.1262619

Polderman, J., & Willems, J. (1998). *Introduction to Mathematical Systems Theory: A Behavioral Approach* (2nd ed.). Springer Verlag. doi:10.1007/978-1-4757-2953-5

Pradani, D. A., Anwar, C., & Armeliza, D. (2021). Pengaruh Pemahaman Good Governance dan Penguasaan Teknik Audit Berbantuan Komputer terhadap. *Artificial Intelligence*, *2*(3), 496–516. Advance online publication. doi:10.21009/japa.0203.02

Pratsri, S., & Nilsook, P. (2020). Design on Big Data Platform-Based in Higher Education Institute. *Higher Education Studies*, *10*(4), 36–43. doi:10.5539/hes.v10n4p36

Provost, F., & Fawcett, T. (2013). Data Science and its Relationship to Big Data and Data-Driven Decision Making. *Big Data*, *1*(1), 51–59. Advance online publication. doi:10.1089/big.2013.1508 PMID:27447038

Provost, F., & Fawcett, T. (2013). *Data Science for Business*. O'Reilly Media.

PushpakumaraH.JayaweeraP.ManjulanW. (2021). *Using the Open Group Architecture Framework (TOGAF) for Quality Assurance in Higher Education Teaching and Learning*. doi:10.2139/ssrn.3808691

Putri, N., & Yusof, S. M. (2009). Critical success factors for implementing quality engineering tools and techniques in malaysian's and indonesian's automotive industries: An Exploratory Study. *Journal Proceedings of the International MultiConference of Engineers and Computer Scientists.*, *2*, 18–20.

Qi, Y., Guo, K., Zhang, C., Guo, D., & Zhi, Z. (2018). A VGI-based Foodborn Disease Report and Forecast System. *Proceedings of the 4th ACM SIGSPATIAL International Workshop on Safety and Resilience, EM-GIS 2018*. 10.1145/3284103.3284124

Quasim, M. T., Johri, P., Meraj, M., & Haider, S. (2019). 5V's of big data via cloud computing: Uses and importance. *Science International (Lahore)*, *31*(3), 367–371.

Quinlan, J. R. (1986). Induction of decision trees. *Machine Learning*, *1*(1), 81–106. doi:10.1007/BF00116251

Quinlan, J. R. (2014). *C4. 5: programs for machine learning*. Elsevier.

R, J., & B, S. (2022). Social Impacts of Data Science in Food, Housing And Medical Attention Linked to Public Service. *Technoarete Transactions on Advances in Data Science and Analytics*, *1*(1). doi:10.36647/TTADSA/01.01.A004

Ragnedda, M., & Muschert, G. W. (2013). *The Digital Divide: The Internet and Social Inequality in International Perspective*. Routledge. doi:10.4324/9780203069769

Raj, A., Bosch, J., Olsson, H. H., & Wang, T. J. (2020). *Modelling data pipelines*. 2020 46th Euromicro conference on software engineering and advanced applications (SEAA), Portoroz, Slovenia.

Raj, A., Bosch, J., Olsson, H. H., & Wang, T. J. (2020). Modelling Data Pipelines. *2020 46th Euromicro Conference on Software Engineering and Advanced Applications (SEAA)*.

Rangaswamy, E., Periyasamy, G., & Nawaz, N. (2021). A study on singapore's ageing population in the context of eldercare initiatives using machine learning algorithms. *Big Data and Cognitive Computing*, *5*(4), 51. Advance online publication. doi:10.3390/bdcc5040051

Ray, A., & Bala, P. K. (2020). Social media for improved process management in organizations during disasters. *Knowledge and Process Management*, *27*(1), 63–74. Advance online publication. doi:10.1002/kpm.1623

Rej, A. (2020, Nov. 27). Artificial Intelligence for the Indo-Pacific: A Blueprint for 2030. *The Diplomat*.

Rencher, A. C., & Schaalje, G. B. (2008). *Linear models in statistics*. John Wiley & Sons.

Ribeiro, M. T., Singh, S., & Guestrin, C. (2016). Why Should I Trust You? Explaining the Predictions of Any Classifier. *Proceedings of the 22nd ACM SIGKDD International Conference on Knowledge Discovery and Data Mining*. 10.1145/2939672.2939778

Ricci, F., Rokach, L., & Shapira, B. (2010). Introduction to recommender systems handbook. In Recommender systems handbook (pp. 1-35). Springer US.

Rieck, D., Schünemann, B., & Radusch, I. (2015). Advanced Traffic Light Information in OpenStreetMap for Traffic Simulations. Lecture Notes in Mobility. doi:10.1007/978-3-319-15024-6_2

Rodriguez, G., Torres, H., Fajardo, M., & Medina, J. (2021). Covid-19 in Ecuador: Radiography of Hospital Distribution Using Data Science. *ETCM 2021 - 5th Ecuador Technical Chapters Meeting*. 10.1109/ETCM53643.2021.9590641

Rogge, N., Agasisti, T., & De Witte, K. (2017). Big data and the measurement of public organizations' performance and efficiency: The state-of-the-art. *Public Policy and Administration*, *32*(4), 263–281. Advance online publication. doi:10.1177/0952076716687355

Rumelhart, D. E., Hinton, G. E., & Williams, R. J. (1986). Learning representations by back-propagating errors. *Nature, 323*(6088), 533-536.

Russell, S., & Norvig, P. (2016). *Artificial Intelligence: A Modern Approach* (3rd ed.). Pearson.

Sales, A. (1991). The Private, the Public and Civil Society: Social Realms and Power Structures. *International Political Science Review/Revue Internationale de Science Politique, 12*(4), 295–312. https://www.jstor.org/stable/1601467

Sambrekar, K., Rajpurohit, V. S., & Joshi, J. (2018). A proposed technique for conversion of unstructured Agro-data to semi-structured or structured data. *2018 Fourth International Conference on Computing Communication Control and Automation (ICCUBEA)*, Pune, India. 10.1109/ICCUBEA.2018.8697432

Samuel, A. L. (2000). Some studies in machine learning using the game of checkers. *IBM Journal of Research and Development, 44*(1.2), 206-226.

Samuel, P., Reshmy, A. K., Rajesh, S., Kanipriya, M., & Karthika, R. A. (2023). AI-Based Big Data Algorithms and Machine Learning Techniques for Managing Data in E-Governance. In AI, IoT, and Blockchain Breakthroughs in E-Governance (pp. 19-35). IGI Global. doi:10.4018/978-1-6684-7697-0.ch002

Sandhu, A. K. (2021). Big data with cloud computing: Discussions and challenges. *Big Data Mining and Analytics*, *5*(1), 32–40. doi:10.26599/BDMA.2021.9020016

Sangiambut, S., & Sieber, R. (2016). The V in VGI: Citizens or Civic Data Sources. *Urban Planning*, *1*(2), 141–154. doi:10.17645/up.v1i2.644

Sankaralingam, K., Ferris, M., Nowatzki, T., Estan, C., Wood, D., & Vaish, N. (2013). *Optimization and Mathematical Modeling in Computer Architecture*. Morgan & Claypool Publishers.

Saragih, A. H., Reyhani, Q., Setyowati, M. S., & Hendrawan, A. (2022). The potential of an artificial intelligence (AI) application for the tax administration system's modernization: The case of Indonesia. *Artificial Intelligence and Law*, (0123456789). Advance online publication. doi:10.1007/s10506-022-09321-y

Sarramia, D., Claude, A., Ogereau, F., Mezhoud, J., & Mailhot, G. (2022). CEBA: A Data Lake for Data Sharing and Environmental Monitoring. *Sensors (Basel)*, *22*(7), 2733. doi:10.3390/s22072733 PMID:35408347

SAS. (2021). *History of Big Data*. SAS. https://www.sas.com/en_us/insights/big-data/what-is-big-data.html

Sawadogo, P., & Darmont, J. (2021). On data lake architectures and metadata management. *Journal of Intelligent Information Systems*, *56*(1), 97–120. doi:10.1007/s10844-020-00608-7

Sboui, T., & Aissi, S. (2022). *A Risk-based Approach for Enhancing the Fitness of use of VGI*. IEEE., doi:10.1109/ACCESS.2022.3201022

Schmidhuber, J. (2015). Deep learning in neural networks: An overview. *Neural Networks*, *61*, 85–117. doi:10.1016/j.neunet.2014.09.003 PMID:25462637

Selbst, A. D., Boyd, D., Friedler, S. A., Venkatasubramanian, S., & Vertesi, J. (2019, January). Fairness and abstraction in sociotechnical systems. In *Proceedings of the conference on fairness, accountability, and transparency* (pp. 59-68). 10.1145/3287560.3287598

Sezer, A., Deniz, M., & Topuz, M. (2018). Analysis of Accessibility of Schools in Usak City via Geographical Information Systems (GIS). *Tarih Kultur ve Sanat Arastirmalari Dergisi-Journal of History Culture and Art Research, 7*(5).

Shaikh, R. A., Sahu, T. P., & Anand, V. (2020). Predicting outcomes of legal cases based on legal factors using classifiers. *Procedia Computer Science*, *167*, 2393–2402. doi:10.1016/j.procs.2020.03.292

Shanmugamani, R. (2018). *Deep Learning for Computer Vision: Expert techniques to train advanced neural networks using TensorFlow and Keras*. Packt Publishing Ltd.

Sharma, G. D., Yadav, A., & Chopra, R. (2020). Artificial intelligence and effective governance: A review, critique and research agenda. *Sustainable Futures, 2*. doi:10.1016/j.sftr.2019.100004

Silver, D., Huang, A., Maddison, C. J., Guez, A., Sifre, L., Van Den Driessche, G., ... Hassabis, D. (2016). Mastering the game of Go with deep neural networks and tree search. *Nature, 529*(7587), 484-489.

Simmons, R. (2018). Big Data, Machine Judges, and the Legitimacy of the Criminal Justice System. *SSRN*, *52*(2), 1067–1118. doi:10.2139/ssrn.3156510

Singh, A. (2019). Remote sensing and GIS applications for municipal waste management. *Journal of Environmental Management*, *243*, 22–29. Advance online publication. doi:10.1016/j.jenvman.2019.05.017 PMID:31077867

Singhal, B., & Aggarwal, A. (2022). *ETL, ELT and Reverse ETL: A business case Study. 2022 Second International Conference on Advanced Technologies in Intelligent Control, Environment, Computing & Communication Engineering (ICATIECE)*, Bangalore, India 10.1109/ICATIECE56365.2022.10046997

Singh, Y. P., Singh, A. K., & Singh, R. P. (2016). *Web GIS based Framework for Citizen Reporting on Collection of Solid Waste and Mapping in GIS for Allahabad City. SAMRIDDHI : A Journal of Physical Sciences*, Engineering and Technology. doi:10.18090/samriddhi.v8i1.11405

Solís, P., McCusker, B., Menkiti, N., Cowan, N., & Blevins, C. (2018). Engaging global youth in participatory spatial data creation for the UN sustainable development goals: The case of open mapping for malaria prevention. *Applied Geography (Sevenoaks, England)*, *98*, 143–155. Advance online publication. doi:10.1016/j.apgeog.2018.07.013

Spencer, M. (2016). *Agile EA – the MVP – enterprise architect-Building the Business Value Chain...* https://enterprisearchitect.wordpress.com/2016/04/11/agile-ea-the-mvp/1/2

stahlesq.com. (2018). *How the IRS Uses Artificial Intelligence to Detect Tax Evaders*. https://stahlesq.com/criminal-defense-law-blog/how-the-irs-uses-artificial-intelligence-to-detect-tax-evaders/

Steiniger, S., Poorazizi, M. E., Scott, D. R., Fuentes, C., & Crespo, R. (2016). Can we use OpenStreetMap POIs for the Evaluation of Urban Accessibility? *International Conference on GIScience Short Paper Proceedings, 1*. 10.21433/B31167F0678P

Strange, M., & Tucker, J. (2023). Global governance and the normalization of artificial intelligence as 'good' for human health. *AI & Society*. Advance online publication. doi:10.1007/s00146-023-01774-2

Strijker, D., Bosworth, G., & Bouter, G. (2020). Research methods in rural studies: Qualitative, quantitative and mixed methods. *Journal of Rural Studies*, *78*, 262–270. doi:10.1016/j.jrurstud.2020.06.007

Sturrock, H. J. W., Woolheater, K., Bennett, A. F., Andrade-Pacheco, R., & Midekisa, A. (2018). Predicting residential structures from open source remotely enumerated data using machine learning. *PLoS One*, *13*(9), e0204399. Advance online publication. doi:10.1371/journal.pone.0204399 PMID:30240429

Subrahmanya, S. V. G., Shetty, D. K., Patil, V., Hameed, B. M. Z., Paul, R., Smriti, K., Naik, N., & Somani, B. K. (2022). The role of data science in healthcare advancements: applications, benefits, and future prospects. In Irish Journal of Medical Science (Vol. 191, Issue 4). doi:10.1007/s11845-021-02730-z

Sutton, R. S., & Barto, A. G. (2018). *Reinforcement learning: An introduction*. MIT Press.

Syynimaa, N. (2015). *Enterprise Architecture Adoption Method for Higher Education Institutions* [Doctoral Thesis]. Informatics Research Centre Henley Business School University.

The Open Group. (2011a). *Architecture Development Method.* The Open Group. https://pubs.opengroup.org/architecture/togaf9-doc/arch/chap05.html

The Open Group. (2011b). *TOGAF 9.1*. The Open Group. https://www.opengroup.org/subjectareas/enterprise/togaf

Thomas, J. C., & Streib, G. (2003). The New Face of Government: Citizen-Initiated Contacts in the Era of E-Government. *Journal of Public Administration: Research and Theory*, *13*(1), 83–102. doi:10.1093/jpart/mug010

Thompson, A. F., Afolayan, A. H., & Ibidunmoye, E. O. (2013). Application of geographic information system to solid waste management. *2013 Pan African International Conference on Information Science, Computing and Telecommunications, PACT 2013*. 10.1109/SCAT.2013.7055110

ThoughtSpot. (2023). *Understanding cloud business intelligence: Definition, benefits, and use cases. Business Intelligence.* ThoughtSpot Inc. https://www.thoughtspot.com/data-trends/business-intelligence/cloud-business-intelligence

Thune, T. (2011). Success Factors in Higher Education–Industry Collaboration: A case study of collaboration in the engineering field. *Tertiary Education and Management*, *17*(1), 31–50. doi:10.1080/13583883.2011.552627

To, H., Kim, S. H., & Shahabi, C. (2015). Effectively crowdsourcing the acquisition and analysis of visual data for disaster response. *Proceedings - 2015 IEEE International Conference on Big Data, IEEE Big Data 2015*. 10.1109/BigData.2015.7363814

Tokyo Metropolitan Government. (2020). *AI Traffic Management Initiative*. Author.

Trad, A. (2021b). The business transformation enterprise architecture framework for innovation: The role of artificial intelligence in the global business education (RAIGBE). The Business & Management Review, 12(1), 82-97.

Trad, A. (2021i). The transformation framework The role security in the global education system. International *Journal of Higher Education Management, 8*(1).

Trad, A. (2023c). *Private Cloud based Transformation Projects (PCTP) for Business Intelligence*. E-Leaders. g-casa.com

Trad, A. (2023f). A Relational DataBase based Enterprise Transformation Projects. *International Journal of Mathematics and Computers in Simulation, 17*, 1-11.

Trad, A., & Kalpic, D. (2018a). Business Transformation Projects-An Intelligence Driven Development for Enterprise Architecture and Asset Management-The Proof of Concept. *ICAMCS Journal*.

Trad, A., & Kalpić, D. (2021b). Transformation and Enterprise Architecture Projects-The Integration of Operational Research. *The 3rd International Conference on Machine Learning and Intelligent Systems (MLIS 2021)*.

Trad, A., & Kalpić, D. (2022a). Business Transformation Projects based on a Holistic Enterprise Architecture Pattern (HEAP)-The Basics. IGI.

Trad, A., & Kalpić, D. (2023a). *SWOT based Transformation's Organizational Risks' Management (STORM)*. E-leaders conference, Check Republic. www.g-casa.om

Trad, A., (2022a). *Using a Generic Artificial Intelligence Pattern for Business Transformation*. Academic Press.

Trad, A. (2015a). *A Transformation Framework Proposal for Managers in Business Innovation and Business Transformation Projects-Intelligent aBB architecture*. Centeris.

Trad, A. (2015b). *A Transformation Framework Proposal for Managers in Business Innovation and Business Transformation Projects-An ICS's atomic architecture vision*. Centeris.

Trad, A. (2021c). *Using a Generic Artificial Intelligence Pattern for Business Transformation. Book*. IGI Global.

Trad, A. (2021d). *The Transformation Framework: The Role of Artificial Intelligence for Military Strategies (RAI4MS). Book: Technological Development and Impact on Economic and Environmental Sustainability*. IGI Global.

Trad, A. (2021e). *The Business, Societal, and Enterprise Architecture Framework: An Artificial Intelligence, Data Sciences-, and Big Data-Based Approach. Book: Handbook of Research on Applied Data Science and Artificial Intelligence in Business and Industry*. IGI Global.

Trad, A. (2021f). The Business Transformation Enterprise Architecture Framework: Intelligent Strategic Development and Operations (iSDevOps). *International Journal of Distributed Artificial Intelligence, 13*(1), 74–101. doi:10.4018/IJDAI.2021010104

Trad, A. (2021g). *The Business Transformation Enterprise Architecture Framework for Innovation-The Role of Artificial Intelligence in the Global Business Education (RAIGBE).* ICBED. doi:10.24052/BMR/V12NU01/ART-08

Trad, A. (2022b). *Business Transformation and Enterprise Architecture Projects: Natural Language Programming (NLP). Book: Handbook of Research on Applying Emerging Technologies Across Multiple Disciplines*. IGI Global.

Trad, A. (2023a). *Academic and Educational Transformation Projects-The Role Team-Based Learning in Polymathics (RTBLP)*. IGI Global.

Trad, A. (2023b). *Academic and Educational Transformation Projects-The Role Team-Based Learning in Polymathics For University Cycle (RTBLP4UC)*. IGI Global.

Trad, A. (2023d). *Business Transformation Project's-The Impact of Rise of Over-the-Top (OTT)*. IGI-Global.

Trad, A. (2023e). *Organizational and Digital Transformation Projects-A Mathematical Model for Building Blocks based Organizational Unbundling Process*. IGI-Global.

Trad, A., & Kalpic, D. (2004). Proactive monitoring and maintenance of intelligent control systems: a design pattern for autonomous systems. *26th International Conference on Information Technology Interfaces*, 637-642.

Trad, A., & Kalpić, D. (2014a). The Selection and Training Framework for Managers in Business Innovation and Transformation Projects-An applied mathematics hyper-heuristics model. *Proceedings of the 2014 International Conference on Mathematical Methods, Mathematical Models and Simulation in Science and Engineering (MMSSE 2014).*

Trad, A., & Kalpić, D. (2014b). *The Selection, and Training Framework selection and training framework (STF) for Manager's in Business Innovation Transformation Projects–Educational Recommendations*. Journal EDEN.

Trad, A., & Kalpić, D. (2014c). *The Selection and Training Framework (STF) for Managers in intelligent city Innovation Transformation Projects-Managerial Recommendations.* IEEE.

Trad, A., & Kalpić, D. (2017a). *An Intelligent Neural Networks Micro Artefact Patterns' Based Enterprise Architecture Model*. IGI-Global.

Trad, A., & Kalpić, D. (2019a). *Using Applied Mathematical Models for Business Transformation.* IGI Global.

Trad, A., & Kalpić, D. (2020a). *Business Transformation and Enterprise Architecture: The Holistic Project Asset Management Concept (HPAMC). Book: Handbook of Research on Strategic Fit and Design in Business Ecosystems*. IGI Global.

Trad, A., & Kalpić, D. (2021a). *The business transformation framework on Knowledge and Intelligence-Driven Development (KIDD). Book: Encyclopaedia of Organizational Knowledge, Administration, and Technology*. IGI Global.

Trad, A., & Kalpić, D. (2021c). Business transformation project's architect's profile (BTPAP). *The Business & Management Review.*, *12*(2), 137–153. doi:10.24052/BMR/V12NU02/ART-11

Tran, K., Barbeau, S., Hillsman, E., & Labrador, M. A. (2013). GO_Sync - A Framework to Synchronize Crowd-Sourced Mapping Contributors from Online Communities and Transit Agency Bus Stop Inventories. *International Journal of Intelligent Transportation Systems Research*, *11*(2), 54–64. Advance online publication. doi:10.1007/s13177-013-0056-x

Truby, J., Brown, R., & Dahdal, A. (2020). Banking on AI: Mandating a proactive approach to AI regulation in the financial sector. *Law and Financial Markets Review*, *14*(2), 110–120. doi:10.1080/17521440.2020.1760454

Tsou, M. H., Jung, C. Te, Allen, C., Yang, J. A., Han, S. Y., Spitzberg, B. H., & Dozier, J. (2017). Building a real-time geo-targeted event observation (Geo) viewer for disaster management and situation awareness. *Lecture Notes in Geoinformation and Cartography*. doi:10.1007/978-3-319-57336-6_7

Tzavella, K., Fekete, A., & Fiedrich, F. (2018). Opportunities provided by geographic information systems and volunteered geographic information for a timely emergency response during flood events in Cologne, Germany. *Natural Hazards*, *91*. Advance online publication. doi:10.1007/s11069-017-3102-1

Ulmer, S. S. (1963). Quantitative analysis of judicial processes: Some practical and theoretical applications. *Law and Contemporary Problems*, *28*(1), 164–184. doi:10.2307/1190728

Ulnicane, I., Eke, D., Knight, W., Ogoh, G., & Stahl, B. (2021). Good governance as a response to discontents? Déjà vu, or lessons for AI from other emerging technologies. *Interdisciplinary Science Reviews*, *46*(1-2), 176–195. doi:10.1080/03080188.2020.1840220

United Nations. (2020). *E-Government Survey 2020*. Author.

USCIS. (2020). *Emma: Virtual Assistant*. U.S. Citizenship and Immigration Services.

Vapnik, V. (1999). *The nature of statistical learning theory*. Springer science & business media.

Veale, M., & Brass, I. (2019). Administration by algorithm? Public management meets public sector machine learning. *Public Management Meets Public Sector Machine Learning*.

Vogl, T. M. (2021). Artificial Intelligence in Local Government: Enabling Artificial Intelligence for Good Governance in UK Local Authorities. SSRN *Electronic Journal*. doi:10.2139/SSRN.3840222

Vom Brocke, J., Hevner, A., & Maedche, A. (2020). Introduction to design science research. *Design science research. Cases*, 1-13.

Wahdain, E. A., Baharudin, A. S., & Ahmad, M. N. (2019). Big data analytics in the malaysian public sector: The determinants of value creation. *Advances in Intelligent Systems and Computing*, *843*, 139–150. Advance online publication. doi:10.1007/978-3-319-99007-1_14

Wasserman, W., & Kutner, M. H. (1985). *Applied linear statistical models: regression, analysis of variance, and experimental designs*. RD Irwin.

Weber, R. H. (2017). Regulating the Internet: The New Battle against Chaos. *International Journal of Communications Law and Policy*.

Wei, L. (2022). Intelligent analysis of e-government influence factors based on improved machine learning. *Neural Computing & Applications*, *34*(15), 12241–12256. doi:10.1007/s00521-021-06657-5

West, D. M. (2004). E-Government and the Transformation of Service Delivery and Citizen Attitudes. *Public Administration Review*, *64*(1), 15–27. doi:10.1111/j.1540-6210.2004.00343.x

West, D. M. (2018). *The Future of Work: Robots, AI, and Automation*. Brookings Institution Press.

Wibowo, S., & Sandikapura, T. (2019). *Improving Data Security, Interoperability, and Veracity using Blockchain for One Data Governance, Case Study of Local Tax Big Data*. 2019 International Conference on ICT for Smart Society (ICISS), Bandung, Indonesia.

Wikipedia. (2021). Polymath. In *Wikipedia*. https://en.wikipedia.org/wiki/Polymath

Wikipedia. (2023). *Complexity management*. Wikipedia.

Williamson, B. (2015). Governing methods: Policy innovation labs, design and data science in the digital governance of education. *Journal of Educational Administration and History*, *47*(3), 251–271. Advance online publication. doi:10.1080/00220620.2015.1038693

Winfield, A., & Jirotka, M. (2018). Ethical governance is essential to building trust in robotics and artificial intelligence systems. *Philosophical Transactions. Series A, Mathematical, Physical, and Engineering Sciences*, *376*(2133), 20180085. doi:10.1098/rsta.2018.0085 PMID:30323000

Wong, W., & Hinnant, C. C. (2022). Competing perspectives on the Big Data revolution: A typology of applications in public policy. *Journal of Economic Policy Reform*. Advance online publication. doi:10.1080/17487870.2022.2103701

Woudenberg, M., & Unis, C. J. (2023). *Systems Thinking-Skills and Insights to Resolve Wicked Problems. Systems Thinking*. https://www.polymathicbeing.com/p/systems-thinking

Xie, X., Zhou, Y., Xu, Y., Hu, Y., & Wu, C. (2019). OpenStreetMap Data Quality Assessment via Deep Learning and Remote Sensing Imagery. *IEEE Access : Practical Innovations, Open Solutions*, *7*, 176884–176895. Advance online publication. doi:10.1109/ACCESS.2019.2957825

Xue, K., Chen, W., Li, W., Hong, J., & Hong, P. (2018). Combining Data Owner-Side and Cloud-Side Access Control for Encrypted Cloud Storage. *IEEE Transactions on Information Forensics and Security*, *13*(8), 2062–2074. doi:10.1109/TIFS.2018.2809679

Yigitcanlar, T., Agdas, D., & Degirmenci, K. (2022). Artificial intelligence in local governments: Perceptions of city managers on prospects, constraints and choices. *AI & Society*, (0123456789). Advance online publication. doi:10.1007/s00146-022-01450-x

Yingwei, Y., Dawei, M., & Hongchao, F. (2020). A research framework for the application of volunteered geographic information in post-disaster recovery monitoring. *Tropical Geography, 40*(2). Advance online publication. doi:10.13284/j.cnki.rddl.003239

Yu, W., Dillon, T., Mostafa, F., Rahayu, W., & Liu, Y. (2019). A global manufacturing big data ecosystem for fault detection in predictive maintenance. *IEEE Transactions on Industrial Informatics, 16*(1), 183–192. doi:10.1109/TII.2019.2915846

Zandia, F., & Tavana, M. (2011). *A fuzzy group multi-criteria enterprise architecture framework selection model.* Elsevier.

Završnik, A. (2018). Algorithmic justice: Algorithms and big data in criminal justice settings. *European Journal of Criminology, 18*(5), 623–642. doi:10.1177/1477370819876762

Zilske, M., Neumann, A., & Nagel, K. (2011). OpenStreetMap For Traffic Simulation. *Proceedings of the 1st European State of the Map – OpenStreetMap Conference.*

Related References

To continue our tradition of advancing academic research, we have compiled a list of recommended IGI Global readings. These references will provide additional information and guidance to further enrich your knowledge and assist you with your own research and future publications.

Abbasnejad, B., Moeinzadeh, S., Ahankoob, A., & Wong, P. S. (2021). The Role of Collaboration in the Implementation of BIM-Enabled Projects. In J. Underwood & M. Shelbourn (Eds.), *Handbook of Research on Driving Transformational Change in the Digital Built Environment* (pp. 27–62). IGI Global. https://doi.org/10.4018/978-1-7998-6600-8.ch002

Abdulrahman, K. O., Mahamood, R. M., & Akinlabi, E. T. (2022). Additive Manufacturing (AM): Processing Technique for Lightweight Alloys and Composite Material. In K. Kumar, B. Babu, & J. Davim (Ed.), *Handbook of Research on Advancements in the Processing, Characterization, and Application of Lightweight Materials* (pp. 27-48). IGI Global. https://doi.org/10.4018/978-1-7998-7864-3.ch002

Agrawal, R., Sharma, P., & Saxena, A. (2021). A Diamond Cut Leather Substrate Antenna for BAN (Body Area Network) Application. In V. Singh, V. Dubey, A. Saxena, R. Tiwari, & H. Sharma (Eds.), *Emerging Materials and Advanced Designs for Wearable Antennas* (pp. 54–59). IGI Global. https://doi.org/10.4018/978-1-7998-7611-3.ch004

Ahmad, F., Al-Ammar, E. A., & Alsaidan, I. (2022). Battery Swapping Station: A Potential Solution to Address the Limitations of EV Charging Infrastructure. In M. Alam, R. Pillai, & N. Murugesan (Eds.), *Developing Charging Infrastructure and Technologies for Electric Vehicles* (pp. 195–207). IGI Global. doi:10.4018/978-1-7998-6858-3.ch010

Aikhuele, D. (2018). A Study of Product Development Engineering and Design Reliability Concerns. *International Journal of Applied Industrial Engineering*, *5*(1), 79–89. doi:10.4018/IJAIE.2018010105

Al-Khatri, H., & Al-Atrash, F. (2021). Occupants' Habits and Natural Ventilation in a Hot Arid Climate. In R. González-Lezcano (Ed.), *Advancements in Sustainable Architecture and Energy Efficiency* (pp. 146–168). IGI Global. https://doi.org/10.4018/978-1-7998-7023-4.ch007

Al-Shebeeb, O. A., Rangaswamy, S., Gopalakrishan, B., & Devaru, D. G. (2017). Evaluation and Indexing of Process Plans Based on Electrical Demand and Energy Consumption. *International Journal of Manufacturing, Materials, and Mechanical Engineering*, *7*(3), 1–19. doi:10.4018/IJMMME.2017070101

Amuda, M. O., Lawal, T. F., & Akinlabi, E. T. (2017). Research Progress on Rheological Behavior of AA7075 Aluminum Alloy During Hot Deformation. *International Journal of Materials Forming and Machining Processes*, *4*(1), 53–96. doi:10.4018/IJMFMP.2017010104

Amuda, M. O., Lawal, T. F., & Mridha, S. (2021). Microstructure and Mechanical Properties of Silicon Carbide-Treated Ferritic Stainless Steel Welds. In L. Burstein (Ed.), *Handbook of Research on Advancements in Manufacturing, Materials, and Mechanical Engineering* (pp. 395–411). IGI Global. https://doi.org/10.4018/978-1-7998-4939-1.ch019

Anikeev, V., Gasem, K. A., & Fan, M. (2021). Application of Supercritical Technologies in Clean Energy Production: A Review. In L. Chen (Ed.), *Handbook of Research on Advancements in Supercritical Fluids Applications for Sustainable Energy Systems* (pp. 792–821). IGI Global. https://doi.org/10.4018/978-1-7998-5796-9.ch022

Arafat, M. Y., Saleem, I., & Devi, T. P. (2022). Drivers of EV Charging Infrastructure Entrepreneurship in India. In M. Alam, R. Pillai, & N. Murugesan (Eds.), *Developing Charging Infrastructure and Technologies for Electric Vehicles* (pp. 208–219). IGI Global. https://doi.org/10.4018/978-1-7998-6858-3.ch011

Araujo, A., & Manninen, H. (2022). Contribution of Project-Based Learning on Social Skills Development: An Industrial Engineer Perspective. In A. Alves & N. van Hattum-Janssen (Eds.), *Training Engineering Students for Modern Technological Advancement* (pp. 119–145). IGI Global. https://doi.org/10.4018/978-1-7998-8816-1.ch006

Armutlu, H. (2018). Intelligent Biomedical Engineering Operations by Cloud Computing Technologies. In U. Kose, G. Guraksin, & O. Deperlioglu (Eds.), *Nature-Inspired Intelligent Techniques for Solving Biomedical Engineering Problems* (pp. 297–317). Hershey, PA: IGI Global. doi:10.4018/978-1-5225-4769-3.ch015

Atik, M., Sadek, M., & Shahrour, I. (2017). Single-Run Adaptive Pushover Procedure for Shear Wall Structures. In V. Plevris, G. Kremmyda, & Y. Fahjan (Eds.), *Performance-Based Seismic Design of Concrete Structures and Infrastructures* (pp. 59–83). Hershey, PA: IGI Global. doi:10.4018/978-1-5225-2089-4.ch003

Attia, H. (2021). Smart Power Microgrid Impact on Sustainable Building. In R. González-Lezcano (Ed.), *Advancements in Sustainable Architecture and Energy Efficiency* (pp. 169–194). IGI Global. https://doi.org/10.4018/978-1-7998-7023-4.ch008

Aydin, A., Akyol, E., Gungor, M., Kaya, A., & Tasdelen, S. (2018). Geophysical Surveys in Engineering Geology Investigations With Field Examples. In N. Ceryan (Ed.), *Handbook of Research on Trends and Digital Advances in Engineering Geology* (pp. 257–280). Hershey, PA: IGI Global. doi:10.4018/978-1-5225-2709-1.ch007

Ayoobkhan, M. U. D., Y., A., J., Easwaran, B., & R., T. (2021). Smart Connected Digital Products and IoT Platform With the Digital Twin. In P. Vasant, G. Weber, & W. Punurai (Ed.), Research Advancements in Smart Technology, Optimization, and Renewable Energy (pp. 330-350). IGI Global. https://doi.org/ doi:10.4018/978-1-7998-3970-5.ch016

Baeza Moyano, D., & González Lezcano, R. A. (2021). The Importance of Light in Our Lives: Towards New Lighting in Schools. In R. González-Lezcano (Ed.), *Advancements in Sustainable Architecture and Energy Efficiency* (pp. 239–256). IGI Global. https://doi.org/10.4018/978-1-7998-7023-4.ch011

Bagdadee, A. H. (2021). A Brief Assessment of the Energy Sector of Bangladesh. *International Journal of Energy Optimization and Engineering, 10*(1), 36–55. doi:10.4018/IJEOE.2021010103

Baklezos, A. T., & Hadjigeorgiou, N. G. (2021). Magnetic Sensors for Space Applications and Magnetic Cleanliness Considerations. In C. Nikolopoulos (Ed.), *Recent Trends on Electromagnetic Environmental Effects for Aeronautics and Space Applications* (pp. 147–185). IGI Global. https://doi.org/10.4018/978-1-7998-4879-0.ch006

Bas, T. G. (2017). Nutraceutical Industry with the Collaboration of Biotechnology and Nutrigenomics Engineering: The Significance of Intellectual Property in the Entrepreneurship and Scientific Research Ecosystems. In T. Bas & J. Zhao (Eds.), *Comparative Approaches to Biotechnology Development and Use in Developed and Emerging Nations* (pp. 1–17). Hershey, PA: IGI Global. doi:10.4018/978-1-5225-1040-6.ch001

Bazeer Ahamed, B., & Periakaruppan, S. (2021). Taxonomy of Influence Maximization Techniques in Unknown Social Networks. In P. Vasant, G. Weber, & W. Punurai (Eds.), *Research Advancements in Smart Technology, Optimization, and Renewable Energy* (pp. 351-363). IGI Global. https://doi.org/10.4018/978-1-7998-3970-5.ch017

Beale, R., & André, J. (2017). *Design Solutions and Innovations in Temporary Structures*. Hershey, PA: IGI Global. doi:10.4018/978-1-5225-2199-0

Behnam, B. (2017). Simulating Post-Earthquake Fire Loading in Conventional RC Structures. In P. Samui, S. Chakraborty, & D. Kim (Eds.), *Modeling and Simulation Techniques in Structural Engineering* (pp. 425–444). Hershey, PA: IGI Global. doi:10.4018/978-1-5225-0588-4.ch015

Ben Hamida, I., Salah, S. B., Msahli, F., & Mimouni, M. F. (2018). Distribution Network Reconfiguration Using SPEA2 for Power Loss Minimization and Reliability Improvement. *International Journal of Energy Optimization and Engineering*, *7*(1), 50–65. doi:10.4018/IJEOE.2018010103

Bentarzi, H. (2021). Fault Tree-Based Root Cause Analysis Used to Study Mal-Operation of a Protective Relay in a Smart Grid. In A. Recioui & H. Bentarzi (Eds.), *Optimizing and Measuring Smart Grid Operation and Control* (pp. 289–308). IGI Global. https://doi.org/10.4018/978-1-7998-4027-5.ch012

Beysens, D. A., Garrabos, Y., & Zappoli, B. (2021). Thermal Effects in Near-Critical Fluids: Piston Effect and Related Phenomena. In L. Chen (Ed.), *Handbook of Research on Advancements in Supercritical Fluids Applications for Sustainable Energy Systems* (pp. 1–31). IGI Global. https://doi.org/10.4018/978-1-7998-5796-9.ch001

Bhaskar, S. V., & Kudal, H. N. (2017). Effect of TiCN and AlCrN Coating on Tribological Behaviour of Plasma-nitrided AISI 4140 Steel. *International Journal of Surface Engineering and Interdisciplinary Materials Science*, *5*(2), 1–17. doi:10.4018/IJSEIMS.2017070101

Bhuyan, D. (2018). Designing of a Twin Tube Shock Absorber: A Study in Reverse Engineering. In K. Kumar & J. Davim (Eds.), *Design and Optimization of Mechanical Engineering Products* (pp. 83–104). Hershey, PA: IGI Global. doi:10.4018/978-1-5225-3401-3.ch005

Blumberg, G. (2021). Blockchains for Use in Construction and Engineering Projects. In J. Underwood & M. Shelbourn (Eds.), *Handbook of Research on Driving Transformational Change in the Digital Built Environment* (pp. 179–208). IGI Global. https://doi.org/10.4018/978-1-7998-6600-8.ch008

Bolboaca, A. M. (2021). Considerations Regarding the Use of Fuel Cells in Combined Heat and Power for Stationary Applications. In G. Badea, R. Felseghi, & I. Aşchilean (Eds.), *Hydrogen Fuel Cell Technology for Stationary Applications* (pp. 239–275). IGI Global. https://doi.org/10.4018/978-1-7998-4945-2.ch010

Burstein, L. (2021). Simulation Tool for Cable Design. In L. Burstein (Ed.), *Handbook of Research on Advancements in Manufacturing, Materials, and Mechanical Engineering* (pp. 54–74). IGI Global. https://doi.org/10.4018/978-1-7998-4939-1.ch003

Calderon, F. A., Giolo, E. G., Frau, C. D., Rengel, M. G., Rodriguez, H., Tornello, M., ... Gallucci, R. (2018). Seismic Microzonation and Site Effects Detection Through Microtremors Measures: A Review. In N. Ceryan (Ed.), *Handbook of Research on Trends and Digital Advances in Engineering Geology* (pp. 326–349). Hershey, PA: IGI Global. doi:10.4018/978-1-5225-2709-1.ch009

Ceryan, N., & Can, N. K. (2018). Prediction of The Uniaxial Compressive Strength of Rocks Materials. In N. Ceryan (Ed.), *Handbook of Research on Trends and Digital Advances in Engineering Geology* (pp. 31–96). Hershey, PA: IGI Global. doi:10.4018/978-1-5225-2709-1.ch002

Ceryan, S. (2018). Weathering Indices Used in Evaluation of the Weathering State of Rock Material. In N. Ceryan (Ed.), *Handbook of Research on Trends and Digital Advances in Engineering Geology* (pp. 132–186). Hershey, PA: IGI Global. doi:10.4018/978-1-5225-2709-1.ch004

Chen, H., Padilla, R. V., & Besarati, S. (2017). Supercritical Fluids and Their Applications in Power Generation. In L. Chen & Y. Iwamoto (Eds.), *Advanced Applications of Supercritical Fluids in Energy Systems* (pp. 369–402). Hershey, PA: IGI Global. doi:10.4018/978-1-5225-2047-4.ch012

Chen, H., Padilla, R. V., & Besarati, S. (2021). Supercritical Fluids and Their Applications in Power Generation. In L. Chen (Ed.), *Handbook of Research on Advancements in Supercritical Fluids Applications for Sustainable Energy Systems* (pp. 566–599). IGI Global. https://doi.org/10.4018/978-1-7998-5796-9.ch016

Chen, L. (2017). Principles, Experiments, and Numerical Studies of Supercritical Fluid Natural Circulation System. In L. Chen & Y. Iwamoto (Eds.), *Advanced Applications of Supercritical Fluids in Energy Systems* (pp. 136–187). Hershey, PA: IGI Global. doi:10.4018/978-1-5225-2047-4.ch005

Chen, L. (2021). Principles, Experiments, and Numerical Studies of Supercritical Fluid Natural Circulation System. In L. Chen (Ed.), *Handbook of Research on Advancements in Supercritical Fluids Applications for Sustainable Energy Systems* (pp. 219–269). IGI Global. https://doi.org/10.4018/978-1-7998-5796-9.ch007

Chiba, Y., Marif, Y., Henini, N., & Tlemcani, A. (2021). Modeling of Magnetic Refrigeration Device by Using Artificial Neural Networks Approach. *International Journal of Energy Optimization and Engineering, 10*(4), 68–76. https://doi.org/10.4018/IJEOE.2021100105

Clementi, F., Di Sciascio, G., Di Sciascio, S., & Lenci, S. (2017). Influence of the Shear-Bending Interaction on the Global Capacity of Reinforced Concrete Frames: A Brief Overview of the New Perspectives. In V. Plevris, G. Kremmyda, & Y. Fahjan (Eds.), *Performance-Based Seismic Design of Concrete Structures and Infrastructures* (pp. 84–111). Hershey, PA: IGI Global. doi:10.4018/978-1-5225-2089-4.ch004

Codinhoto, R., Fialho, B. C., Pinti, L., & Fabricio, M. M. (2021). BIM and IoT for Facilities Management: Understanding Key Maintenance Issues. In J. Underwood & M. Shelbourn (Eds.), *Handbook of Research on Driving Transformational Change in the Digital Built Environment* (pp. 209–231). IGI Global. doi:10.4018/978-1-7998-6600-8.ch009

Cortés-Polo, D., Calle-Cancho, J., Carmona-Murillo, J., & González-Sánchez, J. (2017). Future Trends in Mobile-Fixed Integration for Next Generation Networks: Classification and Analysis. *International Journal of Vehicular Telematics and Infotainment Systems, 1*(1), 33–53. doi:10.4018/IJVTIS.2017010103

Costa, H. G., Sheremetieff, F. H., & Araújo, E. A. (2022). Influence of Game-Based Methods in Developing Engineering Competences. In A. Alves & N. van Hattum-Janssen (Eds.), *Training Engineering Students for Modern Technological Advancement* (pp. 69–88). IGI Global. https://doi.org/10.4018/978-1-7998-8816-1.ch004

Cui, X., Zeng, S., Li, Z., Zheng, Q., Yu, X., & Han, B. (2018). Advanced Composites for Civil Engineering Infrastructures. In K. Kumar & J. Davim (Eds.), *Composites and Advanced Materials for Industrial Applications* (pp. 212–248). Hershey, PA: IGI Global. doi:10.4018/978-1-5225-5216-1.ch010

Dalgıç, S., & Kuşku, İ. (2018). Geological and Geotechnical Investigations in Tunneling. In N. Ceryan (Ed.), *Handbook of Research on Trends and Digital Advances in Engineering Geology* (pp. 482–529). Hershey, PA: IGI Global. doi:10.4018/978-1-5225-2709-1.ch014

Dang, C., & Hihara, E. (2021). Study on Cooling Heat Transfer of Supercritical Carbon Dioxide Applied to Transcritical Carbon Dioxide Heat Pump. In L. Chen (Ed.), *Handbook of Research on Advancements in Supercritical Fluids Applications for Sustainable Energy Systems* (pp. 451–493). IGI Global. https://doi.org/10.4018/978-1-7998-5796-9.ch013

Daus, Y., Kharchenko, V., & Yudaev, I. (2021). Research of Solar Energy Potential of Photovoltaic Installations on Enclosing Structures of Buildings. *International Journal of Energy Optimization and Engineering, 10*(4), 18–34. https://doi.org/10.4018/IJEOE.2021100102

Daus, Y., Kharchenko, V., & Yudaev, I. (2021). Optimizing Layout of Distributed Generation Sources of Power Supply System of Agricultural Object. *International Journal of Energy Optimization and Engineering, 10*(3), 70–84. https://doi.org/10.4018/IJEOE.2021070104

de la Varga, D., Soto, M., Arias, C. A., van Oirschot, D., Kilian, R., Pascual, A., & Álvarez, J. A. (2017). Constructed Wetlands for Industrial Wastewater Treatment and Removal of Nutrients. In Á. Val del Río, J. Campos Gómez, & A. Mosquera Corral (Eds.), *Technologies for the Treatment and Recovery of Nutrients from Industrial Wastewater* (pp. 202–230). Hershey, PA: IGI Global. doi:10.4018/978-1-5225-1037-6.ch008

Deb, S., Ammar, E. A., AlRajhi, H., Alsaidan, I., & Shariff, S. M. (2022). V2G Pilot Projects: Review and Lessons Learnt. In M. Alam, R. Pillai, & N. Murugesan (Eds.), *Developing Charging Infrastructure and Technologies for Electric Vehicles* (pp. 252–267). IGI Global. https://doi.org/10.4018/978-1-7998-6858-3.ch014

Dekhandji, F. Z., & Rais, M. C. (2021). A Comparative Study of Power Quality Monitoring Using Various Techniques. In A. Recioui & H. Bentarzi (Eds.), *Optimizing and Measuring Smart Grid Operation and Control* (pp. 259–288). IGI Global. https://doi.org/10.4018/978-1-7998-4027-5.ch011

Deperlioglu, O. (2018). Intelligent Techniques Inspired by Nature and Used in Biomedical Engineering. In U. Kose, G. Guraksin, & O. Deperlioglu (Eds.), *Nature-Inspired Intelligent Techniques for Solving Biomedical Engineering Problems* (pp. 51–77). Hershey, PA: IGI Global. doi:10.4018/978-1-5225-4769-3.ch003

Dhurpate, P. R., & Tang, H. (2021). Quantitative Analysis of the Impact of Inter-Line Conveyor Capacity for Throughput of Manufacturing Systems. *International Journal of Manufacturing, Materials, and Mechanical Engineering, 11*(1), 1–17. https://doi.org/10.4018/IJMMME.2021010101

Dinkar, S., & Deep, K. (2021). A Survey of Recent Variants and Applications of Antlion Optimizer. *International Journal of Energy Optimization and Engineering, 10*(2), 48–73. doi:10.4018/IJEOE.2021040103

Dixit, A. (2018). Application of Silica-Gel-Reinforced Aluminium Composite on the Piston of Internal Combustion Engine: Comparative Study of Silica-Gel-Reinforced Aluminium Composite Piston With Aluminium Alloy Piston. In K. Kumar & J. Davim (Eds.), *Composites and Advanced Materials for Industrial Applications* (pp. 63–98). Hershey, PA: IGI Global. doi:10.4018/978-1-5225-5216-1.ch004

Drabecki, M. P., & Kułak, K. B. (2021). Global Pandemics on European Electrical Energy Markets: Lessons Learned From the COVID-19 Outbreak. *International Journal of Energy Optimization and Engineering, 10*(3), 24–46. https://doi.org/10.4018/IJEOE.2021070102

Dutta, M. M. (2021). Nanomaterials for Food and Agriculture. In M. Bhat, I. Wani, & S. Ashraf (Eds.), *Applications of Nanomaterials in Agriculture, Food Science, and Medicine* (pp. 75–97). IGI Global. doi:10.4018/978-1-7998-5563-7.ch004

Dutta, M. M., & Goswami, M. (2021). Coating Materials: Nano-Materials. In S. Roy & G. Bose (Eds.), *Advanced Surface Coating Techniques for Modern Industrial Applications* (pp. 1–30). IGI Global. doi:10.4018/978-1-7998-4870-7.ch001

Elsayed, A. M., Dakkama, H. J., Mahmoud, S., Al-Dadah, R., & Kaialy, W. (2017). Sustainable Cooling Research Using Activated Carbon Adsorbents and Their Environmental Impact. In T. Kobayashi (Ed.), *Applied Environmental Materials Science for Sustainability* (pp. 186–221). Hershey, PA: IGI Global. doi:10.4018/978-1-5225-1971-3.ch009

Ercanoglu, M., & Sonmez, H. (2018). General Trends and New Perspectives on Landslide Mapping and Assessment Methods. In N. Ceryan (Ed.), *Handbook of Research on Trends and Digital Advances in Engineering Geology* (pp. 350–379). Hershey, PA: IGI Global. doi:10.4018/978-1-5225-2709-1.ch010

Faroz, S. A., Pujari, N. N., Rastogi, R., & Ghosh, S. (2017). Risk Analysis of Structural Engineering Systems Using Bayesian Inference. In P. Samui, S. Chakraborty, & D. Kim (Eds.), *Modeling and Simulation Techniques in Structural Engineering* (pp. 390–424). Hershey, PA: IGI Global. doi:10.4018/978-1-5225-0588-4.ch014

Fekik, A., Hamida, M. L., Denoun, H., Azar, A. T., Kamal, N. A., Vaidyanathan, S., Bousbaine, A., & Benamrouche, N. (2022). Multilevel Inverter for Hybrid Fuel Cell/PV Energy Conversion System. In A. Fekik & N. Benamrouche (Eds.), *Modeling and Control of Static Converters for Hybrid Storage Systems* (pp. 233–270). IGI Global. https://doi.org/10.4018/978-1-7998-7447-8.ch009

Fekik, A., Hamida, M. L., Houassine, H., Azar, A. T., Kamal, N. A., Denoun, H., Vaidyanathan, S., & Sambas, A. (2022). Power Quality Improvement for Grid-Connected Photovoltaic Panels Using Direct Power Control. In A. Fekik & N. Benamrouche (Eds.), *Modeling and Control of Static Converters for Hybrid Storage Systems* (pp. 107–142). IGI Global. https://doi.org/10.4018/978-1-7998-7447-8.ch005

Fernando, P. R., Hamigah, T., Disne, S., Wickramasingha, G. G., & Sutharshan, A. (2018). The Evaluation of Engineering Properties of Low Cost Concrete Blocks by Partial Doping of Sand with Sawdust: Low Cost Sawdust Concrete Block. *International Journal of Strategic Engineering*, *1*(2), 26–42. doi:10.4018/IJoSE.2018070103

Ferro, G., Minciardi, R., Parodi, L., & Robba, M. (2022). Optimal Charging Management of Microgrid-Integrated Electric Vehicles. In M. Alam, R. Pillai, & N. Murugesan (Eds.), *Developing Charging Infrastructure and Technologies for Electric Vehicles* (pp. 133–155). IGI Global. https://doi.org/10.4018/978-1-7998-6858-3.ch007

Flumerfelt, S., & Green, C. (2022). Graduate Lean Leadership Education: A Case Study of a Program. In A. Alves & N. van Hattum-Janssen (Eds.), *Training Engineering Students for Modern Technological Advancement* (pp. 202–224). IGI Global. https://doi.org/10.4018/978-1-7998-8816-1.ch010

Galli, B. J. (2021). Implications of Economic Decision Making to the Project Manager. *International Journal of Strategic Engineering*, *4*(1), 19–32. https://doi.org/10.4018/IJoSE.2021010102

Gento, A. M., Pimentel, C., & Pascual, J. A. (2022). Teaching Circular Economy and Lean Management in a Learning Factory. In A. Alves & N. van Hattum-Janssen (Eds.), *Training Engineering Students for Modern Technological Advancement* (pp. 183–201). IGI Global. https://doi.org/10.4018/978-1-7998-8816-1.ch009

Ghosh, S., Mitra, S., Ghosh, S., & Chakraborty, S. (2017). Seismic Reliability Analysis in the Framework of Metamodelling Based Monte Carlo Simulation. In P. Samui, S. Chakraborty, & D. Kim (Eds.), *Modeling and Simulation Techniques in Structural Engineering* (pp. 192–208). Hershey, PA: IGI Global. doi:10.4018/978-1-5225-0588-4.ch006

Gil, M., & Otero, B. (2017). Learning Engineering Skills through Creativity and Collaboration: A Game-Based Proposal. In R. Alexandre Peixoto de Queirós & M. Pinto (Eds.), *Gamification-Based E-Learning Strategies for Computer Programming Education* (pp. 14–29). Hershey, PA: IGI Global. doi:10.4018/978-1-5225-1034-5.ch002

Gill, J., Ayre, M., & Mills, J. (2017). Revisioning the Engineering Profession: How to Make It Happen! In M. Gray & K. Thomas (Eds.), *Strategies for Increasing Diversity in Engineering Majors and Careers* (pp. 156–175). Hershey, PA: IGI Global. doi:10.4018/978-1-5225-2212-6.ch008

Godzhaev, Z., Senkevich, S., Kuzmin, V., & Melikov, I. (2021). Use of the Neural Network Controller of Sprung Mass to Reduce Vibrations From Road Irregularities. In P. Vasant, G. Weber, & W. Punurai (Ed.), *Research Advancements in Smart Technology, Optimization, and Renewable Energy* (pp. 69-87). IGI Global. https://doi.org/10.4018/978-1-7998-3970-5.ch005

Gomes de Gusmão, C. M. (2022). Digital Competencies and Transformation in Higher Education: Upskilling With Extension Actions. In A. Alves & N. van Hattum-Janssen (Eds.), *Training Engineering Students for Modern Technological Advancement* (pp. 313–328). IGI Global. https://doi.org/10.4018/978-1-7998-8816-1.ch015A

Goyal, N., Ram, M., & Kumar, P. (2017). Welding Process under Fault Coverage Approach for Reliability and MTTF. In M. Ram & J. Davim (Eds.), *Mathematical Concepts and Applications in Mechanical Engineering and Mechatronics* (pp. 222–245). Hershey, PA: IGI Global. doi:10.4018/978-1-5225-1639-2.ch011

Gray, M., & Lundy, C. (2017). Engineering Study Abroad: High Impact Strategy for Increasing Access. In M. Gray & K. Thomas (Eds.), *Strategies for Increasing Diversity in Engineering Majors and Careers* (pp. 42–59). Hershey, PA: IGI Global. doi:10.4018/978-1-5225-2212-6.ch003

Güler, O., & Varol, T. (2021). Fabrication of Functionally Graded Metal and Ceramic Powders Synthesized by Electroless Deposition. In S. Roy & G. Bose (Eds.), *Advanced Surface Coating Techniques for Modern Industrial Applications* (pp. 150–187). IGI Global. https://doi.org/10.4018/978-1-7998-4870-7.ch007

Guraksin, G. E. (2018). Internet of Things and Nature-Inspired Intelligent Techniques for the Future of Biomedical Engineering. In U. Kose, G. Guraksin, & O. Deperlioglu (Eds.), *Nature-Inspired Intelligent Techniques for Solving Biomedical Engineering Problems* (pp. 263–282). Hershey, PA: IGI Global. doi:10.4018/978-1-5225-4769-3.ch013

Hamida, M. L., Fekik, A., Denoun, H., Ardjal, A., & Bokhtache, A. A. (2022). Flying Capacitor Inverter Integration in a Renewable Energy System. In A. Fekik & N. Benamrouche (Eds.), *Modeling and Control of Static Converters for Hybrid Storage Systems* (pp. 287–306). IGI Global. https://doi.org/10.4018/978-1-7998-7447-8.ch011

Hasegawa, N., & Takahashi, Y. (2021). Control of Soap Bubble Ejection Robot Using Facial Expressions. *International Journal of Manufacturing, Materials, and Mechanical Engineering, 11*(2), 1–16. https://doi.org/10.4018/IJMMME.2021040101

Hejazi, T., & Akbari, L. (2017). A Multiresponse Optimization Model for Statistical Design of Processes with Discrete Variables. In M. Ram & J. Davim (Eds.), *Mathematical Concepts and Applications in Mechanical Engineering and Mechatronics* (pp. 17–37). Hershey, PA: IGI Global. doi:10.4018/978-1-5225-1639-2.ch002

Hejazi, T., & Hejazi, A. (2017). Monte Carlo Simulation for Reliability-Based Design of Automotive Complex Subsystems. In M. Ram & J. Davim (Eds.), *Mathematical Concepts and Applications in Mechanical Engineering and Mechatronics* (pp. 177–200). Hershey, PA: IGI Global. doi:10.4018/978-1-5225-1639-2.ch009

Hejazi, T., & Poursabbagh, H. (2017). Reliability Analysis of Engineering Systems: An Accelerated Life Testing for Boiler Tubes. In M. Ram & J. Davim (Eds.), *Mathematical Concepts and Applications in Mechanical Engineering and Mechatronics* (pp. 154–176). Hershey, PA: IGI Global. doi:10.4018/978-1-5225-1639-2.ch008

Henao, J., Poblano-Salas, C. A., Vargas, F., Giraldo-Betancur, A. L., Corona-Castuera, J., & Sotelo-Mazón, O. (2021). Principles and Applications of Thermal Spray Coatings. In S. Roy & G. Bose (Eds.), *Advanced Surface Coating Techniques for Modern Industrial Applications* (pp. 31–70). IGI Global. https://doi.org/10.4018/978-1-7998-4870-7.ch002

Henao, J., & Sotelo, O. (2018). Surface Engineering at High Temperature: Thermal Cycling and Corrosion Resistance. In A. Pakseresht (Ed.), *Production, Properties, and Applications of High Temperature Coatings* (pp. 131–159). Hershey, PA: IGI Global. doi:10.4018/978-1-5225-4194-3.ch006

Hrnčič, M. K., Cör, D., & Knez, Ž. (2021). Supercritical Fluids as a Tool for Green Energy and Chemicals. In L. Chen (Ed.), *Handbook of Research on Advancements in Supercritical Fluids Applications for Sustainable Energy Systems* (pp. 761–791). IGI Global. doi:10.4018/978-1-7998-5796-9.ch021

Ibrahim, O., Erdem, S., & Gurbuz, E. (2021). Studying Physical and Chemical Properties of Graphene Oxide and Reduced Graphene Oxide and Their Applications in Sustainable Building Materials. In R. González-Lezcano (Ed.), *Advancements in Sustainable Architecture and Energy Efficiency* (pp. 221–238). IGI Global. https://doi.org/10.4018/978-1-7998-7023-4.ch010

Ihianle, I. K., Islam, S., Naeem, U., & Ebenuwa, S. H. (2021). Exploiting Patterns of Object Use for Human Activity Recognition. In A. Nwajana & I. Ihianle (Eds.), *Handbook of Research on 5G Networks and Advancements in Computing, Electronics, and Electrical Engineering* (pp. 382–401). IGI Global. https://doi.org/10.4018/978-1-7998-6992-4.ch015

Ijemaru, G. K., Ngharamike, E. T., Oleka, E. U., & Nwajana, A. O. (2021). An Energy-Efficient Model for Opportunistic Data Collection in IoV-Enabled SC Waste Management. In A. Nwajana & I. Ihianle (Eds.), *Handbook of Research on 5G Networks and Advancements in Computing, Electronics, and Electrical Engineering* (pp. 1–19). IGI Global. https://doi.org/10.4018/978-1-7998-6992-4.ch001

Ilori, O. O., Adetan, D. A., & Umoru, L. E. (2017). Effect of Cutting Parameters on the Surface Residual Stress of Face-Milled Pearlitic Ductile Iron. *International Journal of Materials Forming and Machining Processes*, *4*(1), 38–52. doi:10.4018/IJMFMP.2017010103

Imam, M. H., Tasadduq, I. A., Ahmad, A., Aldosari, F., & Khan, H. (2017). Automated Generation of Course Improvement Plans Using Expert System. *International Journal of Quality Assurance in Engineering and Technology Education*, *6*(1), 1–12. doi:10.4018/IJQAETE.2017010101

Injeti, S. K., & Kumar, T. V. (2018). A WDO Framework for Optimal Deployment of DGs and DSCs in a Radial Distribution System Under Daily Load Pattern to Improve Techno-Economic Benefits. *International Journal of Energy Optimization and Engineering*, *7*(2), 1–38. doi:10.4018/IJEOE.2018040101

Ishii, N., Anami, K., & Knisely, C. W. (2018). *Dynamic Stability of Hydraulic Gates and Engineering for Flood Prevention*. Hershey, PA: IGI Global. doi:10.4018/978-1-5225-3079-4

Iwamoto, Y., & Yamaguchi, H. (2021). Application of Supercritical Carbon Dioxide for Solar Water Heater. In L. Chen (Ed.), *Handbook of Research on Advancements in Supercritical Fluids Applications for Sustainable Energy Systems* (pp. 370–387). IGI Global. https://doi.org/10.4018/978-1-7998-5796-9.ch010

Jayapalan, S. (2018). A Review of Chemical Treatments on Natural Fibers-Based Hybrid Composites for Engineering Applications. In K. Kumar & J. Davim (Eds.), *Composites and Advanced Materials for Industrial Applications* (pp. 16–37). Hershey, PA: IGI Global. doi:10.4018/978-1-5225-5216-1.ch002

Kapetanakis, T. N., Vardiambasis, I. O., Ioannidou, M. P., & Konstantaras, A. I. (2021). Modeling Antenna Radiation Using Artificial Intelligence Techniques: The Case of a Circular Loop Antenna. In C. Nikolopoulos (Ed.), *Recent Trends on Electromagnetic Environmental Effects for Aeronautics and Space Applications* (pp. 186–225). IGI Global. https://doi.org/10.4018/978-1-7998-4879-0.ch007

Karkalos, N. E., Markopoulos, A. P., & Dossis, M. F. (2017). Optimal Model Parameters of Inverse Kinematics Solution of a 3R Robotic Manipulator Using ANN Models. *International Journal of Manufacturing, Materials, and Mechanical Engineering*, *7*(3), 20–40. doi:10.4018/IJMMME.2017070102

Kelly, M., Costello, M., Nicholson, G., & O'Connor, J. (2021). The Evolving Integration of BIM Into Built Environment Programmes in a Higher Education Institute. In J. Underwood & M. Shelbourn (Eds.), *Handbook of Research on Driving Transformational Change in the Digital Built Environment* (pp. 294–326). IGI Global. https://doi.org/10.4018/978-1-7998-6600-8.ch012

Kesimal, A., Karaman, K., Cihangir, F., & Ercikdi, B. (2018). Excavatability Assessment of Rock Masses for Geotechnical Studies. In N. Ceryan (Ed.), *Handbook of Research on Trends and Digital Advances in Engineering Geology* (pp. 231–256). Hershey, PA: IGI Global. doi:10.4018/978-1-5225-2709-1.ch006

Knoflacher, H. (2017). The Role of Engineers and Their Tools in the Transport Sector after Paradigm Change: From Assumptions and Extrapolations to Science. In H. Knoflacher & E. Ocalir-Akunal (Eds.), *Engineering Tools and Solutions for Sustainable Transportation Planning* (pp. 1–29). Hershey, PA: IGI Global. doi:10.4018/978-1-5225-2116-7.ch001

Kose, U. (2018). Towards an Intelligent Biomedical Engineering With Nature-Inspired Artificial Intelligence Techniques. In U. Kose, G. Guraksin, & O. Deperlioglu (Eds.), *Nature-Inspired Intelligent Techniques for Solving Biomedical Engineering Problems* (pp. 1–26). Hershey, PA: IGI Global. doi:10.4018/978-1-5225-4769-3.ch001

Kostić, S. (2018). A Review on Enhanced Stability Analyses of Soil Slopes Using Statistical Design. In N. Ceryan (Ed.), *Handbook of Research on Trends and Digital Advances in Engineering Geology* (pp. 446–481). Hershey, PA: IGI Global. doi:10.4018/978-1-5225-2709-1.ch013

Kumar, A., Patil, P. P., & Prajapati, Y. K. (2018). *Advanced Numerical Simulations in Mechanical Engineering*. Hershey, PA: IGI Global. doi:10.4018/978-1-5225-3722-9

Kumar, G. R., Rajyalakshmi, G., & Manupati, V. K. (2017). Surface Micro Patterning of Aluminium Reinforced Composite through Laser Peening. *International Journal of Manufacturing, Materials, and Mechanical Engineering*, *7*(4), 15–27. doi:10.4018/IJMMME.2017100102

Kumar, N., Basu, D. N., & Chen, L. (2021). Effect of Flow Acceleration and Buoyancy on Thermalhydraulics of sCO2 in Mini/Micro-Channel. In L. Chen (Ed.), *Handbook of Research on Advancements in Supercritical Fluids Applications for Sustainable Energy Systems* (pp. 161–182). IGI Global. doi:10.4018/978-1-7998-5796-9.ch005

Kumari, N., & Kumar, K. (2018). Fabrication of Orthotic Calipers With Epoxy-Based Green Composite. In K. Kumar & J. Davim (Eds.), *Composites and Advanced Materials for Industrial Applications* (pp. 157–176). Hershey, PA: IGI Global. doi:10.4018/978-1-5225-5216-1.ch008

Kuppusamy, R. R. (2018). Development of Aerospace Composite Structures Through Vacuum-Enhanced Resin Transfer Moulding Technology (VERTMTy): Vacuum-Enhanced Resin Transfer Moulding. In K. Kumar & J. Davim (Eds.), *Composites and Advanced Materials for Industrial Applications* (pp. 99–111). Hershey, PA: IGI Global. doi:10.4018/978-1-5225-5216-1.ch005

Kurganov, V. A., Zeigarnik, Y. A., & Maslakova, I. V. (2021). Normal and Deteriorated Heat Transfer Under Heating Turbulent Supercritical Pressure Coolants Flows in Round Tubes. In L. Chen (Ed.), *Handbook of Research on Advancements in Supercritical Fluids Applications for Sustainable Energy Systems* (pp. 494–532). IGI Global. https://doi.org/10.4018/978-1-7998-5796-9.ch014

Li, H., & Zhang, Y. (2021). Heat Transfer and Fluid Flow Modeling for Supercritical Fluids in Advanced Energy Systems. In L. Chen (Ed.), *Handbook of Research on Advancements in Supercritical Fluids Applications for Sustainable Energy Systems* (pp. 388–422). IGI Global. https://doi.org/10.4018/978-1-7998-5796-9.ch011

Loy, J., Howell, S., & Cooper, R. (2017). Engineering Teams: Supporting Diversity in Engineering Education. In M. Gray & K. Thomas (Eds.), *Strategies for Increasing Diversity in Engineering Majors and Careers* (pp. 106–129). Hershey, PA: IGI Global. doi:10.4018/978-1-5225-2212-6.ch006

Macher, G., Armengaud, E., Kreiner, C., Brenner, E., Schmittner, C., Ma, Z., ... Krammer, M. (2018). Integration of Security in the Development Lifecycle of Dependable Automotive CPS. In N. Druml, A. Genser, A. Krieg, M. Menghin, & A. Hoeller (Eds.), *Solutions for Cyber-Physical Systems Ubiquity* (pp. 383–423). Hershey, PA: IGI Global. doi:10.4018/978-1-5225-2845-6.ch015

Madhu, M. N., Singh, J. G., Mohan, V., & Ongsakul, W. (2021). Transmission Risk Optimization in Interconnected Systems: Risk-Adjusted Available Transfer Capability. In P. Vasant, G. Weber, & W. Punurai (Ed.), *Research Advancements in Smart Technology, Optimization, and Renewable Energy* (pp. 183-199). IGI Global. https://doi.org/10.4018/978-1-7998-3970-5.ch010

Mahendramani, G., & Lakshmana Swamy, N. (2018). Effect of Weld Groove Area on Distortion of Butt Welded Joints in Submerged Arc Welding. *International Journal of Manufacturing, Materials, and Mechanical Engineering*, *8*(2), 33–44. doi:10.4018/IJMMME.2018040103

Makropoulos, G., Koumaras, H., Setaki, F., Filis, K., Lutz, T., Montowtt, P., Tomaszewski, L., Dybiec, P., & Järvet, T. (2021). 5G and Unmanned Aerial Vehicles (UAVs) Use Cases: Analysis of the Ecosystem, Architecture, and Applications. In A. Nwajana & I. Ihianle (Eds.), *Handbook of Research on 5G Networks and Advancements in Computing, Electronics, and Electrical Engineering* (pp. 36–69). IGI Global. https://doi.org/10.4018/978-1-7998-6992-4.ch003

Meric, E. M., Erdem, S., & Gurbuz, E. (2021). Application of Phase Change Materials in Construction Materials for Thermal Energy Storage Systems in Buildings. In R. González-Lezcano (Ed.), *Advancements in Sustainable Architecture and Energy Efficiency* (pp. 1–20). IGI Global. https://doi.org/10.4018/978-1-7998-7023-4.ch001

Mihret, E. T., & Yitayih, K. A. (2021). Operation of VANET Communications: The Convergence of UAV System With LTE/4G and WAVE Technologies. *International Journal of Smart Vehicles and Smart Transportation*, *4*(1), 29–51. https://doi.org/10.4018/IJSVST.2021010103

Mir, M. A., Bhat, B. A., Sheikh, B. A., Rather, G. A., Mehraj, S., & Mir, W. R. (2021). Nanomedicine in Human Health Therapeutics and Drug Delivery: Nanobiotechnology and Nanobiomedicine. In M. Bhat, I. Wani, & S. Ashraf (Eds.), *Applications of Nanomaterials in Agriculture, Food Science, and Medicine* (pp. 229–251). IGI Global. doi:10.4018/978-1-7998-5563-7.ch013

Mohammadzadeh, S., & Kim, Y. (2017). Nonlinear System Identification of Smart Buildings. In P. Samui, S. Chakraborty, & D. Kim (Eds.), *Modeling and Simulation Techniques in Structural Engineering* (pp. 328–347). Hershey, PA: IGI Global. doi:10.4018/978-1-5225-0588-4.ch011

Molina, G. J., Aktaruzzaman, F., Soloiu, V., & Rahman, M. (2017). Design and Testing of a Jet-Impingement Instrument to Study Surface-Modification Effects by Nanofluids. *International Journal of Surface Engineering and Interdisciplinary Materials Science*, *5*(2), 43–61. doi:10.4018/IJSEIMS.2017070104

Moreno-Rangel, A., & Carrillo, G. (2021). Energy-Efficient Homes: A Heaven for Respiratory Illnesses. In R. González-Lezcano (Ed.), *Advancements in Sustainable Architecture and Energy Efficiency* (pp. 49–71). IGI Global. https://doi.org/10.4018/978-1-7998-7023-4.ch003

Msomi, V., & Jantjies, B. T. (2021). Correlative Analysis Between Tensile Properties and Tool Rotational Speeds of Friction Stir Welded Similar Aluminium Alloy Joints. *International Journal of Surface Engineering and Interdisciplinary Materials Science*, *9*(2), 58–78. https://doi.org/10.4018/IJSEIMS.2021070104

Muigai, M. N., Mwema, F. M., Akinlabi, E. T., & Obiko, J. O. (2021). Surface Engineering of Materials Through Weld-Based Technologies: An Overview. In S. Roy & G. Bose (Eds.), *Advanced Surface Coating Techniques for Modern Industrial Applications* (pp. 247–260). IGI Global. doi:10.4018/978-1-7998-4870-7.ch011

Mukherjee, A., Saeed, R. A., Dutta, S., & Naskar, M. K. (2017). Fault Tracking Framework for Software-Defined Networking (SDN). In C. Singhal & S. De (Eds.), *Resource Allocation in Next-Generation Broadband Wireless Access Networks* (pp. 247–272). Hershey, PA: IGI Global. doi:10.4018/978-1-5225-2023-8.ch011

Mukhopadhyay, A., Barman, T. K., & Sahoo, P. (2018). Electroless Nickel Coatings for High Temperature Applications. In K. Kumar & J. Davim (Eds.), *Composites and Advanced Materials for Industrial Applications* (pp. 297–331). Hershey, PA: IGI Global. doi:10.4018/978-1-5225-5216-1.ch013

Mwema, F. M., & Wambua, J. M. (2022). Machining of Poly Methyl Methacrylate (PMMA) and Other Olymeric Materials: A Review. In K. Kumar, B. Babu, & J. Davim (Eds.), *Handbook of Research on Advancements in the Processing, Characterization, and Application of Lightweight Materials* (pp. 363–379). IGI Global. https://doi.org/10.4018/978-1-7998-7864-3.ch016

Mykhailyshyn, R., Savkiv, V., Boyko, I., Prada, E., & Virgala, I. (2021). Substantiation of Parameters of Friction Elements of Bernoulli Grippers With a Cylindrical Nozzle. *International Journal of Manufacturing, Materials, and Mechanical Engineering, 11*(2), 17–39. https://doi.org/10.4018/IJMMME.2021040102

Náprstek, J., & Fischer, C. (2017). Dynamic Stability and Post-Critical Processes of Slender Auto-Parametric Systems. In V. Plevris, G. Kremmyda, & Y. Fahjan (Eds.), *Performance-Based Seismic Design of Concrete Structures and Infrastructures* (pp. 128–171). Hershey, PA: IGI Global. doi:10.4018/978-1-5225-2089-4.ch006

Nautiyal, L., Shivach, P., & Ram, M. (2018). Optimal Designs by Means of Genetic Algorithms. In M. Ram & J. Davim (Eds.), *Soft Computing Techniques and Applications in Mechanical Engineering* (pp. 151–161). Hershey, PA: IGI Global. doi:10.4018/978-1-5225-3035-0.ch007

Nazir, R. (2017). Advanced Nanomaterials for Water Engineering and Treatment: Nano-Metal Oxides and Their Nanocomposites. In T. Saleh (Ed.), *Advanced Nanomaterials for Water Engineering, Treatment, and Hydraulics* (pp. 84–126). Hershey, PA: IGI Global. doi:10.4018/978-1-5225-2136-5.ch005

Nikolopoulos, C. D. (2021). Recent Advances on Measuring and Modeling ELF-Radiated Emissions for Space Applications. In C. Nikolopoulos (Ed.), *Recent Trends on Electromagnetic Environmental Effects for Aeronautics and Space Applications* (pp. 1–38). IGI Global. https://doi.org/10.4018/978-1-7998-4879-0.ch001

Nogueira, A. F., Ribeiro, J. C., Fernández de Vega, F., & Zenha-Rela, M. A. (2018). Evolutionary Approaches to Test Data Generation for Object-Oriented Software: Overview of Techniques and Tools. In M. Khosrow-Pour, D.B.A. (Ed.), Incorporating Nature-Inspired Paradigms in Computational Applications (pp. 162-194). Hershey, PA: IGI Global. https://doi.org/ doi:10.4018/978-1-5225-5020-4.ch006

Nwajana, A. O., Obi, E. R., Ijemaru, G. K., Oleka, E. U., & Anthony, D. C. (2021). Fundamentals of RF/Microwave Bandpass Filter Design. In A. Nwajana & I. Ihianle (Eds.), *Handbook of Research on 5G Networks and Advancements in Computing, Electronics, and Electrical Engineering* (pp. 149–164). IGI Global. https://doi.org/10.4018/978-1-7998-6992-4.ch005

Ogbodo, E. A. (2021). Comparative Study of Transmission Line Junction vs. Asynchronously Coupled Junction Diplexers. In A. Nwajana & I. Ihianle (Eds.), *Handbook of Research on 5G Networks and Advancements in Computing, Electronics, and Electrical Engineering* (pp. 326–336). IGI Global. https://doi.org/10.4018/978-1-7998-6992-4.ch013

Orosa, J. A., Vergara, D., Fraguela, F., & Masdías-Bonome, A. (2021). Statistical Understanding and Optimization of Building Energy Consumption and Climate Change Consequences. In R. González-Lezcano (Ed.), *Advancements in Sustainable Architecture and Energy Efficiency* (pp. 195–220). IGI Global. https://doi.org/10.4018/978-1-7998-7023-4.ch009

Osho, M. B. (2018). Industrial Enzyme Technology: Potential Applications. In S. Bharati & P. Chaurasia (Eds.), *Research Advancements in Pharmaceutical, Nutritional, and Industrial Enzymology* (pp. 375–394). Hershey, PA: IGI Global. doi:10.4018/978-1-5225-5237-6.ch017

Ouadi, A., & Zitouni, A. (2021). Phasor Measurement Improvement Using Digital Filter in a Smart Grid. In A. Recioui & H. Bentarzi (Eds.), *Optimizing and Measuring Smart Grid Operation and Control* (pp. 100–117). IGI Global. https://doi.org/10.4018/978-1-7998-4027-5.ch005

Padmaja, P., & Marutheswar, G. (2017). Certain Investigation on Secured Data Transmission in Wireless Sensor Networks. *International Journal of Mobile Computing and Multimedia Communications, 8*(1), 48–61. doi:10.4018/IJMCMC.2017010104

Palmer, S., & Hall, W. (2017). An Evaluation of Group Work in First-Year Engineering Design Education. In R. Tucker (Ed.), *Collaboration and Student Engagement in Design Education* (pp. 145–168). Hershey, PA: IGI Global. doi:10.4018/978-1-5225-0726-0.ch007

Panchenko, V. (2021). Prospects for Energy Supply of the Arctic Zone Objects of Russia Using Frost-Resistant Solar Modules. In P. Vasant, G. Weber, & W. Punurai (Eds.), *Research Advancements in Smart Technology, Optimization, and Renewable Energy* (pp. 149-169). IGI Global. https://doi.org/10.4018/978-1-7998-3970-5.ch008

Panchenko, V. (2021). Photovoltaic Thermal Module With Paraboloid Type Solar Concentrators. *International Journal of Energy Optimization and Engineering, 10*(2), 1–23. https://doi.org/10.4018/IJEOE.2021040101

Pandey, K., & Datta, S. (2021). Dry Machining of Inconel 825 Superalloys: Performance of Tool Inserts (Carbide, Cermet, and SiAlON). *International Journal of Manufacturing, Materials, and Mechanical Engineering, 11*(4), 26–39. doi:10.4018/IJMMME.2021100102

Panneer, R. (2017). Effect of Composition of Fibers on Properties of Hybrid Composites. *International Journal of Manufacturing, Materials, and Mechanical Engineering, 7*(4), 28–43. doi:10.4018/IJMMME.2017100103

Pany, C. (2021). Estimation of Correct Long-Seam Mismatch Using FEA to Compare the Measured Strain in a Non-Destructive Testing of a Pressurant Tank: A Reverse Problem. *International Journal of Smart Vehicles and Smart Transportation*, *4*(1), 16–28. doi:10.4018/IJSVST.2021010102

Paul, S., & Roy, P. (2018). Optimal Design of Power System Stabilizer Using a Novel Evolutionary Algorithm. *International Journal of Energy Optimization and Engineering*, *7*(3), 24–46. doi:10.4018/IJEOE.2018070102

Paul, S., & Roy, P. K. (2021). Oppositional Differential Search Algorithm for the Optimal Tuning of Both Single Input and Dual Input Power System Stabilizer. In P. Vasant, G. Weber, & W. Punurai (Eds.), *Research Advancements in Smart Technology, Optimization, and Renewable Energy* (pp. 256-282). IGI Global. https://doi.org/10.4018/978-1-7998-3970-5.ch013

Pavaloiu, A. (2018). Artificial Intelligence Ethics in Biomedical-Engineering-Oriented Problems. In U. Kose, G. Guraksin, & O. Deperlioglu (Eds.), *Nature-Inspired Intelligent Techniques for Solving Biomedical Engineering Problems* (pp. 219–231). Hershey, PA: IGI Global. doi:10.4018/978-1-5225-4769-3.ch010

Pioro, I., Mahdi, M., & Popov, R. (2017). Application of Supercritical Pressures in Power Engineering. In L. Chen & Y. Iwamoto (Eds.), *Advanced Applications of Supercritical Fluids in Energy Systems* (pp. 404–457). Hershey, PA: IGI Global. doi:10.4018/978-1-5225-2047-4.ch013

Plaksina, T., & Gildin, E. (2017). Rigorous Integrated Evolutionary Workflow for Optimal Exploitation of Unconventional Gas Assets. *International Journal of Energy Optimization and Engineering*, *6*(1), 101–122. doi:10.4018/IJEOE.2017010106

Popat, J., Kakadiya, H., Tak, L., Singh, N. K., Majeed, M. A., & Mahajan, V. (2021). Reliability of Smart Grid Including Cyber Impact: A Case Study. In R. Singh, A. Singh, A. Dwivedi, & P. Nagabhushan (Eds.), *Computational Methodologies for Electrical and Electronics Engineers* (pp. 163–174). IGI Global. https://doi.org/10.4018/978-1-7998-3327-7.ch013

Quiza, R., La Fé-Perdomo, I., Rivas, M., & Ramtahalsing, V. (2021). Triple Bottom Line-Focused Optimization of Oblique Turning Processes Based on Hybrid Modeling: A Study Case on AISI 1045 Steel Turning. In L. Burstein (Ed.), *Handbook of Research on Advancements in Manufacturing, Materials, and Mechanical Engineering* (pp. 215–241). IGI Global. https://doi.org/10.4018/978-1-7998-4939-1.ch010

Rahmani, M. K. (2022). Blockchain Technology: Principles and Algorithms. In S. Khan, M. Syed, R. Hammad, & A. Bushager (Eds.), *Blockchain Technology and Computational Excellence for Society 5.0* (pp. 16–27). IGI Global. https://doi.org/10.4018/978-1-7998-8382-1.ch002

Ramdani, N., & Azibi, M. (2018). Polymer Composite Materials for Microelectronics Packaging Applications: Composites for Microelectronics Packaging. In K. Kumar & J. Davim (Eds.), *Composites and Advanced Materials for Industrial Applications* (pp. 177–211). Hershey, PA: IGI Global. doi:10.4018/978-1-5225-5216-1.ch009

Ramesh, M., Garg, R., & Subrahmanyam, G. V. (2017). Investigation of Influence of Quenching and Annealing on the Plane Fracture Toughness and Brittle to Ductile Transition Temperature of the Zinc Coated Structural Steel Materials. *International Journal of Surface Engineering and Interdisciplinary Materials Science*, *5*(2), 33–42. doi:10.4018/IJSEIMS.2017070103

Robinson, J., & Beneroso, D. (2022). Project-Based Learning in Chemical Engineering: Curriculum and Assessment, Culture and Learning Spaces. In A. Alves & N. van Hattum-Janssen (Eds.), *Training Engineering Students for Modern Technological Advancement* (pp. 1–19). IGI Global. https://doi.org/10.4018/978-1-7998-8816-1.ch001

Rondon, B. (2021). Experimental Characterization of Admittance Meter With Crude Oil Emulsions. *International Journal of Electronics, Communications, and Measurement Engineering*, *10*(2), 51–59. https://doi.org/10.4018/IJECME.2021070104

Rudolf, S., Biryuk, V. V., & Volov, V. (2018). Vortex Effect, Vortex Power: Technology of Vortex Power Engineering. In V. Kharchenko & P. Vasant (Eds.), *Handbook of Research on Renewable Energy and Electric Resources for Sustainable Rural Development* (pp. 500–533). Hershey, PA: IGI Global. doi:10.4018/978-1-5225-3867-7.ch021

Sah, A., Bhadula, S. J., Dumka, A., & Rawat, S. (2018). A Software Engineering Perspective for Development of Enterprise Applications. In A. Elçi (Ed.), *Handbook of Research on Contemporary Perspectives on Web-Based Systems* (pp. 1–23). Hershey, PA: IGI Global. doi:10.4018/978-1-5225-5384-7.ch001

Sahli, Y., Zitouni, B., & Hocine, B. M. (2021). Three-Dimensional Numerical Study of Overheating of Two Intermediate Temperature P-AS-SOFC Geometrical Configurations. In G. Badea, R. Felseghi, & I. Aşchilean (Eds.), *Hydrogen Fuel Cell Technology for Stationary Applications* (pp. 186–222). IGI Global. https://doi.org/10.4018/978-1-7998-4945-2.ch008

Sahoo, P., & Roy, S. (2017). Tribological Behavior of Electroless Ni-P, Ni-P-W and Ni-P-Cu Coatings: A Comparison. *International Journal of Surface Engineering and Interdisciplinary Materials Science*, *5*(1), 1–15. doi:10.4018/IJSEIMS.2017010101

Sahoo, S. (2018). Laminated Composite Hypar Shells as Roofing Units: Static and Dynamic Behavior. In K. Kumar & J. Davim (Eds.), *Composites and Advanced Materials for Industrial Applications* (pp. 249–269). Hershey, PA: IGI Global. doi:10.4018/978-1-5225-5216-1.ch011

Sahu, H., & Hungyo, M. (2018). Introduction to SDN and NFV. In A. Dumka (Ed.), *Innovations in Software-Defined Networking and Network Functions Virtualization* (pp. 1–25). Hershey, PA: IGI Global. doi:10.4018/978-1-5225-3640-6.ch001

Salem, A. M., & Shmelova, T. (2018). Intelligent Expert Decision Support Systems: Methodologies, Applications, and Challenges. In T. Shmelova, Y. Sikirda, N. Rizun, A. Salem, & Y. Kovalyov (Eds.), *Socio-Technical Decision Support in Air Navigation Systems: Emerging Research and Opportunities* (pp. 215–242). Hershey, PA: IGI Global. doi:10.4018/978-1-5225-3108-1.ch007

Samal, M. (2017). FE Analysis and Experimental Investigation of Cracked and Un-Cracked Thin-Walled Tubular Components to Evaluate Mechanical and Fracture Properties. In P. Samui, S. Chakraborty, & D. Kim (Eds.), *Modeling and Simulation Techniques in Structural Engineering* (pp. 266–293). Hershey, PA: IGI Global. doi:10.4018/978-1-5225-0588-4.ch009

Samal, M., & Balakrishnan, K. (2017). Experiments on a Ring Tension Setup and FE Analysis to Evaluate Transverse Mechanical Properties of Tubular Components. In P. Samui, S. Chakraborty, & D. Kim (Eds.), *Modeling and Simulation Techniques in Structural Engineering* (pp. 91–115). Hershey, PA: IGI Global. doi:10.4018/978-1-5225-0588-4.ch004

Samarasinghe, D. A., & Wood, E. (2021). Innovative Digital Technologies. In J. Underwood & M. Shelbourn (Eds.), *Handbook of Research on Driving Transformational Change in the Digital Built Environment* (pp. 142–163). IGI Global. https://doi.org/10.4018/978-1-7998-6600-8.ch006

Sawant, S. (2018). Deep Learning and Biomedical Engineering. In U. Kose, G. Guraksin, & O. Deperlioglu (Eds.), *Nature-Inspired Intelligent Techniques for Solving Biomedical Engineering Problems* (pp. 283–296). Hershey, PA: IGI Global. doi:10.4018/978-1-5225-4769-3.ch014

Schulenberg, T. (2021). Energy Conversion Using the Supercritical Steam Cycle. In L. Chen (Ed.), *Handbook of Research on Advancements in Supercritical Fluids Applications for Sustainable Energy Systems* (pp. 659–681). IGI Global. doi:10.4018/978-1-7998-5796-9.ch018

Sezgin, H., & Berkalp, O. B. (2018). Textile-Reinforced Composites for the Automotive Industry. In K. Kumar & J. Davim (Eds.), *Composites and Advanced Materials for Industrial Applications* (pp. 129–156). Hershey, PA: IGI Global. doi:10.4018/978-1-5225-5216-1.ch007

Shaaban, A. A., & Shehata, O. M. (2021). Combining Response Surface Method and Metaheuristic Algorithms for Optimizing SPIF Process. *International Journal of Manufacturing, Materials, and Mechanical Engineering, 11*(4), 1–25. https://doi.org/10.4018/IJMMME.2021100101

Shafaati Shemami, M., & Sefid, M. (2022). Implementation and Demonstration of Electric Vehicle-to-Home (V2H) Application: A Case Study. In M. Alam, R. Pillai, & N. Murugesan (Eds.), *Developing Charging Infrastructure and Technologies for Electric Vehicles* (pp. 268–293). IGI Global. https://doi.org/10.4018/978-1-7998-6858-3.ch015

Shah, M. Z., Gazder, U., Bhatti, M. S., & Hussain, M. (2018). Comparative Performance Evaluation of Effects of Modifier in Asphaltic Concrete Mix. *International Journal of Strategic Engineering, 1*(2), 13–25. doi:10.4018/IJoSE.2018070102

Sharma, N., & Kumar, K. (2018). Fabrication of Porous NiTi Alloy Using Organic Binders. In K. Kumar & J. Davim (Eds.), *Composites and Advanced Materials for Industrial Applications* (pp. 38–62). Hershey, PA: IGI Global. doi:10.4018/978-1-5225-5216-1.ch003

Shivach, P., Nautiyal, L., & Ram, M. (2018). Applying Multi-Objective Optimization Algorithms to Mechanical Engineering. In M. Ram & J. Davim (Eds.), *Soft Computing Techniques and Applications in Mechanical Engineering* (pp. 287–301). Hershey, PA: IGI Global. doi:10.4018/978-1-5225-3035-0.ch014

Shmelova, T. (2018). Stochastic Methods for Estimation and Problem Solving in Engineering: Stochastic Methods of Decision Making in Aviation. In S. Kadry (Ed.), *Stochastic Methods for Estimation and Problem Solving in Engineering* (pp. 139–160). Hershey, PA: IGI Global. doi:10.4018/978-1-5225-5045-7.ch006

Siero González, L. R., & Romo Vázquez, A. (2017). Didactic Sequences Teaching Mathematics for Engineers With Focus on Differential Equations. In M. Ramírez-Montoya (Ed.), *Handbook of Research on Driving STEM Learning With Educational Technologies* (pp. 129–151). Hershey, PA: IGI Global. doi:10.4018/978-1-5225-2026-9.ch007

Sim, M. S., You, K. Y., Esa, F., & Chan, Y. L. (2021). Nanostructured Electromagnetic Metamaterials for Sensing Applications. In M. Bhat, I. Wani, & S. Ashraf (Eds.), *Applications of Nanomaterials in Agriculture, Food Science, and Medicine* (pp. 141–164). IGI Global. https://doi.org/10.4018/978-1-7998-5563-7.ch009

Singh, R., & Dutta, S. (2018). Visible Light Active Nanocomposites for Photocatalytic Applications. In K. Kumar & J. Davim (Eds.), *Composites and Advanced Materials for Industrial Applications* (pp. 270–296). Hershey, PA: IGI Global. doi:10.4018/978-1-5225-5216-1.ch012

Skripov, P. V., Yampol'skiy, A. D., & Rutin, S. B. (2021). High-Power Heat Transfer in Supercritical Fluids: Microscale Times and Sizes. In L. Chen (Ed.), *Handbook of Research on Advancements in Supercritical Fluids Applications for Sustainable Energy Systems* (pp. 424–450). IGI Global. https://doi.org/10.4018/978-1-7998-5796-9.ch012

Sözbilir, H., Özkaymak, Ç., Uzel, B., & Sümer, Ö. (2018). Criteria for Surface Rupture Microzonation of Active Faults for Earthquake Hazards in Urban Areas. In N. Ceryan (Ed.), *Handbook of Research on Trends and Digital Advances in Engineering Geology* (pp. 187–230). Hershey, PA: IGI Global. doi:10.4018/978-1-5225-2709-1.ch005

Stanciu, I. (2018). Stochastic Methods in Microsystems Engineering. In S. Kadry (Ed.), *Stochastic Methods for Estimation and Problem Solving in Engineering* (pp. 161–176). Hershey, PA: IGI Global. doi:10.4018/978-1-5225-5045-7.ch007

Strebkov, D., Nekrasov, A., Trubnikov, V., & Nekrasov, A. (2018). Single-Wire Resonant Electric Power Systems for Renewable-Based Electric Grid. In V. Kharchenko & P. Vasant (Eds.), *Handbook of Research on Renewable Energy and Electric Resources for Sustainable Rural Development* (pp. 449–474). Hershey, PA: IGI Global. doi:10.4018/978-1-5225-3867-7.ch019

Sukhyy, K., Belyanovskaya, E., & Sukhyy, M. (2021). *Basic Principles for Substantiation of Working Pair Choice*. IGI Global. doi:10.4018/978-1-7998-4432-7.ch002

Suri, M. S., & Kaliyaperumal, D. (2022). Extension of Aspiration Level Model for Optimal Planning of Fast Charging Stations. In A. Fekik & N. Benamrouche (Eds.), *Modeling and Control of Static Converters for Hybrid Storage Systems* (pp. 91–106). IGI Global. https://doi.org/10.4018/978-1-7998-7447-8.ch004

Tallet, E., Gledson, B., Rogage, K., Thompson, A., & Wiggett, D. (2021). Digitally-Enabled Design Management. In J. Underwood & M. Shelbourn (Eds.), *Handbook of Research on Driving Transformational Change in the Digital Built Environment* (pp. 63–89). IGI Global. https://doi.org/10.4018/978-1-7998-6600-8.ch003

Terki, A., & Boubertakh, H. (2021). A New Hybrid Binary-Real Coded Cuckoo Search and Tabu Search Algorithm for Solving the Unit-Commitment Problem. *International Journal of Energy Optimization and Engineering, 10*(2), 104–119. https://doi.org/10.4018/IJEOE.2021040105

Tüdeş, Ş., Kumlu, K. B., & Ceryan, S. (2018). Integration Between Urban Planning and Natural Hazards For Resilient City. In N. Ceryan (Ed.), *Handbook of Research on Trends and Digital Advances in Engineering Geology* (pp. 591–630). Hershey, PA: IGI Global. doi:10.4018/978-1-5225-2709-1.ch017

Ulamis, K. (2018). Soil Liquefaction Assessment by Anisotropic Cyclic Triaxial Test. In N. Ceryan (Ed.), *Handbook of Research on Trends and Digital Advances in Engineering Geology* (pp. 631–664). Hershey, PA: IGI Global. doi:10.4018/978-1-5225-2709-1.ch018

Valente, M., & Milani, G. (2017). Seismic Assessment and Retrofitting of an Under-Designed RC Frame Through a Displacement-Based Approach. In V. Plevris, G. Kremmyda, & Y. Fahjan (Eds.), *Performance-Based Seismic Design of Concrete Structures and Infrastructures* (pp. 36–58). Hershey, PA: IGI Global. doi:10.4018/978-1-5225-2089-4.ch002

Vargas-Bernal, R. (2021). Advances in Electromagnetic Environmental Shielding for Aeronautics and Space Applications. In C. Nikolopoulos (Ed.), *Recent Trends on Electromagnetic Environmental Effects for Aeronautics and Space Applications* (pp. 80–96). IGI Global. https://doi.org/10.4018/978-1-7998-4879-0.ch003

Vasant, P. (2018). A General Medical Diagnosis System Formed by Artificial Neural Networks and Swarm Intelligence Techniques. In U. Kose, G. Guraksin, & O. Deperlioglu (Eds.), *Nature-Inspired Intelligent Techniques for Solving Biomedical Engineering Problems* (pp. 130–145). Hershey, PA: IGI Global. doi:10.4018/978-1-5225-4769-3.ch006

Verner, C. M., & Sarwar, D. (2021). Avoiding Project Failure and Achieving Project Success in NHS IT System Projects in the United Kingdom. *International Journal of Strategic Engineering*, *4*(1), 33–54. https://doi.org/10.4018/IJoSE.2021010103

Verrollot, J., Tolonen, A., Harkonen, J., & Haapasalo, H. J. (2018). Challenges and Enablers for Rapid Product Development. *International Journal of Applied Industrial Engineering*, *5*(1), 25–49. doi:10.4018/IJAIE.2018010102

Wan, A. C., Zulu, S. L., & Khosrow-Shahi, F. (2021). Industry Views on BIM for Site Safety in Hong Kong. In J. Underwood & M. Shelbourn (Eds.), *Handbook of Research on Driving Transformational Change in the Digital Built Environment* (pp. 120–140). IGI Global. https://doi.org/10.4018/978-1-7998-6600-8.ch005

Yardimci, A. G., & Karpuz, C. (2018). Fuzzy Rock Mass Rating: Soft-Computing-Aided Preliminary Stability Analysis of Weak Rock Slopes. In N. Ceryan (Ed.), *Handbook of Research on Trends and Digital Advances in Engineering Geology* (pp. 97–131). Hershey, PA: IGI Global. doi:10.4018/978-1-5225-2709-1.ch003

You, K. Y. (2021). Development Electronic Design Automation for RF/Microwave Antenna Using MATLAB GUI. In A. Nwajana & I. Ihianle (Eds.), *Handbook of Research on 5G Networks and Advancements in Computing, Electronics, and Electrical Engineering* (pp. 70–148). IGI Global. https://doi.org/10.4018/978-1-7998-6992-4.ch004

Yousefi, Y., Gratton, P., & Sarwar, D. (2021). Investigating the Opportunities to Improve the Thermal Performance of a Case Study Building in London. *International Journal of Strategic Engineering*, *4*(1), 1–18. https://doi.org/10.4018/IJoSE.2021010101

Zindani, D., & Kumar, K. (2018). Industrial Applications of Polymer Composite Materials. In K. Kumar & J. Davim (Eds.), *Composites and Advanced Materials for Industrial Applications* (pp. 1–15). Hershey, PA: IGI Global. doi:10.4018/978-1-5225-5216-1.ch001

Zindani, D., Maity, S. R., & Bhowmik, S. (2018). A Decision-Making Approach for Material Selection of Polymeric Composite Bumper Beam. In K. Kumar & J. Davim (Eds.), *Composites and Advanced Materials for Industrial Applications* (pp. 112–128). Hershey, PA: IGI Global. doi:10.4018/978-1-5225-5216-1.ch006

About the Contributors

Olalekan Samuel Ogunleye has worked as the head of Mobile Development, Strategy and Business Innovations at Eyethenticate Computervision Lab, Johannesburg, South Africa. He was a Senior Mobile and Enterprise Application Developer at the Council for Scientific and Industrial Research (CSIR), Pretoria, South Africa. He was also the Academic Content Developer for Google Sub-Saharan Africa, covering Eight Countries (Nigeria, South Africa, Cameroon, Kenya, Uganda, Ghana and Cote D' Ivoire). During his time at CSIR, Dr Olalekan became interested in and developed cybersecurity expertise, particularly in fighting Cyber Crime, Artificial Intelligence, System Development and Implementation, ICDL for Organization Development, Internet of Things, ICT4D for Social Development. His significant IT and ICT interest has centred around Artificial Intelligence, Machine Learning, Data Science and the Internet of Things. He is a social Media Enthusiast and regular. Dr Olalekan has B. Tech (Hons) degree in Computer Science and Engineering from the Ladoke Akintola University of Technology, MSc in Computer Science from University of Cape Town (UCT), Master of Business Administration (MBA) degree from Management College of Southern Africa (MANCOSA). He obtained his PhD in Information Systems from the University of Cape Town, where he investigated and developed a Framework and Model for Supporting Government Service Delivery using Mobile Technology. He has worked as a Senior Lecturer at the School of Information Technology, Monash University, ICT Lecturer for MBA at the MANCOSA, Research Consultant on ICT research at the Faculty of ICT, Tshwane University of Technology, and Technical Research Implementation Consultant for the Department of the Electrical Engineering Mangosuthu University of Technology, all in South Africa. Further to this, Dr Olalekan has consulted for various organizations in Botswana, Nigeria, Ghana, Uganda, South Africa, Swaziland, and Zambia on Cybersecurity Implementation and has developed various Machine Learning Models for the majority of these organizations.

* * *

Munir Ahmad is a Ph.D. in Computer Science. over 23 years of extensive experience in spatial data development, management, processing, visualization, and quality control. He is dedicated expertise in open data, crowdsourced data, volunteered geographic information and spatial data infrastructure. A seasoned professional with extensive knowledge in the field, having served as a trainer for the latest spatial technologies. With a passion for research and over 25 publications in the same field. In 2022, he got PhD degree in Computer Science from Preston University Rawalpindi, Pakistan. He is dedicated to advancing the industry and spreading knowledge through my expertise and experience. #SpatialData #GIS #GeoTech.

Ayotuyi T. Akinola was part of the data lakehouse development project at the Durban University of Technology, which began in 2023 with a cohort of Bachelor of ICT (Honours) students. He was among the team of supervisors for the students who carried out this research at Durban University of Technology. His area of specialization covers Mobile cloud computing, ad-hoc mobile cloud computing systems, and software-defined networking systems with data analytics. He has successfully supervised three Honours' students in the previous academic year and look forward to completing the supervision of two of his students in this project. He also has PhD and Master's students currently under his supervision in these above highlighted areas.

Amir Ahmad Dar is the Faculty in the Department of Mathematics at Lovely Professional University Punjab. The area of interest: Financial mathematics, financial economics, statistics and business mathematics.

Santosh Durugkar has pursued Ph.D in Software engineering from Amity University Rajasthan Jaipur. He has completed U.G. (B.E.) and P.G. (M.E.) from SPPU, Pune. His area of interests are software engineering, Machine Learning, Artificial Intelligence, Database Management, Data Analysis, Data Mining & Information Retrieval.

Aditya Dhar Dwivedi is M.A in Political Science from Dr. Rammanohar Lohia Avadh University. He is currently pursuing PhD from Dr. Rammanohar Lohia Avadh University. Having academic background in Political Science, his interest lies in studying Governance, ethics, artificial intelligence, public administration and what are the key factors that contribute to Good Governance. As a research scholar, he wants to analyze the formal and informal actors involved in the process of decision-making, how these processes can be improved and made more efficient and then implemented in a better way.

Dwijendra Nath Dwivedi is a professional with 20+ years of subject matter expertise creating right value propositions for analytics and AI. He currently heads the EMEA+AP AI and IoT team at SAS, a worldwide frontrunner in AI technology. He is a post-Graduate in Economics from Indira Gandhi Institute of Development and Research and currently perusing PHD from crackow university of economics Poland. He has presented his research in more than 20 international conference and published several Scopus indexed paper on AI adoption in many areas. As an author he has contributed to more than 8 books and has more than 25 publications in high impact journals. He conducts AI Value seminars and workshops for the executive audience and for power users. In the role of a thought leader, he is actively closing the divide between business requirements and serving as a catalyst for analytical capabilities, thereby fostering a culture of analytical thinking that fuels effective business strategies

Ghana Mahanty leads MENA Data science, UAE and Global Data Science Center of Excellent, India for Visa Inc. He is a data enthusiast with expertise in mobilizing the organization to deliver value out of data and specializing in business management, data transformation strategy, and machine learning and artificial intelligence solutions for Retail Banking and Payment industry. He has worked extensively across North America, Asia, Europe and Middle East regions. Currently pursuing PhD. in Economics from Department of Analytical and Applied Economics, Utkal University, Bhubaneswar, India. His research area of interests are machine learning, artificial intelligence, macro econometric and structural data modelling, panel modelling, money, banking and payments.

Devraj Moonsamy is a lecturer in the Department of Information Systems at the Durban University of Technology. He has been an academic for more than 25 years and his area of expertise is in data engineering, data mining, machine learning and artificial intelligence.

Samuel Ibukun Olotu is a Lecturer in the Department of Information Technology, Federal University of Technology, Akure, Nigeria. He obtained a BTech degree in Computer Engineering from Ladoke Akintola University of Technology, Ogbomoso, Nigeria, a MTech and in Computer Science from Federal University of Technology, Akure, Nigeria. He has a PhD in Computer Science from Federal University of Technology, Akure, Nigeria, He has a PhD in Computer Science from Federal University of Technology, Akure, Nigeria, and was in University of Pavia, Italy, for part of his research work. His current research interest include Computer Networks and Artificial Intelligence. He has published papers in learned journals and academic conferences such as International Journal of Vehicular Telematics and Infotainment Systems and International Journal of Advanced Engineering and Technology.

Sulaiman S. Patel is a lecturer in the Department of Information Systems at Durban University of Technology in South Africa. He also co-ordinates postgraduate and research within the Department. Dr Patel completed his PhD in Electronic Engineering in 2018 from the University of Kwa-Zulu Natal, at which point he was heralded as the youngest ever PhD graduate from the university in his field. He had previously completed his Bachelor of Science in Engineering (Electronics) at the same institution Summa Cum Laude in 2015. His research interests span wireless communication systems, socio-technical systems, carbon literacy, the Internet of Things and applications of artificial intelligence.

Sabyasachi Pramanik is a professional IEEE member. He obtained a PhD in Computer Science and Engineering from Sri Satya Sai University of Technology and Medical Sciences, Bhopal, India. Presently, he is an Associate Professor, Department of Computer Science and Engineering, Haldia Institute of Technology, India. He has many publications in various reputed international conferences, journals, and book chapters (Indexed by SCIE, Scopus, ESCI, etc). He is doing research in the fields of Artificial Intelligence, Data Privacy, Cybersecurity, Network Security, and Machine Learning. He also serves on the editorial boards of several international journals. He is a reviewer of journal articles from IEEE, Springer, Elsevier, Inderscience, IET and IGI Global. He has reviewed many conference papers, has been a keynote speaker, session chair, and technical program committee member at many international conferences. He has authored a book on Wireless Sensor Network. He has edited 8 books from IGI Global, CRC Press, Springer and Wiley Publications.

Index

www.ingramcontent.com/pod-product-compliance
Lightning Source LLC
LaVergne TN
LVHW080558300926
849162LV00005B/987
* 9 7 8 1 6 6 8 4 9 7 1 6 6 *